Seductions of Crime

SEDUCTIONS
OF CRIME

Moral and Sensual
Attractions in Doing Evil

JACK KATZ

BASIC

BOOKS

A Member of the Perseus Books Group

Basic Books is a member of the Perseus Books Group
Library of Congress Cataloging-in-Publication Data

Katz, Jack.
   Seductions of crime.

   Bibliography: p. 325.
   Includes index.
   1. Crime and criminals—United States—
Moral and ethical aspects.   2. Criminal
behavior—United States.   3. Compulsive
behavior—United States.   4. Good and evil—
Psychological aspects.   I. Title.
HV6791.K38   1988   364.2′4   88–47691
ISBN 0–465–07615–7 (cloth)
ISBN 0–465–07616–5 (paper)

Designed by Vincent Torre

CONTENTS

PREFACE AND ACKNOWLEDGMENTS

I envy those who can somehow graciously transport themselves to intellectual worlds they have never inhabited before, all the while taking cautious little steps as if they knew in advance where all the traps lie, and ever prepared to demonstrate with a comely humility just what they are doing even as they figure out how to do it. My work on this book, I realized about five years ago, would have to begin pretentiously and crudely, in a style much too unseemly for quick, broad display.

In part my caution in letting this work loose too soon can be attributed to the phenomena addressed. If traced closely, the seductions of crime present great risks for violating the reader's sensibilities. I have done what I could to ground abrupt, sensational changes in mood as features of the offenders' experiences, but no doubt some eyes will still be poked by descriptions of sensual dynamics which jump a bit too suddenly from the text.

Morally as well as sensually, it is likely that some readers will feel personally victimized by my effort to convey the offender's experience. But if guided by empathy, this text does not compel sympathy. The adage "To understand is to forgive" was false when touted by George Herbert Mead and has misguided generations of social researchers on deviance. A trip to "the other side" does not have to be a permanent change in spiritual address. I suspect that readers who follow the text through several chapters will emerge from the various offenders' worlds at least as often in disgust as with acceptance.

A set of fortunate circumstances made it easy to keep my ambitions relatively private until they could be made presentable: an early tenure decision at UCLA, which provided insulation from pressures of the labor market; an early book contract, which provided equally valuable insulation from pressures of academic bureaucracy and careerism; and a sociological research community sustained by Harold Garfinkel, Manny Schegloff, Bob Emerson, and Mel Pollner, in which what is precisely unspeakable can be treated very comfortably as just what is most sought after.

Howard S. Becker, who some thirty years ago laid out a foundation for this work, helped me simultaneously recognize and find a way around more than one major obstacle in the analysis. For encouragement, caution

signs, and practical assistance in locating data, I am very grateful to
Gresham Sykes, Phil Cook, Ted Sarbin, David Luckenbill, Bill Gibson, Mel
Oliver, Bob Emerson, Ivan Light, Henry Lundsgaarde, Dick Berk, Eli An-
derson, Eric Monkkonen, Joseph de Rivera, Mel Lansky, and John Kitsuse.
Steven Fraser repeatedly came up with incisive, sensitive, and eminently
workable editorial suggestions. For research assistance, I am grateful to Jim
Angell, Oanh Dinh, Beth Sammis, and Peter Rosielewski. The index was
composed by Leah Robin.

Last, and most, I would like to thank the people who provided the data:
for chapter 2, three classes of enthusiastic students at UCLA; for chapter
5, Franklin Zimring and James Zuehl; and throughout, the ethnographic
research community. Although I use endnotes to acknowledge researchers
by name, I would like to offer a generalized word of appreciation, and I
hope a measure of encouragement, to those who do the groundwork for
books like this. The fieldwork enterprise has become increasingly precarious in modern social science. Funding agencies, academic bureaucracies,
and professional associations do not adequately recognize the enormous
professional altruism of fieldworkers who take the pains to document
poignant social action outside the auspices of formalized theoretical categories and conventionalized research methodology. But unless that work
gets done, how can we expect new analyses to be broadly grounded in the
lived experience of people in society, rather than in our personal experience, theoretical prejudices, or moral and political sentiments? A good part
of the pleasure in working on this manuscript has come from a sense of
recovering and reliving widely scattered, sometimes almost lost, moments
of fieldwork insight.

My only regret for the book is that the moral and sensual dynamics it
examines do not fit the dedication I would like to use—"A la maja, Elena."

Seductions of Crime

Introduction

The study of crime has been preoccupied with a search for background forces, usually defects in the offenders' psychological backgrounds or social environments, to the neglect of the positive, often wonderful attractions within the lived experience of criminality. The novelty of this book is its focus on the seductive qualities of crimes: those aspects in the foreground of criminality that make its various forms sensible, even sensually compelling, ways of being.

The social science literature contains only scattered evidence of what it means, feels, sounds, tastes, or looks like to commit a particular crime. Readers of research on homicide and assault do not hear the slaps and curses, see the pushes and shoves, or feel the humiliation and rage that may build toward the attack, sometimes persisting after the victim's death. How adolescents manage to make the shoplifting or vandalism of cheap and commonplace things a thrilling experience has not been intriguing to many students of delinquency. Researchers of adolescent gangs have never grasped why their subjects so often stubbornly refuse to accept the outsider's insistence that they wear the "gang" label. The description of "cold-blooded, senseless murders" has been left to writers outside the social sciences. Neither academic methods nor academic theories seem to be able to grasp why such killers may have been courteous to their victims just moments before the killing, why they often wait until they have dominated victims in sealed-off environments before coldly executing them, or how it makes sense to them to kill when only petty cash is at stake. Sociological and psychological studies of robbery rarely focus on the *distinctive* attractions of robbery, even though research has now clearly documented that alternative forms of criminality are available and familiar to many career robbers. In sum, only rarely have sociologists taken up the challenge of explaining the qualities of deviant experience.[1]

The statistical and correlational findings of positivist criminology provide the following irritations to inquiry: (1) whatever the validity of the hereditary, psychological, and social-ecological conditions of crime, many of those in the supposedly causal categories do not commit the crime at issue, (2) many who do commit the crime do not fit the causal categories, and (3) and what is most provocative, many who do fit the background categories and later commit the predicted crime go for long stretches without committing the crimes to which theory directs them. Why are people who were not determined to commit a crime one moment determined to do so the next?

I propose that empirical research turn the direction of inquiry around to focus initially on the foreground, rather than the background of crime. Let us for once make it our first priority to understand the qualities of experience that distinguish different forms of criminality. What concerns can guide such an inquiry? How can the explanation of the qualities of criminality be pursued without starting an undisciplined pursuit of experiential evidence?

The Magic in Motivation

Whatever the relevance of antecedent events and contemporaneous social conditions, something causally essential happens in the very moments in which a crime is committed. The assailant must sense, then and there, a distinctive constraint or seductive appeal that he did not sense a little while before in a substantially similar place. Although his economic status, peer group relations, Oedipal conflicts, genetic makeup, internalized machismo, history of child abuse, and the like remain the same, he must suddenly become propelled to commit the crime. Thus, the central problem is to understand the emergence of distinctive sensual dynamics.

To believe that a person can suddenly feel propelled to crime without any independently verifiable change in his background, it seems that we must almost believe in magic. And, indeed, this is precisely what we must do. When they are committing crimes, people feel drawn and propelled to their criminality, but in feeling determined by outside forces, they do nothing morally special. The particular seductions and compulsions they experience may be unique to crime, but the sense of being seduced and compelled is not. To grasp the magic in the criminal's sensuality, we must acknowledge our own.

A sense of being determined by the environment, of being pushed away from one line of action and pulled toward another, is natural to everyday, routine human experience. We are always moving away from and toward different objects of consciousness, taking account of this and ignoring that, and moving in one direction or the other between the extremes of involvement and boredom. In this constant movement of consciousness, we do not perceive that we are controlling the movement. Instead, to one degree or another, we are always being seduced and repelled by the world.[2] "This *is* fascinating (interesting, beautiful, sexy, dull, ugly, disgusting)," we know (without having to say), as if the thing itself possessed the designated quality independent of us and somehow controlled our understanding of it. Indeed, the very nature of mundane being is emotional; attention is feeling, and consciousness is sensual.

Only rarely do we actually experience ourselves as subjects directing our conduct. How often, when you speak, do you actually sense that you are choosing the words you utter? As the words come out, they reveal the thought behind them even to the speaker whose lips gave them shape. Similarly, we talk, walk, and write in a sense of natural competence governed by moods of determinism. We rest our subjectivity on rhythmic sensibilities, feelings for directions, and visions of unfolding patterns, allowing esthetics to guide us.[3] Self-reflexive postures in which one creates a distance between the self and the world and pointedly directs the self into the world, occur typically in an exceptional mood of recognizing a malapropism, after a misstep, or at the slip of the pen. With a slight shock, we recognize that it was not the things in themselves but our perspective that temporarily gave things outside of us the power to seduce or repel.

Among the forms of crime, the range of sensual dynamics runs from enticements that may draw a person into shoplifting to furies that can compel him to murder. If, as social researchers, we are to be able to explain more variation in criminality than background correlations allow, it appears that we must respect these sensual dynamics and honor them as authentic. But now we seem caught in a new dilemma. How can we simultaneously discredit the determinism of psychological and social background factors while crediting the determinism of sensually dynamic attractions and compulsions? Put another way, how can we find, through studying how people construct their experience as an artifact, the emergence of new forces that shape the actors themselves? Can we really see any novel causal forces in the black box between background factors and subsequent acts? After we have refined correlations between problematic acts and explanatory background factors, is there anything more to say other than that those whose actions do and those whose actions do not line up with predictions just "choose" to act that way?

For clues to the resolution of the dilemma, we may consider the dynamics of interaction between interrogator and interrogee,[4] drawing specifically on the American military experience in Vietnam. The interrogation of Vietnamese peasants routinely included physical assaults—at a minimal level, slapping. Intelligence officers often began a session in the spirit of many routine, civilian work assignments, as an obligation, without marked enthusiasm, only to discover overriding sensual dimensions in the process.

These were not extraordinary happenings. Unless one sets out to do so, it is actually difficult to avoid the development of an involving esthetic in the sounds and rhythms of repeatedly slapping another person. To maintain the controlled assault of an interrogating slapping and pushing, the officer must repeatedly adjust his body in relation to the responding movement of the interrogee. If a resonant slap was used to articulate the imposition of pressure and if the pressure is not to dissipate, the audible universe must be further managed, perhaps through making the subsequent slap louder or through the cunning use of silence. Attention to the esthetics of sound and interrelated body movements is not perverse but practically essential if the significance and spirit of "pressure" is to be maintained.

In the interrogator's attentiveness to rhythm and intensity as essential concerns for sustaining the metaphysics of "pressure," there is a move into the spirit of determinism. The interrogator has created themes that, through their evolving apparent requirements, he must acknowledge. Although he began the line of action, now it constrains his further creativity. He may walk away at any moment, but if he is to keep the pressure on, there are certain things he must now do.

From here, the interrogator may spin off along one of the many alternative paths of determinism. Patterns of slapping freely suggest various metaphors, and authority may be shaped to play out any of the symbolic possibilities that have sprung up. For example, despite repeated slaps that audibly ring in his head, the interrogee will not pick up on requests for information. What does the "ringing" and the refusal to "pick up" suggest? A metaphor, the dictates of which the interrogator may now enact under the rubric, the "Bell Telephone Hour": "You take a field telephone, wire it up around the man's testicles, you ring him up and he always answers."[5]

Another path of escalating determinism became known as the "Americal Rule": "if he wasn't a Vietcong then, he sure as hell is one now."[6] At the start, interrogators were often unsure of the political sympathies of the interrogee, but, in the end, it did not matter. Either the interrogee was a Vietcong sympathizer or, if not, the eminently dispassionate reasoning went, he was likely to turn hostile after being slapped unjustly. In either case, it was reasonable after a while to consider his failure to cooperate as being motivated by malevolence. At that point, the interrogee's hostility is blocking the progress of the interrogation and thus is provocative: the *interrogee* is giving the *interrogator* a hard time!

The moral responsibility, and in a strictly empirical perspective, the causal responsibility has been shifted to the victim. Now the interrogator, just by insistently repeating questions, establishes the interrogee's region of freedom not to respond, emphasizing in turn the constraints of the process on the interrogator's freedom. But if the peasant will not answer the questions, if the peasant's information is beyond the control of Authority, the peasant's suffering is not. The peasant's suffering is conveniently in front of Authority; it offers itself as an object that can be juxtaposed against the interrogator's frustrations and constructed to fit the military will. The dialectic of freedom and restraint has reversed. Just as Authority was beginning to become disciplined to the requirements of the process—doing what is necessary to sustain pressure and responding to the interrogee's hostility—it discovers a new region of freedom.

Occasionally, this process would turn into frenzied slaughter; more commonly, it would cause a modest increase in brutalization. In either case, Authority set into motion a process that it could go with. But this process is always vulnerable to an interruption of its implicit sensual logic. The interrogator, no matter how carried away he may feel, can always stop.

In one instance, a peasant woman "shit in her pants . . . [and became] very embarrassed." In odor and in moral sensibility, the interrogee violated the esthetics and the moral stance underlying the ongoing dynamic. Suddenly her spontaneous bowel movement perfectly if unwittingly reversed the esthetic preconditions and moral thrust of the process. The soldier stopped. "I'm beating up this girl, for what? What the fuck am I doing? I just felt like a shit."[7]

In another incident, a Marine was showing the peasants that the Marines were in charge by recklessly driving a truck. His dominance was spatially and audibly established; up in the noisy truck, he did not bother to count how many he hit. Somehow a 15-year-old boy on a bicycle got caught in the wheels. The driver came down to look and found "this kid who just stared back at him with an absolutely level stare."[8] Silence and spatial equality broke the momentum. The Marine, previously above and behind a wall of noise, was suddenly on the same plane with his victim, with nothingness audibly around. This time, he walked off.

The challenge for explanation is to specify the steps of the dialectic process through which a person empowers the world to seduce him to criminality. On the one hand, we must explain how the individual himself *conjures up* the spirit. On the other hand, we must accept the attraction or compulsion as *authentic*.

It is not a simple matter to raise these spirits. One cannot be blindly enraged, cooly sadistic, or secretly thrilled at will, simply by the conscious choice to be evil, no more than one can transport himself to erotic heights simply and instantly by opting for pleasure. For a person to experience being influenced or determined, he must lose a reflective awareness of the abiding, constructive workings of his subjectivity. Thus, part of the challenge is to recognize steps in raising a spirit of determinism that are sufficiently subtle that their contingencies go unnoticed.

Typically, the person will not be able to help us with the analysis because he is taken in by his efforts to construct the dynamic. If we ask, "Why did you do it?" he is likely to respond with self-justifying rhetoric. But he can help us with a detailed account of the processual development of his experience. If we ask, "How did you do that? And then what did you do?" we are likely to discover some poignant moments. And, because the person constructs his definition of the situation through bodily comprehension, we may catch the conditions of his involvement in exceptional circumstances when it is undermined by an incongruent sensuality. Thus, the interrogator's victim may defecate, triggering a life-saving perception by her torturer that *he* is the shit. Or, to offer an erotic example, the lovers' child may suddenly walk in and prove that what they had sensed as an abandoned involvement was not.

That emotions are contingent on definitions of the situation is a commonplace both in existentialist writing and in the sociological tradition of symbolic interaction. What has been more difficult to appreciate is the ontological validity of passion—the authentic efficacy of sensual magic. In sex, as well as in mock fighting on street corners, initially lighthearted thrusts and parries may turn into the real thing without warning. Such preliminaries to passion are playful in an existentially specific sense: the participants are playing with the line between the sense of themselves as subject and object, between being in and out of control, between directing and being directed by the dynamics of the situation. To complete successfully the transition from subject to object and achieve the emotional extremes of eros or thanatos, a person may have to arrange the environment to "pacify" his subjectivity.[9] He may then submit to forces that transcend his subjectivity even while he tacitly controls the transition.

What phenomenology uniquely has appreciated is not simply that a person's lived world is his artifact but that by experiencing himself as an object controlled by transcendent forces, an individual can genuinely experience a new or different world. By pacifying his subjectivity, a person can conjure up a magic so powerful that it can change his ontology. What begins as idle slapping or fondling may lead to the discovery of rare truths or the acquisition of a new incompetence.[10]

It is necessary to indulge a fiction or invoke a ritual to begin the process, but if one does not hedge on the commitment of faith, otherwise inaccessible phenomena may come into reach, bringing revelations or shutting off part of one's freedom and confirming that the initial commitment was authentic. In religious practice, we may find the results of this dialectical process inspiring; in sex, delightful. As unattractive morally as crime may be, we must appreciate that there is *genuine experiential creativity* in it as well. We should then be able to see what are, for the subject, the authentic attractions of crime and we should then be able to explain variations in criminality beyond what can be accounted for by background factors.

Criminal Projects

Approaching criminality from the inside, social research takes as its subject the morally exceptional conduct that the persons themselves regard as criminally sanctionable in official eyes. Since there is an enormous variety of criminal phenomena, how can one demarcate and set up for explanation a limited number of subjectively homogeneous offenses? I suggest that a seemingly simple question be asked persistently in detailed application to the facts of criminal experience: what are people trying to do when they commit a crime?

The resulting topics will not necessarily follow official crime categories. Crimes, as defined in statutes, surveys of citizens, and police records, take definitional shape from the interests of victims and from practical problems of detection and punishment, not necessarily from the experience of those committing the crimes. But if one begins with rough conventional or folk categories, such as hot-blooded murder, gang violence, adolescent property crime, commercial robbery, and "senseless" and "cold-blooded" murder, and refines the concepts to fit homogeneous forms of experience, one can arrive at a significant range of criminal projects, as represented by the chapter titles: committing righteous slaughter, mobilizing the spirit of a street elite, constructing sneaky thrills, persisting in the practice of stickup as a hardman, and embodying primordial evil.

By way of explanation, I will propose for each type of crime a different set of individually necessary and jointly sufficient conditions, each set containing (1) a path of action—distinctive practical requirements for successfully committing the crime, (2) a line of interpretation—unique ways of understanding how one is and will be seen by others, and (3) an emotional process—seductions and compulsions that have special dynamics. Raising the spirit of criminality requires practical attention to a mode of executing action, symbolic creativity in defining the situation, and esthetic finesse in recognizing and elaborating on the sensual possibilities.

Central to all these experiences in deviance is a member of the family of moral emotions: humiliation, righteousness, arrogance, ridicule, cynicism, defilement, and vengeance. In each, the attraction that proves to be most fundamentally compelling is that of overcoming a personal challenge to moral—not to material—existence. For the impassioned killer, the challenge is to escape a situation that has come to seem otherwise inexorably humiliating. Unable to sense how he or she can move with self-respect from the current situation, now, to any mundane-time relationship that might be reengaged, then, the would-be killer leaps at the possibility of embodying, through the practice of "righteous" slaughter, some eternal, universal form of the Good.

For many adolescents, shoplifting and vandalism offer the attractions of a thrilling melodrama about the self as seen from within and from without. Quite apart from what is taken, they may regard "getting away with it" as a thrilling demonstration of personal competence, especially if it is accomplished under the eyes of adults.

Specifically "bad" forms of criminality are essentially addressed to a moral challenge experienced in a spatial metaphor. Whether by intimidating others' efforts to take him into their worlds ("Who you lookin' at?") or by treating artificial geographic boundaries as sacred and defending local "turf" with relentless "heart," "badasses" and *barrio* warriors celebrate an indifference to modern society's expectation that a person should demonstrate a sensibility to reshape himself as he moves from here to there.

To make a habit of doing stickups, I will argue, one must become a "hardman." It is only smart to avoid injuring victims unnecessarily, but if one becomes too calculating about the application of violence, the inherent uncertainties of face-to-face interaction in robberies will be emotionally forbidding. Beneath the surface, there may be, to paraphrase Nietzsche, a ball of snakes in chaotic struggle. But the stickup man denies any uncertainty and any possibility of change with a personal style that ubiquitously negates social pressures toward a malleable self.

Perhaps the ultimate criminal project is mounted by men who culminate a social life organized around the symbolism of deviance with a cold-blooded, "senseless" murder. Mimicking the ways of primordial gods as they kill, they proudly appear to the world as astonishingly evil. Through a killing only superficially justified by the context of robbery, they emerge from a dizzying alternation between affiliation with the great symbolic powers of deviant identity and a nagging dis-ease that conformity means cowardice.

Overall, my objective is to demonstrate that a theory of moral self-transcendence can make comprehensible the minutia of experiential details in the phenomenal foreground, as well as explain the general conditions that are most commonly found in the social backgrounds of these forms of criminality. This inquiry will best serve those who wish to address evil—not as judged by moral philosophy or imputed by political ideology but as lived in the everyday realities of contemporary society. In the end, I suggest that the dominant political and sociological understanding that crime is motivated by materialism is poorly grounded empirically—indeed, that it is more a sentimentality than a creditable causal theory. Because of its insistence on attributing causation to material conditions in personal and social backgrounds, modern social thought has been unable either to acknowledge the embrace of evil by common or street criminals, or, and for the same reason, develop empirical bite and intellectual depth in the study of criminality by the wealthy and powerful. By opening up systematic, theoretical, and empirical inquiry into the experience of criminality, this study points toward a comparative sociology that is capable of examining the seductions of crime as they are experienced up and down the social and political order. Those who follow the argument to its end may not find encouragement for broad-based social welfare policies, but readers should discover that the domestic deceits and foreign atrocities of our elites are no longer tangential to social research on crime.

Sources and Methods

Chapter 2 is based on reports of shoplifting, burglary, and vandalism that I solicited from classes of university students over three years. Chapter 5 analyzes narrative descriptions of robberies in Chicago that were generated in an original study directed by Franklin Zimring and James Zuehl. In the rest of the manuscript, except for some dissertations and bits in chapters 3 and 4 that were taken from a number of graduate students who have conducted field research in East and South Central Los Angeles, I analyze previously published material. Throughout, I draw on ethnographies and life histories produced by professional social scientists, reconstructions of situated criminality by the police and by academics using police records, autobiographies by self-professed ex-criminals, best-selling biographies of criminals written by professional journalists, and an occasional instance of *cinema verité* or participant observation ("new") journalism.

The evidentiary logic guiding the use of such diverse, qualitative material is that of analytic induction, which forces revisions in theory with each disconfirming or negative case, but which does not produce abstract, summary forms of evidence (sampling designs, statistics of association, tests of agreement among coders, and the like). To appreciate or denigrate the empirical validity of the study, one must work in detail with relevant substantive materials. Because the search for evidence and the development of theory proceed in mutually altering steps, the analytic results do not emerge from a straightforward, deductive, hard or inflexible application of theory to fact. Rather, the methodological quality increases the more theory is pushed around and beaten into shape by frustrated applications. Indeed, one tradition for indicating the methodological strength of studies conducted via analytic induction is to present in text the theoretical wounds that have been suffered on the way to the final, comprehensively validated theory. But such demonstrations are gratuitous and unnecessarily defensive; the working history of rejected and revised rival hypotheses is preserved in the substantive distinctions made in the text itself.[11]

In keeping with the spirit of the work as a whole and in order not to foreclose the utility of the data for subsequent analysts, quoted material has not been edited to correct spelling or grammar. *"Sic"* is used only when readers might otherwise suspect typographical error.

CHAPTER 1

Righteous Slaughter

What is the killer trying to do in a typical homicide? How does he understand himself, his victim, and the scene at the fatal moment? With what sense and in what sensuality is he compelled to act?

Defining the Problem

Aside from deaths from automobile accidents and murders committed in the course of robberies and other predatory crimes, the modal criminal homicide[1] is an impassioned attempt to perform a sacrifice to embody one or another version of the "Good." When people kill in a moralistic rage, their perspective often seems foolish or incomprehensible to us, and, indeed, it often seems that way to them soon after the killing. But if we stick to the details of the event, we can see offenders defending the Good, even in what initially appear to be crazy circumstances.[2]

To press the point with an extreme example, consider this killing through beating of a 5-week-old infant:

The victim . . . started crying early in the morning. The offender, the boy's father, ordered the victim to stop crying. The victim's crying, however, only heightened in intensity. The . . . persistent crying may have been oriented not toward challenging his father's authority, but toward acquiring food or a change of diapers. Whatever the motive for crying, the child's father defined it as purposive and offensive.[3]

This scene differed only in degree from everyday, routine events. It is not unusual for parents to demand respect from children and to respond to defiance with beatings. Nor is it unusual to misinterpret an infant's motives. Parents differ widely in the abilities and comprehension that they attribute to children of various ages.[4]

The father just described may have been crazy in some sense but if he was, presumably he had been crazy for some time before he killed; his craziness would not seem to explain the event. Within the situation of the homicide, whatever insanity haunted him was morally shaped. It appears that he did not kill in the course of doing something conventionally considered bad, such as sexually abusing the child, robbing a third party, or sadistically celebrating violence. He did not suddenly explode and kill while irrationally flailing about. Nor was he simply trying to remove an irritation; a more expedient course would have been to put the child out the door, throw him out the window, or abandon him. When parents beat their children, much less kill them, they are using, at best, an indirect, cumbersome way of ridding themselves of the problems the children are causing.

The interpretation that the father defined the crying as defiant and enacted his violence to honor parental authority, is based on few facts. The interpretation becomes more convincing as a way of understanding such events if it is examined in the context of a wide variety of other cases. Thus, it helps to note that in 112 cases of homicides of children in New York, the assailants were primarily parents (especially mothers), and the means of killing were kickings and beatings—extensions of ordinary means of enforcing parental discipline.[5]

Now consider a classic case of homicide caused by sexual jealousy from Henry Lundsgaarde's study of cases in Houston in 1969. For reasons to be explained, I have not removed what may be sensational details, even though the police may have encouraged the surviving seductress, Mrs. Jones, to spice up the account.

Last night . . . I called Russell at his home. . . . to ask if I could borrow some money from him to pay the rent and the utilities. . . . I guess it was about five minutes to midnight when he got to my house. . . . We were just standing there talking about different things and the troubles me and Jones were having. . . . Russell made some remark about my husband being down at some joint watching the go-go girls. . . . Russell said that I was going to be the talk of the neighborhood because I was standing out front talking to a bachelor. . . . We got in the car. . . . Russell teased me about how my hair looked and he kissed me a few times and then I kissed him back a few times. I kidded him about wrinkling his white shirt and he said that he wasn't worried about his shirt and that it was his tight black pants that were bothering him. . . . I told him to let me see and I felt and he had an erection. This is when he pulled his pants down. . . . [and] told me "It's too late to send me home now!" He reached over and kissed me. About this time I looked over Russell's shoulder and saw my husband. He had a gun. . . . and then Russell said "now listen Jones" or "Wait Jones" and this is when my husband shot him. . . . [I] looked into the car and saw Russell. He was bleeding real bad from the back of his head and he vomited. . . . I grabbed a wet towel from the bathroom and went back to the car and started to wipe stuff off of Russell's face and then I put the rag behind his head. About this time the police arrived and I went back into the house to quiet my children. I told my son to keep the other children in the bedroom.[6]

According to the police, all the participants had been good friends. Mrs. Jones and Russell had been having an affair for two years. Mrs. Jones had suggested divorce to her husband but had not pressed the matter. Mr. Jones had suspected the two and had tried to surprise them in the act. The grand jury refused to bring charges against him. Technically—that is, according to its official treatment—this homicide was not a crime.

Nor was Francine Hughes judged guilty for the highly publicized killing of her spouse, James. James had frequently beaten her, partly because of his violent opposition to her effort to become independent through education. The day of the killing, Francine's 12-year-old daughter called the police while James was beating Francine, but the police did not arrest him. Francine packed to move out, a decision that had the moral support of her children, and then poured gasoline around the bed in which James had fallen asleep, lit the gas, and drove straight to the sheriff's office to make a hysterical confession. The fact that James was asleep when the fire was set made a finding of self-defense difficult. Instead, the jury found Francine temporarily insane because of James's long-term abuse of her. (There was no indication of a belief in her continuing insanity. Francine was freed soon after the administration of psychological tests.)

Both spouse slayings illustrate that the killer's frequently "self-righteous" attitude (a term used by Lundsgaarde) is not necessarily idiosyncratic. Francine had been repeatedly beaten by James for almost fifteen years. On the day of the murder, she had more at stake than the recurrent issue of physical self-defense. A welfare mother, she had enrolled in business college some months before, and James was now prohibiting her effort to improve herself. The version of the Good she was defending was not simply the right to physical self-defense. It was also a version of the American dream that is widely accepted among people of all political persuasions: to better yourself through education and to escape the welfare rolls by applying yourself to serve business. And although the reaction was not universally favorable, her killing of James was considered righteous and as deserving profound respect by some of the national news commentaries on her case and in the tone of a nationally broadcast television drama.[7]

Likewise, Mr. Jones's killing of Russell was not considered wrong, nor was his Texas grand jury idiosyncratic in understanding that he was upholding the traditional sanctity of the marital union. The defense of *flagrante delicto* has been acceptable for centuries in many societies. If Mr. Jones and Francine Hughes both experienced an exceptional moment of temporary insanity, they were rational in claiming that their irrationality would be understood by others as righteously inspired.

The presence of children at the scene of the homicide—close to Russell's erotic behavior with Mrs. Jones and as witnesses to James Hughes's beatings of Francine—is also morally significant. Accounts of homicides of spouses often show the killer postured as a defender of the children's moral sensibilities. The following account, from a Canadian study, is taken largely from the husband's construction of the event:

About two weeks prior to the homicidal act . . . the wife openly told John that he was not wanted anymore and she wanted him to leave home. John begged her to do something and save the marriage for the sake of the children but the wife refused to discuss the matter further. Then John was so upset that he bought a rifle, intending to commit suicide. Just three days prior to the homicide John's wife left home for a lover. . . . When this happened John was crushed emotionally and was looking for ways to hurt himself. . . . After three days (and on Mother's Day) the wife returned home to take the children and go away again. John begged her not to do such a thing to the children but she ignored him. During this argument the children became upset and started crying. Then John turned to his wife and told her what was she doing to the children [sic]. When the wife replied that she "didn't give a damn about the children," John grabbed a knife and stabbed her to death.[8]

The next case of homicide growing out of erotic passions illustrates a different notion of killing in defense of the Good. According to the killer's statement to the police, he and his wife were engaged in sex when she repeatedly called out the name of a fellow he knew to be a former boyfriend. He brought his sexual act to a climax and then shot her. The couple's twin 3-year-old daughters were present.[9]

What is striking in this case is not only the form of the humiliation—the wife's mention of the boyfriend's name is reminiscent of a classic genre of crude jokes—but the husband's claim that he first finished the sex act. On hearing the other fellow's name, he might have lost the will to go on. Attentive to the double entendre, insisting that he would "fuck" her sexually-literally and violently-figuratively, he was transcending the challenge to his virility. Although the legal system was not sympathetic—he was given a life sentence—the killer could consider his act as upholding part of an eternally recognized Good.

The first two killings that were described were among whites, the last was among blacks, and the next occurred in a Mexican-American community. The killer, aged 35, was at home when several people came over to visit his neighbor. One visitor, the neighbor's uncle, aged 50, parked in front of the killer's driveway. After an initial request, the visitor moved his car, but later he again blocked the driveway. The killer, carrying a loaded shotgun, told the visitor that he would kill him if he did not remove his car. The visitor was unarmed and made no response, but he held his ground; then the killer shot him.[10]

In this instance, the killing was formally in defense of property rights, another value that a killer may regard, at the crucial time, as eternal and obviously righteous. In defending his right to control the use of his property, a killer can sense himself upholding the institution of property rights in general. As crazy or foolish as such an incident may appear, it is essential to note that such craziness or foolishness does not occur randomly; the violence erupts in situations that put at stake what the people involved momentarily regard as dimensions of the eternal Good.

That homicidal acts occur in defense of the Good is highlighted by the materially petty, "inconsequential" nature of the conflicts. In the following case, the killer and the victim were black male friends in their twenties. While in a cafe late one Saturday evening, the victim, who had a reputation as a "tough," began picking barbecued food from the killer's plate. The killer complained, but the victim persisted, defiantly splashing hot sauce on the killer. When the fight escalated, the killer pulled out his knife.[11]

To call such fights "childish" may highlight their pathos. But this struggle to control personal property is naturally sensible to all witnesses. Here the killer could expect bystanders to support the defense of his rights, particularly because the victim's reputation as a troublemaker made the issue a community cause.

It is tempting to discount as superficial the claim that such incidents are motivated by morality. There *is* something artificial about the moral explanation. As Peter D. Chimbos noted, in his study of homicides of spouses:

> A common technique in arguments is to refer to old grievances or conflicts no longer relevant except as weapons to argue with. . . . Another typical technique is to attack the spouse's deviations from the culturally approved sex role ideal. . . . For example, a wife may accuse her husband of being a poor breadwinner or an incompetent lover. Similarly, a husband may accuse his wife of being "bitchy," "frigid" or promiscuous. Insinuations that the spouse is not a good mother or father to the children are commonly made.[12]

We are accustomed to think that, surely, these people are not *really* killing because they regard a piece of food or a blocked driveway as so important. But it is essential not to overlook the moral form of common homicide. This form does not explain (much less justify) the killing, but it defines the killer's experience and thus sets up the problem so it can be explained.

Frequently, both the killer and the victim agree that "the Good" is at stake, as is illustrated in the following account of a wife's murder of her husband:

> A woman, a 35-year-old Black female, had gone to a local cafe to get her husband to come home. . . . She apparently yelled that she was tired of seeing her husband fooling with "them whores" in the cafe and he was overheard to shout that she should remove her eyeglasses. They fought on the sidewalk and during the fight the woman took a .22 caliber pistol from her purse and fired. A witness said that the man tried to raise himself after the first shot had been fired and that the woman then shot him once more. . . . Homicide detectives were able to interview the husband before he died and he stated that he was willing to prosecute the person who had shot him but that he didn't know who had done it![13]

It is not uncommon for victims to refuse to prosecute assailants who are lovers or family members. In this case, the wife was defending the traditional rights of her status. As he was dying, the husband seemed to concede that his wife had a right to shoot him.

Of course, these accounts only sketch the participants at the crucial moments. But it is striking that a "righteous" posture fits such a wide variety of the best sketches available in research on homicide. Consider one final example—a killing recounted by the 15-year-old daughter of the couple involved:

> This morning my mother told my stepfather that she was going to cash a check. He told her that he was going to cash the check to pay the car note. Mother told him that he could not pay the car note this week because he had other bills to pay. Mother was sitting on the footstool in the living room reading the paper. My stepfather was sitting in another chair in the same room. He got up and went into the bedroom and got the gun off the bookcase at the head of the bed. He told mother he was tired of this goddamn shit and he said that when he had the gun in his hand. He put the gun in his pocket. Mother told him, "That is what I wanted you to do. Now that you have got the gun, use it!" She told me to go gather up the clothes for the laundry. I left the room and went to get the clothes. I heard three shots. I ran back into the room to see what had happened. My stepfather told me that he had killed my mother and for me to go and call the police.[14]

In many important senses, this killing was not about who would pay which bill; other, more fundamental, sources of tension must have been at work. But in an initially important sense, the fatal fight was literally over which bill would be paid first. In *form,* both the husband and the wife were trying to position themselves to appear to be good people to the world, to creditors—to outsiders—who would think better of them if they paid their bills. Each was trying to defend the Good, not an idiosyncratic value.

One feature of the typical homicide, then, is its character as a self-righteous act undertaken within the form of defending communal values. The next feature is its lack of premeditation. From a law-enforcement perspective, homicides are relatively easy to solve. The police believe they have grounds to make arrests in from 75 to 90 percent of their homicide cases, compared to perhaps 25 percent of their robbery cases and 15 percent or fewer of their burglary cases.[15] The lack of premeditation in the typical homicide is suggested by the number of killers who make no attempt to escape and wait for the police[16] and by the rapidity with which police "solve" the crime. As Marvin Wolfgang reported in his classic Philadelphia study, "Two-thirds of the offenders in criminal homicide who were taken into custody by the police were arrested on the same day they committed the crime."[17] Even when the offenders run away, their simple and unsuccessful "escapes" indicate that they had not realized that they would become killers until they did.[18]

These homicides are not morally self-conscious acts on the order of calculated political assasinations or coldly executed acts of vengeance. They emerge quickly, are fiercely impassioned, and are conducted with an indifference to the legal consequences. Thus, the second feature of this form of homicide is that the attacks are conducted within the spirit of a quickly developing rage. In addition to explaining how one could come to see one's attack as a defense of the Good, then, I must explain how one becomes enraged.

The third notable feature of these homicidal attacks, which points to a third explanatory task, is suggested by the arbitrary relationship between what the assailants are attempting to do and their practical results. As many researchers have noted, criminal homicides that are not part of a robbery are substantially similar to assaults. It is artificial to take a "killing" as the act to be explained. What the nonpredatory assailant is attempting to do is more accurately captured by the concept of sacrifice: the marking of a victim in ways that will reconsecrate the assailant as Good. The victim's *death* is neither a *necessary* nor a *sufficient* element of the assailant's animating project.

Thus, I arrive at a definition of the problem to be explained as "righteously enraged slaughter," or an impassioned attack through which the assailant attempts to embody in his victim marks that will eternally attest to the assailant's embrace of a primordial Good. The explanation I propose is in three parts:

1. The would-be-killer must interpret the scene and the behavior of the victim in a particular way. He must understand not only that the victim is attacking what he, the killer, regards as an eternal human

value, but that the situation requires a last stand in defense of his basic worth.

2. The would-be-killer must undergo a particular emotional process. He must transform what he initially senses as an eternally humiliating situation into a rage. In rage, the killer can blind himself to his future, forging a momentary sense of eternal unity with the Good.

3. The would-be-killer must successfully organize his behavior to maintain the required perspective and emotional posture while implementing a particular project. The project is the honoring of the offense that he suffered through a marking violently drawn into the body of the victim. Death may or may not result, but when it does, it comes as a sacrificial slaughter.

Respectability's Last Stand

The impassioned killers described here were upholding the respected social statuses of husband, mother, wife, father, property owner, virile male, deserving poor/self-improving welfare mother, and responsible debtor. These killers were defending both the morality of the social system and a personal claim of moral worth.

Several patterns in homicide situations indicate that the killers develop a righteous passion against the background of taking a last stand in defense of respectability. First, the behavior of their victims gives them reason to believe that they will no longer be able to ignore a fundamental challenge. David Luckenbill constructed narrative accounts from information in the official files of 71 transactions that culminated in murder in an urban California county over a ten-year period. He found that the roles played by the victims and killers often reversed from the beginning to the end of the event.[19] A study of 159 cases of criminal homicide and assault that were not related to other offenses found that "in most cases, most of the victim's actions were aggressive, indicating that they, [sic] at least partially caused the outcome."[20] This was the most recent in a long line of studies that have provided evidence, in one manner or another, of precipitation by the victims.[21]

Precipitation by victims usually is physical, but the significance of the victim's attack is moral as well. At a minimum, the studies on this phenomenon indicate, in a high percentage of cases, that the person who turns out to be the victim was not trying to escape. To the (eventual) killer, the (eventual) victim, by not trying to brush off or avoid the conflict, is indicating that neither party may escape the implications of what is to transpire.

Thus, in each of the killings described earlier, it may be noted that there were indications that the victim either teased or dared the killer to resolve the conflict. The lurid police account depicts Mrs. Jones teasing her husband to resolve the ambiguous status of their marriage by the openness of her two-year relationship with Mr. Jones's friend Russell; at the fatal moment she and Russell were in a car in front of her house.[22] In the infanticide, the baby was, in the killer's eyes, defying parental orders by persistently crying. In the erotically inspired spouse killing, the killer's wife unwittingly teased him during sex by repeatedly calling out the name of an old boyfriend. In the shotgun, "property rights" killing, the victim, when warned by the killer that he would be shot if he did not clear the driveway, said nothing but held his ground. In the fight in the cafe, the victim teased the killer by "borrowing" his food to the point of daring him to do something about it. In the penultimate case reported here, the husband-victim agreed to fight, telling his wife to take off her glasses. And in the last case in this series, a couple fought over who would pay which bill, and the wife-victim, seeing her husband threaten her with a gun, urged him to use it.

Even the Francine Hughes case, with its strong theme of physical self-defense, involved a dare on other issues in conflict. When Francine Hughes set her sleeping husband on fire, she was reacting to his destruction of her school materials and to his prohibition of her return to school, in essence daring her to defy him and to escape degradation.

From the killer's perspective, the victim either teases, dares, defies, or pursues the killer. In all cases, the victim sustains a sense in the killer-to-be that there is no escape from the issue at hand. In the last case, the wife's urging was not necessarily a narrow demand that her husband kill her, but a means of expressing that she, too, felt that the situation was too awful to bear and that something had to be done immediately to resolve the conflict. Most generally, in all these incidents (except that of the infant), the victim could have tried to escape but did not. That the victims did not try to escape physically indicated to the would-be assailants that they could not escape morally.[23]

That the killer feels compelled to respond to a fundamental challenge to his worth is indicated as well by the frequent presence and the role of an audience. We might expect that homicides would typically occur in private or in circumstances that would give the killer reason not to worry about witnesses. But in the majority of the cases he studied, Luckenbill found that an audience was present, either supporting the violence—urging the combatants on, pointing out an offense, or supplying a weapon—or observing.[24] In no case did the audience oppose or attempt to defuse the situation. When a potentially humiliating conflict occurs in public, an insulted party has grounds to take for granted that he or she cannot simply walk away from the challenge, especially when others are offering such comments as, "Did you hear what he said about you?"; "Are you going to take that?"; and "Here, use this." In any case when bystanders are present, a potential assailant is apt to realize that the audience may develop and carry away its own version of the scene, staining the assailant's reputation beyond any visible limit. What is happening "now," the would-be assailant senses, will determine my identity "then," in the open-ended future. Thus, the killer acts not to affect the image he will have at any envisioned time or place but to escape the premonition of an unbearable "then."

Finally, the distribution of nonpredatory homicides in social time and space is also significant. In many respects the most serious act one can commit, homicide ironically takes place most often in casual settings. It does not occur at work in those infuriating moments when people are humiliated by their bosses or realize that their careers may have been irreparably damaged by the backstabbing of co-workers. It does not happen at serious social occasions, such as weddings and funerals, when the community gathers to manifest a collective agreement that matters of fundamental importance are at hand. Rather, it takes place at times of sexual intimacy or while one is relaxing at home, out for a good time on Saturday night, kidding around with friends, or having an otherwise unremarkable evening at a tavern.[25] And although many killings occur in bars, even these killings typically occur outside an occupational context: "It is less common for a patron to kill a bartender than another person, even though they are all in the same social situation and may have the same demographic characteristics."[26] Victims and assailants are usually kin, friends, or at least acquaintances.[27]

It should be noted that the patterns of homicide do not display a simple, dialectical relationship between Eros and Thanatos. "Mere acquaintance" relations and strangers who met shortly before the fatal event constitute a category of victims as significant as that of spouses, children/parents, and old friends. The casual nature of the setting is more clearly important than the emotional depth of the relationship.

The temporal patterning of homicide further details the ironically casual background of this most serious act. Marvin Wolfgang examined the distribution of homicides over the weekly calendar and described a decisively nonrandom pattern. He found that 65 percent of the homicides occurred on the weekend. Wolfgang noted that homicides pick up dramatically as the weekend starts, reach their height at about midnight Saturday, and taper off as the weekend comes to a close.[28] He also found that the offender and/or the victim were drinking in two-thirds of the cases, a finding that has been replicated frequently.[29]

Although these situational patterns do not speak directly of the understanding of participants, they can be interpreted as consistently indicating a paradox: the casual nature of the setting enhances the sense of challenge to personal identity. No doubt, humiliation is broadly experienced over the workweek and across all types of social settings. Certainly, workers often feel they are treated without respect and even insulted on the job. Why, then, do they not attack their bosses more often? Why do they instead kill their mates, friends, or slight acquaintances? When tensions arise on the job, one may feel severe humiliation but there are possible escapes: other people, other times, other social places in which one can expect to be free of the humiliation. Thus, one may bear the humiliation one receives from a superior by entertaining visions of the appreciation one will receive at night in bed, of the relaxed approbation one will enjoy on the weekend with friends, or of the drink that waits at the end of the day. Casual life, affectionate relationships, the weekend and Saturday night, or drinking and cruising Main Street—all the characteristic social settings for non-predatory homicide—are distinctively places of last resort for the pursuit of relaxed fun. If one cannot escape serious personal challenges then and there, it may seem as if there were nowhere else to go.

From Humiliation to Rage

When people sense that they have no resort but to confront a challenge to their ultimate personal worth, they need not respond with a violent attack. A common alternative is to turn the challenge against the self and endure humiliation. Transforming humiliation into rage is a second contingency of righteous slaughter.[30]

As with emotions in general, persons who become enraged must create the sensuality that makes them its vehicle. Thus, the analyst must account for a dialectical process in which assailants make themselves the object of forces beyond their control but retain the possibility of abandoning the process.

The situations from which righteous slaughters emerge are either conventionally humiliating, or involve the victim's self-conscious efforts to ridicule or degrade, or include the assailant's perception that the victim's actions are defiant and disrespectful. In some cases, however, the assailant's rage emerges so suddenly and silently that only when it appears does a preceding experience of humiliation become visible. The challenge here is posed not by a lack of evidence but by the subtlety of the phenomenon. Frequently, the assailant does not acknowledge the humiliation to himself until he attempts to transcend it in rage.

Thus, mortal assaults often arise directly from attempts by the killer to deflect the insult with an air of indifference or cool superiority, which is abandoned only in the attack itself. Anger, he realizes, is a concession. That is, the would-be-assailant often anticipates that if he should respond with a display of anger, he would retrospectively acknowledge that the attempted insults of the victim had hit home and that beneath his pretense, he had been on the edge of humiliation. This acknowledgment may itself be humiliating.

When the assailant suddenly drops his air of indifference, he embraces and creates his own humiliation. He then makes public his understanding, not only that he was hurt by the victim, but that he was falsely, foolishly, and cowardly *pretending* not to care. In this double respect, the once-cool but now enraged attacker acknowledges that he has already been *morally* dominated just as he moves to seek *physical* domination. He becomes humiliated at the same time and through the same action in which he becomes enraged.

That humiliation may be constituted in juxtaposition to a simultaneously constituted rage has an important implication for empirical theory. In order to analyze the move from humiliation to rage, we must simultaneously analyze the construction of humiliation *in* rage. That is, we should not err by treating rage as an escape from humiliation. There is an essential link between rage and humiliation. As a lived experience, rage is livid with the awareness of humiliation.

Rage constructs and transforms humiliation so quickly and smoothly that talking and writing about the process can very easily become artificial and obfuscating. In order not to lose sight of the phenomenon, the best approach is to take the rapid and smooth quality of the dynamic as a focus for this analysis.

It is not always easy to move from certain emotional states to certain others, for example to go from sadness to laughter. Humiliation and rage are as opposite as emotions can be, but the switch can be made quickly. How can that be? And how does rage propose to resolve the problems experienced in and through humiliation? How does rage simultaneously recall and transform the experience of humiliation? What is the logic of rage, such that it can grow so smoothly and quickly from humiliation and lead to righteous slaughter as its perfectly sensible (if only momentarily convincing) end?

These questions may appear a bit odd because the process seems so automatic. But it is contingent: not all who experience humiliation become enraged. Moreover, the experience is a personal construction. Although the assailant typically does not perceive himself as having chosen to become humiliated and enraged—although he believes that he was forced into humiliation and carried away by rage—we can unravel the process by which the assailant constructs the sense of logically smooth coherence in the transition from one state of compulsion to another.

The argument is threefold: (1) As experiences, rage and humiliation have certain identical fundamental features. (2) Like images in a mirror, rage and humiliation inversely reflect each other. (3) Righteousness is not the product of rage; it is the essential stepping stone from humiliation to rage. Like a person who passes in front of a cracked mirror and recognizes a reversed and flawed depiction of himself, the would-be assailant needs only the most fleeting encounter with the principle of moral reflection to move from humiliation to rage. The "righteous" thrust of the resulting attack does not develop through discursive reasoning; the attack is not a "statement" of moral superiority. It is the outcome of the embrace of righteousness as a means to the perfect resolution of humiliation through the overwhelming sensuality of rage.

HUMILIATION AND RAGE

In both humiliation and rage, the individual experiences himself as an object compelled by forces beyond his control. That is, his control of his identity is lost when he is humiliated. We say, for example, that a person has become an object of ridicule. Thus, a husband knows that others know he is a cuckold, and he senses that they always will see him that way. Suddenly, he realizes that his identity has been transformed by forces outside his control in some fundamental way. He has become morally impotent, unable to govern the evolution of his identity.

It is not by chance that homicides among mates so often spring from complaints about sexual performance and acknowledgments of sexual infidelity. Humiliation always embodies an awareness of impotence. The vocabulary for expressing humiliation takes for granted the feature of impotence: "she has made me a cuckold," "he has made a fool of me," or "he has 'unmade' me by revealing my pretentiousness, my fraud." If the vulnerability to impotence is often metaphorical, when it is sexual, the step from insult to humiliation is especially short.

A loss of control over one's identity may seem irremediable when injury has been inflicted on one's public image; image or reputation is social and, therefore, outside one's personal control. The experience of public degradation carries the fear of bearing the stigma of disgrace eternally.[31]

Humiliation may be passively acquired. For you to become humiliated, you need not do anything new. Humiliation may be experienced when there is a revelation to you about the conduct of others. Thus, you may become humiliated at the sudden revelation of the misleading and immoral acts by which others have long treated you as a fool.

Of course, one may humiliate oneself, for example, by confessing dreadful truths. But the exercise of personal autonomy in beginning the process does not contradict the sense of being controlled by others in the experience itself. Within humiliation, there is a profound apprehension of the power of others to control one's soul.

Although deeply spiritual, the sense of vulnerability in humiliation is neither abstract nor speculative: the person can prove to himself that it is true. Thus, when feeling humiliated, the person often tries to envision a future in which the memory of the disgrace will have faded, but as long as he stays in humiliation, he discovers that he cannot. He tries to abolish the unbearably awful feeling by reciting folk recipes: "time heals all wounds"; "he's drunk, he doesn't mean it and won't remember it"; "she's upset because of her period"; "life goes on"; "I don't need him, I'll leave"; or "I'll move, and my new associates won't know about my past." Despite the conviction that these propositions are rational, the person who feels humiliated confronts undeniable evidence that these propositions do not work: the humiliation persists.

As is true of humiliation, when enraged one's existence as a social object overpowers one's will. As in humiliation, angry people often talk becalming wisdom to themselves or attempt to control their rage (by, for example, counting to ten) and discover that it won't work; the irritation continues to mount toward rage. Indeed, they are often aware that they might well be foolish or irrational to become angry, and this awareness itself can speed the mobilization of rage: "So, I'm acting like a fool, am I?," one may hear in the private echo of an outward expression of indignation.

Humiliation either washes over the self or provokes ceaseless resistance as it threatens to seize one's being. Rage also exists on a dynamic dimension. Irritation always threatens to ripen into anger, anger threatens a self-reinforcing progression to rage, and rage has already lost a sense of developmental boundaries. As suggested by the dual meanings, anger and insanity, that have historically been associated with being "mad," rage always carries the threat of chaos.

After their lethal attacks, killers often retrospectively acknowledge a determining sense of compulsion. They frequently say, "I got carried away"; "I didn't know what I was doing"; "I wasn't myself." These are not only face-saving devices or ploys to reduce punishment, since, as was already mentioned, killers often do not attempt to escape or spontaneously call the police and confess. At times, the urgency with which they bring in the authorities and condemn themselves seems to be an attempt to prove that they have regained control of themselves—that they are typically rational and that the killing was an aberrant moment that disrupted their characteristic state of moral competence. Thus, the killers may be truly disturbed by the question, "Why did you do that?"

Humiliation and rage are holistic feelings, experienced as transcending bodily limitations. In humiliation, the person is overcome with an intolerable discomfort. Humiliation forces him to feel himself as soul, to become intensely aware that his being is spiritual, not protected by physical barriers between the internal and the external. Unlike embarrassment, which may afflict only the face through blushing, humiliation is not confined to the stomach, like a mild anxiety; limited to the top of the head, like a giddy feeling; or located narrowly in the chest, as in a recognition of unrequited love. Humiliation takes over the soul by invading the whole body. The humiliated body is unbearable alive; one's very being is humiliated.

Like humiliation, rage draws the whole body into its service. It disciplines parts of the body that often work out of harmony into coordinated action. When we speak of getting one's adrenalin up to counter physical challenges aggressively, the reference is not only to an unusual level of effort but to a new esthetic that unites all the parts of the body. Athletes and performers of martial arts naturally understand the connection between the energy level and the esthetic flow of effort. The successful execution of aggressive plays requires the precise movements of specific parts of the body, but the dependence on a part can draw consciousness to it and make it overly sensitive and thereby independent of the player's body as a whole. Getting "psyched out" refers to a real problem in such activities. To restore a prophylactic sense of flow, performers may simulate expressions of anger. If they shout, snarl, and stamp enough, maybe they will achieve a "deep acting" that will restore their transcendent sense of holistic identity.

By becoming humiliated, a person has already constructed certain fundamental elements of rage. Once a person has become humiliated, he need not lose control to be carried blindly into a raging violence. Humiliation has already accomplished that. The righteous killer need not lose himself in rage; he need only acknowledge that he is already lost in humiliation. And if he is to take a last violent stand in defense of his basic worth, humiliation has already constructed the moral profoundity and metaphysical totality of the moment.

To put the point another way, when a person becomes enraged, he confirms his humiliation through transcending it. In rage, he acknowledges that his subjectivity had been overcome by implicitly acknowledging that he could not take it anymore. But now the acknowledgment is triumphal because it comes just as rage promises to take him to dominance over the situation.

FRUSTRATION, SHAME, HUMILIATION, AND RAGE

The rage that carries an assailant into a righteous attack also shares a fundamentally social focus with humiliation. In this sense, one must distinguish humiliation from *frustration.* People who are frustrated may direct their anger toward another, but only after a transition through which they first socialize their discontent. Humiliation, however, is already a socialized emotion, reflecting an immediate, unquestionable connection between one's discomfort and another's attack. Thus, humiliation is a qualitative leap closer to rage than is frustration.

Because of the essential continuity between the internal dis-ease and the external hostility that provokes it, humiliation is also closer to rage than is shame. Both shame and humiliation are social and moral emotions in the sense that in both, one feels isolated from a community one regards as sacred. But only in shame does the person acknowledge failings or moral inadequacy. Thus, I may "become ashamed of myself" but I do not become humiliated of myself. Instead, I "am humiliated"; I am acted on by one or more persons who morally assault me by challenging my competence or trying to ridicule me. You may shame me while I remain shameless, but if you humiliate me, I feel it. The loyal trusting wife may experience deep humiliation but not shame from the discovery of her husband's long-practiced infidelity. Although shame acknowledges a personal failing or incompetence, humiliation verges on humility and is compatible with innocence.

If others are trying to help me, I may experience shame because they are reinforcing a public awareness of my condition, but I will not feel humiliation unless I perceive an aggressive, demeaning spirit in their "help," for instance, that they are patronizing me like a charity case. I feel shame in front of those who are trying to love me; I feel humiliation if I am the butt of ridicule. Hence, in humiliation, I presume a self-conscious and overt intention by others to degrade me. If I realize that they silently perceived my incompetence, I will be ashamed. If I understand that they conspired to share and hide their degrading view of me, then I will also be humiliated. And then I may well get mad.

RAGE AGAINST HUMILIATION

Even though humiliation and rage are both experienced as aggressive powers reaching into the soul, they are, of course, different forms of experience. The explanation of the swiftness and smoothness of the transition from one to the other lies precisely in the perfection of their opposition. Humiliation becomes rage when a person senses that the way to resolve the problem of humiliation is to turn the structure of his humiliation on its head.

Both humiliation and rage are experienced on a vertical dimension. Dictionaries define humiliation as an experience of being reduced to a lower position in one's own or another's eyes. Humiliation drives you down; in humiliation, you feel suddenly made small, so small that everyone seems to look down on you. Humiliation often moves through the body by warming the top of the head; then moving to the face, where its acknowledgment may create the blush of shame; and then working itself through the self, ultimately to envelope it from top to bottom. Etymologically, humiliation shares roots with "humble." All manner of degrading, debasing, deflating attacks may produce humiliation.

In contrast, rage proceeds in an upward direction. It may start in the pit of the stomach and soon threaten to burst out of your head. "Don't blow your top" and "hold your lid on," we counsel the angry. In Chicago in the late 1960s, one of the most militant youth publications was called *Rising Up Angry*. Members of militant movements understand implicitly that angry people "rise up" and that to affiliate with symbols of sitting down would express a calm resolution in protest.

If one looks back further in etymology, one finds that *humiliation, humble,* and related terms in English grew out of the Latin for *humus*—the same humus prized by gardeners—the organic, wet, fertile earth that is the most natural foundation for what human beings can grow to sustain life.[32] The wetness of humus is reflected in the liquid character of the experience of humiliation and its family of related feelings. Embarrassment, shame, and humiliation flow through the self. The blush of shame is a sudden wave of blood to the face. Humiliation threatens to drown one's being. When we have made fools of ourselves or have been made fools by others, we may wish or feel we are sinking into the earth. Someone who is completely wrong is "all wet."

Children use water balloons, not balloons with air or helium, to play at humiliation. Practical jokers place water buckets over doors and push victims into swimming pools. One of the most universal conventions for degrading someone is to spit at them. Somehow spitting, which casts a liquid on someone, significantly conveys disrespect; while blowing at someone, though a substantially similar physical act, carries other meanings. To humiliate others in an extreme way, you might urinate on them. You would then expect them to become "pissed off," their response being in opposition to the liquid provocation. An "angry young man" is said to be "full of piss and vinegar," on the understanding that anger is stimulated by the irritating qualities natural to these caustic liquids.

Humiliation as a drowning liquid and rage leaping up like a fiery gas share a boundary-defying holistic quality. Liquids and gases both seep over the edges of containers; neither has any apparent internal divisions. But they are also intrinsically opposed. Rage is a hot gas, a fire; it burns. As fire is to water, so rage is to humiliation. The heat of rage ontologically transforms the liquid of humiliation. Thus, a person "boils" in anger and then, like Yosemite Sam after he has been humiliated by Bugs Bunny, "blows off steam."

Cartoons are useful for understanding the emotional construction of experience. Popular cartoons represent imagery that has proved effective for representing emotions. Like the images of dreams and poetry, cartoon images make sense according to a symbolic logic that operates ubiquitously in everyday life but that somehow resists expression in the conventions of discursive reasoning. So, just as we know automatically that it is appropriate to say that a person might "blow up" in rage and that it is obviously wrong to say that a person might "blow down" in anger, cartoonists naturally illustrate rage as an explosion coming out of a character's head, not his or her foot. In color cartoons, the enraged character might be depicted as progressing from an initially pink irritation through deepening shades of red anger into purple rage and then into an explosion in the hues of a fire.

Tales that children find effective also reveal the symbols that are natural vehicles for emotions in a given culture. That certain patterns make dramatic sense and are persistently fascinating suggests that they fit with the structure of emotions as experienced in everyday life. Metaphoric oppositions, such as those between liquid and gas, cold and hot, and upward and downward movement, are frequently used to juxtapose good and evil.

Take, for example, the death of the evil witch in *The Wizard of Oz*. Dorothy's lethal attack, launched in rage after the witch had snatched one of her silver shoes, consists of throwing on the witch a bucket of water. This is a moral attack, a status-reducing expression of disgust by the young girl from a self-confident stance. Dorothy responds to the witch, whose power is symbolized by the control of fire, by assuming the confident posture of a little princess toward an unspeakably inferior subject, dousing her enemy with a super-spit. The witch then shrinks down to the dirt, ultimately dissolving into nothingness.[33]

Finally, the sexual oppositions. In some social circles, an erection is an "angry" penis. Today, impotence is so fundamentally linked to humiliation that in virtually all modern languages the terms for describing impotence are reliable means of effecting ridicule. If rage is red, hot, and explosive, it is like a penis threatening to ejaculate and it is also like the screaming, red-faced birth of a self. Whichever of these metaphors might be more relevant to a given individual, the language and the symbolic structure of the experience of humiliation is metaphorically the perfect opposite: a return to the womb.[34] The etymology of humiliation points to the centrality of the metaphor of the womb through humus—wet, fertile soil enriched by decayed vegetable matter—that is the most natural source of all terrestrial life: Gaea, "Mother Earth."

To disparage someone, a contemporary American might readily say that he or she "sucks," a usage that points back to the womb as a reference to the infant's sucking at the breast (as well as to the female in fellatio). Not only what we say but also what we feel in shame and humiliation is symbolically summarized by the metaphor of a return to the womb. In its sensuality, humiliation makes one feel small. In humiliation, one feels incompetent and powerless as if one's stature has been reduced to that of a baby.

Rage is specifically, intensely an oppositional emotion. Thus, humiliation threatens to be endless and diffuse, while rage searches for a target to extinguish itself. In emotional logic, rage has already found its perfect target in humiliation.

When moral attack has us pressed toward humiliation, we may construct rage through a flash recognition of the principle of opposition. The path to rage is right there before us, in the structure of whichever metaphoric features of humiliation may have become most compelling to us long ago, through cartoons, language usage, fairy tales, erotic fantasies, or other regions of popular culture. Along one or the other of the oppositions of upward and downward, static and active, liquid and gaseous, inward and outward, and male and female, we know just where to find an escape route.

Rage does not emerge spontaneously from the common killer's humiliation. What draws the would-be killer to turn his humiliation on its head and into rage? What triggers the spiritual reversal? To understand the emotional process through which humiliation leads to righteous slaughter we must examine the interconnections in the flow of experience among humiliation, rage, and the Good.

In the tale that the Mouse relates to Alice, Fury tells a mouse that they must go to trial:

> Said the mouse to the cur,
> "Such a trial, dear sir,
> With no jury or judge, would be wasting our breath."
> "I'll be judge, I'll be jury,"
> Said cunning old Fury;
> "I'll try the whole cause, and condemn you to death."[35]

Rage is a sophisticated incompetence. It is deaf in the sense of being indifferent to reasoned argument and dumb in the narrow sense of being inarticulate. Fury judges but without hearing arguments and it does not pause to explain its reasons, not even to itself. Rage is also blind, but it is not stupid. Rage is not necessarily expressed in chaotic thrusts; the common killer does not go beserk, striking at any proximate object and killing only when the victim stumbles by accident in the path of a randomly aimed blow. Rage is often coherent, disciplined action, cunning in its moral structure. Would-be killers create their homicidal rage only through a precisely articulated leap to a righteousness, which logically resolves, just for the crucial moment, the animating dilemma.

Righteousness shares with rage a blindness to the temporal boundaries of existence. Humiliation is a painful awareness of the mundane future, a vivid appreciation that once I get out of the current situation I still will not be able to get away from its degradation. I become humiliated just as I discover that despite my struggles to do so, I cannot really believe that the meaning of the moment is temporary. But rage is mercifully blind to the future. And righteousness, concerned only with what always has been and always will be right, is justly indifferent to the historical moment. In this way, the Good serves as the springboard for the leap into blind rage.

Rage is not blind to the details of the immediate context. On the contrary, in rage, the person is vividly aware of otherwise imperceptible significances in the most minor details: of the angle of the other person's head, which only now can be seen to reveal contempt; of the cumbersome nature of his own comportment as he throws an initial blow that brings him more pain than it inflicts; and of the stupid redundancy of the current conflict with innumerable fights he has been in before. Rage focuses consciousness completely on the here-and-now situation with an unparalleled intensity. Rage so powerfully magnifies the most minute details of what is present that one's consciousness cannot focus on the potential consequences of the action for one's subsequent life.

Stunned with premonitions of endless humiliation, unable to grasp any tolerable path from the "now" to concrete situations "then," the would-be killer leaps to a righteous plateau from which he can perceive eternal truths in the situation here and now. His attack enacts a feature of his social identity that he presumes will always be communally regarded as valuable: his status as father, husband, property owner, virile male, and so forth. Although the period of moral rest on his righteous perch may turn out to be short lived, in his tortured experience the person in rage searches frantically for something that will end what cannot be taken anymore—and an eternal moral peace.

The blindness to the practical future implications of the moment gives rage, with all its fury, a soothing, negative promise that humiliation painfully lacks. This is its great comfort. Like the promise of an erotic drive, rage moves toward the experience of time suspended; it blows up the present moment so the situation becomes portentous, potentially an endless present, possibly the occasion for a destruction that will become an eternally significant creativity. This is the spiritual beauty of rage.

The irony of artifice and essence in homicide may now be explained. In many motivational respects, it is patently artificial to think that homicide is committed in defense of the Good. A man who kills a stranger who has parked in his driveway or who kills the friend who has taken a piece of his barbecued food does not "really" kill because he values so highly his status as owner of these items of property. But, whatever the deeper psychological sources of his aggression, he does not kill until and unless he can fashion violence to convey the situational meaning of defending his rights. Without the moral artifact, violence would not work even momentarily as an existential escape.

Sacrificial Violence: the Embodiment of Righteous Rage

Although those who kill in righteous rage are attempting to settle matters once and for all, they often have tried many times before. The fatal blow is one of a family of acts that form a coherent field of aggressive conduct. To understand the lived experience of homicides committed in everyday settings in defense of the Good, we must understand a range of related phenomena. Why all the shouting and cursing? Why the shoving and pushing? How do the acts that are distinctive to violent attacks—"belting" and "stomping" and "cutting up" the other—seem especially fitting to one who is attempting to transcend humiliation with a righteous passion?

A practical project guides and shapes the aggression. Moral attentions after the event focus on the negative, destructive results. But within the event, the impassioned attacker is destroying his victim only to create something for himself. The positive achievement that the attacker pursues can best be seen after we consider the relationship between assault and homicide.

The practical objective of those who kill is not necessarily to kill. In the nonpredatory assault *or* homicide, "much of the violence is of an impulsive nature. An argument gets out of hand or two old enemies meet on the street, and a fight ensues. It is often difficult to tell who is the victim and who is the offender."[36]

Recognizing these findings, contemporary writers on homicide and assault routinely note that whether an event ends in a criminal homicide or an aggravated assault depends on such chance factors as the distance to the hospital;[37] the quality of medical services available; whether a gun was used and, if so, its caliber;[38] whether "a head reeling from a punch strikes a rail or concrete floor";[39] or whether the knife chanced to hit a vital organ.[40]

Research on family violence has indicated the hidden or "dark figure" of violent attacks that, but for chance factors, might have ended as homicides. Because victims are reluctant to complain officially, for a variety of reasons ranging from sympathy for the offender to fears of retaliation and self-incrimination, such attacks are notoriously unrepresented in crimes reported to the police. A national survey, whose results were based on what interviewees were willing to admit, found that

> every year about one out of every six couples in the United States commits at least one violent act against his or her partner. . . . The rates for actually *using a knife or gun* on one's spouse are one out of every two hundred couples in the previous year, and almost one out of twenty-seven couples at some point in the marriage. . . . *over 1.7 million Americans had at some time faced a husband or wife wielding a knife or gun, and well over 2 million had been beaten up* by his or her spouse.[41]

That a large percentage of homicides by gun are effected by a single shot has been interpreted as evidence that there is no specific intent to kill: if the first shot misses, another might not be taken.[42] In attacks that result in death, the attack often ceases long before the end of the victim's life, when there is clear evidence of serious injury but equally clear evidence of persistent life: cries of pain, pleas for mercy, moves to retreat. As Philip Cook noted:

In a large proportion of assaults with deadly weapons, the assailant ceases the attack by choice, rather than because of effective victim resistance. We can infer in unsustained attacks of this sort that the assailant's intent is to injure or incapacitate the victim—that there is no deliberate, unambiguous intent to kill.[43]

In short, there are many indications that the victim's death is not a *necessary* concern in either aggravated assaults or the typical criminal homicide. Perhaps a more striking way to draw attention to the practical perspective animating the assailant is to note the indications that the victim's death may not be a *sufficient* concern. In a "stomping," the attacker may announce to his victim the objective of "kicking your eyes out of your head." The specific practical objective—to remove precisely the condition of the attacker's humiliation, the victim's offending gaze—is more imaginatively related to the project of transcending humiliation than would be the victim's death. Sacrificial violence does not particularly seek the neat end of death; rather, it attempts to achieve the existentially impossible goal of obliteration, of annihilating or wiping out the victim.

To "blow away" or wipe out a person goes beyond death, which only takes life from a body but leaves the body: a wipe out leaves no trace of what was removed. It reflects a specifically transcendent project in which death may be "too good" for the victim, as in the following case:

> I was a good provider for my family and a hard worker. . . . I told her if she stopped with the divorce, and that I would promise to act better and . . . but she wouldn't buy any of it. I got angrier and angrier. . . . I looked at her straight in the face and said, "Well, X, you better start thinking about those poor kids of ours." She said, "I don't care about them: I just want a divorce."
>
> My hate for her exploded then, and I said, "You dirty, no-good bitch", [*sic*] and started pounding her in the face with my fist. She put her arms up and covered her face, so I ran and got my rifle and pointed it at her. I said, "Bitch, you better change your mind fast or I'm going to kill you." She looked up and said in a smart-ass way, "Go ahead then, shoot me." I got so mad and felt so much hate for her, that I just started shooting her again and again. . . .[44]

At times the attack persists past death, in a spirit that suggests that the assailant wishes the victim would stay alive or return to life, so the strange joy of killing might be sustained through repetition. It is arbitrary to assume that while the attack persists, the victim's death is the objective. Indeed, the victim's death may frustrate the attacker's purpose.

When the victim's death terminates the violent attack, one should still question whether death was the killer's objective or whether it was a means in a symbolically and emotionally compelling project that transcends death. When one mate slays the other after a series of impassioned fights mobilized by charges of sexual disloyalty, it sometimes seems that the killer specifically wants the victim dead. The relationship had become intolerably humiliating; the killer—like Ruth in the next example—"couldn't take it anymore"; he or she simply wanted to end it.

> Ruth seemed to be secretive about her marital problems because of her pride. She was only separated from her second legal husband and did not want people to know about her common-law relationship [with the victim]. . . . He was teasing her about another woman he met who was nicer and more attractive than Ruth. He also ceased giving any physical affection to Ruth. This bothered Ruth a lot as she started to believe that he was going to leave her for the other woman. The day the homicide occurred. . . . he came back with another woman [and] . . . a bitter quarrel ensued. Ruth could not remember what happened after that. . . . She had stabbed to death the man she had lived with for two years. According to neighbours her last remark before the murder was "If I can't have you, nobody else can!"[45]

The goal of ending the relationship is inadequate to understand the sense of such killings. Ruth's problem, for which the killing was a resolution, could not be solved by her leaving her lover, her suicide, or her lover's death, since the relationship was about to end anyway.

From within the assailant's perspective, killing a deserting lover makes sense as a way of *preserving* a relationship that otherwise would end. If he leaves her or if she leaves him, the relationship they had may well become, in both their romantic biographies, a relatively unremarkable chapter in a series of failed relationships. By killing her mate, Ruth made their relationship last forever; in the most existentially unarguable sense, she made it the most profound relationship either had ever had. Then no one else could have him; no one else could develop a relationship with him that would retrospectively extinguish the special significance they shared. Killing him was her means of honoring and protecting the transcendent significance of their relationship.

MARKING THE OFFENSE IN SACRIFICE

The practical project that the impassioned attacker, lashing out against insistent humiliation, is trying to accomplish is analogous to the practices of criminal punishment under the ancien régime, as analyzed by Michel Foucault.[46] When absolutist regimes punish theft by chopping off limbs, death becomes more likely, but it is not a necessary objective of this righteous vengeance. And when punishment persists beyond death, to dismemberment and torture of the dead body, it is clear that "capital punishment"—death—is not sufficient to accomplish the penal project.

The eighteenth-century critique of torture as barbaric and irrational called for a utilitarian penology in which the punishment was made to fit the crime. But the details of punishment by torture were given great care by the ancien régime just so the punishment would fit the crime. The punishment of major crimes called for ingenuity in the creation of new methods of torture, as reflected in the time and money spent to construct novel racks for inflicting novel forms of pain. A person who attempted regicide might be tortured for days—and for long after death transpired—first with horses to draw and quarter his body, then by hacking off the remaining limbs, then by piercing the corpse with heated metals, and so on.

Why expend all this effort? Why not make short work of the execution? According to Foucault, the object was to construct the truth of the crime. The nature and gravity of punishment defined the offense of which the condemned was guilty. To sustain the symbolism of the king's regal sensibilities, each affront to the king's rule must be given idiosyncratic punishment. The extent of the offense was defined for all to see by the pains the offender was forced to experience. The callous desecration of the criminal's body was a method of celebrating the precious sensibility that the crime had offended.

Such punishments exacted in the name of divine right were continuous with ancient traditions of sacrifice that demonstrated respect for the sacred. When a lamb's throat is slashed in a religious ceremony, the production of a dead animal is not the objective. A ritual slaughter might follow, the choice parts to be burned in a deferential offering. On other occasions, the drawing of blood, the scarring of a body, or a nonmortal dismemberment might demonstrate sufficient respect. Overall, the practical project—the concern that organized the bloody, righteous behavior—is the manifestation of respect for the sacred. It is not enough to feel the devotional spirit. Respect has to be objectified in blood.

If we must go back to the early eighteenth century to find an official system in the West that organized criminal punishment according to this understanding, we need only go to the details of contemporary assaults and homicides in families and against friends to find evidence of its persistent appeal. What is at stake in everyday contemporary violence is not a king's divine right but the sacred core of respectability that the assailant is defending and defining through his violence.

Sometimes the correspondence between the assailant's sense of offense and the marking he or she accomplishes is relatively direct. In an incident reported by M. Goldstein, a couple living in a trailer camp near his army base began fighting about music. "I felt like I wasn't being allowed to listen to the music, and she went out to the car and she wrecked my tapes." He then went "roaring back into the trailer" and, after "knocking over Patsy's record player," beat her with a rubber hose.[47] Before beating her, he attacked her record player, drawing a quick parallel between his attack on her and her offense to his musical tastes. In the Hughes killing, Francine set a fire around the bed in which her husband was sleeping—a strikingly peculiar way to kill someone—only after, earlier that day, he had compelled her to burn her school books in a barrel.[48] The form of her attack on him linked her aggression not just to his physical attack on her but to his attack on her educational version of self-worth.

In the details of the assault, the project of sacrificial violence recreates the truth of the offense received. Sometimes the correspondence is drawn in exquisite detail; more often, it is crudely accomplished. We must look carefully at the several levels of correspondence between the offense received and assault undertaken to grasp just how the enraged person finds physical attack compellingly seductive.

Consider cursing. Most studies of impassioned violence reveal a great deal of attendant cursing. Although impassioned attacks sometimes occur without verbal forewarning, it seems natural to move into the assault with shouts of "bitch," "you fucking asshole," "rat bastard," "punk mother-fucker," "nickel-and-dime drunk," "bull-dagging bitch," "cock-sucking piece of shit," and so forth. Why? If attackers were focused on killing their victims, they might be expected to express wishes of that result, for example in the clean pronouncement, "I wish you were dead." If attackers were focused on "venting anger," they might be expected to emit conventional phrases like, "I hate you." If the purpose was to mobilize the body for the attack and perhaps intimidate the opponent, incoherent, guttural cries like those used in martial arts would be most fitting.

Instead, attackers curse, at times visibly struggling against the pressure of rising emotion to discipline the mouth into a vehicle for coherent vilification. They curse, not in the superficial sense of throwing "dirty" words in the vicinity of their victims (for example, by ejecting the asides that seem natural to people when irritated), but in the more profound, ancient sense of casting a spell or invoking magical forces to effect degrading transformations in a polluting offender. Such cursing is at best an indirect way of venting anger and is often useless or even counterproductive in removing the irritant. But it is a direct and effective way of doing just what it appears to do: symbolically transforming the offending party into an ontologically lower status. As in a cartoon, a wife becomes a barking dog. An acquaintance loses his recognizable personal appearance and becomes nothing more than an anus penetrated at will by anonymous others. A person who a moment ago was a friend with a recognizably human name now has become fecal material animated in fellatio.

Cursing is an eminently sensible way of making a subsequent attack into a service honoring the sacred. Now the attack will be against some morally lower, polluted, corrupted, profanized form of life, and hence in honor of a morally higher, more sacred, and—this bears special emphasis—an eternally respectable realm of being. Guttural cries are idiosyncratic, but curses draw on the communal language and its primordial sensibility about the relationship between the sacred and the profane. If the other is shit, attacking him becomes a community service—a form of moral garbage collection performed on behalf of all decent people. Who, after all, wants to touch shit or scum or a bitch or a dirty whore? Cursing at once makes the accursed repulsive and conjures up an altruistic overlay for an attack on him or her. Now the attack will honor not just the attacker but the Good, in a presumptively primordial sense. In the terms in which cursing defines the battle, who would take the side of bitches against human beings, of fecal material against the sanctity of human life? Cursing sets up violence to be a sacrifice to honor the attacker as a priest representing the collective moral being. If the priest is stained by the blood of the sacrifice, by contact with the polluting profane material, that is a measure of the priest's devotion to society.

In addition to the cursing, the assailant often utters other distinctive preliminaries. Again, these are typically not literal threats or promises of physical injury, prosaically described, such as "I will kill you" or "I will disable you for a long time." They are powerfully portentous words, more like omens than promises or mundane threats: "I'm going to cut up your ass," "I'll kick your eyes out of your head," "I'll cut off your balls and hand them to you," "I'll fuck you up good," "I'll blow you away."

The promise is of a marking that will serve as a permanent witness that the offense previously suffered by the attacker has been transcended. The marking may be a scarring ("I'll cut you up real bad") or a blindness that will remain a visible sign ("I'll kick your eyes out"). It may be a violation of the victim's moral order ("I'll mess you up real bad") and thereby a sign of the transcendence of the assailant's moral coherence over the victim's resulting "mess." Or it may be a threat of obliteration ("I'll blow you away" or "wipe you out"), not just of the victim's future existence, but of any trace of his or her prior existence on earth. Like wiping out, a stomping is an action peculiar to sacrificial violence. Kicking occurs by accident, in sports or in joking behavior. But to attempt to stomp someone specifically seeks to leave the normal universe of routine behavior, with its multiple, morally inconsequential motives, and to enter a battlefield, where the stakes are incomparably higher— where Good and Evil fight for a final victory with a passion that understands the nature of the stakes.

Words are not necessary to make violence a means of honoring offended respectability. The general project is to mark the offense as a sacrifice taken in the victim's sensuality. In some instances, the lack of verbal forewarning is helpful.

> She more or less tried to run me and I said no, and she got hysterical and said, "I could kill you!" And I got rather angry and slapped her in the face three or four times and I said "Don't you ever say that to me again!" And we haven't had any problem since.[49]

In this instance, slapping was a device for the sensual manifestation of meaning—sounds were created, pain inflicted, and a sudden move was made. It was effective, in this recollection, in establishing the seriousness of the offense received from the wife and in reestablishing the order of the domestic community.

After the attack, what offenders recall provides further evidence that their objective was a marking. A black eye hidden under sunglasses or kept private by a spouse who stays at home for days, fearing to appear in public, is a naturally satisfying symbolic transcendence of the offense. The organ-source of the offending gaze is now darkened and perhaps shut closed in proved deference to the offended party. Attackers remember black eyes. They also detail the number of stitches required to sew the victim up, the number of bones that were broken, and the length of time the victim was in the hospital; recall the piece of finger or ear that was bitten or cut off; and note that the head was "cracked open." And they talk of blood: how much blood ran, where it ran, and the bloody mess that resulted.[50]

Like the shouting that was the corporeal vehicle for the cursing, the blood and the bones that are the noted results of impassioned attacks bespeak the seriousness of the attacker's purpose. It is not incidental that the marks of sacrifice are signs of the body penetrated and its normally hidden elements revealed. Physical attack is seductively sensible as a device for bringing to the surface what is most fundamental in life. Attackers may understand their victims to have been acting artificially with them, for example, by providing transparent excuses for suspected adultery or by making promises that were made before and subsequently betrayed. The very recurrence of physical fights between spouses makes language more and more superficial and violence increasingly attractive. When words have lost their ability to articulate credible meaning through too-casual use, violent attack is an ultimate way of conveying the message: "Cut the bullshit. Be real with me. This is important to me, more important than anything else, deadly important." In the physical thrust, the attacker focuses on matters of vital significance; the attack reaches bone and spills blood, it aims to go beneath the surface of the everyday persona to reveal what is usually deeply hidden, the essential structure of life.

The imagery of sacrificial marking, however bizarre it seems, is usually not strange to those who kill. National data indicate that about 80 percent of those arrested for murder or nonnegligent manslaughter in 1970 had previous arrests. Among homicide offenders arrested in the United States between 1970 and 1975, almost 70 percent had previous arrest records.[51] A study in Kansas City found that, in the two years preceding domestic homicides, police had intervened in a domestic disturbance at the address of the victim or suspect in about 90 percent of the cases, and that for about half the cases, the police had been at the location for a disturbance call at least five times.[52]

If sacrificial violence is not exactly a practiced art, it is often a recurrent practice over careers of violent acts. The attackers, however wild and impassioned they appear at the moment, know deeply and in some detail just what they are doing. The typical killer is familiar with the victim, feels at home in the setting, and has often practiced variations on the themes of sacrificial violence.

Humiliation, Rage, and Sacrificial Violence

Obviously it is possible to feel humiliated without becoming enraged; to become righteously enraged without launching an assault; to perform ritual sacrifices in a pacific, pietistic spirit; and so on. None of the conditions that create a seduction to righteous slaughter, when jointly experienced, independently calls out the others. But the interpretive, emotional, and practical conditions of righteous slaughter often depend on each other. Should one fail, not only will the prospects of an attack fade, the others are likely to be dismantled.

First, it should be noted that assailants do not necessarily construct the conditions of righteous slaughter one by one or in any particular temporal order. Commentators usually place the passion in homicidal and assaultive events before and as the immediately determining cause of the attack—often with metaphors suggesting catharsis or an image of the mind as a munitions dump. Thus, they describe the attackers as finally feeling that they cannot take any more pressure and "exploding" into violence, as "giving vent" to their disturbance through attacking, and as "exhausting" or "expending" their passion through violence. But close accounts reveal a frequent pattern in which an assailant moves into an attack and then rage builds.

In the following account of a fight, the attacker and his brother, after drinking with the victim in a bar, paid for a cab and "a couple of six packs" to take to the home of the victim. On their arrival, the victim announced that the two brothers, who had expected to spend the night, would have to leave. Some curses and threats were exchanged as the brothers moved to leave:

The dude said, "That's right, get your fucking ass out of here now," and pushed me once more. I said to myself, "Fuck it, that's it, I'm going to fuck him up." I hit him with a right hook, went berserk, and grabbed a lamp and busted him over the head and downed him. I yelled, "You punk motherfucker, I'll kick your eyes out of your head" and stomped him in the face.[53]

After being pushed repeatedly by the victim, the attacker first decided no longer to respect his brother's remonstrations not to attack and began in a relatively civil manner ("with a right hook," as if in a boxing match). Only then did his rage accelerate, generating curses and a wild method of attack. The motions of battle sometimes call up the emotions that would sustain them.

Physical involvement in the style of sacrificial violence commonly precedes the height of rage. In yelling curses, one is deepening the significance of the conflict not only in symbolism but in the physical process as one's whole body is being mobilized for the expression. If anger is a confined experience (for instance, getting red in the face) and rage is a holistic experience (one is in rage or "en-raged"), shouting, screaming, or yelling is a conveniently intermediary step that sensually paves the way for enraged violence.

Family fights often begin in verbal hassling and physical tussling that have an ambiguous status. In such cases, rage does not precede and cause a violent attack; conflictual motions initiated without a source in deep anger may elicit symbolic themes of violent attack that are then taken up in rage. The next quote is from an observer who found himself in the middle of a family battle.

> It started sort of slowly . . . so I couldn't tell for sure if they were even serious. . . . In the beginning they'd push at each other, or shove, like kids—little kids who want to fight but they don't know how. Then, this one time, while I'm standing there not sure whether to stay or go, and them treating me like I didn't even exist, she begins yelling at him like she did.
>
> "You're a bust, you're a failure, I want you out of here, I can always get men who'll work, good men, not scum like you." And they're pushing and poking with their hands, like they were dancing. She pushes him, he pushes her, only she's doing all the talking. He isn't saying a word.
>
> Then all of a sudden, she must have triggered off the right nerve because he lets fly with a right cross that I mean stuns. I mean she goes down like a rock! And he's swearing at her, calling her every name in the book.[54]

Not only does rage sometimes develop after the violence begins, its persistence frequently is contingent on the practical success of violence. If it appears that violence will not succeed, the attacker may put an abrupt stop to rage, anticipating that otherwise he or she risks reverting to a more profound humiliation. In the following case of a fight in a jail cell, the attacker called his victim "crazy" and then was knocked down:

> I really got hot. I just thought I wanted to kill that dirty s.o.b. I jumped up to my feet and pulled out a fingernail file that I had on me. But then

I thought, "This file won't stop him, and he's too fucking big to fight without something more than this. I better back off." After I backed up a few feet, I said, "Motherfucker, don't you ever turn your back near me; you've busted my fucking nose, and I'm going to get you for it." He looked at me and said "Come on, do it right now." I just said, "I'll catch you later" and walked off fast, real fast.[55]

This attacker, however enraged he was, still had the composure to back off with a face-saving curse and a promise of revenge.

Notice how each of the three conditions of righteous slaughter was dismantled in that situation. First, the attacker suddenly realized the practical project of sacrificial violence could not be successfully organized ("he's too fucking big to fight"). His rage then quickly faded, threatening to turn back into humiliation. The further result was a reintepretation of the situation as no longer calling for a last stand. There will be other opportunities to settle this, the would-be attacker announced with a now-calculated bravado, "I'll catch you later."

In other events, the causal conditions become undone in a different order. The first step back may come when the assailant seizes on grounds to hope for a future acknowledgment of respectability, as in this account:

I was at home looking for the t.v. guide when I found a note written by my wife. It said that she owed somebody $6 for babysitting for her twelve hours. I thought to myself "Where in the living hell could she have been gone for twelve hours?" My mind then turned to her stepping out with someone behind my back, so I called her. When she came in the room, I said, "What in the hell is this note about?" She grabbed the note out of my hand and said, "Oh, it's nothing." I said, "What in the hell do you mean that it's nothing? Where in the hell were you for twelve hours?"

Then she started giving me some story about going shopping and to the hairdresser's. I said, "Bullshit, that crap doesn't take any twelve hours to do." She said, "Well, maybe the twelve hours that I wrote on the note is a mistake." I said, "Don't hand me that bullshit; you're fucking around with someone." She said, "No, no, I'm not." Then I yelled, "You no-good tramp, dirty whore, you better tell me where in the hell you have been." She said, "You are acting like nothing but a bum: I'm not going to tell you anything." I thought to myself, "I'm going to beat the damn truth out of that no-good, rotten bitch." I started thinking about tying her up and beating her until she talked, but then I thought that if I went that far, she might leave me, so I dropped it. I was scared that if I did do it, then I would end up losing her.[56]

In this recollection, the alleged adultress denied the accusation ("No, no, I'm not."). There were further curses, but after the denial, the offended spouse did not need to treat the dispute as a last stand, and he turned from being in hell, surrounded by bullshit, to the mundane future—to what life would be like on the other side of a terminal conflict. Then he abandoned the transcendent aspiration of rage. By labeling his accusations as the crude acts of a "bum," his wife threw out a hint of respectability: they should rise above mean suspicions, they are suited to a more refined level of understanding. And, this time anyway, he jumped at that hint and quickly abandoned what he sensed was an even more precarious last stand.

Even when the parties are enraged and are familiar with the ways of sacrificial violence, the interactive character of the relationship with the victim builds a further dimension of uncertainty into the event. The victim may not sustain the pressure of humiliation but back off, redefining the situation as not requiring a last stand.[57] These battles are processes of negotiation over how much is practically required before the pressure to humiliate is over, before the last stand is dismantled, and before an objective reconstruction of offended respectability is deemed accomplished. Rage may seem powerful, both to the enraged person and to analysts, but rage itself does not demand an attack on the body of the humiliating party. If a sacrifice is to be taken, it may be made in the forms of inanimate targets, for example, by punching holes in a wall, smashing chairs on tables, shooting out windows, or throwing about objects that are precious to the offensive party.

There are multiple situational contingencies on the road to righteous slaughter. That there is no inevitability to the event is not due to the defects of methodology or theory or solely to the frequently interactional character of the violence. As experienced by the participants, the event is inherently uncertain in at least two respects.

First, much of the conflict leading to sacrificial violence is conducted not in a controlling attitude but in the stance of prayer. Pushing, shoving, shouting—these characteristic aggressive moves are inadequately understood simply as punitive. Why shove or shout? What damage does that do? Pushing is incomprehensible as "irrational" behavior somehow randomly growing out of "explosive anger." It is pellucid as a way of trying to move the other out of his or her posture to end the humiliation and reverse the pressure to take a last stand. Shouting is loud—not so loud to hurt the other's eardrums but loud enough momentarily to block out one's own openness to the other's definition of the situation. If the other would not shout back, if he or she would "just shut up," perhaps that would be enough. If these moves appear in one light to assume postures of dominance, in another, more obscure way, they are prayers that acknowledge the uncertainty of the evolving moment. These common openings to righteous violence signify a still-engaged moral inclination for peace even as they prepare to honor the Good in blood.

Second, the performance of sacrificial violence is an opening of the self to fate. If the attacker does not know just what the practical result of his attack will be—whether the bullet will hit a vital organ, whether his victim will be strong enough to survive, or how long it will take for medical assistance to arrive—he knows that he does not know. He could know. As I will detail in chapter 8, killers can meditate on and preside over their administration of a coup de grace. They can envision a dead body while they plan an escape and they can arrange corpses after the fact to shape the scene that will greet subsequent discoverers. As can be seen in most modern methods of capital punishment—when carefully balanced chemicals are injected to produce death instantly, painlessly, and without marring the resulting corpse—killing a person can be made the precise, efficient, specific objective of an act.

But distinctive to righteous slaughter is an objective that makes such attentions obscenely mundane: the project of transcending one's existential future. After humiliation makes one painfully aware that what has just now happened cannot be reconciled with a respectable vision of oneself in any imaginable, concrete future, rage rises to block out concern for what will be, "then." These criminal killings are the results of leaps into blind faith. Impassioned slayings are both morally familiar moves typically taken on familiar grounds and acts that make no sense unless they attempt to go beyond the familiar, to produce an irreversible, unprecedented transformation. Ultimately, the open character of sacrificial violence is due not to failings of evidence or to features of interaction, but to the phenomenological fact that its final seduction is the unknown.

Phenomenal Foreground and Structural Background

In the United States, police departments, coroners' offices, federal and state departments of justice, and the U.S. Bureau of the Census routinely produce data on crime. The choice of the variables that are covered in the official data is structured by a multitude of historical and political-institutional forces; causal social theory has played little discernible part in this process.[58] Surely, the contours and lived contingencies of criminal experience are far removed from the definitions of crime and the demographic factors that such data trace. Still, the government's regular and statistically massive production of crime data has been, to judge from the contents of professional journals, a powerful seducer of academic social scientists.[59]

What can one learn about the relationship of background factors to homicide if one sticks with data that describe the offenders within their backgrounds? By making the understanding of criminal experience the first priority, we do not abandon inquiry into the relation of demographic and socioeconomic factors to crime. On the contrary, we discover phenomenologically grounded leads to a comprehensive theory. In the next sections, I discuss social class and gender. To understand the disproportionate representation of blacks in homicide requires a discussion of some themes that, to avoid redundancy, are taken up in chapter 7, which treats the even greater overrepresentation of blacks in robbery.

SOCIAL CLASS

Marvin Wolfgang, among others, has asserted that criminal homicide, especially its impassioned form, is committed primarily by those of low socioeconomic status. In addition to examining quantified police data, analysts such as Wolfgang have read extensive underlying evidentiary documents and have personally observed the investigatory process.[60] The strength of their conviction comes not so much from quantified class data as from the absence of evidence of homicides among the middle and upper classes.[61]

To date the best inquiry into middle- and upper-class homicides found not only that the crime is rare but that these rare events are qualitatively different from killings that have the qualities of righteous slaughter. The researchers examined 119 cases of upper-class socioeconomic killers reported in the *New York Times* between 1955 and 1979. They found that

> only 2.5% of the upper-class homicides, as compared to between one-third and one-half (in other studies) of the lower-class homicides, were the result of a trivial altercation. . . . Of the lower-class killers, 25.5% in the Wolfgang study, 37.9% in the Voss and Hepburn study, and 22% in the Curtis study could claim some mitigation of the offense by virtue of the initial show of force by the victim. In contrast, none of the upper-class killers in the present study was provoked by a victim's overt act of force. . . . None of the lower-class spouse-killings but 26.9% of those in the upper-class, were linked to pecuniary motives such as insurance benefits or property inheritance, while 28.6% were attributed to profound mental depression. Of the 56 upper-class spouse-slayers, almost one-fifth (six husbands and five wives) hired someone else to do the job.[62]

Suicide followed homicide in 27 percent of the affluent cases, compared to a range from 0.8 percent to 9 percent in other U.S. studies of all homicides, regardless of class.

Because it was based on newspaper reports, this study is far from ideal. The researchers first tried to locate a sample by contacting law enforcement agencies, but despite a cooperative response, they could not locate more than a handful of cases. The people in the best position to know, know that the cases are not there. If the affluent are more capable of covering up their crimes, such a facility would be less relevant to righteous slaughters than to murders done for profit. And there is no reason to suspect that newspapers are biased to report murder among the affluent only when it is done coldly for gain. The Jean Harris case—of the headmistress of a prestigious Eastern girls' school who shot the "Scarsdale diet doctor" to death—fit the form of a righteous slaughter and certainly did not lack news coverage.

Unfortunately, the available data are inadequate to determine whether homicide is concentrated among the poor, diffused throughout the working class, at the lower margins of the working class, in a steadily inverse relationship to socioeconomic status at the bottom region of the social structure, or whatever. A double irony captures what is known, through qualitative evidence, about the relationship of social class to righteously enraged homicide. First, although impassioned homicides are extreme attacks on perhaps the most fundamental communal taboo, to the killers they are efforts to defend what they, often idiosyncratically, take to be eternal, collectively shared values. Second, if it is the working and underclasses who are doing virtually all the righteously enraged criminal killings, they are killing to honor not only values often associated with the lower classes (male virility and *machismo*), but values typically labeled as middle class or bourgeois: the sanctity of the marital union, respect for property rights, and the importance of being a responsible debtor. Why should it be the members of the lower working and underclasses who kill (each other) so passionately to defend middle-class values?

An answer is suggested by the oddity of Jean Harris's killing of Dr. Tarnower, which was strikingly similar to common lower-class killings in its dynamics. Caught in the passions of sexual jealousy, after a series of humiliating outbursts in which competing mistresses tore and smeared feces on each other's clothes found in Doctor Tarnower's home, Jean Harris arrived late at night at her lover's home, admittedly with a gun and, in retrospect, obviously without a good plan of escape. Perhaps the most appealing part of her defense was that she did not have an escape plan. But the lack of an escape plan is not unusual in lower-class passion killings. In effect, Ms. Harris relied on her ability to convey a "classy" impression to keep the jury from considering her case a lower-class killing.[63]

The Harris-Tarnower killing is an exception that indicates the rule—a "negative case" strategically valuable for understanding why social class would ordinarily be related inversely to homicide. Ms. Harris had just learned that she would lose her job and perhaps much of her respectable reputation. What was new in her life was not the destruction of her love relationship—she had been pushed aside by her lover long before—but the threat to her career. Her trip to the doctor's home on the fateful night began not as a murder plot but as a desperate effort to rescue her respectability. The association of lower-class status and homicide is understandable as a product of this sort of convergent disrespect in a person's occupational and intimate life.

Before further speculation is warranted on possible causal connections between homicides of passion and class status, many more close studies are needed of negative cases and of the personal contexts in lower-income settings within which homicidal passions commonly develop. Economic pressures are only occasionally visible within the situated homicide interaction and, even then, one must wonder how the offenders previously managed to handle the pressures. And as to the relative lack of murders of passion in the higher classes, it is too easy to speculate that, given the social structure of his life, the upper-middle-class male has more opportunities to escape humiliation.

There is at least widespread evidence that the modal times and places for homicide track the escape routes of the male working class. This evidence supports one side of the causal theory relating social class to murders of passion. That is, if experience at work becomes intolerably degrading, the worker can fantasize about respect and sensual pleasure at home. If tensions at home become intolerable, he can escape to the neighborhood bar. But at some point on this route, there may be no further escape.

Elijah Anderson vividly conveyed the risks of the neighborhood tavern as one stop on the escape route of urban black poor men. Working as a participant-observer, Anderson was taken home by his informant, Herman, who bragged to his sister that Anderson, who was, at the time, a Ph.D. candidate, was a "doctor." Overhearing this statement as a showy claim of respectability by association, Butterroll, Herman's common-law wife, made sure that Herman heard her tell her sister-in-law that Anderson was just another "wino" from Jelly's, Herman's favorite corner tavern. With that remark, Herman and Anderson left. Anderson explained about Herman and his associates at Jelly's:

> This setting often becomes the thick of their social life. Here are the others they really care about impressing. . . . this general audience of peers . . . gains the real capacity to accept or reject the selves exhibited. . . . Here people can gather freely, bargaining with their limited resources, their symbols of status, and their personal sense of who and what they are against the resources of their peers and against what their peers see them *really* to be. . . . It is here among intimate peers that selves on display may be meaningfully accepted, "shot down," "blown away," tried and tested, or simply ignored.[64]

I cannot confidently suggest that escape routes (the office as a respectable retreat, private space and business trips for diversions from the horrors at home, or the power of money to buy shows of respect in consumer transactions) are more readily available to the middle class because no one knows whether people in all the classes experience humiliation in a similar way. The available qualitative data show what humiliation is like when it leads to violent assault. The lives of those who are higher in the social class system are likely to be so thoroughly different that not just the response but the emergence and shape of humiliation may also be radically different.

GENDER

Independent of the influence of social class, region, race, and all other socioeconomic and demographic factors that have been examined in relation to homicide, men commit criminal homicides at much higher rates than do women. U.S. data show that males are responsible for about 80 percent of the homicides, a relatively low level compared to societies in other parts of the world and especially to nonliterate societies.[65] The data describing the sex of the offenders and victims in criminal homicides are also consistent. In about 60 percent of the homicides in the United States, males kill males; killings of women by women are significantly uncommon, currently constituting less than 3 percent of all criminal homicides.[66]

These figures seem to fit well the notion of sex-related, generalized psychological or socialized proclivities to violence. But if *machismo* or male cultures of violence have much effect on homicidal behavior, the effects must not be powerful, given the rarity of the event. And such notions seem contradicted by the minor measure of the predominance of men in family homicides. For homicides within families in the modern West, the rates for males are not always higher than the rates for females, and when they are, the edge is often only slight.[67] The overall preponderance of male homicides consists largely of felony murders by males and fatal fights among male acquaintances. A recent study found that women committed about 40 percent of the family homicides in several American cities (see table 1.1).[68]

TABLE 1.1

Percentage (and Number) of Homicides Committed by Women by City and Type of Homicide, 1978

City	Family Homicide	Stranger Homicide
Oakland	50.0(5)	10.0(1)
Chicago	49.2(30)	4.5(4)
Newark	46.2(6)	16.7(4)
Dallas	39.5(17)	8.3(5)
Memphis	37.5(6)	9.1(2)
"Ashton"	36.8(7)	6.3(1)
St. Louis	33.3(9)	2.9(1)
Philadelphia	27.9(12)	0
Total	39.7(92)	5.7(18)

SOURCE: Marc Riedel and Margaret Zahn, *Nature and Patterns of American Homicide* (Washington, D.C.: Department of Justice, National Institute of Justice, 1985), p. 41.

But whatever the exact balance of male and female homicides in contemporary society, there are distinctive male and female forms of the project. Although the basic dimensions of the causal process of impassioned murder are essentially uniform, differences are notable in the versions of the Good, in the constitution of the "last moral stand," in the experience of the transition from humiliation to rage, and in the style of sacrificial marking that each sex finds compelling.

As attacks undertaken to mark offenses received in sacrifices taken, male-to-female and female-to-male physical abuse, even when counted as equivalent by surveyors, do not necessarily have identical meanings. Men may take pride in the black eyes they have planted on their mates, which force the women into a short-lived purdah, their shame confining them at home or, should they go out, compelling them to wear veils constructed of heavy makeup, sunglasses, and hats. The male's appreciation of such scarring depends on his community's understanding of proper gender roles, which do not include pride in the abuse of men by women. Nevertheless, curses may scar when blows would glance off. A woman can distinctively mark a man by ridiculing his virility and, whether or not the woman works, by shaming him for failing to uphold the traditional, symbolic male responsibility for the economic status of the household.[69]

A recent study by Angela Browne of "battered women who kill" suggested another difference in the ways men and women in homicidal relationships may take pleasure in sustaining the other's pain. The subjects, forty-two women from fifteen states, were not randomly selected from female offenders but were found through the efforts of their defense lawyers to document histories of physical abuse.[70] Several of the women recounted sadistic sexual practices by their mates following the males' vicious attacks. Although the sample is systematically biased, the finding is significant because there are no comparable indications in the literature of an erotic reward for females who may physically attack their male mates. But, although Browne's research did not include data on the male perspective, she noted that the women tended to be from a higher social class than did the men. The women's accounts so strongly attest to their superior refinement and moral sensibility that it seems likely they somehow gave just that impression, not only to their interviewer after the killing but during the life of the doomed relationship to their mates.

As in the cases reviewed earlier in this chapter, in the homicides committed by the women in Browne's study, the victims sustained the offenders' sense that the here and now required a last stand. As Browne stated, "In the eventual homicide incidents, many of the men *dared* their partners to kill them, or ran against the gun as the women were firing."[71] Moreover, the women's sense of the need to take a last stand was frequently constructed for the women by the men's threats to hunt them down and kill them if they attempted to walk out on the relationship.

Perhaps the strongest statistical finding in this area is a negative one—

the rarity of women killing women. Within the social circles in which homicides by women typically occur, women seem so exclusively to place their self-esteem on their relations with men that only their mates, or occasionally a female rival, can press them to a last moral stand. Homicides by women are tightly tied to female roles at home. In contrast to homicides by men, the victims of female criminal killers are much more often family members,[72] the event typically occurs in the home,[73] and there is even some provocative evidence that the act is more often performed in a context—in the kitchen, with knives—suggesting the traditional female role in the home.[74] Within the home, differences in the social identities of men and women more clearly shape the process than the probability of homicide.

Jane Totman's study of female killers incarcerated in California portrayed an extreme degree of isolation. Many of Totman's subjects had suffered histories of violent attacks by their mates and despaired of having any alternatives; they had no employment prospects, no educational opportunities, not even hobbies or interests outside their families. Of the thirty-six women who killed mates, no woman expressed pleasure or interest in previous academic or vocational experiences:

> Very few ever imagined, even as a child, doing anything with themselves other than getting married and having children. . . . The women interviewed wanted to feel loved by their men. . . . "Life" can perhaps be defined as their circumscribed mate relationship.[75]

Men stand up for virility in its traditional folk meaning when they fight it out with other men in bars and on the street. Women who kill likewise defend traditional versions of the female identity.

As to the emotional process of moving from humiliation to rage, the evidence does not indicate a constitutional or socialized incompetence among female killers. If violence is a vehicle of masculine sensuality, that is, if rising up in hot, angry physical aggression embodies a phallic metaphor, women are not especially put off by the unfeminine character required to do battle with men. Even in traditional societies in which women's killing of their mates is virtually nonexistent, there are often patterns of female killing of children and disciplinary practices in which physical attacks are routine.

If anything, the evidence is that women's transition to rage is even more sudden than is men's. A study of family violence conducted at a rural medical clinic found, that in cases of assaults, "the violence by women was related to a direct threat to life and usually came as a surprise since they themselves were unaware of the extent of their rage."[76] Browne's volume elaborated on this theme with evidence from several cases in which the women so thoroughly portrayed themselves as long-suffering martyrs that they could not make sense of the moment in which they finally and fatally moved into an aggressive posture.[77] There is virtually no evidence that any of the women had become angry, much less physically counterattacked, before. These women retrospectively reported the abandonment of passivity as an automatic, alien process. It is as if they regarded the embodiment of rage as so out of character that they could achieve it only by refusing to recognize themselves as authentically engaged. Thus, as Browne described:

> Suddenly, Karen was just tired of being threatened this way and never knowing if she was going to live or die. . . . The next thing she remembers, she was standing in the kitchen and realized that Hal was shot. . . .

> The next thing Kim remembers is standing in the living room facing Billy, putting a 7mm rifle to her shoulder and firing once. She remembers a huge sound. . . .

> Bella thinks she said, 'How could that happen?' She wondered how the fire could have started. It was like she was in a daze; she didn't really think she did it. . . .

> Mary Wheeler was found at the scene of Chuck's death in a state of profound shock, by police officers who responded to a call from a neighbor.[78]

Women do not live the offense by stumbling about, shooting erratically, setting fires haphazardly, or acting with an air of uncertainty while they are committing it. The blackout comes afterwards. They appear to have a distinct problem in self-consciously acknowledging the sacrificial rage that they were able to effect, apparently quite naturally, at the fatal moment. The experience of traumatic shock that they authentically construct suggests a direct and desperate effort to reconstruct a posture of innocence. The innocence most deeply at issue is not a matter of legal responsibility for the homicide; with respect to legal difficulties, they are generally in as difficult a position as are men who are spontaneous passion killers. Their more distinctive problem is to explain *to themselves* how, after so many cycles of receiving physical abuse from and extending forgiveness to their male mates, they could have accomplished the killing so naturally. The ability to execute righteous slaughter at the first try may imply something inconsistent with their autobiographies of martyrdom: that they had long been living the anger and practicing the elements of righteous sacrifice, but in ways that previously left no public scars. Perhaps rituals of forgiving abusive mates can substitute for rites of cursing; surely, as visible marks of sacrifices taken and respectability honored, tears and wrenching pleas can substitute for blood. When battered wives make a sudden switch from suffering to avenging martyr, they are often concluding an epic moral tale characterized on one side by a series of attacks in which the male exacts testimony to his respectability from the body of the female and on the other by recurrent cycles of reconciliation in which the female is honored by pleas for forgiveness and acts of humbled contrition.[79]

In short, with the limited evidence now available for comparative analysis, it appears that both men and women construct impassioned murders through roughly the same steps but frequently in distinctive styles. On the one hand, murder is too rare an event and male and female homicide rates within families are too close, for the study of homicide to be an important source of knowledge about differences in male and female identity. On the other hand, the study of gender differences is essential to the study of homicide. Killing a mate is too important an act not to reflect the shape one has given his or her sexual being.

CHAPTER 2

Sneaky Thrills

Various property crimes share an appeal to young people, independent of material gain or esteem from peers. Vandalism defaces property without satisfying a desire for acquisition. During burglaries, young people sometimes break in and exit successfully but do not try to take anything. Youthful shoplifting, especially by older youths, often is a solitary activity retained as a private memory.[1] "Joyriding" captures a form of auto theft in which getting away with something in celebratory style is more important than keeping anything or getting anywhere in particular.

In upper-middle-class settings, material needs are often clearly insufficient to account for the fleeting fascination with theft, as the account by one of my students illustrates:

> [82] I grew up in a neighborhood where at 13 everyone went to Israel, at 16 everyone got a car and after high school graduation we were all sent off to Europe for the summer. . . . I was 14 and my neighbor was 16. He had just gotten a red Firebird for his birthday and we went driving around. We just happened to drive past the local pizza place and we saw the delivery boy getting into his car. . . . We could see the pizza boxes in his back seat. When the pizza boy pulled into a high rise apartment complex, we were right behind him. All of a sudden, my neighbor said, "You know, it would be so easy to take a pizza!" . . . I looked at him, he looked at me, and without saying a word I was out of the door. . . . got a pizza and ran back. . . . (As I remember, neither of us was hungry, but the pizza was the best we'd ever eaten.)

It is not the taste for pizza that leads to the crime; the crime makes the pizza tasty.

Qualitative accounts of *initial* experiences in property crime by the poorest ghetto youths also show an exciting attraction that cannot be explained by material necessity. John Allen, whose career as a stickup man living in a Washington, D.C., ghetto will be examined in detail in chapter 6, recalled his first crime as stealing comic books from a junkyard truck: "we destroyed things and took a lot of junk—flashlights, telephones." These things only occasionally would be put to use; if they were retained at all, they would be kept more as souvenirs, items that had acquired value from the theft, than as items needed before and used after the theft.[2]

What are these wealthy and poor young property criminals trying to do? A common thread running through vandalism, joyriding, and shoplifting is that all are sneaky crimes that frequently thrill their practitioners. Thus I take as a phenomenon to be explained the commission of a nonviolent property crime as a sneaky thrill.

In addition to materials collected by others, my analysis is based on 122 self-reports of university students in my criminology courses.[3] Over one-half were instances of shoplifting, mostly female; about one-quarter described vandalism, almost all male; and the rest reported drug sales, non-mercenary housebreaking, and employee theft. In selecting quotations, I have emphasized reports of female shoplifters, largely because they were the most numerous and sensitively written.

The sneaky thrill is created when a person (1) tacitly generates the experience of being seduced to deviance, (2) reconquers her emotions in a concentration dedicated to the production of normal appearances, (3) and then appreciates the reverberating significance of her accomplishment in a euphoric thrill. After examining the process of constructing the phenomenon, I suggest that we rethink the relationships of age and social class to devious property crime.

Flirting with the Project

In the students' accounts there is a recurrent theme of items stolen and then quickly abandoned or soon forgotten. More generally, even when retained and used later, the booty somehow seems especially valuable while it is in the store, in the neighbor's house, or in the parent's pocketbook. To describe the changing nature of the object in the person's experience, we should say that once it is removed from the protected environment, the object quickly loses much of its charm.

During the initial stage of constructing a sneaky thrill, it is more accurate to say that the objective is to be taken or struck by an object than to take or strike out at it. In most of the accounts of shoplifting, the shoplifters enter with the idea of stealing but usually do not have a particular object in mind.[4] Indeed, shoplifters often make legitimate purchases during the same shopping excursions in which they steal. The entering mood is similar to that which often guides juveniles into the short journeys or sprees that result in pranks and vandalism.[5] Vandals and pranksters often play with conventional appearances; for example, when driving down local streets, they may issue friendly greetings one moment and collectively drop their pants ("moon") to shock the citizenry the next. The event begins with a markedly deviant air, the excitement of which is due partly to the understanding that the occurrence of theft or vandalism will be left to inspirational circumstance, creative perception, and innovative technique. Approaching a protected property with disingenuous designs, the person must be drawn to a particular object to steal or vandalize, in effect, inviting particular objects to seduce him or her. The would-be offender is not hysterical; he or she will not be governed by an overriding impulse that arises without any anticipation. But the experience is not simply utilitarian and practical; it is eminently magical.

MAGICAL ENVIRONMENTS

In several of the students' recountings of their thefts, the imputation of sensual power to the object is accomplished anthropomorphically. By endowing a thing with human sensibilities, one's reason can be overpowered by it. To the Alice in Wonderland quoted below, a necklace first enticed— "I found the one that outshone the rest and begged me to take it"—and then appeared to speak.

[15] There we were, in the most lucrative department Mervyn's had to offer two curious (but very mature) adolescent girls: the cosmetic and jewelry department. . . . We didn't enter the store planning to steal anything. In fact, I believe we had "given it up" a few weeks earlier; but once my eyes caught sight of the beautiful white and blue necklaces alongside the counter, a spark inside me was once again ignited. . . . Those exquisite puka necklaces were calling out to me, "Take me! Wear me! I can be yours!" All I needed to do was take them to make it a reality.

Another young shoplifter endowed her booty, also a necklace, with the sense of hearing. Against all reason, it took her; then, with a touch of fear, she tossed it aside in an attempt to exorcise the black magic and reduce it to a lifeless thing.

[56] I remember walking into the store and going directly to the jewelry stand. . . . This is very odd in itself, being that I am what I would consider a clothes person with little or no concern for accessories. . . . Once at home about 40–45 minutes after leaving the store, I looked at the necklace. I said "You could have gotten me in a lot of trouble" and I threw it in my jewelry box. I can't remember the first time I wore the necklace but I know it was a very long time before I put it on.

The pilferer's experience of seduction often takes off from an individualizing imputation. Customers typically enter stores, not to buy a thing they envisioned in its particularities but with generic needs in mind. A purchased item may not be grasped phenomenally as an individualized thing until it is grasped physically. Often, the particular ontology that a possession comes to exhibit—the charm of a favorite hat or an umbrella regarded as a treasure—will not exist while the item sits in a store with other like items; the item will come to have charm only after it has been incorporated into the purchaser's life—only when the brim is shaped to a characteristic angle or the umbrella becomes weathered. But the would-be thief manages to bring the particular charm of an object into existence before she possesses it. Seduction is experienced as an influence emanating from a particular necklace, compact, or chapstick, even though the particular object one is drawn to may not be distinguishable from numerous others near it.

In some accounts, the experience of seduction suggests a romantic encounter. Objects sometimes have the capacity to trigger "love at first sight."[6] Seduction is an elaborate process that begins with enticement and turns into compulsion. As a woman in her mid-thirties recalled:

> A gold-plated compact that I had seen on a countertop kept playing on my mind. Heaven knows I didn't need it, and at $40 it was obviously overpriced. Still, there was something about the design that intrigued me. I went back to the counter and picked up the compact again. At that moment, I felt an overwhelming urge.[7]

Participant accounts often suggest the image of lovers catching each other's eyes across a crowded room and entering an illicit conspiracy. The student next quoted initially imagines herself in control and the object as passive—she is moving to put it in her possession; but at the end of her imagining, the object has the power to bring her pocket to life.

> [67] I can see what I want to steal in plain sight, with no one in the aisle of my target. It would be so easy for me to get to the chapstick without attracting attention and simply place it in my pocket. . . . I'm not quite sure why I must have it, but I must.

On the far side of "It would be so easy" is an appreciation of the object already in her pocket. Now she has imagined not just the thing and a secret, collusive relationship with it; she perceives the thing as having transcended her personal boundaries and as residing in her pocket. The thing has demonstrated its power to act in her world by bringing her pocket into experiential existence.

The ordinary customer, even one being seduced to a purchase by the charm of an object, would not be aware of the pocket in which she would place her purchase until, through inserting the object, she would sense herself creating her sensual awareness of the pocket. But a flirtation with the project of theft can make the pocket exist for the person before the object has entered it, and through the powers of the object itself. Through nothing more than the sheer power of a slight bit of deviant intention, a pocket can magically become alive. In more detailed accounts, we would find descriptions of just how the pocket is sensually alive: perhaps hot or perhaps begging to be filled.

Like a wanderer in an enchanted land, the thief or vandal seems to be captive of an environment that knows just what she needs or what he wants to do. Ten brand-new subway cars, shiny new, at rest overnight, no guards around—just perfect; it would be so easy! The keys are hanging in the ignition of that sports car, as if the car knew just where it should be and when—as if it was just waiting for me to come along; it would be so easy! Having secretly reentered the country club after all the members left for the night, I suddenly feel the need to defecate. There, just at the right time, is the cash register drawer, with compartments in just the right shape. It's not that I came in with this in mind but, my God! it would be so easy! By chance, seeing the green necklace lying on top of the pile, she suddenly realizes that it is just what she has been looking for; she glances around and notices an oblivious environment. The setting seems almost to look the other way, respectfully allowing the new intimacy to develop in private.

'IT WOULD BE SO EASY'

An environment that is sensually endowed; items capable of speaking, hearing, or lighting up an awareness of usually dead parts of clothing; a "Eureka!" or "my God!" at the recognition that the situation is miraculously constituted perfectly for the emergent project in deviance—these are signs of success in conjuring up magic. This is not a magic used to trick the audience of observers who are not in on the magician's sleight of hand; this is a magic that takes in its magician-creator. In some sense, the would-be thief is imputing to objects and the scene the sensual capacities to seduce. But, just as obviously, in some other sense the would-be thief must be accomplishing the imputation tacitly for the feeling of temptation to be raised.[8]

The initial movement toward the dialectics of sneaky thrills is into the culture of deviance. "It would be so easy" is experienced as compelling within a broader awareness that what is to follow will be a deviant privacy maintained within a realm of public conventionality. The reference in "It would be so easy" is at once to the budding project in deviance and to the particular object to be stolen, vandalized, or broken into. Only because she is contemplating theft does it make sense for her to appreciate how easy it would be to acquire the object.[9] The excitement of the challenge in the deviant project—an excitement that the acquisition would not have were it not deviant—is experienced as an external provocation that works independently on the self.

Some of the details that would make the deviant project hard or easy really are not up to the would-be shoplifter. In part the facility of the project is a matter of environmental arrangements for which she has no responsibility. While she is appreciating the object as a possible object of theft, she considers it at a particular angle. She will approach it from this side, with her back to that part of the scene, taking hold of it at just that part of its surface. In her experience that "It would be so easy," she is mobilizing herself to concentrate on the tangible details of the object. Thus the would-be shoplifter's sense of the facility of the project is constituted not as a feature of her "intent" or mental plan, but as a result of the position of the object in the store and the posture the object takes toward her.

To specify further how the would-be shoplifter endows the inanimate world with a real power to move her, we might consider why the initial stage of magical provocation is part of the project of sneaky thrills and not of other, equally fascinating, forms of deviance. Not all projects in deviance begin with the seductive sense, "It would be so easy." Indeed, some projects in deviance that are especially attractive to young people begin with an appreciation of the difficulties in becoming seduced to them.

Often novices to deviant activities enter with a self-conscious awareness that they are unsuccessfully struggling to conjure up compelling forces in the world. Consider the path into marijuana smoking. The sensual pleasure typically emerges only after some repeated use and the mastery of new practical tasks, (such as sucking in smoke and holding it down), and then only after learning how to interpret the new experiences as pleasurable.[10]

There is no evidence that prospective users, before they come to appreciate the unusual possibilities of the substance, experience any seductive power emanating from it. During initial attempts, would-be marijuana users often are struck by the mundane character of the technical requirements of the activity: how to roll a joint, how to hold onto the tiny lengths that are being passed around, how long to hold in their breath, and so on. In initial experiences with many types of contraband substances, the novice often seems to sense the trial as consequential and possibly intimidating—not as an act that the substance itself draws them to perform. Only after they develop the competence to enjoy illicit substances do they come to see items that are associated with its sustained use—such as "roach" clips, crooked little "hash" pipes, and shiny little "coke" spoons—as charming. And, depending on numerous further contingencies, they may develop a feeling of compelling attraction to the substance itself.[11]

Objects already defined as deviant by social convention may reveal their seductive powers only after practiced use. Whether the novice is becoming acquainted with marijuana smoking in a group or privately, he knows that the activity is regarded as deviant before he begins. His initial responsibility is to master the technical requirements of the practice; the construction of the moral significance of the activity has already been taken care of by society. With sneaky, thrilling property crimes such as shoplifting, however, a conventional object, like a chapstick on a store counter, becomes fascinating, seductively drawing the would-be shoplifter to it, only and just because she is playing with imposing a deviant project on the world.

Thus, it appears that the origin of the seductive power of the objects is in the person's *origination* of the deviant character of the event. "It would be so easy" signals to her not simply that no external obstacles stand firmly in the way, but a secret, internal desire to be deviant. The person's fascination with the particularly attractive features of the object—the paint and the wall that are in irresistible proximity, the stillness of the car that could so quickly be driven away, and the chapstick on the counter—is the outside of the person's fascination in discovering his or her deviant creativity.

As the budding shoplifting project brings the object of deviance to life, the person and the object enter a conspiratorial relationship. "It would be so easy" contains a touch of surprise in the sudden awareness that no one else would notice. The tension of attraction/hesitation in moving toward the object is experienced within a broader awareness of how others are interpreting one's desires. For all *they* know, one's purposes are moral and the scene will remain mundane. The person's situational involvement in sneaky property crimes begins with a *sensual concentration on the boundary between the self as known from within and as seen from without.*

In this first stage of sneaky thrills, the metaphysical magic of the deviant project takes the person in. She knows that as she plays with appearances to manipulate others' perceptions of her, the object may come into her life in uniquely provocative ways. Depending on how she manipulates the object and the boundary between self and others, *they* may soon manipulate her as a dependent creature suddenly at their mercy, held deeply within their world. What happens depends not just on how she handles the object, but on whether others are watching it as closely as she is.

The Reemergence of Practiced Reason

Independent of the would-be shoplifter's construction of a sense that she might get away with it are any number of contingencies that can terminate the process. For example, the sudden attentions of a clerk may trigger an intimidating awareness of the necessity to produce "normal appearances."[12]

At some point on the way toward all sneaky thrills, the person realizes that she must work to maintain a conventional, calm appearance up to and through the point of exit. The timing of this stage, relative to others in the process, is not constant. The tasks of constructing normal appearances may be confronted only after the act is complete; thus, during the last steps of an escape, vandals may self-consciously slacken their pace from a run to normal walking, and joyriders may slow down only when they finally abandon the stolen car.

In shoplifting, the person occasionally becomes fascinated with particular objects to steal only after appreciating an especially valuable resource for putting on normal appearances. In the following recollection of one of my students, the resource was a parent:

[19] I can clearly remember when we coaxed my mom into taking us shopping with the excuse that our summer trip was coming up & we just wanted to see what the stores had so we could plan on getting it later. We walked over to the section that we were interested in, making sure that we made ourselves seem "legitimate" by keeping my mom close & by showing her items that appealed to us. We thought "they won't suspect us, two girls in school uniforms with their mom, no way". As we carried on like this, playing this little game "Oh, look how pretty, Gee, I'll have to tell dad about all these pretty things."

Eventually a necklace became irresistible.

Whichever comes first, the pull of the person toward the object to be stolen or the person's concentration on devices for deception, to enact the theft the person must bracket her appearance to set it off from her experience of her appearance, as this student's account shows:

[19] My shoplifting experiences go back to high school days when it was kind of an adventureous thing to do. My best friend & I couldn't walk into a store without getting that familiar grin on our faces. . . . Without uttering a word, we'd check out the place. . . . The whole process pretty much went about as if we were really "shopping" except in our minds the whole scene was different because of our paranoia & our knowledge of our real intentions.

Sensing a difference between what appears to be going on and what is "really" going on, the person focuses intently on normal interactional tasks. Everyday matters that have always been easily handled now rise to the level of explicit consciousness and seem subtle and complex. The thief asks herself, "How long does a normal customer spend at a particular counter?" "Do innocent customers look around to see if others are watching them?" "When customers leave a store, do they usually have their heads up or down?" The recognition that all these questions cannot possibly be answered correctly further stimulates self-consciousness. As one student expressed it,

> [19] Now, somehow no matter what the reality is, whether the salesperson is looking at you or not, the minute you walk in the store you feel as if it's written all over your face "Hi, I'm your daily shoplifter".

Unless the person achieves this second stage of appreciating the work involved—if she proceeds to shoplift with a relaxed sense of ease—she may get away in the end but not with the peculiar celebration of the sneaky thrill. Novice shoplifters, however, find it easy to accomplish the sense that they are faced with a prodigious amount of work. "Avoiding suspicion" is a challenge that seems to haunt the minute details of behavior with an endless series of questions—How fast should one walk? Do customers usually take items from one department to another without paying? and so on.

To construct normal appearances, the person must attempt a sociological analysis of the local interactional order. She employs folk theories to explain the contingencies of clerk-customer interactions and to guide the various practical tasks of the theft. On how to obscure the moment of illicit taking:

> [44] The jewelry counter at Nordstroms was the scene of the crime. . . . I proceeded to make myself look busy as I tried on several pairs of earrings. My philosophy was that the more busy you look the less conspicuous.

On where to hide the item:

> [15] Karen and I were inside the elevator now. As she was telling me to quickly put the necklace into my purse or bag, I did a strange thing. I knelt down, pulled up my pants leg, and slipped the necklace into my sock! I remember insisting that my sock was the safest and smartest place to hide my treasure. I knew if I put it in an obvious place and was stopped, I'd be in serious trouble. Besides, packages belonging to young girls are usually subject to suspicion.

Some who shoplift clothes think it will fool the clerks if they take so many items into a dressing room that an observer could not easily keep count, as this student recalled:

> [5] We went into a clothing shop, selected about six garments a piece (to confuse the sales people), entered separate dressing rooms and stuffed one blouse each into our bags.

Others, like the following student, think it sufficiently strategic to take two identical garments in, cover one with the other, and emerge with only one visible:

[46] We'd always take two of the same item & stuff one inside the other to make it seem like we only had one.

Many hit on the magician's sleight of hand, focusing the clerk's attentions on an item that subsequently will be returned to hide their possession of another.

[56] [While being watched by a clerk] I was now holding the green necklace out in the open to give the impression that I was trying to decide whether to buy it or not. Finally, after about 2 minutes I put the green necklace back but I balled the brown necklace up in my right hand and placed my jacket over that hand.

In its dramatic structure, the experience of sneak theft has multiple emotional peaks as the thief is exposed to a series of challenges to maintaining a normal appearance. The length of the series varies with the individual and the type of theft, but, typically, there are several tests of the transparency of the thief's publicly visible self, as one student indicated:

[122] I can recall a sneak theft at Penny's Dept. store very well. I was about 12 years old. . . . I found an eyeshadow kit. I could feel my heart pounding as I glanced around to make sure that others weren't watching. I quickly slipped the eyeshadow in my purse and sighed heavily with relief when I realized that no one had seen. I nervously stepped out of the aisle and once again was relieved when I saw that there was no one around the corner waiting to catch me. I caught my friend's eye; she gave me a knowing glance and we walked to the next section in self satisfaction for having succeeded so far.

When the person devises the deviant project in advance, even entering the store normally may be an accomplishment. Having entered without arousing suspicion, the would-be shoplifter may relax slightly. Then tension mounts as she seizes the item. Dressing rooms provide an escape from the risk of detection, but only momentarily, as in this student's account:

[19] So, here we were, looking at things, walking around & each time getting closer to the dressing room. Finally we entered it & for once I remember feeling relieved for the first time since I'd walked into the store because I was away at last from those "piercing eyes" & I had the merchandise with me. At this point we broke into laughter. . . . We

stuffed the items in our purses making sure that they had no security gadgets on them & then we thought to ourselves "well we're half way there." Then it hit me, how I was safe in the dressing room, no one could prove anything. I was still a "legitimate" shopper.

Then a salesperson may come up and, with an unsuspecting remark, raise the question of transparency to new heights:

[19] I remember coming out of the dressing room & the sales lady looking at me & asking me if I had found anything (probably concerned with only making her commission). I thought I would die.

Finally there is the drama of leaving the store:

[19] Walking out the door was always a big, big step. We knew that that's when people get busted as they step out & we just hoped & prayed that no one would run up to us & grab us or scream "hey you"! The whole time as we approached the exit I remember looking at it as a dark tunnel & just wanting to run down it & disappear as I hung on to my "beloved purse."

Once they have hidden the booty and so long as they are in the store, the would-be-shoplifters must constantly decide to sustain their deviance. Thus, the multiple boundaries of exposure offer multiple proofs not only of their ability to get away with it but of their will toward immorality:

[5] We went into the restroom before we left and I remember telling Lori, "We can drop all this stuff in here and leave, or we can take it with us." Lori wanted to take everything, and as we neared the exit, I began to get very nervous.

Many of these shoplifters understand that clerks or store detectives may be watching them undercover, in preparation for arresting them at the exit door. They also believe that criminal culpability is only established when they leave with the stolen goods. As they understand it, they are not irretrievably committed to be thieves until they are on the other side of the exit; up to that point, they may replace the goods and instantly revert from a deviant to a morally unexceptional status. Were they to believe that they were criminally culpable as soon as they secreted the item, they would continue to face the interactional and emotional challenges of accomplishing deception. But because they think they are not committed legally until they are physically out of the store, they experience each practical challenge in covering up their deviance as an occasion to reaffirm their spiritual fortitude for being deviant. One student described the phenomenon this way:

[56] I guess I had been there so long that I started to look suspicious. I was holding a bright lime green necklace in my left hand and a brown Indian type necklace in my right. A lady, she must have been the store manager, was watching me. She was about 20 ft. away from me and on my left. I could feel her looking at me but I didn't look directly at her. . . . I remember actually visualizing myself putting back both the necklaces and walking out the store with pride and proving this bitch she was wrong and that I was smarter than her, but I didn't. . . . I started out the store very slowly I even smiled at the lady as I passed by the cash register. It was then that she started toward me and my mind said okay T. what are you going to do now. There was a table full of sweaters on sale near me and I could have easily drop the necklace on the table and continued out the door. I knew I could and I considered it but I wouldn't do it. I remember just holding the necklace tighter in my right hand. As she was coming toward me I even thought of dropping the necklace and running out the door but I continued in a slow pace even though the thought of them calling my mother if I was caught and what she would do to me was terribly frightening.

In addition to focusing on the practical components of producing a normal appearance, the would-be shoplifter struggles not to betray the difficulty of the project. This is the second layer of work—the work of appearing not to work at practicing normal appearances. The first layer of work is experienced as the emergence of a novel, analytical attention to behavioral detail; the second, as a struggle to remain in rational control, as the following statement by a student illustrates:

[19] You desperately try to cover it up by trying to remember how you've acted before but still you feel as if all eyes are on you! I think, that's the purpose of settling in one area & feeling everything & everyone out. It's an attempt to feel comfortable so that you don't appear obvious. Like maybe if I'm real cool & subtle about it & try on a few things but don't seem impressed w/ anything, I can just stroll out of here & no one will notice.

In the sensual character of the experience, the person literally embodies the issue of transcendence that is at stake. The would-be thief is attempting to prove that outsiders cannot perceive the deviance of which the thief is internally aware. Correspondingly, the thief experiences a struggle to keep her insides from becoming telltale signs on the outside. Some part of the body threatens to reveal the secret deviance; the project seems "written all over your face," knees may feel like they will give way, the stomach threatens to erupt or drop to the floor, and the heart suddenly puts the coverup at risk by racing or trying to leap out of the chest:

[56] She stopped me about 5 ft. from the door, my heart was beating so hard, not fast just hard like it was going to jump out of my chest. The lady asked me "Didn't you find anything you liked?" I knew she was trying to see if I was nervous and to let me know she had seen me earlier. I said no, that I hadn't discovered anything that I couldn't live without. I remember trying to phrase the sentence as grownup as possible so she wouldn't think I was a dumb little kid. Then she said "What about that green necklace I saw you holding." . . . I said "I simply don't own anything to go with it so I hung it back on the rack." She said "Oh" and started toward the rack, so I continued out the door.

Being Thrilled

Usually after the scene of risk is successfully exited, the third stage of the sneaky thrill is realized. This is the euphoria of being thrilled. In one form or another, there is a "Wow, I got away with it!" or an "It was so easy!" A necklace shoplifter stated:

[56] Once outside the door I thought Wow! I pulled it off, I faced danger and I pulled it off. I was smiling so much and I felt at that moment like there was nothing I couldn't do.

After stealing candy with friends, another student recalled:

[87] Once we were out the door we knew we had been successful! We would run up the street . . . all be laughing and shouting, each one trying to tell just how he pulled it off and the details that would make each of us look like the bravest one.

The pizza thief noted:

[82] The feeling I got from taking the pizza, the thrill of getting something for nothing, knowing I got away with something I never thought I could, was wonderful. . . . I'm 21 now and my neighbor is 23. Every time we see each other, I remember and relive a little bit of that thrill.

Success brings in its wake emotions that go far beyond the joy of material acquisition. The "it" in "getting away with it" is not just the object, but something significantly shameful. Thus, the other side of the euphoria felt from being successful is the humiliation from being caught. What the neak thieves are avoiding, or getting away with by not being caught, is he shame they would feel if they were caught:

[19] I remember visualizing for a split second that she had snatched the jacket off my arm and was leading me off by the arm and I was crying hysterically because my mother was going to kill me. I had about 27 dollars in my purse at the time and the necklace couldn't have cost half that much.

To these young thieves, being caught is an experience of degradation. Just as success can bring a thrill to one's entire being, so failure can threaten one's moral existence. The discovered thieves often feel that their parents will "kill" them:

[44] It was a lady about 35 yrs. with a big shopping bag in her hands. We looked at each other and then at her and realized she was talking to us. My stomach dropped to the floor and I suddenly felt faint. . . . The lady wrote up everything and Betsy just sat there mouthing at me "My mom is going to kill me." . . . Boy did we get it when we got home. It was so degrading to face my parents and tell them what I did. They were so disappointed in me and couldn't believe that their perfect little angel would ever do anything so awful.

In a literal sense, the successful thieves were being thrilled: they shuddered or shook in elation, often to the rhythms of laughter. For many, whether successful or not, the experience of youthful shoplifting was profoundly moving, so moving that they could vividly recall minute details of the event years later. Juvenile and adult nonprofessional shoplifters typically experience arrest with a genuine moral horror.

"This is a nightmare," said one woman pilferer who had been formally charged with stealing an expensive handbag. "It can't be happening to me! Why, oh why can't I wake up and find that it isn't so," she cried later as she waited at a store exit, accompanied by a city and a store policeman, for the city police van to arrive. "Whatever will I do? Please make it go away," she pleaded with the officer. "I'll be disgraced forever. I can never look anyone in the face again."

Store detectives report that the most frequent question women ask is, "Will my husband have to know about this?" Men, they say, express immediate fear that their employers will be informed of their arrest. . . . Children are apprehensive of parental reaction.[13]

The thrills of sneaky thrills are metaphysically complex matters. On the one hand, shoplifters and vandals know what they are doing is illegal; the deviant character of the practice is part of its appeal. On the other hand, they typically register a kind of metaphysical shock when an arrest induces a sense that what they are doing might be treated as a *real* crime. It appears that an essential attraction of these practices is that although they are risks taken in the real world and hence not just play, they are accomplished in a playful spirit. Once an arrest occurs, the shoplifting career typically ends in response to an awareness that persistence would now clearly signal a commitment to a deviant identity.[14]

In contrast, boosters (professional shoplifters), who are comfortable with being seen and with explicitly seeing themselves as part of a criminal subculture, may take for granted and treat their arrest as a cost of doing business.[15] Just because it is not an inevitable result for all thieves, the achievement of euphoria, which can make sneaky property crime thrilling, must be explained.

For a sneaky property crime to produce a thrill, the person must understand that it incorporates several challenges that have personal, existentially fundamental, significance outside the act of theft. The experienced profundity of the event—both as deeply moving in the moment of success or failure and as one of the rare, brief events of private life that can be recalled vividly years, even decades, later—embodies the awareness of its multiple metaphoric implications.

For the typical amateur, sneaky property crime is a symbolically protean experience that simultaneously mobilizes metaphors of (1) the self and its boundaries from other selves, (2) scoring in a game, (3) the defilement of the sacred, (4) sexual intercourse, and (5) the existential interdependence of deviance and charisma.[16]

THE SELF AND ITS BOUNDARIES

Sneak theft and vandalism test one's ability to bound the authentic morality of the self from others' perceptions. At stake is an exemplary experimentation with interactional metaphysics. This point is illustrated by the following account of theft of cash from a co-worker's drawer:

[91] I watched carefully as they all drove off then I ran to my desk draw [*sic*], got my purse out & took out the keys. I was excited. I felt I was on the verge of a new discovery. I was almost like a kid the first time he discovers something new. I was like a child looking in a mirror for the first time and discovering that the image you saw was yourself. The image did everything you did.

Sneaky property crimes are especially well constructed to transform any ubiquitous concerns about the transparency of the self that the thief may harbor into a concrete problem of situated interaction. Vandalism and shoplifting create a practical reason to worry about what others are seeing of oneself; they specify precisely what the deviance is that others might suspect in oneself, and they delimit an occasion for transcending others' perceptions.

The young shoplifter, in particular, puts the perceptions of adults to a series of tests. By discovering that clerks and house detectives in department stores cannot prove that she has deviant intentions, the young shoplifter may acquire confidence that adults cannot detect that she harbors other forms of deviant spirit, shameful inclinations, or personal incompetence. As he invades another's boundaries of private rights, the vandal publicly proves that he can "get away with it." If successful, the vandal or the shoplifter leaves with objective proof that he or she can bound a morally unacceptable self from powers that are materially motivated to detect it.

THE LUDIC METAPHOR

Sneaky thieves do not necessarily or only consider their criminal experience to be an experiment with the boundaries of the self. If the implications of the experience are metaphysically rich, immediately the experience is a lot of "fun." One dimension of the thrill is ludic: the process is a kind of game.[17]

More clearly than any other crimes, sneaky property crimes resonate with the structure of ambulatory sports contests. Like games, shoplifting and vandalism can be tried again and again, with no more justification than that it seems to be fun. Like games, sneaky property crime occurs in a field of delimited space and within time constraints. Temporally, the starting and ending whistles may be blown privately, but the contest begins and ends at defined moments and locations. And like all ambulatory games, there is a provision for "time out," such as when the shoplifter retires to the safety of a dressing room.

Spatially as well, the player knows at all times whether he is in or out of risk. In all his locations, the criminal player knows he is either on or off the playing field. The analogy is perhaps strongest with such forms of theft as shoplifting and burglary in which, as compared to vandalism, a formally defined spatial boundary must be crossed to achieve victory. But even with joyriding and vandalism, the sense of a getaway implies at least an amorphous goal line.

Unlike most conventional concerns or relationships in life, sneaky property crimes produce a clear winner and loser. Like the athletic contestant, the shoplifter and the vandal know just when and where they can sigh with relief and burst into euphoria. In contrast, those who suffer from anxious self-consciousness frequently review scenes that they managed with apparent aplomb, only to raise new questions of how they might unwittingly have divulged some form of inner ugliness.

As in familiar sports contests, there is a zero-sum outcome to sneaky property crimes, as well as a way of calculating the margin of victory or defeat. You either get away with it or you do not, and, at least in the case of success, there is a way of calculating precisely how much you have won. In each flush of victory, the margins of success among clearly independent contests can be compared in detail.

In contrast to the structure of diffuse, everyday anxieties (such as those attending membership in a social clique), the thief and the vandal, like athletes on a team, participate in a contest with relatively clear sides. In shoplifting, it is always clear which side you are on and who is on the other side. The shoplifter and the vandal, like a player guiding a ball down a field, focus on "psyching" and "faking out" perceived opponents, although they realize that they may be intercepted by surprise from a blind side.

As in games, there is an infinite variety of plays in sneaky property crimes. In shoplifting, as in all the major ambulatory sports contests in the Western world, there is a mutually agreed-on thing of value that the player tries to carry toward a goal line while the opposing side tries to frustrate him or wrest it away. Shoplifters who work in teams may devise pre-planned codes and secretly communicate defensive signals that provide warnings about their opponents' countermoves. If an opponent draws too near, a player, responding to a signal, may pass off the booty in a tricky move.

The analogy of sneaky property crimes and ambulatory sports contests becomes ambiguous if pushed too far. Property crime is likely to be treated by the opponents as more than a game. The analogy also fails with respect to the opponent's freedom to choose to play. Stores must be suited up and ready to play at all times, although they might not consider the contest fun, and vandals' victims often have no chance to adjust their defenses. In other respects, sneaky property crimes are less serious than games. As a game, shoplifting is only child's play; if the thief does not like the approaching outcome, she often assumes that she may drop the goods and call it off, like a child who takes his ball away rather than lose.

But the ludic metaphor is distinctively applicable to sneaky property crimes, as opposed to other forms of criminality. For example, drug dealers are not so sure of when and where they may be caught; the possession of contraband, financial arrangements, and distribution networks may keep them so constantly involved that they enjoy no "time out." Robbers also have no chance for "time out" once they publicly define the situation as a stickup. And unlike the ludic aspect of sneak thefts, robbery risks consequences so serious that, as I will show later, the crime must be justified as profitable. In murders of passion, the winner of a fight often regards himself as a loser only a few moments later; the calculation of success and failure is much more confusing. Unlike assailants in fights, which often erupt without forewarning, the sneaky property criminal can make up plays in advance and may estimate the magnitude of risk. Each of these other types of criminality have their own form of excitement, but the form is not as close to that of the game.

THE RELIGIOUS METAPHOR

The dramatic possibilities of sneaky property crimes are not exhausted by the metaphysical structures of games. "Property" has boundaries separating insiders, or authorized users, from outsiders, or unauthorized occupants, and these boundaries are often sensed as sacred. In many sneaky criminal acts, part of the sensuality of the sneaky thrill is that of a secret defilement; the process can be experienced as a black sacrament with identifiable stages.

In the first stage, the person secretly and in the spirit of a desecration penetrates another's world. The means of penetration vary; vandalism usually involves some "foreign" or profane object, such as a rock or paint; shoplifting, perhaps the person's hand and purse; and burglary, the person's whole body. No doubt the emotional embodiment of the spirit of violation depends, in subtle ways, on the way and the extent to which the deviant's body pierces the sanctity of the victim's world.

The spirit of violation that accompanies the penetration is derived from a tacit collective agreement between the deviant and the victim to regard the penetration as a violation. In much of the property crime committed by young people, the possibility of achieving a sneaky thrill is strongly supported by economically irrational, intensely moral sensibilities surrounding property. The criminals are likely to anticipate correctly that those they would make "victims" will so define themselves. Why the latter should do so, however, is often not immediately obvious, since the items that are taken typically are petty and the damage that is done is often only a minor nuisance to repair. The shock at finding a gang name painted on one's garage, one's car sitting on the opposite side of the street from where it had been parked, or beer cans mysteriously taken from one's refrigerator and left empty on the kitchen counter cannot be accounted for in utilitarian terms.

After the initial trespass of a boundary that has been collectively consecrated, the thief or vandal must, if he is to continue to build the drama of the sneaky thrill, do something to prove that the invasion has occurred. This is the organizing objective of vandalism, but in theft it is, perhaps surprisingly, a key step as well. On the surface, the thief's purpose is to take something away, but as I mentioned before, the targeted object is often without sacred or motivating character, independent of or outside the theft. More deeply, on the way to a sneaky thrill, the criminal's aim is to project something negative into the victim's world, deposit proof of his deviance, or create a moral stain.

One of my students described an elaborate fascination with nonacquisitive burglary. The following is my summary of her lengthy account:

When she was 13, she would enter neighbors' homes and roam around. Somehow being in a neighbor's house without express permission made the otherwise mundane environment charged. She had been invited into all these homes before but by entering without notice through an unlocked door or an open window, she found that a familiar kitchen or living room was magically transformed into a provocative environment. The excitement was distinctly sensual. She would feel objects in various rooms; in a sense they would feel her, creating a variety of exotic sensations through her touch. But she rarely took anything. Instead she might simply rearrange the furniture. It seems she was not so much "playing house" or decorating to fit her tastes as she was trying to leave evidence that someone had been there. Many years later, recollecting her year or so of nonmercenary burglary, she thought the events were "crazy." She had never told anyone about them. But she could still recall the thrill of the experience. The pattern stopped the day that neighbors unexpectedly came home and almost caught her.

Victims of burglary often return to find human feces in the middle of their homes. Although the rhythm of excitement in the act may promote bowel movement and the circumstances may make the usual proprieties of the bathroom seem dispensable, the larger patterns in property crime suggest that some trespassers defecate to desecrate. Elliott Leyton described the following incident that may serve as an example:

> Carrying a crowbar, 13 year old Tyrone entered his neighbour's new bungalow. Swinging the bar wildly, he smashed an expensive mock-antique mirror and then turned his destructive attention to every piece of glass and furniture in the house. His work completed, he squatted to leave a pile of excrement on the living room floor, and left.[18]

Usually the symbolism of desecretion is less obvious. The shoplifter who shakes from the risk of the act anticipates shaking up the victim's world. Even if the victim never discovers that the item is missing, the thief and the vandal understand that the moral order of the victim's objective world will have been altered. Recall the shoplifter who took the brown necklace that she deemed capable, when addressed in the safety of her bedroom, of understanding her reproving speech. Within the magical world of sneaky thrills, the thief and the vandal take the objective world of their victims to be a knowing presence. If the victim never notices that the item is missing or damaged, still the *place* or the *order* of things there will retain the character of a deviant past.

Once the theft has been accomplished, the character of its place is unalterably changed in the experience of the thief. Forever (or, at least, so it seems at the time of the event) it will be the scene of the crime. Although all the clerks may change and although months or years may pass, the place has been magically transformed. It will have a special charm, perhaps tinged with the threat of discovery, whenever it is reentered. If hallowed places convey the presence of a sacred host by their special aura, the places that are stolen from have been negatively hallowed for the thief. They remain haunted for some time after, perhaps for eternity, by the memory of his previous, deviant presence. That haunting is a continuing testimony to desecration.

THE SEXUAL METAPHOR

From a sensitivity to the sacred metaphor implicated in sneak theft, the person can, with a short step, appreciate the sexual references of the act. In many of the accounts of shoplifting, there is an experience of seduction turning into irrational compulsion, a rush of excitement as contact is made with the item and another as it is guided across personal boundaries and inserted into a private place, then a physical process of movement in which the body is guided to a point of climax. For the sophisticated perpetrator, there are phases of rest and opportunities to play with the transcendence of successive boundaries of risk. And, finally, there is the experience of shameful failure or euphoric success (which many youths naturally follow with the ceremonial smoking of a cigarette).

As one student stated, "Every time I would drop something into my bag, my heart would be pounding and I could feel this tremendous excitement, a sort of 'rush', go through me." The sexual analogy, if implicit at the time, later became obvious to some offenders:

> The experience was almost orgasmic for me. There was a build-up of tension as I contemplated the danger of a forbidden act, then a rush of excitement at the moment of committing the crime, and finally a delicious sense of release.[19]

A necklace thief quoted earlier recalled: "It's really funny being 23 years old now and in writing this, I can't stop feeling how thrilling it was, certainly a feeling much like the anticipation of sex."

The accounts in this chapter come largely from females, and the sexual metaphor they describe may be shaped to represent sex from a feminine perspective. Various incidental features of the shoplifting accounts indicate a secret attempt to realize female sexual identity. Thus the items stolen do not represent a random collection of the things that might be stolen. Money itself is only rarely the objective. Instead, the young girls seem especially seduced by items of makeup, jewelry, and clothes: things used to cover-up the naked female self, to give the body the appearance of the mature female, and to make the self dazzlingly attractive to a world blinded to the blemishes underneath. Females take symbols of adult female identity—cosmetics, jewelry, and sexy underwear—while males take gadgets, cigarette lighters, and wallets. It is notable that female shoplifters, rarely steal items to give to men or children.[20]

Other objects of theft implicate the body in other ways: items used on the beach, such as suntan lotion, and various forms of food that, like the proverbial forbidden fruit, become especially tasty when illegally acquired. The sexual metaphor is also implicated in criminal methods. Shoplifters hide things on their body, often beneath their clothes, in one case, in a "beloved purse." One of my students worked as a detective in the campus store. She reported an unaccountable proclivity of female shoplifters to steal underwear.

The sexual reference of shoplifting by young amateurs is doubly illicit. Not only is the young shoplifter projecting into a criminal project an experience prohibited at her age, but the form of sex is illicit. The sneaky property criminal is not participating in a consensual act; the pleasure is distinctly asymmetrical. Colloquially, the thief and the vandal fuck their victims.

We may now see the richly isomorphic, extraordinarily protean symbolic structure of sneaky property crimes. Each of the metaphoric layers reson-ates independently with more general themes of consciousness: the meta-physical problem of bounding the self, the primitive religious dread of defilement, the fun of ambulatory games, and the development of a sexual identity. In addition, each layer resonates with each of the others. A description of the metaphysical metaphor experienced in sneaky property crime borders on a description of sexual intercourse; an analysis of the ludic structure of sneak theft could readily describe sacred spaces and ritual degradations; familiar ambulatory games recreate the imagery of sexual intercourse, as do such familiar folk phrases of double entendre as "scor-ing"; and so on. And there is at least one more metaphoric layer to examine.

THE INTERDEPENDENCE OF DEVIANCE AND CHARISMA

The thief who would take by stealth opts to construct a paranoia. She makes a usually abhorrent emotional condition suddenly functional: the more you are aware of how others are watching you, the more likely you are to get away with it. The thief makes herself "self-conscious" by creat-ing a practical reason for others to suspect that she harbors a deviant spirit. One student described her thoughts this way:

[19] What kept running through my mind was this idea of self-centeredness. I felt like everyone was watching me, following me & and like the whole store was at a stand still just concentrating on my next move.

As a practical matter, this self-consciousness, which before the theft may have been only a burdensome threat to the smooth projection of a desirable self into the world, has, under the discipline of the criminal project, become a positive resource promoting theft. The positive moral achievement of sneaky property crimes signals perhaps their most elusive metaphoric layer. The thief is not just enacting her deviance; through being secretly deviant, she is discovering charisma.

The sneak thief and the vandal achieve a resonant metaphoric relationship between positive and negative, between the capacity to violate and to transcend moral constraint, and between deviance and charisma.[21] In the getaway, after having pulled off a particularly cunning method of faking out house detectives, the sneaky thief knows with all her being that "that was beautiful." By doing something ugly to another, the sneak thief or vandal establishes that she can bring beauty into the world. Appreciated from within, a sneaky property crime by an amateur is not a failure of social control but a personal esthetic triumph.

In the first stage of sneaky thrills, when the sense "It would be so easy" guides the person to a particular material focus for her deviant project, the seductive powers of objects sway her. Then she faces a test of whether she can maintain a personal "cool" and execute the sneaky theft through willful, calculating manipulations. If she can, she has proved that she will not "freak out" from the pressures of pulling it off. The euphoria that rewards success, then, embodies the awareness that the sneak thief can allow herself to be seduced by the world without fear. Through taking from others, sneak thieves may learn that they can let themselves go, that they can safely be taken by the secret charm and black magic in the world. Like charismatic personalities, they may discover that the mysterious forces of the universe are on their side. Others walk in fear of the unknown; they confront the unknown and walk away with the goods.

The consequences of sneaky thrills are not usually to launch criminal careers or otherwise to define the future self. On the contrary, the protagonists in sneaky property crime more often thrill to the expanded possibilities of the self, in the knowledge that they have opened up ways of being that previously seemed inaccessible.[22] Social theorists have resisted strongly the recognition that deviance is not merely a reaction against something negative in a person's background but a reaching for exquisite possibilities. Researchers like to point out the popular error of considering as essentially deviant people who, whatever their crime or infraction, overtly commit deviant acts only during rare moments of their lives. But deviant persons also appreciate the economy of doing evil for characterizing the self generally: it is literally wonderful. Through being deviant for a moment, the person may portray his or her general, if usually hidden, charismatic potential.

The Sensual Metaphysics of Sneaky Thrills

Although they know they are breaking the law, nonprofessional shoplifters and vandals commonly feel when they are arrested, an irresistible
protest that "this can't be happening to me!" It is as if they lived the
process of the crime like a character moving in a myth or a dream. And
in the emotional meaning or sensual dimension of the event, they do.

Sometimes the mythical quality of the experience is highlighted. The
13-year-old housebreaker who would enter neighbors' homes not to take
things but in search of she knew not what and who would run the risk of
being caught by suprise to rearrange items, is reminiscent of Goldilocks
entering the home of the Three Bears.[23] More commonly, if less obviously,
the mythical meaning of the event is experienced emotionally. To understand the experience of sneaky thrills, we must appreciate how the structure of everyday sensuality is continuous with the structure of fantasy
worlds.

As Alfred Schutz specified, there are fundamental contrasts between
experience in mundane activities and in various alternative "worlds," such
as those of the theater, night and day dreams, and jokes or laughter.[24]
Experience in the mundane world of practical reality is confined by time,
space, and social boundaries. People conduct practical social action with
the limiting awareness that they are acting in a specific "here," during a
specific "now," and in a particular type of publicly recognizable social
situation. Dreams, fantasies, and various meta-mundane worlds do not
respect these limitations.

The dreamer (asleep, while daydreaming, in the theater, or caught up in
listening to a fairy tale) suspends the focus of his consciousness on the
historical time and the geopolitical space he is in and the socially bounded
process of sleeping and dreaming that he is going through. As a member
of the audience who becomes absorbed in the theatrical drama, he "suspends disbelief" on these three dimensions. He dulls his awareness of the
clock time during which the drama transpires, the physical location of the
theater, and the fact that he is watching a dramatization of life. The
dreamer witnesses movements through time, over space, and across the
boundaries that usually separate internal awareness and externally visible
expression and that are inconsistent with what he rationally knows of the
structures of everyday practical life.

The world of everyday practical life and dream worlds are not existentially inconsistent. (And indeed, they may always be co-present. Even in
the deepest sleep, we maintain an awareness of time, space, and social
situations; we are not lost to the noises around us or the pressures of our

autonomous physical selves.) Thus pilferers do not move through department stores as sleep walkers or day dreamers, but neither do they construct their sneaky crimes simply as exercises of self-reflective reason. Through their feelings and the evolving sensuality of the event, they walk through its mythical dimensions.

In a metaphysically similar way, although within a different transcendent project, so do the killers examined in chapter 1. For both the pilferer and the passion killer, a dash of reality is often an effective "cure," although in the latter case it comes much too late. Those who murder in a passionate effort to dramatize their defense of the Good, like shoplifters who are arrested, are surprisingly without emotional defenses. Many wait for the police to arrive or confess quickly; few make good on escapes. Brought to the fatal moment by a leap to a timeless, primordial version of the Good, the impassioned killer momentarily transcends the demand to relate his behavior "now" to the meaning it will have "then." When he returns to practical everyday concerns a few moments later, he realizes that he must innovate an escape if he is to have one.

Similarly, the essence of the sneaky thrill is an attempt to transcend an existential dilemma, but, in this case, the dilemma is to relate the inner to outer identity. The shoplifter goes about her sneaky efforts to see if she can get away with it—"it" being a freely drawn, playfully artificial projection of the self into the world. Must I appear to be who I know I am? Need I struggle to shape what I know about myself into an acceptable appearance to others, or can I play with it? Can I dispense, not with moral appearances but with the *struggle* to produce moral appearances? Thus, the thrill embodies an awareness that the experience is essentially a play about dilemmas of moral authenticity arranged on a public staging of the self.

Those who pursue sneaky thrills appreciate this perspective with emotional immediacy. They know it sensually, not self-reflectively. Ask, and they may cite one of the stock background explanations, such as peer pressure; find the causation mysterious; or simply state, because it's fun. To appreciate the distinctive character of this phenomenon, we must ask, Why the mystery? What explains the odd metaphysical mood of the event? How can doing *this* be fun? The immediately relevant answer lies not in the problems of personal or social group background nor in mundane material results, but in a project with distinctively transcendent pretensions.

Foreground and Background in Sneaky Thrills

ADOLESCENCE

It is tempting to move the analysis from the foreground of sneaky thrills to the background of adolescence and to suggest causes rooted in this stage of the life cycle. If the thrill of accomplishing a sneaky property crime is, in part, a recognition that the person has been successfully opaque in public, surely that is an especially meaningful message for adolescents. Through sneaky property crimes, we may easily conclude, adolescents can metaphorically enact the double dilemma that promotes their self-consciousness. They are becoming anxious about many forms of internal ugliness that it would be shameful to display—of all the unseemly things that threaten to leap out of the body into the world—from pimples to sexual desires; of manifold, unpredictably displayed, telltale signs of intellectual inferiority; and of parochial attitudes linked to ethnic or class identity. And they are becoming aware that mature moral competence in society means that they should not only maintain privacy over the ugly parts of their identities, but they should be graceful in the process, covering up the process of covering up.[25]

Add to the extraordinary self-consciousness of adolescence the extraordinary social machinery for producing interpersonal transparency that is the school. Surrounded throughout the day with more or less the same people, the young student is forced to strip in virtually every literal and figurative way imaginable; any wart, whatever its region of physical or intellectual location, will have its moment of public display. The members of this constant audience are selected by age, neighborhood, and even intellectual level to be homogeneous and, as such, they are uniquely capable of discerning inner realities through reading external signs. There will usually be an overlap between out-of-school associates and schoolmates, which promotes a ubiquitous concern with transparency. Moreover, the same group follows the student from year to year, which fosters the accumulation of a collective memory that may never allow him to escape far from his initial reputation. If this were not enough, schools often structure time in ways that are so boring that peers have nothing more fascinating to do than to attempt telling observations.

With all this in the background, surely it is easy to understand why sneaky property crimes are especially attractive to adolescents as devices for proving that they can be deviant in society and get away with it. To test themselves on socially approved criteria of personal competence, adolescents have a multitude of socially institutionalized opportunities: courage and physical prowess may be challenged in sports, cosmetic attractiveness may be put on the line in the dating market, and intellectual capacity may be tested in school or, perhaps more profoundly, in informal repartee. A wide and popular range of nonsneaky violent forms of crime, from reckless driving to group fights, offer adolescents additional opportunities to take risks openly and prove they are not afraid of physical harm. The distinctive appeal of the sneaky property crimes that seem to have a special salience for adolescents—shoplifting, vandalism, joyriding, and nonmercenary breaking and entering—is the particular dialectic of being privately deviant in public places.

There are at least two reasons for resisting a quick analytical shift from the phenomenal foreground of adolescent property crime to the psychological and social structures in the background of adolescence. The first is that the apparent association may well be circular and spurious. Shoplifting may be concentrated in adolescence, but it may well peak before puberty,[26] and it clearly continues long after. Our enthusiasm for examining the nature of adolescence as the causal background of sneaky property crime should be restrained by the recollection that, as recently as 1964, Cameron had to argue, against a substantial body of criminological opinion, that shoplifting was not a response to a different phase in the age cycle, this one gender specific: the crisis of menopause.[27]

For obvious reasons, preadolescents are less likely to be picked up by official statistics on shoplifting. And postadolescents may steal from employers at a higher rate than adolescents shoplift and vandalize, and from a variety of nonutilitarian attractions to the practice. When the thief is old enough to work in the shop, the crime no longer fits the category of "shoplifting."[28] Before we push off adult property crime as obviously more practically minded than the adolescent varieties, we should explore the contrast more closely. Like adolescent shoplifters, embezzlers[29] and corrupt politicians and tax frauds[30] often suffer intense shame on arrest and no less than adolescents, they may take from successful deceptions and cover-ups an emotionally meaningful measure of faith in their abilities to obscure areas of routine personal incompetence.

Within the context of this study, the more important reason not to move too quickly toward theorizing about the etiological background of sneaky crimes is the danger of misrepresenting the quality of the phenomenon. Explanations of the structures of adolescence may jump into the reader's mind because the data here, for reasons of convenience, were largely limited to recollections of youthful experiences. But it is not clear that the sneaky property criminals we have been examining are precisely concerned with the structures of adolescence. Indeed, the attractive power of the experience is essentially dependent on its ambiguous, indirect significance for the rest of the person's life. To preserve the emotional power of the thrill, the process should implicate more than one metaphor. A single meaning would threaten to make the practice too literal and mundane.

If sneaky property crime was simply a form of practical therapy for the dilemmas of adolescence, it would not be fun. But shoplifting, while it tests the transparency of the self also follows the structure of a game. As a game it can be erotically evocative; however, it is not just a sexual play. The relevance of particular metaphoric frameworks varies from one form of sneaky property crime to the next. Vandalism plays up desecration and plays down the potential to prove a superior ability to manipulate perceptions of moral character in face-to-face interactions. One shoplifting episode may be structured in a particularly effective way along the lines of a sex act; another, accomplished by using the mother's presence as a shield, may carry a special message about independence. It is just because it can resonate with any and all these meanings from one moment to the next that sneaky property crime can convey the experience of a thrill.

SOCIAL CLASS

The data I have used, which come from an overprivileged group, perhaps overemphasize the irrelevance of material objectives.[31] These shoplifters often had sufficient money in their pockets to pay for what they stole and, if not, they often knew that they could readily obtain the necessary funds from parents or friends. Even when the object was economically beyond their reach, their aim was not necessarily to use the booty. In marked contrast, studies of preadult working-class "serious" thieves emphasize the practical use of the products of sneak theft to sustain a materially improved lifestyle.[32] But just as it is with age, it is easy to misconstrue the relation of economic status or social class and the thrilling quality of sneaky property crime.

Vandalism does not appear to be a class-specific form of delinquency. If this hedonistic adolescent offense runs parallel to adolescent theft, should we not reconsider the relevance of materialist motives for both?[33] Even with respect to shoplifting and burglary, at least up to the point of the initial arrest, the animating attraction toward sneaky property crimes appears to be some form of thrill, even for youths who, in middle-class eyes, must have pressing material needs. Recall the autobiographical excerpt presented earlier of John Allen, a poor black youth from Washington, D.C., who went on to a serious criminal career.

Researchers who let their subjects do the sociological analysis for them often get folk theories that emphasize material causes and objectives. In his interviews with black gang members in Philadelphia, Barry Krisberg was sometimes told that their initial thefts were done to satisfy material needs, but when he checked into official records on the events in question, he found contrary indications. For example, one interviewee claimed that he committed his first theft to feed his family, but Krisberg found in records of an arrest related to the event that the fellow had been stealing a gun to use in fights between peer groups.[34] And there are indications that even in desperately poor areas, adolescent thieves turn to theft for emotionally compelling rather than materially necessary reasons. A study of thieves in the low castes in India found that the initial victims of theft were frequently the youths' parents.[35]

The initial experiences in sneak thefts of poor, working-class, and middle-class youths, alike, appear to be more clearly projects in constructing sneaky thrills than efforts to satisfy previously defined material needs. Thus, there is no basis for assuming any particular social-class pattern in the background of sneaky thrills.

Yet, for *persistent* or "serious" property thieves, repetition itself tends to undercut the experimental, discovery foundations of sneaky thrills. In a rare participant-observation study conducted in lower- and working-class areas in Toronto, Canada, Gordon West described "serious adolescent property offenders" who cooperate in "casing" targets, sharing tips on places to victimize, collectively arranging the "fencing" of stolen items, and lending each other money when one is down on his thieving luck.[36] Because they often steal to resell, these serious thieves may appear to be stealing for material objectives, rather than for the thrill. In addition, they often make a calculated choice to abandon thievery at the age of majority, when penalties substantially increase. Many of these patterns were recently documented by Mercer Sullivan among poor Hispanic and black youths in New York City.[37] Nothing in this chapter speaks to the social-class factors that may lie behind such "serious" short-term careers or behind long-term careers in nonviolent, sneaky property crimes like burglary, boosting, and confidence games.

But even in the case of "serious" thieves, I would suggest, we should not too readily assume that material objectives are dominant. If we looked more closely at how they define material needs, we might get a different image of these "serious" thieves. West's thieves, at times, go out specifically to steal for such "needs" as buying Speed and entertaining friends in a flashy manner. The drugs and clothes differ in Sullivan's settings, but the theme is similar. In lower-class areas, adolescent theft satisfies the objective needs common to the class—buying food, paying rent, and acquiring clothes—less obviously than it supports a form of material taste that the youths can only satisfy through more theft. It is also notable that older thieves, in their recollections of "big" scores, commonly report the value of the item at its retail price rather than at the discounted price realized through fencing; the situational charm of the event to the thief apparently does not decline quite as much as does the market value of the stolen items. And although with persistent practice, the thrills of sneaky property crimes may diminish, the various metaphors that make up the thrill of the event do not necessarily become irrelevant. Rather, they may become diffused throughout a way of life in which situated property crimes, by themselves, may not be the most exciting, deviant, or risky moments. At least, this often appears to be the case for "career" stickup men, whose complex relationships between material and transcendent purposes will be taken up in chapter 6.

CHAPTER 3

Ways of the Badass

In many youthful circles, to be "bad," to be a "badass," or otherwise overtly to embrace symbols of deviance is regarded as a good thing. How does one go about being a badass? How can that become a compelling project?

One can develop a systematic understanding of the ways of the badass by distinguishing among three levels or degrees of intimating aggression. Someone who is "real bad" must be tough, not easily influenced, highly impressionable, or anxious about the opinions that others hold of him; in a phrase, he must not be morally malleable. He must take on an existential posture that in effect states, "You see me, but I am not here for you; I see you, and maybe you are here for me."

The second stage in becoming a badass is to construct alien aspects of the self. This construction may be achieved barbarically, by developing ways of living that appear hostile to any form of civilization, or by inventing a version of civilization that is not only foreign but incomprehensible to native sensibilities. If being *tough* is essentially a negative activity of convincing others that one is not subject to their influence, being *alien* is a more positive projection of the world in which one truly fits. The existential posture of the alien states in effect, "Not only am I not here for you, I come from a place that is inherently intractable by your world." The foreigner may often be charming; the alien is unnerving. Managing the difference between appearing to be interestingly foreign and disturbingly alien is a subtle business; much of the work of the adolescent badass plays on the fineness of the distinction.

Either alone or in combination with a posture of toughness, the perfection of an alien way is not sufficient to achieve the awesomely deviant presence of the badass. Toughs who set off sparks that call for attention but never explode risk being regarded as "punks." And many who elaborate alien ways achieve nothing more than the recognition of being "really weird." In addition to being tough and developing an alien style, the would-be badass must add a measure of meanness.[1]

To be "bad" is to be mean in a precise sense of the term. Badasses manifest the transcendent superiority of their being, specifically by insisting on the dominance of their will, that "I mean it," when the "it" itself is, in a way obvious to all, immaterial. They engage in violence not necessarily sadistically or "for its own sake" but to back up their meaning without the limiting influence of utilitarian considerations or a concern for self-preservation. At this level, the badass announces, in effect, "Not only do you not know where I'm at or where I'm coming from, but, at any moment, I may transcend the distance between us and destroy you. I'll jump you on the street, I'll 'come up side' your head, I'll 'fuck you up good'—I'll rush destructively to the center of your world, whenever I will! Where I'm coming from, you don't *want* to know!"

To make vivid sense of all the detailed ways of the badass, one must consider the essential project as transcending the modern moral injunction to adjust the public self sensitively to situationally contingent expectations. The frequent use of phallic metaphors is especially effective for making this process bristle with sensational moves. At the end of the chapter, I will clarify the distinctive relevance of masculine sexual symbols and suggest why being a badass is so disproportionately seductive to males. In chapter 4 I will relate class and ethnic status to differences in adolescent cultures of deviance. In chapter 6 knowledge of the ways of the badass will contribute to the explanation of the self-consciously criminal careers of hardened stickup men.

Being Tough

The ways of being tough may be summarized along two lines. First, a tough appearance may be accomplished by using symbols and practical devices that suggest an impenetrable self. Here we can place the attractions, to those who would effect a tough appearance, of leather clothing and metal adornments. Here, too, we can understand the connection of a publicly recognizable "toughness" with signs that unusual physical risks have been suffered and transcended; scars are an example. High boots frequently enhance a tough look, in some styles suggesting cowboys or motorcyclists, in other styles implying that the wearer has passed or expects to pass through some sort of disagreeable muck.[2]

Prominent among the devices of toughness are dark sunglasses. As the street name suggests, "shades," unlike sunglasses in general, pull down a one-way curtain in face-to-face interaction, accomplishing nicely the specific interactional strategy that is toughness. On the folk assumption that the eyes are windows to the soul, in face-to-face interaction we regularly read the eye movements of others for signs of the focus of their consciousness, to grasp their subjective location, and to track what is "here" to them. Simultaneously, we manage the direction of our gaze to shape the perception by others of what is "here" to us. Thus, we usually avert our gaze from passersby after an implicitly understood interval, so that our apparent continued attentions do not suggest an improperly intimate interest; conversely, if we want to suggest that the other is intimately "here" for us, we do not avert our gaze. Shades permit the wearer to detect what is "here" to passersby, while the wearer's focus of consciousness remains inaccessible to them. When this interactional reading does not hold, for example, when we know the wearer is blind, darkly tinted glasses will not work as a device for intimating toughness.

Because toughness manifests that one is not morally or emotionally accessible, one recognizable style of being tough is to maintain silence, sometimes referred to as a "stony" silence, in the face of extensive questions, pleadings, comic antics, and other efforts to evoke signs of sympathy. As an audible analog to the eyes' "shades," when "tough" guys have to say something to get things from others, they may mumble or speak in a voice muffled by gum, a tightly closed mouth, or a downcast face.

The symbols and devices of impenetrability are a simple ready-made way of being tough; many of them can literally be bought off the rack. What is culturally more complex and individually more challenging is the requirement to offset the moral malleability inevitably suggested when one enters communicative interaction. I may easily appear tough to you when I am not attempting to shape your understanding to any effect other than that I am tough. But if I want to do any other sort of business with you, my apparent rigidity will, sooner or later, become a problem. If I want to communicate substantive desires, I must attend to whether you have correctly interpreted my messages; if not, I am constrained to alter my expression to get the point across—all of which risks suggesting that, to shape your experience of me, I am willing to shape and reshape myself and, hence, that I am not so tough.[3]

It is common for young people to take on the first layer of toughness without being accomplished in the second. What appears to be a hard-and-fast toughness often dissolves in the first moments of substantive interaction. Thus, in the privacy of a bedroom, one may drape the body in leather and chains, practice a hard look in the mirror, apply apparently permanent but really erasable tattoos of skulls and crossbones, and so forth. When one enters a store to buy cigarettes, however, it may feel impossible not to wait one's turn with the clerk politely, and even to finish the transaction with a muttered "thanks."

The openings and closings of face-to-face interactions in public are routine occasions for indicating that one has the moral competence to be in society. With "How are you?" we often formally open and move into an interaction. The response, "And how are you?" without a pause is accepted and thus the interaction proceeds smoothly without either party explicitly responding to the question.[4]

The primary project of the questioner is usually to indicate that he is the sort of person who cares. Even though his failure to await a response might logically be taken to indicate just the opposite, the move makes sense to the participants because it indicates that the speaker is open to moral concerns. He has used convention to indicate that he is open to change based on the state of the other's being. Here is a little ceremony performed to ritualize the beginning of interaction, a ceremony in which each indicates to the other that he is capable of mediating his existence with others through social forms.

Compare a common ritual opening of interaction among adolescents who are attempting to be tough. When boys in American junior high schools pass each other in the halls while changing classes, they sometimes exchange punches aimed at each others' shoulders. They may then continue past each other or, even more oddly, they may abruptly abandon the dramatization of hostilities and pause for a short interchange of affable comments that make no reference to the opening blows. Literally, the thrust of the message is the thrust of the message. Familiarity with this ritual breeds a competition to be first in detecting the other's presence and to land the first punch. In a little ceremony performed to mark the initial moments of interaction, each attempts to indicate to the other that he exists for the other in the first instance physically, independent of civility and social form.

Note that not only is the implicit statement the inverse of that made by the customary civil ritual, so is its irony. The tactful adult shows that he is the sort of person who cares by inquiring about the other's sensibilities and then proceeding without pausing for a response. But the playfully combative adolescent shows that he is present most fundamentally in his socially unrestrained physical being, by more or less artfully employing a well-established social form.

One of the most elemental ways of being tough is to mark the beginning and the ending of an interaction gutturally, with a sound that emanates from deep in the body and whose form indicates that the sound maker ("speaker" would not be quite accurate here) exists outside of civil conventions. Members of street gangs in Italian sections of Brooklyn in the 1950s would often signal their entrance into a streets corner assemblage of their fellows with an "eh" (or "ay") that would trigger a cycle of responsive "ehs."[5] This utterance is guttural, both in significance and sensual practice; the physical exertion indicates to the others that he is present for them from his stomach—not from his mind or from any socialized sensibility.

Endings of interactions are again typical occasions for expressing a competently socialized moral character. The strength of the moral demands made during an interaction is revealed by the amount of culture and proficiency of skill required to end an interaction without retrospectively undermining its moral framework. Such verbal and written civil endings as "Take Care," "Yours Truly," and "Have a Nice Day" reaffirm the person's competent social sensibility. Despite a near-universal awareness of the banality of these forms, they remain difficult to avoid.

Such ritual endings are executed because people who have been interacting anticipate that a new threat will emerge at the end of the interaction. This threat is not to the future of their relationship (these conventions are used as much, perhaps more, among strangers who may well never see each other again as among friends), but to the reinterpretation of what has just transpired. Often formally prospective *(Have* a nice day: I *remain* sincerely yours, *take* care, best *wishes),* these devices are implicitly and more fundamentally retrospective. In effect, farewells assert that even though my care for you is so limited that I can now move on to other cares—even though by ending this interaction I may suggest that I have not been authentically here for you—I really have been deeply, sensitively involved with you all the while. The misleadingly prospective direction of the form is essential to suppress awareness of the implicit retrospective doubt, the existential doubt that either participant was (and perhaps ever can be) really "here" for the other. As phenomenal worlds begin objectively to separate, civil interactors rush to reaffirm that those worlds really were isomorphic and that each person really was morally sensitive to the other. I anticipate your sense that if I can break off abruptly from you, you may reflect, "He never really gave a shit about what I felt in the first place!"

To produce toughness is, in part, a matter of failing to perform these prophylactic rituals on the moral health of everyday life, but it is also a matter of inventing substitutes. Consider as a striking example of a guttural exiting ceremony, the *cholo's* "Shaa-haa!" In East Los Angeles, adolescent *vatos, cholos,* or "homeboys" frequently mill about in a casual mood that shows no particularly malevolent spirit until the assemblage is brought to a close when one of the participants utters a forceful or cool statement of bravado to which he appends a "Shaa" or "Shaa-haa," which the others join in.

The following instance was part of a homeboy's recollection of his first day in the tenth grade at Garfield High School in East Los Angeles. He was "holding up the wall" with fellow homeboys from his *barrio*—a traditional practice in which groups congregate at traditional spots, lean against the wall, and look out at groups clustered in other spots. The school bell rang to call students to class. The homeboys continued to mill about, aware that with time, their passivity would take on an increasingly deviant significance as a tacit rebellion against the school's attempt to control their interaction. A vice principal came over to urge the group to go to class, and one homeboy responded, " 'Say, professor, don't you have something better to do? If you don't take my advise, go sit on the toilet and flush yourself down. Shaa-haa!' "[6]

Like "eh," "Shaa-haa" (which can be short or long and more syncopated or less, depending on the occasion) comes from deep in the body, from the very bottom of the throat, if not from the guts. It involves letting out a burst of air audibly, over a jutting jaw, with mouth open but without shaping lips to form letters, all to accomplish a broad, deep, serpentine hiss that is often succeeded by a machine-gun burst of belly laughing. Having publicly defined the interaction that preceded the termination as one in which all the boys were present in a gutturally direct, socially uninhibited way, the aggregation can disband and the participants can head toward class.[7] With this utterance, a group of young men can harmoniously articulate a common moral posture of being tough without fear that the medium will contradict the message.

In addition to opening and closing interactions, those who would be tough must routinely counter the moral vulnerabilities suggested in the very nature of human existence. For human beings eating, for example, is a figurative, as well as a literal, opening of the self. For tough guys, eating (and defecating, ejaculating, extracting mucus from the nose and throat, and so on) must be carefully cultivated to offset the breach of self inherent in the process. Sweating, however, should require no special ceremony for toughs: perspiring occurs simply in a transpiring; no act of opening the body is necessary to make visible these drops from inside.

In adolescent cultures, toughness is commonly displayed as a subtle negativity, barely glossed onto an otherwise morally sensitive interaction. Consider two everyday ironies from black street life, hand-slapping rituals and the use of "shit" to begin a turn at speaking in conversation. Handshaking is a conventional form for displaying a civil sensibility when face-to-face interactions begin or end. It expresses a gentle man's spirit by physically enacting a moral malleability and a moral vulnerability: I open my hand, my self, to feel the force of your presence, and vice versa; we are united by social form, such that each may be influenced by the other's will.

Young men in black ghettos have constructed from this convention a means of displaying a paradoxical form of social contract. With the hand slap, the moral malleability suggested by the handshake becomes a cooperative hitting—I hit you and I let you hit me. The moral vulnerability suggested by the offer and acceptance of physical contact is simultaneously countered by its opposite. The hitting or slapping, an action that in other contexts might be humiliating punishment, usually passes as an unremarkable gloss of toughness.

This dialectical principle is elaborated within ongoing group interactions as speakers and listeners seek and confer agreement. The more a listener agrees with a speaker, the harder he hits him, and conversely. As R. Lincoln Keiser noted:

> In general, when a hand-slapping episode occurs during social interaction it emphasizes agreement between the two parties. If an individual has said something someone thinks particularly noteworthy, he will put

out his hand to be slapped. By slapping it, the alter in the relationship signals agreement. Varying the intensity of the slap response indicates varying degrees of agreement. A Vice Lord may say, "Five Lords can whup fifty Cobras!" and then put out his hand, palm up. Another club member responds by slapping the palm hard, thus indicating strong agreement. The first Vice Lord might then say, "I can whup ten Cobras myself!" and again put out his hand. This time, however, the second individual may respond with a much lighter slap.[8]

The more the listener indicates that he has been moved by the speaker, the more emphatically he simultaneously acknowledges and counters his malleability through enacting aggression.

"Shit," pronounced melodically over long vowel sounds ("Sheee-it"), has had an extraordinary run of popularity in black street life. It is a way for a speaker to begin a turn in conversation or to mark publicly the movement of his consciousness from one theme to another within a monologue. Compare, as the inverse in form and function, the British use of "Right" to begin a turn in conversation, for example, the Bobby's "Right, what's going on here?" the Mexican's use of "Bueno, es que" to begin a response to a question; and the use of "okay" by white middle-class adolescents in the U.S. to begin a turn and repeatedly to reorient a narrative account in a conversation. Although with "shee-it" the speaker pulls himself out of a communal moral order even as he audibly begins to enter it, "Right," "Bueno," and "Okay" invoke a transcendent moral order to tie people together into a conversation at moments when the coordination of their sensibilities has become problematic. With "Right," the Bobby invokes a framework of moral approbation to begin the assertion of his authority. With "Bueno, es que," the Mexican begins to respond to a question by formally overcoming the dim, horrific possibility that the asking has inexorably alienated the speakers. With "okay, okay, okay," the young suburban American asserts his moral commitment to sustain order in conversation just as he anticipates that, because of problems in the evolving structuring of a narrative, it may soon fall into doubt.[9]

"Sheee-it" is elegantly negative, both in content and in form of delivery. When pronounced in a descending melody, the phrasing gives the word, even apart from its content, a cynical, negating tone. In content, shit is about as purely negative an image as any that could be thrown into a conversation. The existential fact that we are, each of us, literally (if also narrowly), walking, talking containers of excrement is remarkable for its typical absence from overt public attention. When used to start a speaker's turn in conversation, "shee-it" brilliantly executes a simultaneous expression of two dialectically related themes: (1) the fact that I speak to you coherently displays my ability to shape myself to fit into your understanding and (2) the fact that I begin by tying your impression of me to shit suggests that the social form I take on is but a thin veneer over a nature that is obdurately beyond social domination. The following example, which illustrates the point both in form and content, came from an interview with a member of a black street gang in San Francisco:

> I feel my high school education is the most important thing in my life right now. That's how I feel.
> [Interviewer:] How long have you felt this way?
> Shit. Maybe a year.[10]

These subculturally varied devices for producing a veneer of toughness are all counterveiling commentaries on the image of personal moral openness that is persistently implied in social interaction. To sustain interaction while remaining tough, one can repeatedly negate the continuously resurrected implication that one is sensitive to others by throwing shit onto the scene, with guttural outbursts, by physically hitting at the image of moral sensibility, and so forth. Attacks on the conventions and cliches of civil demeanor constitute one of the stock ways of being tough. An account of street gang violence in Glasgow, Scotland, provides a final illustration. According to one retelling by members of the "Young Team" of an attack on a solitary victim, the victim, a boy aged 14, rolled himself into a ball for self-protection and was then stabbed seventeen times in the back. Just before the attackers ran off, Big Sheila, a barmaid who was sympathetic to the Young Team, created a memorable closing line by dropping a handkerchief on the boy and offering: "That'll help ye tae mop yir brow."[11]

Being Alien

Being tough is essentially a process of negation, achieved either with a visual block, a symbolic sartorial shield, an audible muffle, or a maneuver that inverts the suggestions of a morally open self that are inevitably born in such everyday activities as eating, meeting friends, and conversing. Of course, being tough is not sufficient to construct a deviant identity; we admire poker players, respect businessmen, and honor political leaders who appear to be "tough." In all cases, the quality being celebrated is a negative moral capacity—an ability not to give away, not to give up, and not to give in.

By developing ways of being alien, adolescents can move positively beyond the negativity of a tough posture without abandoning it and without embracing respectable conventions. In congruence with the statement made from the stance of toughness, "I am not here for you," adolescents have fashioned an ever-expanding set of subcultures in which they can style great swaths of their everyday lives with indications that they come from some morally alien place.

Across subcultures would-be badasses exploit the hermeneutic possibilities in walking. Young blacks who would strike up the admirable image of the "bad nigger" work on orchestrating their pace to a ghetto "bop." John Allen, a black from Washington, D.C., who became a "professional" stickup man, recalled that when he was first committed to a juvenile detention facility,

> I learned a lot of things. . . . it was a place where you fought almost every day because everybody trying to be tougher than the next person. As a kid you pay so much attention to how a dude's supposed to be a bad nigger, he really having his way around the joint with the counselors and with everybody. . . . So you wanna be like him, you wanna act like him and talk like him. I think down there I must of changed my voice about hundred times 'cause I had a high-pitched voice and was bothered being small. And I changed my walk from supercool to ultracool.[12]

In East Los Angeles, the night before his first day in high school, a barrio homeboy anxiously anticipated humiliating challenges. He debated whether to take a gun to school and practiced his "barrio stroll": "a slow, rhythmic walk with ample flamboyant arm movement, chesty posture, and head up towards the heavens."[13]

Each of these styles transforms walking from a utilitarian convention into a deviant esthetic statement made routinely in the practice of getting from here to there. Each suggests that the walker takes some special pleasure in the existential necessity of putting one foot in front of the other to get ahead. Each suggests that the walker will not take a simple "straight" path through the social structure. He will take up more attention and more space in his social mobility than is called for by civil routines, perhaps, with those flamboyantly swayed arms and his side-to-side gait or slightly jumping bop causing problems for pedestrians who are attempting to pass unnoticed in the other direction.

Most notably, each style of walking suggests not only that the walker is not here for the others around and "walks to a beat of a different drummer," but he is from a morally deviant place. The *ghetto* bop and the *barrio* stroll, identify the walker as a native of a place that is outside and antagonistically related to the morally respectable center of society. Similarly, the streetcorner male's habit of repeatedly making manual contact with his genitals and hoisting up his pants is a prominent way of pointing to the walker's animal life, a life carried on somewhere beyond the perception of respectable society. The currently popular "sag" look makes the same point by inverting these symbols. Pants are held by tight belts below the buttocks, where they permit the display of a "bad" ass covered by florid boxer shorts, which are often worn over a second, unseen pair of underpants.[14]

From Japan to Scotland to East Los Angeles, tattoos are appreciated as devices for embracing a deviant identity. Tattoos may be used minimally to suggest toughness by drawing attention to the skin as a barrier between the tattooed person and others. They also conjure up toughness by suggesting that the person has suffered and survived pain. Tattoos are not necessarily ominous, but often their content conveys an additionally "bad," alien theme by suggesting a totemic relationship with evil. In one circle of street fighting young men in Glasgow in the early 1970s, "Mick . . . sported on his forearm a red dagger entering the top of a skull and reappearing through its mouth. It was considered to be the finest tattoo in the neighbourhood."[15] Los Angeles cholos are partial to black widow spiders and death skulls. Hell's Angels sport swastikas, German crosses, and skulls-and-crossbones.

These symbols suggest that the wearer presumes himself fundamentally rooted in a world of deviance and so is unresponsive to conventional moral appeals. What is more interesting is that the same effect is often achieved with tattoos that are traditional, respectable symbols of moral content—of "Mom," "love," and American Eagles; in the Japanese criminal subculture of *yakuza*, the whole body may be tattooed with chrysanthemums.[16] Beyond suggesting toughness and almost regardless of content, tattoos emphasize personal intransigence and are symbols of permanent loyalty to a particular subgroup's interpretation of the Good. They seem to say, "Wherever I am, whatever is going on, without my even trying, this will be fundamental to who I am." Even when the moral commitment is to "Mom" or to the American flag, the tattoo will often have threatening, deviant overtones. (Contrast the morally innocuous wearing of pins bearing club or patriotic images: unlike tattoos and like college ties and tieclips, these can be taken off.)

Like walking, the would-be badass may also fashion talking into a deviant esthetic. John Allen, the professional "bad nigger" whose recollections of his street education in a juvenile detention facility were quoted earlier, noted: "There was a big thing there about talking. You had to express yourself, and you saying, 'Damn, jive, Listen man' and going through all the motions and changes."[17] In Glasgow, young street fighting men use a slang, reminiscent of Cockney forms, that hides its meaning through a multistep process of alteration from conventional expression. Thus, "It's jist yir Donald" means "It's just your luck": "Donald" calls up "duck," and "duck" rhymes with "luck." "Ya tea-leaf ye!" means "You thief!," which, if pronounced with their accent, would sound something like, tea-eef. "Ah fancy yir tin flute" means "I like your suit."[18]

The ethnographer who recorded these phrases grew up in Glasgow but was initially frustrated in attempting to understand the young toughs' everyday conversations. As Allen indicates with regard to the United States, "jive" talk is not a natural talent of ghetto blacks.[19] Within the local context of ghettoes, these argots are resources for taking the posture of an alien presence, a being who moves cooly above the mundane realities of others. As with being tough, being alien is not necessarily a posture taken toward conventional society. It is a way of being that may be taken up at any moment. As Allen's quote made clear, being ultra cool is most essential in the company of other tough young men. Being alien is a way of stating, "I am not here for you," when anyone—friend, family, or foe—may be the "you."

The ways of being alien begin to define an alternative deviant culture. As such, they call for the study of their distinctive esthetic unities. Here, I can only indicate a few lines of analysis that might be elaborated by investigations devoted solely to ethnographic documentation.

THE CHOLO

A coherent deviant esthetic unites various manifestations of the low-income youth culture of the barrio known as *la vida loca* and identified with the cholo, vato loco, or Mexican-American homeboy. Language, body posture, clothing fashions, car styles, and graffiti exhibit a distinctive, structurally similar, "bad" perspective. As individuals, young people in the barrio take on and shed this esthetic from situation to situation and to different degrees, but they continuously take for granted that affiliation with it will signify, to their peers and to adults alike, the transcendence of a line of respectability and the assumption of a high-risk posture of moral defiance.

In its essential thrust, the cholo esthetic assumes an inferior or outsider status and asserts an aggressive dominance. In body posture, this dialectic is achieved by dropping below or falling back and simultaneously looking down on others. Thus, when Mexican-American young men wish to take up a cholo or "bad" posture for a photograph, they often squat, placing their buttocks just off the ground, sometimes on their heels, while they throw their heads slightly back to a position from which they can glare down at the camera. This posture is not easily sustained; its accomplishment is at once an athletic test and an esthetic demonstration of "bad" toughness.[20]

This position might be characterized as an aristocratic squat. Reminiscent of a resource known to peasants throughout the world, the cholo's squat creates a place for him to sit when there are no chairs. But by throwing his head sharply back, the cholo takes on a paradoxically aristocratic air. Once in the lowered and reared-back position, a sense of superiority is attached to him, as it is to one who is born to privilege: naturally and necessarily, like a law of nature.

Faced by a squatting cholo, an observer sees himself observed by a down-the-nose glance, like the stereotype of a peasant under the regard of an aristocrat. For his part, the cholo accomplishes something magical: he simultaneously embraces and transcends an inferior status. Before your very eyes and dressed in an undershirt that has no sleeves to put anything up, the cholo drops down to the ground, becoming lower to you in physical position but putting you down morally. Miraculously, the cholo manages literally to look down on you from beneath you.

The dialectical structure and aggressive symbolic force of this body posture is also carried out in the classic *pachuco* stance and in the contemporary "barrio stroll." Unlike the cholo's aristocratic squat, the pachuco style is both historically dated and well-known outside Mexican-American barrios, in part because of the popularity of the play and then movie, *Zoot Suit*. Although the pachuco's Zoot Suit or "drapes" were fashions of the 1930s and 1940s, contemporary cholos proudly, and sometimes self-consciously, continue elements of the pachuco style, wearing overly large, multiply pleated, sharply pressed khaki pants and pointed, brightly shined black shoes. And if the narrator of *Zoot Suit* took an exaggerated back-leaning stance, the contemporary cholo is similarly inclined.[21]

When being photographed, a group of cholos will often divide up into some who squat, lean forward, throw their heads back, and cast their eyes down to meet the camera and some who stand, maintaining the wide angle between their side-pointed feet that the squatters also adopt, throwing the trunk slightly back, throwing their heads back even more, and casting their eyes down to meet the camera. This standing position is put into motion in the barrio stroll. In forward movement, the foot position adopted by squatting and stationary cholos is maintained, but now it becomes far more noticeable, causing a ducklike waddle. To balance out the waddle and the backward slant of the trunk, the barrio stroller bends his elbows sharply, drawing the hands up parallel to the ground.

In the stationary position and in the stroll, the "being low" of the squat is replaced by a "being outside." While the squatting cholo is in a remarkably low social position, the backward-inclined, standing and strolling cholo is remarkably beyond reach. The magical effect is that while being emphatically beyond conventional reach, the cholo appears to be unusually aggressive and assertive as he strides into your world.

The low position of the cholo's aristocratic squat is repeated in the automobile esthetic of the low rider. By altering stock shocks and springs, cholos make cars ride literally low. If the rear is lowered more than the front, the driver will naturally incline backwards. Even without mechanical alterations, they may achieve the same effect by driving with their arms fully extended, their trunk and head inclined back, and their eyes cast down at the world above.

The overall effect is less an approximation of the advertised modern man in an up-to-date car than a fantasy image of a prince in a horse-drawn chariot, sometimes racing with other chariots and sometimes promenading slowly through public boulevards. The cars themselves are restored and dressed up at a substantial expense. The challenge is to demonstrate a transcendent esthetic power by raising the dead and discarded to a vividly displayed superiority. The low-rider is a distinctively American construction of alien being; foreign cars are not used, but the style is pointedly different from anything Detroit has ever tried to get Americans to buy.

The form of graffiti that is popular among Mexican-American youths in Los Angeles also has an emphatically alien esthetic and a backward leaning slant. In New York City, graffiti, produced by blacks, Puerto Ricans, and others, is often colorful and graphic, sometimes extensively narrative, and cartoon figures are often mixed in with individual and gang names, threats, and ideological slogans. New York graffiti writers consider one of their highest achievements to be the creation of an integrated set of images running over up to ten subway cars. In East Los Angeles, graffiti is primarily monotonic calligraphy; as one writer put it, everything is in the line:

> Graffiti is all the same line, the same feeling, even though different people use it for a different purpose. . . . Anyway, I dig that line, I dug that line. That's how I got involved. It's my thing—that line.[22]

Experienced graffiti "writers" in New York denigrate "tags" (writing only a name or nickname) as amateurish and unsophisticated. But in Los Angeles, graffiti is called *plaqueasos*—from *placa,* which in various contexts means a car license plate, a policeman's badge, or a plaque announcing one's business to the world. The plaqueasos of Los Angeles are elaborated in line and adornment far beyond the "tags" derided by New York writers.

Mexican-American plaqueaso writers appear to be working from traditions that are so ancient and foreign as to make the content of their graffiti routinely indecipherable to outsiders, often even to residents of their own barrios. The emphasis in the content is on individual and gang names, phrases of bravado and threats, nightmarish (black widow spiders, laughing skulls) and deviant (the number 13 for the letter "M" for marijuana) iconography, and a protective curse (*Con Savos* or *Con Safos,* often written simply as C/S) that is reminiscent of those inscribed on Egyptian tombs. Individual letters in words, designed in a style that is unfamiliar to any written tradition known in the barrio, are often mixed with symbols (for instance, stars between letters), as in a hieroglyphics.

In a sensitive study of East Los Angeles graffiti, Jerry and Sally Romotsky argued that major styles of plaqueasos are based on Old English, Gothic, Dürer-like calligraphy.[23] Perhaps the style that is most difficult for outsiders to decipher is what plaqueaso writers call the "point" style. Romotsky and Romotsky showed that the point style is achieved essentially by tracing the outlines of blocky, Old English-style letters. In effect, plaqueaso writers achieve a strange, alien appearance by working out of Anglo-Saxon cultural traditions in a disguised way. They achieve a distinctive presence by the ingeniously simple device of negation, that is, leaving out the substance of letters.

A superior posture for plaqueaso is achieved by using the same dialectical technique that is used in body posture. When drawn in three dimensions, the letters sometimes march to one side or huddle together like colorful cartoon characters engaged in a light, comic spirit. But in their "bad" forms—when they announce the names of gangs or make ominous declarations, three-dimensional letters often rear back and come down heavily on the observer as they declare their author's existence.[24]

The same esthetic runs through clothing and language. Cholos favor armless undershirts, as if to embrace a sign of the working-class status that has been abjured by conventional fashion. Unlike garments that are manufactured to be worn as "tops," these tops are also bottoms: traditionally worn beneath shirts, their display is a negation that emphasizes what is not worn. And by studiously maintaining their undershirts in brilliant white, cholos proclaim their transcendence of dirty work. Plaid shirts, referred to in the barrios as "Pendletons," are part of the everyday uniform of many school-age cholos. Worn over a bright white undershirt, the Pendleton recalls the cotton plaid shirts common among impoverished Mexican immigrants as well as the expensive wool shirts associated with the Oregon manufacturer. As a practical matter, the style is alien to the reality of the cholos, whose first days of classes in the fall often have temperatures topping 100 degrees. With colorful bandanas wrapped around their foreheads, cholos look like they come from rural Indian areas rather than urban barrio neighborhoods.

Homeboys in East Los Angeles speak and write graffiti with elements from Calo, a unique amalgam of Spanish and English that continues a "pachuco" argot whose roots are in pre-World War II, Mexican-American gang life.[25] On the one hand, cholos often ridicule recently arrived Mexicans who are incompetent in English.[26] On the other hand, their version of Spanish is incomprehensible to native Mexicans as well as to many of their U.S.-born parents. Pachuco or Calo is not a foreign language; it is ubiquitously alien.

In sum, the cholo-pachuco style is a deviant posture of aggressive intrusiveness made from a position that is proudly outside the reaches of the various societies it addresses. Through the stationary and the walking body and in clothing, cars, everyday language, and stylized writing, the pachuco-cholo-homeboy-vato loco conjures up a deviance rooted in a world that is self-consciously and intrinsically alien. The special claim of this esthetic is not just that its bearers are tough, but that they are from a spiritually rich, morally coherent place that Anglo authorities, native Mexicans, parents, or conventionally styled peers may only grasp minimally and at a distance as existing somewhere over "there."

THE PUNK

Consider next the novel way in which the punk culture locates its bearers in an alien moral system. An observer of the original British working class-based punk culture offered this summary:

> The punks turned towards the world a dead white face which was there and yet not "there." These "murdered victims"—emptied and inert—also had an alibi, an elsewhere, literally "made up" out of vaseline and cosmetics, hair dye and mascara. But paradoxically, in the case of the punks, this "elsewhere" was a nowhere—a twilight zone—a zone constituted out of negativity.[27]

The alien character of punk culture has been achieved in several ways. One is to embrace as appearance enhancing the devices that, according to strong moral injunctions and contemporary fashion, ought to be kept hidden. Thus, safety pins and sanitary napkins are worn as adornments on shirts and skirts, lavatory chains are draped like a necklace on the chest, and makeup is applied in degrees and places that ensure that its application will be seen. And hair is not only dressed in unconventional ways but is dyed blue, green, intense red, yellows, and combinations of these colors that are not found naturally on any humans. The suggestion is of an alien culture whose standards are the opposite of conventional esthetic standards. The thrust of punk culture is not only foreign or "weird" but consistently antipathetic.

The alien theme in punk culture has not been limited to dress and appearance. Dancing "was turned into a dumbshow of blank robotics." The pogo—a dance style of jumping up and down, hands clenched to the sides, as if to head an imaginary ball, the jumps repeated without variation in time to the strict mechanical rhythms of the music—"was a caricature—a reductio ad absurdum of all the solo dance styles associated with rock music." Bands took names like the Unwanted, the Rejects, the Sex Pistols, the Clash, and the Worst and wrote songs with titles like "I Wanna be Sick on You" and "If You Don't Want to Fuck Me, Fuck Off." There was a "wilful desecration and the voluntary assumption of outcast status which characterized the whole punk movement."[28] A memorable example was a sort of pet hairdo constructed by carrying live rats perched on the head.[29]

Another alien theme, one that was given a particular reading in punk culture but that has had broad appeal to many "bad" youth cultures, might be called, being inured to violence. Clothes display holes and rips that suggest not wear but war; hair is shaped into daggers; makeup may suggest bruises, scars, and black eyes. In this theme, the suggestion of an alien origin for the punk is that he or she has just come to the instant social situation, to what is going on here, from a place that is, to all in civil society, somewhere inhospitably "there."

Despite radical differences in the substance of their symbols, the punk and cholo cultures dramatize a tough invulnerability and the status of a visitor in the conventional world. For the individual adolescent, the adoption of the cholo or punk style has often meant a weighty decision of moral citizenship. On the one hand, the bearer sets himself off as a member of an alien culture in the eyes of school and police authorities, parents, and conforming peers. On the other hand, the alien style enables even the loner to induct himself, through what sociologists call collective behavior, into a deviant community.

Punk culture was manifested during its classic stage in the mid-to-late 1970s by an informal social organization underlying a strong esthetic coherence. The punk style inevitably became commercialized, softened, and sold to "normal" adolescents and to middle-aged adults through beauty salons, high-priced boutiques, and mass-marketed music. But for several years, tens of thousands of adolescents were working out a personal style and helping to produce the emerging collective esthetic. By acquiring pieces of used clothing, costume jewelry, and miscellaneous "junk"; altering items already in their closets; and applying makeup and assembling outfits with a care for detail; adolescents, male and female, were literally fitting themselves into a controversial collective movement. That the culture as a whole achieved a persistent coherence even while the details of the punk "look" constantly changed could be taken by individual members as proof both of the autodidactical, idiosyncratic creativity of individual punks and of the existence of a common spiritual bond running through the age group, cutting across formal divisions of school classes, neighborhoods, sex, and ethnicity.

Many adolescents live alien subcultures with far more everyday meaning than simply that of a bizarre dressing ritual. Beyond exploring the reactions of conventional others, adolescents who are dressed in an alien style are recurrently challenged to behave in a distinctively cholo or punk (or "bad nigger," or Hell's Angel) style in routine interactions. How, for example, does one order food at a restaurant in punk style? How does one answer a teacher's question like a cholo?

If the alien adolescent is in exile from a society that does not and never has existed, we still must appreciate the transcendent loyalties that are being evoked. Alien adolescent subcultures are collective movements on the way toward class consciousness, but they rarely reach explicit self-awareness or survive efforts to organize them formally. The cholos' aristocratic squat and other elements of arch style suggest their inchoate collective efforts to weave themes from their unique historical reality: the Mexican peasant origins and U.S. agricultural exploitation of earlier generations combined with a revolutionary tradition in which battles between peasants and aristocrats were joined by bandit leaders. Just as the black ghetto pimp, dressed in a white suit and a planter's hat, defiantly embodies the stereotype of slave owners he has never known, so the cholo, looking down on his environment by taking up a stance beneath and outside, unwittingly but defiantly gives expression to his people's historical subjugation.

The punk movement in the United States emerged in the mid-1970s, coincident with the recession, rapid inflation, and the passage into political quiescence of the "sixties" generation. It emerged after the withdrawal from Vietnam, after the culmination of Watergate, and as the oil crisis was beginning to push up prices throughout the economy. Meanwhile the sixties generation, which originally gained collective self-consciousness, in part by taking over radio station formats and displacing the pop stars of the fifties, was now in its thirties, moving into higher income brackets, but still holding onto its cultural representation of youth. In rock music, the arena in which adolescents uniquely attempt to detect and define the waxing and waning of generations, scores of bands struggled for mass recognition in a youth market that was tenaciously dominated by stars and styles nearing middle age. Styled like a militant vanguard, the punk band represented, in the market of collective symbols, the distinctive historical struggle of the emerging generation. The punk movement was bitterly antihippie; rumors of attacks on sixties youth types were constant. And the punk music and performance style was not simply raucous but a move back to an historical era before the sixties. It was an effort to get back to the fertile, earliest, crudest days of rock and roll in the fifties, as if to begin the youth culture again but in a way in which the currently young could take their place.

To regard these as more than speculations is to miss the open-ended, protean quality of the subculture. What the movement is about in terms of collective material interest and historical position is necessarily unclear as long as it retains the openness to individual esthetic creativity that makes it a compellingly exciting process to its members. But not to speculate on underlying, implicitly sensed themes of collective class interest is to miss an essential element in the excitement of being in these movements. The alien subcultures of adolescence are vehicles for cooperative speculation, means of exploring, through the reactions of others to clothing and new speech forms, which devices "work" and which do not; which fit the alien soul and which are incomprehensible in it; and which compromise the alien order by evincing a subtle sympathy to mainstream conventions. To the extent that young people who do not know each other can create, through indirect interactions and informality, a rich coherence among such minor details as the shape of a line in graffiti, the colors painted on hair, a rag worn around the head, a stirring accent, or a memorable phrase uttered before a class, they can sense the reality of an alien spiritual home—a place as yet concretely present in no definable geography, but surely "there."

THE ANIMAL AND THE COOL

Cutting across the various alien adolescent subcultures is a dualism between the animalistic and the cool. One way to indicate that you are not just tough but essentially outside contemporary civilization is to manifest an animal incapacity for moral responsiveness. Hell's Angels embraced this folk anthropology with their studied affinity for dirt. Inverting the practice of teenagers who shrink "designer" jeans through multiple washings before wearing them skin tight in public, Hell's Angels would train new denim jackets through multiple baths in dirt and grease before wearing them on the road. To shock outsiders, they turned rituals of civil society into occasions for displaying their animal natures, as when one 250-pound Hell's Angel would greet another in a bar by taking a running jump into his arms and planting a wet kiss on his lips.[30] To be animal is to suggest chaotic possibilities—that, through you, at any moment, forces of nature may explode the immediate social situation.

Being cool is a way of being alien by suggesting that one is not metaphysically "here" in the situation that apparently obtains for others, but is really in tune with sensually transcendent forces in another, conventionally inaccessible dimension. To be cool is to view the immediate social situation as ontologically inferior, nontranscendent, and too mundane to compel one's complete attentions. A common way of being cool is to realize or affect a moderate drug mood: the "cool cat" of black street life has its origins in the culture of the heroin world.[31] In Los Angeles barrios, an analogous, drug-related phenomenon is *tapaoism,* an air of being so into a deviant world *(la vida loca)* that one cannot "give a shit" about any situational restraints. In contexts of extreme poverty, a cool version of a "bad" look may be achieved by a self-consciously exaggerated display of luxury in the form of flashy styles worn casually. In their ghettoes, the pachuco who is "draped" in overflowing fabric and the black cat who is "dripping" in jewelry imply sources of wealth that must exist at a distance from conventional morality, in some underground realm, perhaps that of the pimp or the drug dealer.[32]

The two emphases of alien style have spawned different descriptions of fighting. On the animal side, in Puerto Rican street gangs in New York in the 1970s, to be beaten up was to be "dogged up." In many black ghettoes, group attacks on isolated individuals are described as "rat packing" or "wolf packing." In East Los Angeles, attempting to intimidate others with a fierce expression is known as doing a "maddog" look.

On the cool side, to Chicago's Vice Lords of the early 1960s, a fight was a "humbug," and some of the West Side branches became known as the "Conservative" Vice Lords. With "conservative" as with "humbug," they were assuming a pose of calm reserve toward what others find extremely upsetting. It also is cool to refer to risky deviant activities with a diminutive. John Allen, the "professional" stickup man, liked to talk about a period in his life in Washington, D.C., that was nicely organized—a time when he could do "my little sex thing," "my little drug thing," and "a little stickup."[33]

As used in black street culture, "shit," "jive," and "stone" have been used to express both the animal and the cool sides of an alien posture. To talk "jive" is to talk in a cool, poetically effective way, but it may also be to talk nonsense and to bullshit, as in the pejorative "don't give me that jive talk!" or "you jive motherfucker!" "Jive" and "shit" also refer to a gun. In this sense they suggest an overwhelming force that puts the individual beyond the restraints of civilized morality. To be "stoned" is, in one aspect, to be drugged beyond competence for morally responsive interaction. Stone is also a cool object; metaphysically, it emphasizes a hard, unmovable reality, as in the praiseworthy, "He's a stone motherfucker," or in The Black P. Stone Rangers, a famous gang name in Southside Chicago in the 1960s. The gang's name was supercool, since it exploited a double entendre ("stone" played off the name of a local street, Blackstone). Actually, the phrase was ultracool, in that it fortuitously created a triple or quadruple entendre; the club's name was celebrated by poetically inserting a "P" within the street name, which audibly set "stone" apart from "black" just long enough to register racial as well as metaphysical connotations.

Finally, a lack of expressiveness is used widely to construct alien adolescent subcultures in both animal and cool forms. "Animals" in fraternity houses and on sports teams represent a frequently admired way of being "bad" by showing themselves, in loud and wild forms, as being governed by inarticulate, uncivilized forces. On the cool side is the use of silence to affect the style of the professional killer or the Mafia chief. When asked by a sociologist, "What would you like to be when you grow up?" it is cool to answer, "an assassin."[34]

More elaborately, it is dramatically "bad" style to exercise power publicly through silent codes. Turtle, "the Chicano 'Fonz,'" first verbally dressed down homeboys from another barrio in a dangerous face-to-face confrontation and next gave a hand signal and walked away; then twenty or so of *his* homeboys "spontaneously" attacked in unison.[35] This move is "supercool" or extraordinarily "bad" owing to its doubly silent structure. It is a silent message that mobilizes a more profoundly silent dialectic. That is, the most minimal imaginable physical move causes a major physical attack, a momentary shift in posture produces a permanent change in being, a silent signal creates screaming pain, and a cool move turns on the heat and burns the victim.

No attack need follow such a silent message, however. A gesture by one, apparently undifferentiated, man that turns all the others in a place into his servants—for instance, in a bar, at the snap of a finger, an aisle is cleared and a central table is left vacant—also shows a bad "cool." Watching the silent signal and its results, both the participants and bystanders suddenly appreciate a powerful, alien presence. The indications are not only that a structure of authority clearly exists in the group, but that it is implicitly illicit: no formal indicia demarcate those who act as waiters, chauffeurs, and couriers from those who are served as customers, car owners, and chiefs. Exercised with an aura of mystery, "bad" because it cannot show its sources publicly, this power always exists at a distance from the situation that obtains here and now. For those under its spell, its sources are always in some unreachable location vaguely apprehended as over "there."

Being Mean

The person who would be tough must cultivate in others the perception that they cannot reach his sensibilities. Adolescents who would achieve a foreign and hostile presence in interaction must go further and participate in a collective project to produce an alien esthetic. But the shaping of a tough image and the practice of an alien sensibility are insufficient to ensure that one will be "bad." Those who would be bad are always pursued by powerful spiritual enemies who soften tough postures and upset the carefully balanced cultures of alienation, making them appear silly, puerile, and banal and thus undermining their potential for intimidation. To survive unwanted imitators, you must show that unlike the kids, you're not kidding; unlike the gays, you're not playing; unlike the fashionable middle class, you understand fully and embrace the evil of your style. You must show that you mean it.

By being mean, I refer to a distinctive sensuality worked into the experience of interaction. To complete the project of becoming a badass, it is necessary to impress on others the apprehension that, however carefully they may maintain a respectful comportment, you might suddenly thrust the forces of chaos into their world. If he is serious about being tough and alien, the would-be badass can inundate the routine social settings of his everyday life with this "awe-full," ominous character. But how can he show that he means it so clearly that he is never confused with childish, playful, or otherwise inauthentic imitators?

The key distinction is not between physical action and its symbolic representation. If the badass is to make everyday social situations routinely ominous, he cannot, as a practical matter, depend simply on violently harming others.[36] As has frequently been found in studies of street "gangs," those with the "baddest" reputations are not necessarily the best nor even the most frequent fighters. And in the qualitative materials which follow, the actual infliction of physical harm seems always imminent but is not.

Whether through physical attack or via dramatization at a distance, the badass conveys the specific message that he means it. If we ask, what is the "it" that he means? we miss the point. To construct and maintain an awesome, ominous presence, the badass must not allow others to grasp the goals or substantive meaning of his action. He must seem prepared to use violence, not only in a utilitarian, instrumental fashion but as a means to ensure the predominance of his meaning, as he alone understands it, whatever "it" may be.

To make clear that "he means it," the badass celebrates a commitment to violence beyond any reason comprehensible to others. For example, at a dance hall in Glasgow, Tim, a dominant personality in the Young Team, turned to Dave and pointed to a bystander, " 'Ah don't fancy the look o' his puss. Go over an' stab him fur me.' Dave had duly carried out the request."[37] From London's East End, an ex-skinhead recalled, "We only 'it people for reasons, didn't we? . . . like if they looked at us."[38]

In conflicts between street gangs, there is little room for a reasoned exchange of grievances; "discussion" and "debate" risk suggesting a deferential bow to rational order that would undermine the project of the badass. Manny Torres, a member of the "Young Stars" in Spanish Harlem in the late 1950s, recalled that in his work as "warlord," debate was not a means of avoiding conflict but a signal that a fight was inevitable:

> My job was to go around to the other gangs, meet with their chiefs, and decide whose territory was whose. And if we had any debate about it, it was my job to settle on when and where we would fight it out and what weapons we would use.[39]

Physically, badasses are always vulnerable; in U.S. ghettoes, someone can always "get to" them, since guns are widely available. But if they communicate that they will persevere without limitation until they dominate, then they force others to confront the same choice: are they willing to risk bodily injury, and even if they escape injury, are they willing to risk arrest? Is a momentary sensation of dominance worth it? The badass's logic of domination is to mean nothing more or less than meanness. He succeeds by *inducing others* to reason, to reflect on the extraneous meaning of violence, to weigh the value of experiencing dominance against the fear of physical destruction and legal punishment, when *he* will not make the calculation. Now and again, he must go at least a little bit mad.

Ethnographic details demonstrate the would-be badass's awareness of the necessity to dramatize his transcendence of rationality. Badasses are not irrational or antirational, and they certainly are not stupid. They understand precisely the nature of rationality and they position themselves carefully to manifest that their spirit, their meaning, is not limited by their need to make intelligible to others or even to themselves the purposive coherence or utilitarian sensibility of their action. Within this framework, we can understand the following comments by black Philadelphia street toughs to sociologist Barry Krisberg not as evidence of intellectual incompetence or moral insensitivity, but as the opposite. A group leader named William told Krisberg that he "wouldn't argue with someone—just stab them."[40] There was no need to argue or explain because: " 'whatever comes to my mind, I know it got to be right because I'm thinking of it.' "[41] Another leader, Deacon, characterized his everyday posture with:

> Doesn't have to be anything, it could be just the principle of a conversation. If I thought it was justifiable, like, they was trying to, like fuck over me, I would shoot them, whatever way that came into my mind at that moment.[42]

Where badasses congregate, showdowns are likely. In showdowns, we can sometimes see the eminently rational use of seemingly irrational violence to manifest a transcendence of rationality. In the following incident, drawn from R. Lincoln Keiser's ethnography of Chicago's Vice Lords, there is no suggestion of sadism or even of much anger; rather, there is a mutual recognition of the meanness required to be a badass. The background is a fight between two cliques within the Vice Lords, the Rat Pack and the Magnificent Seven. The speaker, a member of the Rat Pack, began a fist-fight with Fresh-up Freddie of the Magnificent Seven:

> He couldn't touch me, so I said, "I quit," and I dropped my guard. That mother fucker, he hit me in the nose, hit me in the mouth, and my mouth started bleeding. Now Cool Fool had my jive [gun]. I said, "Fool, gimme my jive!" and Fool, he gave me my gun. I said to Fresh-up, "I ought to shoot you!" Now Fresh-up got the intention of snatching the gun. He done snatched three or four guns out of different fellows hands, and he started walking at me. He said, "Shoot me if you want to. I don't believe you going to shoot me." I knew what he's going to do when he got close, he going to grab the gun. I didn't want to kill him so I shot him in the arm. I had to shoot him. You see, if I hadn't done it, he would of took my gun away from me.[43]

Fresh-up was attempting to be the baddest, first by manifestly not limiting himself by principles of honor or conventional morality (he struck out at the speaker after the latter had "quit") and second, in moving to snatch the gun away, by demonstrating the other's moral weakness—the other's fear not of him but of the consequences of using the gun he possessed. The speaker shot, not necessarily out of fear that Fresh-up would take the gun and shoot him, but so Fresh-up would not transform the speaker's pretense of meanness into an evident bluff.

Being mean, then, is a pristinely rational social logic for manifesting that one has transcended rationality. Having grasped its paradoxical rationality, we can now more readily understand various ways in which badasses breathe awesomely mean airs into everyday life. To the would-be badass, being mean is not an abstract commitment but an exciting world of distinctive phenomena. Becoming a badass becomes seductive when one senses in interactional detail the transcendent significance of manifesting meanness. I will trace three segments of esthetically and sensually compelling ways of being mean under the categories: "Soulful Chaos," "Paraphernalia of Purposiveness," and "Mind Fucking."

SOULFUL CHAOS

The ominous presence of the badass is achieved in one respect by his ways of intimating chaos. The person who is most fearsomely beyond social control is the one who does not appear to be quite in control of himself because his soul is rooted in what, to us, is chaos.

The following is a poem written by an ex-skinhead.

> Everywhere they are waiting, In silence.
> In boredom. Staring into space.
> Reflecting on nothing, or on violence. . . .
> Then suddenly it happens. A motor-cycle
> Explodes outside, a cup smashes.
> They are on their feet, identified
> At last as living creatures,
> The universal silence is shattered,
> The law is overthrown, chaos
> Has come again. . . .[44]

In this poem, chaos is represented as the force that moves one from boredom to liveliness, awakening one's senses, providing essential energy, making the world a seductive place again. The suggestion is that chaos is at the very source of one's spiritual being.

If badasses are not often poets, they are most fundamentally creators of a special culture. Consider the explanation offered by Big L, a member of a Puerto Rican gang in Brooklyn in the 1970s, of why the Bikers have the reputation of being the baddest:

> Rape old ladies. Rape young girls. Kick people out of their homes. Steal. Vandalize the whole neighborhood. Burn cars and all this. And they're bad. That's why they consider them bad. They're bad.[45]

Beyond the specific acts cited, the Bikers have, for Big L, a transcendent, ringing reality as bad, real bad, the baddest: his description quickly becomes a recitation in which the intonation of evil goes on and on, resonating in choruses of awe.

Rape and mayhem may sometimes be useful to construct a bad reputation, but as a routine matter, the badass will exploit a more cultured, symbolically economic means of sustaining an awful presence. He may dramatize a sadistic pleasure in violence to suggest that chaos is natural to him and, therefore, that it is always his potential. Skinheads described cutting someone with a razor as "striping," as if there was an esthetic appeal, a matter of artistic achievement, in the process of destruction. In Glasgow, another place where knives have been a favorite instrument of group violence, "team" fighters distinguish between being "slashed" and being "ripped" (the latter involving a special turning of the knife) and they further distinguish a method of kicking aimed at opening the wound.[46] When gangs have successfully established terrifying reputations, they are often accorded myths of bestial sadism. Ellison reported that in the 1950s in Brooklyn, members of the most feared gang, the Puerto Rican Flyers, were said to drink blood.[47]

By celebrating hedonism as the underlying motivation for their violence, badasses avoid the interpretation that their violence is contingent on the prospect of extrinsic rewards and, therefore, ultimately controllable by others. A Vice Lord explained to Keiser the essential attraction of "wolf packing":

> Wolf packing—like for instance me and some other fellows go out and knock you down 'cause we feel like it. That's what it is. I might take your money, but I really want to kick some ass anyway, so I decide to knock the first thing in my way down.[48]

Across various sociocultural settings, badasses sometimes seem to attack victims because they "need" a beating. A graffiti writer from the South Bronx recalled a time when a few Black Spades arrived at their clubhouse with guns, turned lights on, and discovered that some of those present were not of their group: "first they took and beat up a couple of guys because, though they weren't in a gang, they just needed a good ass-kicking at the time."[49] There is an ambiguity in this statement as to who "needed" the beating, the attackers or the victims. In some contexts, badasses posture virtually as altruistic servants of their victims' "need" for a beating. At other times, the "need to kick ass" is more clearly their own. In either case the suggestion is of soulful chaos: of a nature governed by overwhelming, destructive forces that demand release through the instrumentality of the badass or of irresistibly seductive weaknesses in victims that compel the badass to attack, like a priestly servant who is duty bound to preserve a certain harmony of evil in the world.

Being mean is achieved with a special economy by attacks directed at especially vulnerable victims and especially respectable places. Accompanying a Glasgow gang, Patrick described a rush into a public library. They began setting fire to newspapers in the Reading Room, knocked a magnifying glass out of the hand of an elderly man, and en route to the street, a male attendant in a green uniform was punched and kicked out of the way. "Some, behind me," he noted, "could hardly run for laughing."[50]

Ex-skinheads recalled an excursion to London's Hyde Park: "When we got to the Park we just went wild." Disturbing "Pakis," for example, by putting fingers in the way of a man taking pictures of his wife and children, was a focal activity. At the local park, they would throw stones at ducks; go to the cafe, order food, and not pay; and hide behind bushes waiting for a boat to come by, say to the child in it, "give me a lift, mate," and then collectively jump in, promptly sinking the boat.[51] Their targets were "nice" in a conventional moral sense. The attacks had no utilitarian purpose; many were treated exclusively as "fun." With these elements of context, meanness may be manifest with remarkably little physical effort.

In fights, meanness may be demonstrated by exceeding moral limitations and utilitarian justification. From the white ethnic gang scene of 1950s Brooklyn, Ellison recited

> the primer for gang kids. . . . When he's down, kick for the head and groin. . . . gang warfare is typified by a callous disregard for Marquis of Queensbury rules, or for that matter, rules of simple decency. When they fight, they are amoral . . . totally without mercy . . . almost inhuman. A cat that's down is a cat who can't bother you, man! Stomp him! Stomp him good! Put that lit cigarette in the bastard's eye! Wear Army barracks boots—kick him in the throat, in the face, kick him where he lives. Smash him from behind with a brick, cave in his effin' skull! Flat edge of the hand in the Adam's Apple! Use a lead pipe across the bridge of his nose—smash the nose and send bone splinters into the brain![52]

PARAPHERNALIA OF PURPOSIVENESS

All manner of weapons contribute to the badass's project of being mean. From a Philadelphia black gang leader, Krisberg recorded this spontaneous expression of affection:

> I love shotguns. . . . And if anybody ever bother me, that's what they better look out for. Cause I'm going to bring it. . . . Cause I know I ain't going to miss you.[53]

In adolescent "bad" society, weapons and their incidents are matters for sacred ritual. In the South Bronx in the early 1970s, the Savage Nomads were ordered by their leader to clean their guns meticulously twice, sometimes three times, in weekly, group sessions.[54] In Chicago, Ruth Horowitz observed Mexican-American gang members' fascination with the special instruments of violence.

One afternoon I was sitting on a bench talking with the Lions. Suddenly all conversation stopped and attention was focused on Spoof and Fidel, two Senior Nobles in their mid-twenties. Spoof flipped his keys to the nearest Lion and told him to get his lounge chair from the trunk of the car. His orders were carried out silently. Spoof settled comfortably in his chair. He proudly produced three bullets: one had a cutoff head, one had a flattened head, and the third was unmodified. He carefully described just how each of the bullets reacted inside the body. Everyone listened quietly and a few asked technical questions. No one was allowed to hold the bullets. . . . Then we were treated to a show and history of their scars while the Lions nodded their approval and were properly awed. Even after the two departed, the Lions discussed nothing else for the rest of the evening.[55]

As Ellison observed in Italian gangs in 1950s Brooklyn, "the weapons of the gang kid have a charm all their own." In this setting, the charmed objects resembled a medieval knight's battery of arms: garrison belts with razor-sharp buckles to be wrapped around fists, raw potatoes studded with double-edged razor blades, zip guns, barracks boots with razor blades stuck between toe and sole, and Molotov cocktails.[56] One fellow drew special attention for possessing a flare-shooting Navy Very pistol. As Robert DeNiro effectively captured in the movie *Taxi Driver* (after he asks the mirror, "Are you looking at me?"), would-be badasses may spend hours practicing the rapid production of a knife or a gun with a special flourish.[57] Among Chicago's Vice Lords, a three-foot sword was, for a time, a popular weapon for robbing passengers on the El. A gang member named Cupid recalled the time "my mother came up and busted me with six shotguns!" including a buffalo gun, and Cupid will

never forget this. It was . . . crazy ass King Solomon, [in a fight with the Comanches] he had one of these little Hookvilles. It's a knife, a linoleum knife. Got a hook on the end. . . . [which he used when he caught "Ghengis Khan" and] Cut the stud's whole guts out![58]

Among the fighting teams in Glasgow, a member named Baggy kept a "sword" in his scooter and would often recount how, in a battle with the Milton Tongs at a bowling center, he had rushed to his scooter, taken up his sword, cut one boy, and watched the rest scatter. When stopped by bouncers at a dance hall, members of the Young Team were required to give up a concealed hatchet and bayonet, but one got by with a hidden, open razor. In a fight outside a dance hall, Tim charged into battle, brandishing his open razor, but only after grabbing a wine bottle that he broke on the wall, cutting his hand badly. Later, Tim embroidered his account of the fight, adding an air rifle. "The open razor and the broken wine bottle he had carried were apparently not sufficient to create the image he hankered after."[59] In the United States today, we might find the objects of awesome charm to be Uzi machine guns and Ninja stars.

Fascinated, charmed, seduced—the badass is completely taken by the paraphernalia of his purposiveness. Note that although some of these objects might fit presumptions about the power of phallic imagery, others (stars, garrison belts, and linoleum knives) surely do not. Note also that the fascination persists apart from any envisioned practical context of the use of these objects. Just to have these things, to hold them, inspect them, and observe them swiftly introduced into the focus of the moment is exciting. These objects suggest that others will have to take seriously the intentions of the badass who controls them, whatever those intentions may be—that he will mean it, whatever he may make of "it."

We might attribute the significance of these things to the power they represent, but "power" is an impoverished metaphor for this world of experience. "Being mean" picks up the evil undertones set off by the display of these objects. Many of these weapons are notable not just for their power but for their brutish, sadistic character; others, fitted for covert possession, are notably illicit in design. In contrast to "power," "being mean" captures the project at stake: to assume a tough, alien posture beyond all danger of mockery and metaphysical doubt that ensures that one will be taken seriously. These things excite by attesting to a purpose that transcends the material utility of power.

MIND FUCKING

In various languages, badasses have a special affinity for the culture of "fuck you!" Chas, an East Los Angeles graffiti writer, recounted his transformation from "Chingaso."

A friend gave me that nickname. Started calling me that about three years ago. . . . Now it's funny. I don't like "Chingaso" any more because it's too "bad," it's too heavy. "Chingaso" means the one who's a fucker. Not a stud, just one who fucks people up. I don't like that. I feel like I'm not saying the right thing out there. I like it, but I think I'm telling the right people the wrong thing. So I write "Chas" now.[60]

In Glasgow, both the police and the street toughs they attempt to control are deeply involved in the same culture. In the following account, Patrick, Tim, and Dave from the Young Team were at Saracen Cross, on their way to a dance hall:

Tim was prevented from moving forward by the approach of two policemen, one of whom shouted across at him: "So fuckin' Malloy is oot again? Is yir fuckin' brothers still in fuckin' prison?" Tim's answers also made liberal use of Glasgow's favourite adjective. The second policeman turned to Dave and me, and, noticing the marks on Dave's face he began: "So ye goat fuckin' scratched, trying' tae get yir fuckin' hole."[61]

The confrontation ended when one of the policeman said, "Weil, get aff this fuckin' Cross, or Ah'll fuckin' book ye."

Used gramatically in myriad ways and conveyed through posture and conduct perhaps more generally than in explicit verbal form, the distinctive thrust of the "fuck" culture is captured nicely in the English form, "fuck you!" Although it may seem obvious, it is worth a moment's pause to articulate just what makes this phrase so effectively "bad." To wish sex on another is not necessarily negative, but this is clearly not an alternative form for "Have a nice lay." Nor is the use of "fuck" for denoting sex necessarily negative; the phrase is universally "bad" while crude sex is not.[62]

At the essence of "fuck you!" is the silent but emphatic presence of the "I." "Fuck you!" implies the existence of the speaker as the key actor (compared to "get fucked!" and the appropriately feminine form, "fuck off!"). It is the assertion of an anonymous insertion—a claim to penetrate the other in his most vulnerable, sensitive center, in his moral and spiritual essence, without revealing oneself to the other. "Fuck you!" thus achieves its force through projecting an asymmetry of the most extreme sort between the fucker and the fucked; I will force myself to the center of your existence, while you will not grasp even the most superficial indication of my subjectivity.

In its essence, then, "fuck you!" is a way of being mean as a transcendent existential project. "Fuck you!" equals "I'll thrust my meaning into your world, and you won't know why, what for, what I mean; I'll hide the 'I' from you as I do it." Of course, in context "fuck you!" may connote anything from a dare to a muted message uttered on retreat. But with the existential significance of "fuck you!" in mind, we may more readily grasp, as devices for mind fucking, several widespread, practical strategies of would-be badasses that are otherwise deeply enigmatic.

THE BUMP

Consider the "accidental" bump, used either to begin a fight or to force a humiliating show of deference. Manny Torres recalled from his adolescent years in Spanish Harlem,

> walking around with your chest out, bumping into people and hoping they'll give you a bad time so you can pounce on them and beat 'em into the goddamn concrete.[63]

In the literature on adolescent street violence, there are innumerable analogous examples of fights beginning from what in one light appears to be accidental and minor physical contact. Sometimes the badass is the one arranging the accident, sometimes he is the one who is accidentally bumped. Thus, when some laborers accidentally nudged Pat at a Glasgow bar, he challenged them to a fight, immediately moving his hand into his jacket as if he had a weapon. Wee Midgie hit the laborers on their heads with a lemonade bottle, Pat and others kicked them in the face, and Tim cracked a bottle over their heads. The fighting team suddenly exited when someone shouted, "Run like fuck."[64]

To understand specifically what is happening in these scenes, it is insufficient to interpret the attackers as "looking for a fight." The enigmatic aspect is the dramatization of a "bump"—an accidental physical clash—as the necessary condition or catalyst of the violence. Pat and his friends seemed so intent on attacking these laborers that one wonders why they waited for the chance, unintentional nudge.

Nor will it do to project onto the attackers a felt necessity to neutralize moral prohibitions against unwarranted attacks, that is, that the attack would make no compelling sense to them until and unless they had the "excuse" of a bump. The same young men can be seen at other moments proudly attacking without the moral necessity of any excuse or justification, as when the party attacked is treated simply as one who "needs his ass kicked."[65] Attackers often arrange bumps that are publicly, self-consciously transparent. Why do they bother to feign accidents?

Because their focus is not on physical destruction or moral self-justification, but on the transcendent appeal of being mean. The feigned accident is not a moral necessity for attack; it is, however, a delightful resource for constructing from the attack the stature of the attacker as badass. Manny and Pat did not "have to have an excuse" to attack. Nor were they compulsive sadists "getting off" on physical destruction. They were seduced by the bump. They rejoiced in the special reverberations that could be given the interaction by making the attack the product of a transparently "accidental" bump.

At its first, most superficial, level of appeal, the bump clarifies and enhances the meaning of a subsequent physical attack as the work of a badass. After a bump, an attack inevitably reflects the spatial metaphor the existential dilemma of "here" and "there" with which all the ways of the badass are concerned.

The badass does not invent the revolutionary moral potential in the bump; he simply seizes on it. When you and I, two polite members of civil society, bump into each other, there is at once a literal and figurative invocation of the toughness of each of us. Wishing to avoid giving offense with bated breath we race each other to the stage of apology. Through my apology, I drop any possible pretense of toughness, showing you that I am morally responsive to your well-being. In apologizing, I enact a shameful recognition that the bump occurred because, as far as I could tell, or phenomenal worlds had been independent; I had practiced an apparent indifference to your existence.

In the bump, what had been "here" to you, bounded off from me, penetrates my phenomenal isolation and becomes "here" to me, and vice versa. As quickly as polite members of civil society scurry to avoid the moral tensions that they sense have suddenly become potential, so can the badass flood the situation with awful possibilities. By treating the accidental bump as an obdurate, unforgettable fact of history, the badass opens up a glorious array of nasty courses of action.

No matter who was at "fault" for the bump, once the "bump" has occurred the badass can exploit a precious ambiguity to charge the situation with the tensions of a moral crisis. Any fool can see and only a coward would deny that the bump takes each into the other's phenomenal world. In the bump, you become "here" for me and I become "here" for you. The bump provides the grounds for each to wonder, Was it accidental? Or were you "fucking" with me, thrusting yourself into my world for purposes I could not possibly grasp?

At this stage, the least the would-be badass can do is obtain public testimony to his badass status. If the other tries to ignore the bump, the badass can easily make this attempt an obvious pretense for repeating the bump. He may stop at any point in this process, taking as his sole booty from the situation the victim's evidently artificial posture that "nothing unusual is happening."

More enigmatically, immediately after he has produced an intentional bump or received an obviously accidental bump, the badass may launch an attack without waiting for an apology, whether sincere or pretended. This, an even tougher, "badder" move, plays off the metaphor of mind fucking.

Once we have accidentally bumped for all to see, everyone knows that you must wonder whether I will let it go as an accident or charge you with an intentional attack. Everyone knows that you are wondering about my purpose and spirit and that merely by wondering, you are taking me into your world of moral judgment and putting me at risk of negative judgment. In other words, the bump suddenly raises the momentous possibility that "you are fucking with me." I can now, without more provocation, strike out physically to "fuck you up" as a transcendent response to your publicly visible "fucking with me."

Before examining elaborations on this interaction, we should take special note of the profound explosion of meaning that has already occurred. Through the most inarticulate, most minor physical contact between two individuals, without any apparent plan, intention, or reason, without any forewarning any man could detect, a small moral world has suddenly burst into full-blown existence. Once the bump has occurred, for whatever original cause or antecedent reason, everything has forever changed; the bump cannot be removed from moral history. A chain reaction can then sensibly follow in a spirit of coherent determinism. The badass, as it were, struts out as the Great Creator, capable of arranging the most transcendent cosmological experience from the chance encounters of everyday life; with a little bump, he has occasioned a moral Big Bang.

But this is only the first theme of significance that may be drawn by the badass from the "accidental" bump. That the accidental quality of the bump should be put in quotes is not only obvious to the would-be badass; he may arrange the bump so that it is obvious to all that the fictive accidental character of the bump is obvious to him, to the victim, to all. And with this move into universal moral transparency, the would-be badass moves the drama to the level of what might be called on the streets, "royal mind fucking."

'WHACHULOOKINAT?'

In perhaps all subcultures of the badass, there is a homegrown version of a mind-fucking strategy that is deeply rooted in the danger of eye contact. It is recognizable with the opening phrase, "Whachulookinat?"

A badass may at any moment treat another's glancing perception of him as an attempt to bring him symbolically into the other's world, for the other's private purposes, perhaps to "fuck with" him. This may be treated as a visual bump. As with the physical bump, the badass may allow the victim to cower his way out of danger by enacting a transparently artificial display of deference, for example, through offering profuse excuses and literally bowing out of the situation.

Of more interest are those situations in which the badass wishes further to exploit the potential to construct a transcendent theme of evil. Victims of "Whachulookinat?" frequently answer "Nothing"; with this response, they open up what sometimes seems to be an irresistible opportunity to fill the air with awesomely threatening meaning. "You callin me nothin?" is the well-known reply.

Just as he thought he had regained a measure of self-protective control over the situation through an effusive display of deference, the victim realizes that he has damned himself, for he has been caught in a lie. *He* is now the immoral party. Everyone knows that he had glanced at the badass. "Nothing" was intended as a ritual of deference, but the badass will not go along with the fiction. The badass suddenly adopts the posture of the only honest man in the transaction: he's being lied to, as all can see. But, he now has the right to ask, why? What malevolence moves the victim to lie and answer, "Nothing?" Has he been fucking with the image of the badass in the privacy of his mind? What is he covering up?

From this point, the badass can readily build tension by playing for a while with the victim, tossing him from one to the other horn of his dilemma. Now the badass treats the victim's "Nothing" as a lie, a fiction designed to cover up a shameful or hostile perspective. Next, the badass insists on a literal interpretation, that the victim's response should be taken as a claim that the existential value of the badass is really "nothing." Then, the badass mocks his own metaphysical stance; everyone knows that the badass knows that the "Nothing" was artificial and, therefore, that the badass's indignation is artificial. All know, as they have known all along, who is the victim and who is the badass—who is attempting to avoid any association with evil and who is embracing it.

In short, all recognize that by feigning victimization, the badass is really mind fucking the victim. The universal transparency of the badass's moral posturing makes it "royal mind-fucking"—a high art that may be practiced through a variety of analogous strategems. Thus, analogous to the simple mind fucking of attacking after a bump is the strategy described by Yablonsky of a New York boy who

> will approach a stranger with the taunt, "What did you say about my mother?" An assault is then delivered upon the victim before he can respond to the question.[66]

And analogous to the royal mind fucking constructed from the visual bumping of "Whachulookinat?" is the Vice Lords's practice of wolf packing. With several mates present, a Vice Lord begins an interaction with a stranger passing by with the formal request, but informal demand, "Hey, man, gimme a dime!" As Keiser noted, "If a dime were given, then a demand for more money would be made until finally the individual would have to refuse."[67]

Physical dominance is not the key concern, since it often seems a foregone conclusion. And, what is even more interesting is that, as some of the Glasgow incidents showed, it sometimes seems not to matter to the badasses that they might lose the battle. From the standpoint of physical power and outcome, these mind-fucking maneuvers are gratuitous. After all, one could physically destroy victims without entering into any interaction with them, for example, by shooting them without warning from a distance and without emerging from camouflage. The ambush of a stranger might maximize one's physical success, but it would not necessarily construct an identity as a badass.

Mind fucking, however, shows the badass in control of the meaning of the situation. Bumps are accidents or intentional provocations, depending on what the badass has in mind. The badass controls the moral ontology of the moment. On the one hand, he may allow life its little bumps, its give and take, recognizing that, owing to imperfections in the nature of social life for which no one is responsible, men must have at least small spaces free from responsibility. On the other hand, he may make life inexorably purposive, affording a man no rest from the moral implications of his conduct. The badass rules the moment as the master of its metaphysics.

Moral pretenses become real and unreal as if by magic, at the snap of his finger. At his discretion, words mean just what they say on the surface or are revealed to mask shamefully hidden intentions. "Nothing" will mean nothing at all or everything fateful, as he chooses. Apart from physical dominance, mind fucking allows the badass to demonstrate the transcendent character of his meaning.

Foreground and Background: The Sex of the Badass

I have attempted to demonstrate that the details of the distinctive adolescent culture of the badass can be grasped as a series of tactics for struggling with what the adolescent experiences as a spatially framed dilemma—a challenge to relate the "here" of his personal world to the phenomenal worlds of others who he experiences as existing at a distance, somewhere over "there." Thus, being tough positions the self as not "here" for others. Being alien goes further, indicating that the self is not only not here for others but is native to some morally alien world, inevitably beyond the intimate grasp of others who are present here. And being mean produces its awful air by intimating that where the self is coming from is a place that represents chaos to outsiders and threatens constantly to rush destructively to the center of their world, attacking their most intimate sensibilities.

The ultimate source of the seductive fascination with being a badass is that of transcending rationality. What "rationality" means to the adolescent, as a challenge that stimulates his seduction to a world of deviance, is not primarily legal authority, institutional discipline, or social expectations of an ordered and integrated competence to reason. These phenomena may, at times, become the foils for badasses of all types, but more routinely, the provocative issue is a matter of demonstrating rationality as the modern moral competence to adjust the self to situationally specific expectations.

To understand the seductive quality of this project and why the data have been overwhelmingly though not exclusively from males, we might consider what, after all, makes the phallus so powerful a symbol for the badass. Phallic imagery is obviously prominent in the ways of the badass, from the "hardness" of the tough posture, to the "hot rodder" style, to the "cool" quality conferred on speech by random thrusts of "fuck," to the drama of "mind fucking." But the motivating, emotionally compelling concerns of the badass cannot simply be reduced to a sexual metaphor; the distinctive presence of the badass is not particularly erotic. Posed like a phallus, the badass threatens to dominate all experience, stimulating a focus of consciousness so intense as to obliterate experientially or to transcend any awareness of boundaries between the situation "here" and any other situation, "there." And in this appreciation, the phallus has the further, socially transcendent power to obliterate any awareness of boundaries between the ontologically independent, phenomenal situations of different people. The fascination here is with the paradoxical, distinctively masculine potential of the phallus: by threatening to penetrate others, the badass, this monstrous member of society, can absorb the whole world into himself.

CHAPTER 4

Street Elites

Considered as a social form of violence, street fighting between adolescent groups shares several features with homicide committed in the passionate spirit of righteous slaughter: the irrelevance of utilitarian calculations, a provocative vocabulary of cursing, and a semiotics of violence in which injuries inflicted on victims attest retrospectively to the profundity of the attacker's offended dignity. But there is no evidence of a special delight among violent spouses for the militaristic weapons that group fighters in the ghetto have found charming, such as garrison belts, sawed-off shotguns, flare guns, Ninja stars, switchblades, and rope knives. Unlike the typical impassioned killer, violent youth groups often make elaborate, detailed plans; indeed, they plan and discuss battle tactics far more often than they attack. Perhaps weeks after an insult has been registered, a youth group may surprise its enemies in a moment of domestic calm, as when shots are fired into a family living room by a passing car.[1]

Fights are conducted for distinctive symbolic rewards. When the reputation of a militant youth group has been offended, satisfactory vengeance sometimes can be accomplished by harming any member of the rival group, or even any young person from the offending neighborhood. At times the Vice Lords of Chicago's West Side in the early 1960s, one of the most fearsome groups documented by modern ethnography, were satisfied if their enemy ran away: "The first who runs, that's it right there."[2]

The practice of peer violence by adolescent groups is also distinguished by an egocentric, at times masochistic, focus. In contrast to impassioned violence among spouses and friends, adolescent attackers of other adolescents may never get close enough or stay around long enough to witness their victims' destruction. But their own "battle scars" are sure to be reviewed repeatedly in intimate collective settings. In an hour-long documentary film on Mexican-American barrio fighters in Oakland, California, the young men are shown on two occasions collectively reviewing the holes and scars they carry from enemy attacks, tracking, in detail, the paths the bullets and knives traveled through their bodies.[3] Short-lived battles can be eternally resurrected by fascinated commentaries such as: "See, it went in here and then came out there." "If you hadn't been wearing your pants high (as a Homeboy should), your belt wouldn't have slowed down the entry and you'd be dead." "Oooh, can I touch it?" The animating concern is less a sadistic consumption of the suffering of others than the construction within one's circle of proof of a heroic commitment to the group's grandiose stature.

In short, the phenomena of gang violence are unique and thus call for their own explanation. But before launching a causal inquiry, I should note that something about the "gang" rubric is itself a bit off the mark.

Ever since Frederic Thrasher's study appeared in 1927, students of juvenile delinquency have had a special fascination with gangs.[4] Since that time, sociologists of various theoretical perspectives have continued to assume that it makes sense to address the problem of "the gang." Meanwhile, the subjects' have been stubbornly recalcitrant about accepting this definition of the phenomenon. An inside joke that has been shared by field investigators over several decades is that subjects freely refer to their enemies as members of gangs but instruct an observing sociologist that their collective commitment is to a "club," an "organization," a "clique," a "barrio," a "mob," a "brotherhood," a "family," an ethnic "nation," a "team," or a "crew."[5] Often, they expressly deny membership in a "gang."

Although it has sometimes been suggested that "gang" members resist being so labeled because they are uncomfortable with the negative connotations,[6] this resistance is common even in groups with names like the Vice Lords, Savage Nomads, Devil's Disciples, Reapers, Tongs; as well as among "homeboys" from Los Angeles barrios who proudly dress like the 1940s gangsters and occasionally blast shotguns at enemies in imitation of scenes from movies set in the days of Prohibition. "Gang" is a troublesome term not because it conveys an impression of evil but because the evil implied by an admission of gang membership is not sufficiently grand. Real, adult, serious "gangsters" do not call their groups "gangs." The media tells us that adult gangsters use euphemisms: Cosa Nostra or This Thing We Got, the syndicate, the organization, the Family or La Familia, and the Black Hand. These terms are more serious, more cool, more adult; "gangs" are for kids. Furthermore, loyal members do not confess the deviant status of their groups to outsiders. Since "gangs" are units of deviance that have already come under the cognitive powers of social researchers and other agents of social control, however, "gang" members have no hesitation about designating rival groups as gangs because the label is a relative minimization, a combative depreciation.

This pride in displaying the symbols of terrifying evil may be used to delineate a particular form of deviance. The distinctive features of violence already noted—strategic calculation, militaristic delight, symbolic representation of enemies, and melodramatic self-absorption—indicate a pride in ruling the streets by terror. Accordingly, I will take as the problem to be explained a socially widespread and recurrent problem of twentieth-century British and American juvenile delinquency: street elites, or adolescent groups that maintain terrifying claims to dominance in urban areas.

As with the other forms of crime treated in this book, my explanation will be of a project constituted in three individually necessary, jointly sufficient stages. The first section analyzes the ways in which groups of adolescent males have constructed the appearance of one or another form of ancient, barbaric, feudal, or supernatural elite that maintains its rule through physical intimidation. In the United States and Great Britain, elite, evil guises have been especially seductive to poverty-level and working-class urban adolescents of varying ethnicities. The common features of their posture may be highlighted by comparing the forms of collective deviance among white middle-class youths.

Second, the project of street elites faces a special practical challenge. By parading in public in bizarre, menacing disguises like those that are associated with feudal knights, they risk being thought of as engaging in child's play. So seen, this form of deviance is humiliating; it continues into adolescence the patterns of geographic, age, and sex relationships that are distinctive to the social organization of childhood. Thus, members must engage in practical activities that convince others that they mean it. Here, we can understand the centrality of the geographic metaphor in the shaping of intergroup violence. "Turf" wars and other forms of violence by ghetto youth groups are essential, literally and figuratively, to ground the myths of natural antagonism among the combatants.

The third essential condition is an emotional process. In the members' experience, "being in" such a group is constantly precarious. Terrifying postures of evil may be adopted for parading around the burger palace on Saturday night, to be replaced at home by a benign outlook on traditional values of family and friendship. What keeps members "in" is their cooperative mobilization of challenges to the personal competence to move socially from the subjectively familiar "here" of local childhood relations to a larger, more vaguely anticipated, social world that exists somewhere out "there," or, as they often refer to it, "on the streets." In this regard we can understand the fascination with parading in menacing postures, the logic of the special tactics of street elites for opposing school authority, and the group's support of various facets of street life.

The final section emphasizes a particular connection between the phenomenal life of street elites and the social conditions in their members' backgrounds. When juxtaposed against the humbled populations in their neighborhoods or in their parents' generation, these groups dramatize a superior moral ability to transcend local communal boundaries and move in a spirit of freedom and emphatic self-respect without accepting social limitations. Writing about gangs from the outside, social researchers and commentators have usually assumed that the key causal forces lie in the distance between their own world and that of the "gang." Members of street elites have been more vividly aware of the proximity of groups that they would place beneath them in social disrepute.

The Posture of the Street Elite

Despite the importance of urban, lower-income, ethnic-minority status for theories of the gang, social-class variables have rarely been examined comparatively to hone in on the thing to be explained.[7] Some authors have offered themes that are supposedly specific to lower-class delinquency but without considering carefully just how these themes are distinctive to their class setting.[8] The prevalence of reckless driving and of illegal drug cultures should serve as a reminder that even in the most respectable, affluent suburbs, adolescents have a special attraction to excitement, trouble, tests of autonomy, and proofs of toughness, as well as an apparently romantic tendency to abandon life to fate. Indeed, on a purely actuarial basis, the attraction of white middle-class youths to these values may be more physically self-destructive than is the violence of ghetto "gangs."[9]

Over the past thirty years, there have been sharp differences in collective forms of youth deviance across class and ethnic lines. To highlight the distinctive pretensions of ghetto street elites, I will, for the most part, neglect intermediary types, such as working-class groups that have combined patterns of "hippie" drug hedonism familiar in suburban middle-class settings with physically intimidating "greaser" styles.[10] On the "street elite" side, most of my materials represent groups from what were at the time of the relevant study ethnic minorities in low income urban centers in the United States. But some, such as the examples from Glasgow and London, clearly are of low income but not ethnic minority youths. And some of the Mexican-American groups with relevant patterns of intergroup violence are from communities that, although ethnically isolated, enjoy an economic status that is markedly above poverty levels. On the other side of the contrast, middle-class adolescent deviants delight in imitating working-class forms, literally inviting class and sometimes ethnic confusions. I will treat punks here in their American incarnation, as an example of a middle-class form, even though the historical origins of the symbolism elaborated in the "punk" movement may be traced to working-class British groups. At the end of the chapter, I try to explain the relationship of social class and form of collective youth deviance. Here, the task is to set up the association that calls for an explanation.

CELEBRATING VERSUS OBSCURING TIES TO HOME

A fascination with spatial mobility expressed through geographic metaphors runs throughout the social lines of adolescence. But across class and ethnic lines, the symbolic slant runs in opposite directions.

Consider the proud self-label, "homeboy," which Mexican-American and black adolescents from low-income areas in Southwestern cities use to signal their loyalty to neighboring peers. Homeboys take great risks to write the name of their neighborhood on walls and to carry its "colors" in their clothing; they anticipate that they may be asked questions about their street or barrio affiliation on the understanding that the "wrong" answer may lead to great personal harm. More generally, neighborhood names have inspired American ghetto adolescents to collective violence against other adolescent groups, from at least the New York Irish of the turn of the century; to Eastern Europeans in Chicago in the 1920s; to Southern Europeans in New York in the 1950s; and to Puerto Rican, Mexican, and black youths in major U.S. cities over the past twenty-five years.[11] A universal rationale for violence among street elites is their claims to control landmarks of a particular residential area: street boundaries, "turf," local food outlets, parks, or particular benches in parks.

In contrast, when middle-class white American adolescents develop forms of collective deviance, they make a special effort to conceal the location of their primary family. Whether in the style of beatniks hanging around Greenwich Village in the 1950s, hippies congregating in San Francisco's Haight-Ashbury in the late 1960s, or punks "slam dancing" in Hollywood clubs in the late 1970s, middle-class white adolescents have attempted to appear as natives of bohemian cultures and lower classes, obscuring their residential ties to, respectively, Westchester County and Long Island, Marin County and Berkeley, and West Los Angeles and the San Fernando Valley.[12] For these middle-class adolescents to have been considered by their peers as socially tied to the locale of their homes in the middle-class suburbs and emotionally tied to their families would have triggered feelings of shame, rather than pride.

SEGREGATING VERSUS INTEGRATING THRUSTS

Since at least the end of World War II, middle-class white adolescents have been attracted to deviant movements, trends, and cultural themes—to what sociologists call "collective behavior." In contrast, ghetto and working-class adolescents have often banded together in more or less formally organized deviant groups, sometimes with designated leaders, "war counselors," official symbols, induction procedures, clubhouses, and a territorially defined jurisdiction. These formal indicia of collective unity tempt outsiders to refer to ghetto groups as "gangs." When collections of middle-class youths have been seen as physically threatening, for example, punks slam dancing in music clubs or hippies protesting in parks, they have achieved no more than the minimal formal status of "mobs" or unruly "crowds."

This social structural difference is itself related to the different slants taken by the two youth groups on the metaphor of geographic mobility. Organized formally into residentially based fighting groups, ghetto adolescents generate mythical distinctions within otherwise homogeneous social groups. Most gang violence is within ethnic and class lines. One group of young Chicago blacks, for example, organizes under the banner of the Blackstone Rangers to fight a neighboring group of young Chicago blacks organized under the name, the Devil's Disciples, with no distinction between the two groups in social origin or philosophy other than that each is linked to a territorially different home base.[13] In the ghetto, adolescent forms of collective deviance are committed to the artificial *construction* of segregating geographic boundaries.

On the other side of the class and ethnic tracks, white middle-class adolescents delight in the use of deviant forms of collective behavior to affect the symbolic *destruction* of geographic boundaries. Hippies did not express their ties to particular places. Instead, they became a national and then international movement by dressing in the culture of transience and—as symbolized by "flower" children reaching out to embrace horrified passersby—by celebrating a spirit of universal understanding. Punk originated in working-class white English adolescent society and was picked up across class and national lines in the United States and continental Europe. Punks of different nationalities and social classes who could not speak to each other, formed an international street show under a common symbolism of deviance.

In the collective worlds of adolescent deviance, ethnic-minority members distinctively and ironically promote segregation. Throughout this century in the United States, urban male adolescents who have been subject to segregation because of their ethnic identities—the Irish in 1900s New York, Eastern European ethnics in Chicago in the 1920s, Italians in Brooklyn in the 1950s, blacks in Chicago in the 1960s, and Mexican-Americans in Oakland barrios in the 1970s and 1980s—have drawn battle lines to enforce neighborhood boundaries. In contrast, an integrating thrust characterizes the forms of collective deviance embraced by ethnic-majority young men. Thus, the Hell's Angels made a practice of flying "colors" while taking trips far from their residential neighborhood, the hippies congregated in a hedonistic mood in public areas, and middle-class suburban and small-town adolescents "raise hell" by traveling to other cities to vandalize property, play tricks on unsuspecting citizens, and commit property theft.[14]

ARISTOCRATS VERSUS RABBLE

In the ghetto, congregations of adolescents style themselves as elites; outside poor ethnic-minority communities, adolescents fashion deviant styles by dressing up as commoners, working-class militants, or members of a mass. The naming conventions that have been widely popular among ghetto fighting groups declare an inborn right or power to rule. Some track the status terms of ancient and medieval royalty and aristocracy: Lords, Nobles, Knights, Pharoahs, Kings, Emperors, Viceroys, Crusaders, and Dukes. Others pick up "classy" terms of style: Diplomats, Saints, and Savoys. Another tradition of nomenclature ties ghetto youth to regal levels of the animal world: Lions, Eagles, Panthers, and Cobras. Still another points upward cosmologically, to Stars and Jets. Yet another turns toward the uppermost levels of the underworld: Satan's Angels and the Devil's Disciples.[15]

In contrast, the hippie styles of white middle-class youths were continuous, in such details as hair style and then in such broad themes as political sympathy, with a humbly named music group, the Beatles. More recently, the bands associated with the punk movement have provided a long list of symbols of low, disgusting, rejected, offensive, conventionally depreciated regions of experience.

The beatnik, hippie, and punk movements have all been distinguished by symbols of low social status. Hippies not only dressed in ways to suggest vagrancy, they developed a form of begging or panhandling as a characteristic street activity.[16] The punk movement is the latest in a series of styles elaborated by white middle-class youths from those originated by British youth groups who were overtly and proudly working class. In Paris in the 1980s, casually destitute middle-class *poseurs* mixed with hard-core unemployed working-class youths around Les Halles.[17]

Jeans and a dishevelled look were de rigueur for hippies; punks, despite their pronounced antagonism to hippies, wore high boots associated with working-class occupations and clothes seemingly torn in a life of hard knocks. In contrast, for "bad" black ghetto adolescents, to look "clean" has long meant to look good. Oddly, ghetto adolescents dramatize deviance with a metaphor similar to the one that middle-class whites have long used to dramatize conventional or "straight" moral affiliations: looking "clean" and "sharp" (sometimes rendered as "keen") and "neat." Thus, at the time when hippies in Chicago's Lincoln Park were provoking public outrage with unkempt long hair and dirty clothes, a few miles south, across 63rd Street, a leader of the most feared "gang" of the day, the Blackstone Rangers, became furious on discovering that a shirt in his closet, recently retrieved from the cleaners, had been borrowed by a brother and now bore minor wrinkles.[18]

The more we focus on the symbolism used to make aristocratic status manifest, the more we illuminate aspects of deviance that have had a distinctive appeal to street fighting groups. Eighteenth-century European aristocrats caked white powder on their faces to emphasize their social distance from field laborers, as if the sun cast an indelible moral stain on the humble classes who worked the soil. Today, barrio homeboys insist on daily rituals of washing and ironing that keep their undershirts brilliantly white and a super-sharp crease in their pants.[19] In the early 1970s, members of fighting teams from Glasgow's poor areas often played soccer in the mud without changing out of the "Edwardian" suits they favored.

> Dan McDade informed me, with admiration on his face, that Dick [the "King" of a large fighting "team"] would throw the suit away and change into another for the evening. The boys were unanimous in telling me that Dick always played while wearing a suit. In fact, once during the summer, he had "done his goalie" wearing a stolen mustard-coloured suede coat, "divin' intae the mud an' everythin'."[20]

HORIZONTAL VERSUS VERTICAL DIRECTIONS OF HOSTILITY

White middle-class adolescents collectively form a deviance that reaches out horizontally to include peers in far-flung places in an antagonistic spirit that is directed upward in the social class and age structure. Their deviant movements tend to take on politically leftist themes, while ghetto fighting groups mobilize aggression primarily horizontally, against peers, and gravitate to the symbolism of right-wing political power.

Following in the legendary traditions of samurai in service to Japanese *daimyo,* criminal gangs bound to Chinese warlords, knights allied with European landlords, and the Mafia in Southern Italy, contemporary ghetto elites conduct violence as agents of aristocratic privilege devoted to the oppression of the poor who live in their neighborhoods. In contrast, portraits of adolescent deviance outside the ghetto typically show a solitary group directing its deviance against adult authority.[21] Outside the ghetto, collective forms of youth deviance regularly turn into rebellion against police authority. Because of the way they dressed themselves and decorated their vehicles, marginal working-class, urban-based Hell's Angels, white Southern "rebels," and middle-class hot rodders have shared the similar, practical problem of police intervention, a ubiquitous contingency that makes driving an inevitably deviant affair.

In contrast, ghetto fighting groups, while enjoying moments of antagonism with the police, often appear remarkably indifferent to official, adult authority. Many autobiographies of ex-ghetto group fighters recall an informal understanding between the police and adolescents by which the police would stay on the sidelines as long as fighting remained among peers.[22] Antigang activities by the police sometimes draw violent attacks from ghetto adolescents,[23] but such events are rare. Ghetto fighting groups seem to be less inclined to attack the representatives of the power of the larger society in which they live than to act as if they live in a country that is foreign to and independent of the one the police represent.

Hippies and punks have been distinctively opposed to adult values, often scandalizing parents and generally promoting critiques of the adult value system. In contrast, while ghetto fighting groups are often abhorred by adults and members' parents in the ghettoes, they ironically embrace adult values. Formally, insults to "mothers" frequently serve as the sensible way to begin fights. Perhaps especially in Hispanic ghetto areas, "wars" between adolescents representing different barrios are, in surface rhetoric at least, often understood as outgrowths of insults to family honor (for example, to protect a sister's reputation or avenge an attack on a brother).[24]

A recent study of a violent youth group in an affluent white suburb of Chicago should, by way of contrast, bring into high relief the aristocratic airs that are distinctive to collective adolescent deviance in the ghetto. This group was that rare sociological find, an exception—a formally self-conscious, violent adolescent group in an upper-middle-class white area— that, in its inverted social patterns, demonstrates the rule in the relation of class and deviant form among adolescents.[25]

First, the group's name: "the Losers." Minority-group youths from impoverished urban areas are delighted to identify with all manner of devil and beast, but affiliation with a deviant status on conventional *moral* standards is usually balanced by a simultaneous claim of superiority in *power and prestige.* Thus, a few years before the Losers were formed in one of the most affluent communities in the nation, a few miles to the southwest, in one of the poorest areas in the United States, the Vice Lords were battling the Spanish Counts. In naming themselves the Losers, working- and middle-class white adolescents in an affluent suburb were expressing a cynicism about adult values in a way that is anathema to minority fighting groups in poor areas. What was most peculiar for such a formally self-conscious, violent adolescent group was that there were no other "gangs" for the Losers to fight. When they spray painted "the Losers" on a railroad overpass, they were not challenging another gang's graffiti: theirs was the only tag in town. The thrust of their graffiti was, like the group's ironical name, directed against the town's self-concept as a community of "winners."

The Losers had a shifting core of ten to fifteen members, but, unlike many ghetto "clubs," there were no initiation rituals or membership formalities. As Gene Muehlbauer and Laura Dodder noted, "Michelle [one of the Losers] put it rather succinctly: 'As long as you were tough, and talked loud, and smoked a little pot or drank a little beer or were willing to try those things they'd accept you.' "[26] The Losers did not attempt to "run" or "own" a residential neighborhood. Like rockers at English seaside towns and *zonards* who congregate in the elegant renovated Forum des Halles in Paris,[27] the Losers provoked controversy by congregating on public property, at the beach, and, especially, at the center of town. Identified first in the style of the hippies, the Losers socialized in the town square and in a park on a major street near the public library. Cruising to show off cars and to pick up girls was the initial attraction. Next, taunting shoppers, the police, and private guards at the center of town became fun. Finally, maneuvering around the police to mobilize parties at public beaches and parks became a focal activity.

Overall, the Losers were very much of the contemporary sociopolitical scene. Their dress and their battles against local authority tied them to the national youth movements against "the Establishment." When, after about six years, the Losers resorted to violence, it took the form not of attacks against neighboring peers but of firebombings of the cars of the chief of police and a vice-principal of the high school.

OPPOSING VERSUS TRANSCENDING AUTHORITY

Collective movements of deviance created by middle-class ethnic-majority adolescents are elaborated in opposition to conventional forms of authority. In the early 1970s, police resistance spurred the informal process of recruitment to antiwar protests, adding a political charm to the street display of such symbols of deviance as long hair and drug paraphernalia. In the late 1970s and early 1980s, when the punk scene in Los Angeles was at its height, the local periodical, *Slash,* regularly covered clashes with the police at punk clubs; its allegations of abusive police power were the most specific rallying cries of the movement's moral energies.

Innumerable dramas were played out when hippie and then punk students devised styles in clothing, cosmetics, and hair to ridicule the codes of school authorities. Particular movements have grown as their members locate and create juxtapositions to the elements of personal style that provide middle-class adults with the means of assuring themselves that their worlds are rationally ordered. Thus, at one historical moment or another, there may be a violation of all "neat" boundaries in personal dress and demeanor, a celebration of chaos in audible dimensions, a fervent commitment to protect the freedom to take gratuitous personal risks (for example, riding motorcycles without helmets or ingesting drugs without knowing what they contain), or a delighted confusion over gender.

In their posture, ghetto street elites stand independent of rational-legal authority, poised as aristocrats, as regal animals, as underworld creatures, or, in a recently popular style, as barbarians (Mongols, Nomads, Barbarians, and Outlaws). For details, members of street elites seem to draw on any bit of historical lore that recalls a pre-nineteenth-century elite. The ethnographer R. Lincoln Keiser noted that the list of original Vice Lords "reads something like the catalog of warriors in the *Iliad.*"[28]

For enemies, the Vice Lords found, among others, the Egyptian Cobras, a group that invoked not the Egypt of today but that of the pharaohs. *Con safos,* written on contemporary barrio walls as an omen to protect graffiti writing against future invaders, recreates the ancient institution of the curse. Mexican-American youths have innovated styles that conjure up long-moribund Mexican Indian civilizations; in Chicago in the 1950s, the first fighting groups formed under the rubric the "Sons of Azteca";[29] today's cholos favor bandana-headbands.

The charm that draws ghetto youths to imagine continuities with socially distant cultures is not simply the charm of the foreign. When black ghetto styles of deviance take on allusions to Africa, they are not to contemporary leaders dressed in Western styles, but to prehistoric or colonial images. In the United States, the famous picture of Black Panther leader Huey Newton, sitting in a naturally woven sedan chair, recalled African colonial rule; in black ghettoes in Great Britain, dread locks call up the Rastafarian mystique, which professes a tie to peoples of ancient Ethiopia.[30] In cars, in styles of dress, in trends in music, the American ghetto adolescent is not particularly drawn to European models or futuristic images. The fascination is with being, by birth, the natural heir to an elite status.

Graffiti writers in East Los Angeles achieve a certain grace by writing "El" or "Sir" as a preface to their name. In this fashion, they are transformed from persons to personages, promoting an otherwise ordinary name to the stature of a title that can be treasured as a public testament to nobility.[31] As was often the case among the small elites who were literate in pre-Enlightenment societies, the quality of the handwriting is the cardinal preoccupation of Mexican-American graffiti writers. "Chingaso" made the sociological connection explicit when he sensed the continuities with Mandarin calligraphy in East Los Angeles graffiti:

> It's like the old Oriental cultures. If somebody was appointed to a government cabinet position, he not only had to be a big general, valiant at war, but he also had to write poetry. And he had to have a beautiful script, because you can tell a person's character by his script.[32]

"Heart" is experienced specifically in relation to the modern rational definition of personal competence. It is displayed as an insistence on receiving respect, without weighing alternatives, envisioning consequences, or even systematically organizing the precise execution of a combative plan. This "heart" is not a sympathetic organ, and its logic is not a "reason," as Keiser's description illustrates:

> A Cobra swung on one of the fellows, and he come down with his knife out. That means he's not scared to take that man's life if he wished to. That's what you call a lot of heart—not scared to go to jail and pay whatever the consequences is.[33]

In Glasgow, being "gemmie" ("game," as in "I'm game for anything.") has a meaning analogous to heart. "This is the mark of the 'gemme boay': someone who is ready to fight, whatever the odds, even if defeat or physical punishment is inevitable."[34]

Heart often is identified with aristocratic stature in references to being "classy." A self-described barrio warrior who became an undergraduate at the University of Southern California (USC) recounted the challenge issued by Bruno, a "rich" Anglo USC football player, to Duke, a homeboy visiting the author in his dorm. Bruno said to Duke, " 'You think you're big shit! Well, I think I'm bigger. I challenge you to do the most craziest thing you can think of." Bruno threw a sofa out a window; then he took a knife and cut the rug, some walls, another student, finally himself. Duke retorted with an outrageous challenge of Russian Roulette: he would pull the trigger twice for each pull by Bruno. After the first round, "Suddenly, Duke began to go insane, he began yelling 'There's no need to fear, the Duke is here! Cha-haa-haa! Duke! Duke! Duke!' Duke then pulled the trigger on himself three more times, gratuitously, but Bruno declined to continue. What is most revealing in this possibly embellished account is the author's interpretation of the moral of the tale: heart, not money or conventional social status, proves class:

> The wild behavior of a mad football player was no match for the intrepidly courageous Homeboy element. The football player's madness is an academic act. For the Homeboy, barrio madness is a way of life. . . . The risks involved did not matter, rather what counted was one's courage, machismo and prestige of one's social status. The Homeboys had class, and they flamboyantly showed it to the USC crowd.[35]

EMPHASIZING VERSUS OBSCURING GENDER DIFFERENCES

Whatever the realities of private relations between the sexes, the public life of the street elite expresses male dominance in an overt manner that further elaborates the group's claims to a privileged status. In contrast, whatever the reality of private relations, the public display of beat, hippie, and punk identities have been accomplished as much by females as by males. Gender distinctions in white middle-class movements of adolescent deviance are blurred by various means: in the hippie style, jeans and long hair for everyone; in the punk movement, makeup for males as well as females.

Females who are associated with street fighting groups are either kept apart or visibly kept down. Observers in several areas noted the practice of seclusion from women (New York in the 1950s)[36] and an absence of public socializing between the sexes (Chicago in the 1960s).[37] In the Red Hook section of Brooklyn, which was Italian in the 1950s, Harlan Ellison noted, "The female's position in the social structure of a street gang is cut and dried. She is property."[38] In the East End of London, a couple of girls hung out around the original skinheads, but the boys, in their own retrospective accounts, were embarrassed to be seen with girls and treated them with snickering, lewd disrespect.[39] In Glasgow, physical intimacy through sex with females was explicitly regarded as inferior to intimate physical contact through fighting with other males:

> Big Fry, the boy "wi' aw the answers", who was easily the most fluent and effusive member of the gang, described the sensation [of fighting] as follows: "See the feelin' in yir belly goin' intae battle, it's like the feelin' ye have when Rangers are attackin' the Celtic goal. Yir heart's racin', ye feel sick; it's better'n sex." The others agreed that gang fighting was what really mattered to them; sex came a poor second in their list of priorities.[40]

Studies of female gangs have described a derivative status. After six years of observing gangs in Mexican-American communities in Los Angeles, Malcolm Klein concluded:

> The female gang is smaller (from 5 to 25 members), less seriously delinquent, and less stable than its male counterpart. It forms in response to the male structure and dissolves as the boys' group loses cohesion.[41]

Anne Campbell summed up her ethnography of black and Puerto Rican girls in New York gangs as follows:

> As they assume a more three-dimensional representation [than they had in previous studies], girls appear increasingly as sisters in the gang instead of as molls. But it cannot be said that their roles have altered substantially. They exist as an annex to the male gang, and the range of possibilities open to them is dictated and controlled by the boys. Within the gang, there are still "good girls" and "bad girls," tomboys and fallen women. Girls are told how to dress, are allowed to fight, and are encouraged to be good mothers and faithful wives. Their principal source of suffering and joy is their men. And though the girls may occasionally defy them, often argue with them, and sometimes patronize them, the men remain indisputably in control.[42]

In the culture of street elites, sharply contrasting gender styles are common, such as the contemporary cholo in khakis, hair combed straight back, with a bandana sweat band and the chola, with creased levis, halter top, up to three pairs of false eyelashes, and white eyeshadow.[43] Street elites have, at times, adopted sartorial styles shared by males and females (jeans and denim or leather jackets displaying a club insignia). But other features of the group indicate that similarity should be read not as equality of the sexes but as the females' imitation of the males' style. As Suttles noted about the differences in the dress of inner-city youths as a whole: "The males show much greater differentiation in their apparel. They seem the primary bearers of those emblems of clothing that express ethnic differences and it is among them that examples of this differentiation are most apparent."[44]

SPECIFYING AGE COHORTS WITHOUT TEMPORAL REFERENCE

Middle- and working-class styles of deviance among ethnic-majority youths tend to blur age differences within an emphasized period of adolescence. Hippie, biker or rocker, and punk styles may be picked up by youths aged 12 to 20 with roughly equal ease. In contrast, running across ethnically, geographically, and historically separate ghetto fighting groups is the pattern of formalizing short age cohorts into separate subgroups, while formally negating the use of age as the criterion.

Thus, "cliques" (usually pronounced in a way that, like a finger snap, audibly suggests disciplined unity, as "clicks" or in Mexican-American groups, "klikas") of about two-year age spans are formalized almost universally. As Horowitz observed in one of the large major Mexican-American neighborhoods in Chicago:

> There are eight major gangs in the area, each of which is segmented by age: miniatures (ages eleven to twelve), midgets (thirteen to fourteen), littles (fifteen to seventeen), juniors (eighteen to twenty-one), and seniors (twenty-one and over).[45]

Frias, a barrio warrior from East Los Angeles whose clique was Los Pequeños, realized on entering high school in the tenth grade that he did not know the homeboys from his barrio, Los Chicos, who were in the upper grades. Keiser charted the age divisions in numerous neighborhood groups of Vice Lords in Chicago in the 1960s and found "Seniors, Juniors, Midgets, in some even Pee Wees."[46]

That street-fighting groups organize the social relations of members around short age cohorts has been almost universally recognized by researchers on gangs. What has not been sufficiently appreciated is the special appearance that members create for the criterion of age. Urban lower-class fighting gangs convert the time metaphor in age into some other metaphor—most typically one of physical size or institutional tenure—which avoids the direct assertion of differences in chronological age. In any institutional framework, "Veterans" are usually older than "Seniors," who are usually older than "Juniors," but not necessarily so in the gang. "Dukes," "Counts," and "Cyclones" have no necessary age ordering. Princes may be older than Kings. Barrio cliques are known by a variety of terms that refer to small stature rather than to young age: los tynies, los enanos (dwarfs, midgets), los pequeños, los chicos, and los cherries.[47]

Violence and the Generation of Dread

Our problem is the recurrent involvement of American and British youths in groups that sustain terrifying claims to dominate urban areas. The first condition for such a group is the detailing of an elitist posture. The street elite saunters onto neighborhood streets in the posture of an aristocratic group of males who rule local landmarks, in opposition to similarly postured neighboring groups, on the basis of a power that transcends the demands of rational authority.

Violence is the second condition, and the deepest challenge to which it responds arises not from other youth groups but from internal moral dangers. Violence is essential so that membership may have a seductively glorious, rather than a mundane, indifferent, significance.

Combative adolescents and middle-class observers generally agree that the evil specter of "gang organization" is responsive to antecedent, independently existing, terrible realities. In the fearsome inner city, it is practically useful, at times essential, to walk on the streets with an aristocratic bearing that supports a self-confident association with terrible power. It would then only be prudent to maintain the social principles of primary loyalty to mates who reside in close proximity.

But not all young men in the ghetto are members of fighting groups. And even if those outside the fighting groups are sometimes subject to harrassment, the hyperbole that membership is necessary for "survival" does sociological understanding a grave disservice. Adolescent street warriors must continuously prove the enormity of the dangers they face. In effect, they work together to provoke fights and create a culture of violence that sustains the image that "it's a jungle out there," that those are "mean streets," that everytime they step out of their homes they are on a "battlefield."[48]

The economic and emotional realities of contemporary ghettoes may be terrible, but the violence to which adolescent fighting groups primarily respond is not that of muggers, rapists, child abusers, robbers, or desperate drug addicts; it is the violence of other adolescent ghetto fighting groups. The violent threat and the militaristic response exist in the same social circle. In a usually implicit, cooperative manner, adolescent street elites collectively sustain antagonistic relations in which each effectively causes the other's existence. Street elites are collective phenomena in a double sense: as multimember, self-conscious, symbolically formal entities and as groups whose raison d'être depends on the existence of structurally similar oppositional groups.

To understand the violence of street elites, I suggest that we turn the folk perspective around. We will then see that the violence of these groups does not necessarily follow from the nature of the ghetto as an oppressive social background; rather, groups must use violence to create an oppressive background if they are to bring into relief their effective presence as an elite on city streets. For without the violence, would-be street elites would appear to be bound to the social world of childhood.

THE TRANSFORMATIVE MAGIC OF VIOLENCE

Just at the time in life when many middle-class white American adolescents are drawn to deviant movements that obscure their social-class and neighborhood origins, transcend narrow age grades, break down sex segregation, and replace the heroic, fantastic caricatures of childhood play with contemporary symbols of political and social class struggle, groups of street fighters are cooperating to create a world of deviance in which sticking close to home (being homeboys),[49] identifying with the primary family (fighting to avenge an attack on a brother or a disparaging remark about a sister's morality), hanging out with peers of the same sex and age cliques, and adorning the self with images of fearful power first encountered in childhood fables (vampires, black widow spiders, skulls, serpents, and dragons), will be matters of awesome struggle and heroic loyalty.[50] In essence, the violence of street elites does the double service of transforming into an awesome presence what might otherwise appear to be the social structure and culture of childhood, and intimidating awareness of the transformation.[51]

One who adopts the adolescent ghetto posture of an elite who wields the powers of terror, without backing it with material violence, risks humiliation. Preadolescents in ghetto areas are often ridiculed for imitating the terrifying flourishes of comic-book toughs. From his youth in Pittsburgh, John Wideman recalled that when his brother, Robby, began hanging out with tough friends, their father would ridicule Robby as "Sluggo."[52] A student in a continuation school in East Los Angeles was aware that

> when we wear kakis or cuffed levis with a pendleton shirt or a tee-shirts and spit shine shoes most of the teachers laugh at us and say thing like, "Oh Tommy, you look like a wino or a killer."[53]

In high schools in East Los Angeles, "wanabe," a noun created by merging "want to be," is used, among other things, to deride recent immigrants who have only begun to take on aspects of the cholo/chola look.[54] Among graffiti writers in New York, use of the word *toy* in reference to an experienced writer is considered to be a powerful denunciation, and it is used in face-to-face confrontations with experienced writers only in anticipation of an argument or a fight.[55]

An ex-skinhead, encountering young skinhead types on London streets, recalled his own painful apprehension of ridicule:

> When a younger kid of say fifteen "screws" you in the street. . . . You don't really know what to do. . . . Sometimes you turn away but are embarrassed, but you would be even more embarrassed if you continued looking at them and the little kid ended up kicking you or something. . . . Maybe the best thing to do is just to smile; we can laugh at them, mainly because we were like them when we were their age. You have to laugh at them, the same as people laughed at us when we were fifteen.[56]

By overwriting the principles of childhood socialization in blood, violence transforms the limitations of the social worlds of adolescent street elites into boundaries that are consecrated in meanness. The Sandman, a figure from the folklore of childhood, becomes an ominous name in the South Bronx when the violent activities of those who wear Sandman colors give "putting to sleep" the awesome meaning made famous in old gangster movies. Violence brings comic-book symbolism to life: Manny Torres stated that the most feared member of the Bishops (a New York gang of the 1950s) was Batman, who wore a cape and "was a stone-cold killer" at age 14; once, Batman murdered a youth by shotgun because he assumed the youth was out to get him.[57] Violence makes the liberty to cross a street—an early parental acknowledgment of the child's developing competence—a proof of manhood. Sticking close to the neighborhood, a parental restraint on the young child, becomes a matter of pride. The Sex Boys, who took their name, in part, from Essex Street, could brag, "We walk all over East New York—everywhere"; because of intergroup violence, a small section of Brooklyn may be spoken of without pause as "everywhere." Degrees of "badness" show bravado and are measured with the handy, local geographic metaphor; people call the Bikers the "baddest," but, bragged Big L, the Sex Boys are badder because they go into the Bikers' turf but the Bikers will not go into the Sex Boys' turf.[58]

The passive fact of living around the primary family home, just being there, may be treated as a heroic feat of "surviving" once intergroup "warfare" has become sufficiently impressive. The protagonist in a video focused on Las Sesentas, a Mexican-American barrio fighting group, introduced the viewer to his world with, "only the fast people survive. . . . this isn't Alameda, Hayward, San Leandro. . . . It's East Oakland." That East Oakland is the measure of the dangers of the larger world would surely be contested by warriors from distant barrios, such as Ruben: "East Los Angeles is the baddest area around—in all of California."[59]

Occasionally, particular incidents will illustrate directly the significance of group violence for transcending humiliating treatment that dismisses the street elite's arrogant, evil posture as childish. The following murder by Chicago Vice Lords was described similarly in two ethnographic interviews, in widespread newspaper coverage, and in judicial proceedings. Keiser's account was as follows:

> One night we was coming from the Golden Dome. The papers said there were thirteen, but they only busted thirteen. They questioned everybody that was there, but they let me go. What happened, we asked this man for a nickel or a dime or something—and he got smart. This fool ["The Fool"], Wine, asked the man for a nickel. And he answered, "I ain't got no nickel."
> Wine said, "You're going to have to give me a nickel!"
> The stud said, "I'm not your daddy!"
> The fool ["The Fool"], Wine, said, "I know you're not my father!"
> And Bull, he hit the man and knocked him down. The man tried to get back up. He was a judo expert. When he got back up again, I guess he was trying to get into position, and somebody hit him again. Boom! He went down. The poor soul, that's the last time he ever stood up ... they stomped him to death. I forgot if he was dead on arrival or not.[60]

VIOLENCE AND SOVEREIGNTY

In that incident, violence was used to overturn an attempt to ridicule evil pretentions as childish; the victim's "I'm not your daddy," which implied that despite his physically intimidating gestures, Wine was presenting himself as a child (perhaps an illegitimate child in search of his father), was catalytic. But other details of this incident are also significant.

Note just how the money was demanded. Surely, the killing cannot be understood simply as a response to poverty. If acquiring money was the object, why ask only for a nickel? Had a nickel been given, it is unlikely that the drama would have ended. But if more would have been demanded, why not simply ask immediately for all the passerby possessed? Why not conduct the encounter straightforwardly as a robbery? The Fool was employing a familiar gambit of street humiliation: to ask for a minimal sum and, if acquiescence is forthcoming, to keep raising the demand in small increments until the victim must realize he is being robbed.

Although the ending is unusual, this incident began with a device commonly used by street elites to make literal the symbolic demand that is implicit in their posture as a whole—that tribute be paid. The insistence is for a monetary token of respect in the form of a toll imposed for passage through their territory. The collection of such payments indicates the presence of a ruling regime. These tokens will not enrich those who collect them, but they will attest to their sovereign control.

When a quarter is demanded of an unaffiliated student in a "gang-controlled" high school, it is the metaphor, not the money that is irresistible. In an Orange County, California, continuation school, Juan bragged that when he is with his barrio homeboys, others "treat us like if we're big shit. Man, we even take money away from some of them."[61] The threat of violence explodes small change into big shit. As a way of dramatizing that it is "their park," a group of Los Angeles cholos approached a picnicking priest dressed in street clothes and "asked" for drinks from the provisions he had assembled on his blanket in a tone indicating that their concern was moral satisfaction, not thirst.[62]

For the members of urban street elites, violence has the instrumental value of stimulating metaphors that make the group a real presence as a militant force of sovereign rulers. In neighborhoods where graffiti or the wearing of group "colors" has suggested that militant collective organizations are about, a relatively few incidents of violence can suddenly conjure up the metaphor of "gang warfare." In the context of militarized tensions, the associational principles of the adolescent street elite—loyalty to mates, an exclusive male society, close ties to a home base, fantastic inspirational symbols, and internal differentiation by length of tenure—become the sturdy framework of a manly social order.

Group members and the metropolitan press alike are charmed by the military metaphor. Much attention is given to the display of "weapons," a category that, in the context of the gang, includes everyday implements, such as hammers and kitchen knives; a collection of such "weapons" is known as an "arsenal." In black and Puerto Rican areas, particular members have been known as "war counselor" or "sergeant at arms" or "minister of defense." Within the context of gang "warfare," a girl who is known to "sleep with" (perhaps just date) members of two rival gangs may be regarded as involved in a "spy/counter-spy" intrigue.[63] Outsiders may be issued passports for visits to the neighborhood, as was a journalist who was granted safe passage into the headquarters of the Blackstone Rangers on the basis of a napkin signed "Fox [,] Black (P) Stone 21."[64] In group settings, wounds are often exhibited and discussed as "battle scars." The crossing of a neighborhood boundary may be readily referred to as an "invasion." Much discussion may be given to military tactics, such as Who should "attack" first and with what "weapons"? If they come first, which way will they approach? Should we try an "ambush"? It follows naturally that gang "wars" may be avoided or ended with "peace talks."

Military-like uniforms are also commonly attractive, although the style, again, suggests not the drab, dull, anonymous uniformity of modern working-class or peasant armies outfitted in khaki greens or plain ("Red" Chinese) jackets, but the flamboyant, colorful, personality-expressive uniforms of royal guards. "Colors" may be sported on handkerchiefs or bandanas in a touch that suggests Indians fighting as renegades against the domesticating forces of modern civilization. If feathered plumes are not worn on hats in a style reminiscent of ancient helmets, they might be carried in the design of birds of prey painted or sewn on the backs of group jackets.[65]

Turf wars, which might, in the childhood analogy, suggest king-of-the-hill play, take on dimensions of political seriousness when they become part of wider claims to symbols of sovereignty. In the sixties and early seventies, in southside and westside Chicago, the most famous adolescent fighting groups boasted of multiple, allied subgroups joined together in transcendent "nations," as in the Black P. Stone Nation, or, only slightly more modestly, in their own "city." As Cupid explained in his interview with R. Lincoln Keiser:

> You was out there. You was holding that street twenty-four hours a day. And you just had to constantly fight life and death out there. Lots of times the police even threatened us. . . . We was a little city. That's why they called it Vice Lord City.[66]

These claims of sovereign rule achieve an especially compelling, glorious ring. To be a "nation" in the primordial sense is to have, in addition to a territorial claim, a collective, ethnically distinctive character. The cultural dimension of nation is achieved through various flamboyant styles: berets and headbands, symbols drawn on or woven into jackets, nonconventional boots and gloves, and so forth. In some Mexican-American communities, adolescents do not treat their barrio just as a neighborhood. With the loyalty due a national homeland, they self-consciously continue elements of the styles associated with prior generations of barrio adolescents, for example, by drinking the same brand of beer as did the defenders of their barrio's pride in previous decades.[67]

By linking their street styles to violent claims over turf, ghetto adolescents avoid another risk of ethnic nations, becoming patronized as a quaint subculture, which occurred for a short while in the 1980s with break dancing, until street gangs began adopting this art form as they had previously adopted grafitti writing, to promote conflict with rival groups. Despite its culturally creative and traditional elements of dress, street talk, and "stroll," the barrio warrior style is not likely to be celebrated along with mariachis, hat dances, and fiesta costumes in the civic center on the Cinco de Mayo in Los Angeles. Nor is it likely that the distinctive esthetics of black ghetto gangs will be celebrated along with gospel singing, inspirational preaching, and myths recalling the African heritage on Martin Luther King, Jr., Day.

Street elites use violence innovatively to elaborate the theme of sovereignty. It is as if a member grasps one or another of the array of activities that nations characteristically perform and, with friends, brings the metaphor to life with the creative magic of violence. Consider initiation ceremonies, for example. Although initiation ceremonies are not universal features, many fighting groups of ghetto adolescents have found them attractive over the years. In contemporary Mexican-American barrios, they commonly take the form of brief, casually arranged episodes of submission to group fist pounding. On the East Coast among white ethnics in the fifties and among Puerto Ricans in the sixties, initiation procedures were described as formalized, elaborate, painful, and terrifying. They are rarely mentioned in the ethnographies of black urban gangs of the sixties. When they are performed, initiation rituals most directly work like a metaphysical immigration ceremony, granting membership in an ontologically higher order.

"Council" meetings may be held with fastidious trappings of diplomacy. Enemy groups at times send reciprocal feelers through emissaries who set up meetings of rival leaders with all the gravity of summit sessions held by chiefs of great nations. Particular sites in no-man's land, such as movie theaters, public schools, and athletic clubs, are discussed as locations that one or another group "has," "controls," or "runs," even though neither group collects the box office receipts, shapes the curriculum, or hires the club's staff. But then, conquering armies of real nations likewise capture hills, fields, regions, and whole countries from enemies, and all may understand that the area has been "taken," even though the only control exercised by the victor is to exclude the rival army. A member of the Vice Lords put it this way:

> Our motivation was to be the baddest, toughest, roughest gangbanger, or streetfighter, and what showed a cat was powerful was turf. We needed land to establish our identity and we really didn't own land. But we thought this was ours and we paraded the streets and occupied certain corners. . . . Or you would tell a cat, "Well, dig, man, I want the movie." He say, "I ain't gonna give it to you. If you gonna take it, I'll be at the show next Sunday." That's an automatic challenge, so next Sunday whoever runs whoever out of there runs the movie. Then the word spreads that so-and-so took the show from so-and-so. Next you take the swimming pool, then the park, then two blocks, three blocks, until he doesn't have any territory at all. The only thing left for him to do is to become a member or move out of the area.[68]

Like flags staked to mark territorial boundaries, the graffiti of ghetto adolescents lay claims to sovereignty. On the wall of a West side high school is written, "Vice Lords Run It." On a highway overpass in East Los Angeles is scrawled, *Hoyo Maravilla Rifa* [rule]. In the bathroom of a Glasgow pub frequented by the Young Team is a notice:

Wild
Young
Catholic
Team
Rules
O.K.[69]

The violence of ghetto adolescents has frequently succeeded not only in channeling the movements of adolescents but also in shaping the ways in which social workers, sociologists, and even the police conduct their activities. The police officers who, through effective "intelligence gathering," incarcerated numerous leaders of an infamous gang center in the South Bronx were careful to knock on the clubhouse door and wait to be admitted: "We'd knock on the door and announce ourselves. They appreciated that touch of formality—it showed respect."[70] Group members may rejoice in the recognition that gang "intelligence" squads have attempted to trace their domains, even to the point of offering to "correct" the lines drawn on police maps. With task forces and spy activities, police departments—big groups of serious, tough-looking, gun-bearing, flesh-and-blood adult men—organize their work lives along units that are dictated, in effect, by metaphors designed by the ghetto's adolescents. What greater proof of sovereignty than the ability to draw official maps of urban geography![71]

Despite the sometimes desperate poverty of the citizens of these adolescent ghetto "nations," despite their inability to shape the lives of nonadolescent local residents, despite the irrelevance of their violence for any voting or economic franchise of their own, their violence routinely suffices so that members take for granted claims that the groups "control" or even "own" their neighborhoods. Nations, after all, need not engage in any particular business or practically intervene in the lives of most citizens. But if they are recognized as possessing territory, if they successfully defend their claims to turf, nations have a sovereign existence.

VIOLENCE AND THE CONSTRUCTION OF DREAD

In the hands of adolescent street elites, violence has a constructive power sufficient (1) to transform the significance of their principles of association from demeaning indications of childhood to the social requirements for glorious combat, (2) to establish a metaphor of sovereignty respected by peers, observed by the police, and duly reported by the mass media, and (3) most essentially, to sustain the claim of elite status in an aura of dread. It should be emphasized here that these are not unwitting consequences but tacitly understood themes. Ghetto adolescents know that if they are to rule their streets as an elite, they must do so by dread. Violence is but one means of conjuring up dread.

Group names imply an elite whose authority may be questioned only with dreadful results. In the 1960s, in Chicago, the Vice Lords epitomized the combination of aristocratic and evil themes that are distinctive of adolescent fighting groups. These naming conventions continue long-standing patterns. Commenting on the European-immigrant "gangs" of 1920s Chicago, Thrasher noted an order of grandiose, "high-sounding" names like "Golden Palace Athletic Club," and an order of "names suggesting murder, blood, banditry, and piracy. . . . 'The Vultures,' the 'Forty Thieves,' the 'Murderers,' . . . [the members of which] get a great 'kick' out of feeling how diabolical they are and, hence, how superior to the world at large."[72] Likewise, the "detached" social workers who were assigned to New York City street gangs in the 1950s found names of "conflict gangs" that tracked neighborhoods, reflected high statuses, or symbolized evil personages (such as the Daggers, the Stompers, and the Killers).[73]

Group names are only the most obvious indicators of an effort to generate dread behind an elitist stance. George, the leader of the Reapers in the famous "Fort Apache" area of the South Bronx in the early 1970s, added a sartorial detail to this theme by carrying a mahogany cane that concealed a sword—a touch of class covering a terrible, hidden power.[74] In an ethnically mixed, poor and working-class area of Chicago in the early 1960s, a group of Mexican-American youths who "openly embraced the stance of a fighting group," made up cards that "introduced them as the 'Fabulous Taylor Barracudas.' "[75] Given the then-popular television show, *Paladin,* whose main character identified himself to strangers with the calling card, "Have Gun Will Travel," this device reflected the calling card of an aristocratic cowboy-knight. At about the same time, in the deepest West Side poverty area, the Vice Lords wore black capes with gold lettering and earrings; using a top hat, canes, and gloves, they created a logo worthy of a collaboration between Noel Coward and the devil. Their canes were arranged to spell out CVL (for Conservative Vice Lords); the top hat was set on a skeleton's head that hovered over a bow tie; and, in the middle of the skull, was a cigarette holder and a stream of exhaled smoke.[76]

Unlike black and Puerto Rican groups in the Midwest and on the East Coast, Mexican-American barrio warriors have not often shown commitments to these themes in their collective names. Nevertheless, both themes have been elaborated in their symbolic world. On the West Coast, for example, the conquistador/devil style of facial hair is popular; in this style, a triangular mini-beard is maintained under the lower lip, sometimes framed, with allusions to myths of Mexican outlaws and a "bad" oriental image, by narrow mustache lines running from the nose to the chin. In chapter 3, I noted the aristocratic squat and related manifestations of the proud, down-the-nose posture of the "bad" barrio youth culture. One more detail is: instead of the leather jackets and embroidered sweaters associated with East Coast youth gangs of the 1950s, West Coast barrio warriors (and some black groups as well) use the strikingly simple sartorial device of an upturned bill on a cap to signify membership in a "bad" group. The barrio name is commonly painted on the underside of the brim, and circular letters in the barrio's name frequently are drawn and punctuated to suggest eyes. When turned up, the bill of the cap has the "bad" youth peering down on passers-by with a collective identity drawn from underneath. And if there is no "evil" image in the barrio's name, the members wear, as a substitute, colorfully painted T-shirts showing vampires with mouths dripping blood over the legend, Dracula; devils grinning sadistically while slaughtering pathetic victims; and self-portraits of the wearers engaged as terrifying superheros brutally beating down enemies of inferior stature.[77] The symbolism of that eternal aristocrat of evil, Count Dracula, is commonly embraced by contemporary cholos.

I suggest that adolescent fighting groups find violence compellingly attractive as a means of sustaining the aura of dread that is an essential element in their project of elite rule. From the vignettes of intergroup violence by detached social workers in the 1950s to the more detailed accounts in recent ethnographies, a number of catalytic scenes and provocative actions continuously reappear. The peculiar contingencies of violence between street elites are situational opportunities to construct dread.

In her observational study of fighting groups in Mexican-American barrios in Chicago, Ruth Horowitz gave an example of the instigation of conflict through one group's seizure of an irresistible opportunity for provocative behavior toward an "enemy" group. The Dukes and Lions spoke of each other as opposed groups, but, as Horowitz observed, "Lions from 32nd Street frequently visited relatives on 40th Street, where several rival gangs were located, with no trepidation." But when a Lion took possession of a Duke's sweater, even though it was by chance discovery in the park, keeping the sweater became an irresistible and a fateful act that, the Lions assumed, meant that they could not longer enter the Dukes' territory with nonchalance. As a Lion said:

> If we go wandering around 40th Street then the Dukes know that we're out looking for them and we got to be careful 'cause its dangerous and we're likely to get shot at. They know who we are and they don't like us 'cause we got one of their sweaters.[78]

Note that the passive act by the Lions of retaining possession of the Dukes' sweater created an aura of dread, first *for the Lions themselves.* Perhaps the Dukes also realized that intergroup relations had become deadly serious or perhaps not. But the theft of the sweater instantly and naturally made the Lions' otherwise mundane movements through neighborhoods into arrogant acts of aristocratic conquerors. For the Lions, holding onto the sweater brought to life the portentious metaphor of sovereignty. The sweater became a flag and its possession, a declaration of war. The Lions understood that nations at peace may freely allow border crossings by each other's citizens, but when they are "at war," border crossings, if not challenged with at least an inquiry about one's national identity, undermine claims of sovereignty.

If they often plead self-defense as a motive for interrogating outsiders, in their own culture, members of street elites not only recognize but celebrate the willful generation of dreadful tensions with other groups. In Glasgow's fighting "teams," members use "puttin' the mix in" as "their expression for contriving a quarrel where none existed."[79] In Southern California barrios, there are reliable methods for acquiring the awesome status of a "psyco" [sic] or *vato loco*. In graffiti, for example,

> the crossing out of a barrio's sign and gang members' names can lead to violent upheavals and confrontations, resulting many times in death for those individuals who dared cross-out their opponents' barrio's name and/or persons' names. Any person who crosses out another barrio's name or gang member's names and who identifies himself by writing his name and his barrio on that same wall is a courageous example of a *vato loco* who does not care what happens to him if the gang members he crossed out are out to get him.[80]

Perhaps, somewhere lurking behind the violence of street elites, there are pathetic, negative conditions: an anticipatory fear of failure in adult careers, resentment over social or racial injustice, irrational and short-sighted lower-class values, and so forth. But what is visible in the process of generating violence is a positive relish, even to the point of self-destruction. The sweater of the rival group is retained and the insulting graffiti is signed, *in spite of* the prediction of a violent response. In Glasgow, "Big Sick" was on trial for using a razor to slash. As Patrick noted, "the case for the defence collapsed . . . when Big Sick boasted in the witness box that the attack was 'the biggest rippin' Ah've done.' "[81] The delight in violence is disastrous from the perspective of defense but irresistible for constructing dread.

Perhaps fatal conflicts resulting from a "stolen" sweater or the writing on a wall of one group's name over another's—not to mention a craftsman-like pride in knifing a victim—indicate psychological pathology. Indeed, even the adolescents involved may label the provocateur as "Fool," a "vato loco," or "Big Sick." But, from Los Angeles to New York to Glasgow, graffiti on walls attest to the *collective* celebration of the acts of the vato loco, the "psyco," the group that has been accorded a reputation as "mental." Although the point may be made less routinely in real blood than in red paint dripping from the mouth of a vampire on a T-shirt, the point is the same. To rule the streets as an elite, arrogantly, as if with an inborn right to rule, the youth group understands it must rule by dread.

Evoking the Spirit of Street Elites

My subject throughout this volume is the lived experience of criminality, in this instance, being in a group that sustains terrifying claims to dominate an urban area. "Being in" this world of experience is not simply a matter of detailing a posture and using violence to raise the specter of terror. It is also a contingent sensual involvement.

Ethnographic research on gangs reveals several recurrent processes of involvement. Each is a way of dramatizing the gang member's project of moving, in a self-respectful, practically successful manner, from the "here" of his small, subjectively familiar social world into a vaguely apprended, broader, more anonymous society that the adolescent experiences as a challenging presence somewhere out "there." By evoking this transcendence on the field of an immediate social situation, members lend the group significance as a means of exploring feelings on an irresistibly compelling dimension from pride to humiliation.

COLLECTIVE ARRANGEMENT OF SPONTANEOUS VIOLENCE

Occasionally, the tacit cooperation underlying the violence of street elites comes to the surface. Recalling his research in the 1960s with Fred Strotbeck on Chicago's black West Side, James Short gave a memorable example.[82] A newly formed black gang in a housing project attempted to stimulate the reorganization of the Egyptian Cobras, another black group that was virtually defunct. The aggressive group was intent on provocation, despite the lack of insults and harms to redress; they sought conflict with the Cobras because the latter, although inactive as a fighting gang for several months, still had a formidable "rep."

Reviewing social workers' field notes from New York City in the 1950s, Irving Spergel was exceptionally clear on the self-conscious maintenance of hostilities between conflict groups:

> It was also important to guard against conditions which might destroy opportunities to have gang fights. Bobby said, "It was best if the Noble Lords didn't go to the Regal's territory or the Regals to the Noble Lord's territory, otherwise we would get to know each other and become too friendly, and then it would be hard to bop."[83]

More commonly, an artificial origin of intergroup conflict is indicated by the ritual invocation of hollow insults. As Spergel illustrated:

> Pro forma, Brave Eagle, a Regal who was tiring of the month-long peace, went over to Lucy, the girlfriend of Flash Gordon, one of the leaders of

the Noble Lords, at the community-center dance, and said loudly so that all those nearby could hear, 'You're getting fat, honey. Flash must be f———g you too much.' The Noble Lord-Regal conflict broke out again the following day.[84]

Similarly, in East London in the early 1970s, the original skinheads were often "searching out provocative situations, looking for 'aggro.' "[85]

For one's provocation of others to become their provocation of oneself, some magic must be worked. One must simultaneously do the dualistic work of manufacturing an irritation of others and not experiencing the resulting tension as one's artifact. In part, the fascination with posturing as a member of a street elite consists of experiencing this magical generation of malevolent action. An alumnus of the skinheads reminisced: "We only 'it people for reasons, didn't we? . . . like if they looked at us."[86] With friends, you generate a terrifying style, then take it to the street. When others curiously take note, you experience "aggro"; suddenly, "they" are "screwing" you. Suddenly, the otherwise mundane phenomena of behavior in public are transformed into the stuff of mortal challenge.[87]

Between predatory inclination and the practice of violence, there is an intermediary process in which the responsibility for the attack is transferred to the other side. The youths' collective creation suddenly takes on a spontaneous, independent life. Such a process is both logically absurd and experientially real.

Dances at clubs or parties, encounters in school corridors, and in bars (in Britain more than in the United States) have frequently been reported as the sites of intergroup violence.[88] The casual settings that bring members of different street elites together are fertile for conflict because the opportunity for elaborating a dreadful aura is exceptionally tempting and in crowded contexts, the collective arrangement of spontaneous violence is geometrically facilitated. To each locally styled elite, these places represent a social world that exists out "there," at a distance from the home base. As such, they are especially salient to the transcendent project of street elites.[89] When the public character of a setting attracts numerous members to strut about in the guise of rulers of the scene, the line between intentional offense and "accidental" bumps may suddenly vanish in any number of chance encounters.

Gang violence has often been attributed to overblown commitments to traditions of honor and revenge, especially among the latest ethnic representatives of this social problem in urban America, Hispanics.[90] But insults to family need not be either delivered or received with passion to be treated by fighters as determining causes. What is essential for a compelling involvement is that one group challenge the seriousness of another's elitist pretensions. And this challenge may be accomplished as a simple extension of the posture of arrogant domination. After all, one of the prerogatives of an inviolable elite is to deliver insults to subordinates as the spirit moves them, without regard to such petty matters as valid foundation.

Once received, however, an insult must be treated as an offense to honor or else the target group will have acknowledged that it cannot sustain an aura of dread. Thus, systems of honor may appear to move enemy groups into real combat, even though the insults may be collectively understood to be artificial. That the insulting party may not know the sister said to be a whore or that the braggart is obviously inventing his liaisons with the insulted party's mother (who may not even be alive) makes no difference.[91] Everyone understands the message that cannot be dismissed: "We're not taking you seriously; we regard you as punks. Prove you mean it by being mean" ("it" being all those pretensions you convey in your talk, walk and dress). At the extreme, there need be no insult at all; a mere "bad look" can puncture another group's pretensions, unless the other group strikes back, as the following account indicates:

> Badman of the Clowns was famous for the manner in which he could look over the enemy. A dirty look from Badman was the equivalent of a slap in the face or a stab in the heart. One evening he was given a work assignment of helping collect tickets to a club dance at the door of his lounge. Several younger members and the president of an opposing group entered to go to the dance. They handed their tickets to Badman. Slowly he accepted their tickets, tore them in half, returned them to the boys, looked them up and down, turned his nose away, and indicated they should enter. The group was furious. Although this incident seems trivial, four youngsters lost their lives over a period of two years, and at least 20 were imprisoned as a result of a gang fight which ensued.[92]

Once an attack by another group becomes public knowledge, a failure to respond threatens to make retrospectively ridiculous the pretensions of all in the attacked group. Members of the attacked group who are related to or friends with the victim are expected to effect the revenge; if they refuse, they may face more danger from within the group than from outside it.[93] At this point, the history of posturing arrogance by the attacked group suddenly becomes a heavy commitment. What had been playfully under the group's control is now out of its hands; the group may no longer determine unilaterally to back off because other elite-styled groups see a prize in its defeat. Whether it delivers or receives the first blow, it has become controlled by its own symbolism.[94]

Virtually all ethnographies of street violence among adolescent elites describe fights generated by interrogations or spontaneous declarations of group membership on public streets. Manny Torres's account of his adolescence in New York City's Spanish Harlem, recounts how Manny woke up in the hospital after miscalculating the audience for his shout of bravado one afternoon in a movie theater, "Young Star Here!"[95] In Glasgow, fights would often start as quick responses to the simple question, here asked by Big Dave of a boy he happened to meet: "Who rules? Whit team are ye in?"[96] And Keiser reported the dramatic way in which the Vice Lords occasionally announced their presence:

> There weren't but two of us—me and Ringo. So Ringo, he yells, "We're Vice Lords, mighty Vice Lords!" He yelling to a man coming up the street. This stud said, "Well, you all Vice Lords, huh!?" We said, "Yeah!" And by the time he was reaching for his back pocket . . . I guess he didn't get out what he wanted to get out before I got what I got out. I shot him in the leg or foot or something, and he ran down the street . . . hollering like a dog! I don't even know if he a Cobra, but it was in the Cobra's hood.[97]

Note that no insult was stated in these incidents. The violent response did not redress an attack on personal, family, or group honor in any conventional sense. What was being formally stated was a simple question or fact of membership. What was being enthusiastically declared was dominance of the streets. What was being conveyed was not an insult but a dare. To one who has been strutting arrogantly, not to take up the dare reverses the meaning of a multitude of prior intimidations, changing their status from an elite's dominance to a punk's bluff.

PARADING

Some gangs of ghetto adolescents have been credited in sensational news stories with organized extortions of local merchants or of running drug markets;[98] some have elaborated an independent social order to the extent of conducting such civil niceties as marriage ceremonies.[99] But the ethnographic record is clear that despite the deep appeal of the metaphor—despite the regular jaunts in which they oversee their lands, the occasional tribute they exact on passersby, and the innovation of social rituals like initiation ceremonies—the "rule" of these rulers is superficial, not only to their communities but, without more, to their members' lives.

Indeed, perhaps the greatest danger to the survival of the fighting group as an entity that embraces the lived experience of members is not the strength of other gangs or pressure from the police, but boredom.[100] In addition to violence, a number of routine practices are universally employed to raise the spirit of the group. Virtually all ethnographies of youth groups that boast terrifying postures describe parading on local streets as a recurrently thrilling practice. Parading is a process of walking in apparent unison past a relatively stationary public while displaying "colors" or other insignia of membership in a diffusely threatening group. Three members of a Glasgow gang were all reminiscing about the time the assembled Young Team had travelled across to Saracen Cross in Possilpark in as many as twelve to fifteen taxis. "It wis some sight. Aw thae taxis in a big line-up." (The phrase "line-up" provoked considerable laughter from the other two, as it was normally used to describe the queue of boys waiting to have sexual intercourse in one of the "gang bangs.") "We came pourin' oot, aw jazzed up in wir tin flutes [sharp suits], aw drunk and blocked up wi' the goofies. Great, man."[101]

Or the thrill of the parade may be achieved by reversing the relationship between viewer and viewed, as when members pace about a public loca- tion, gesturing defiance and shouting insults at will. No practice of violence is necessary. The essential element for sustaining the member's involve- ment in the group is the passerby, whose anonymity represents the world out "there" and makes being in the group a meaningful vehicle for moving from what is subjectively familiar to members to what is less intimately known "on the streets."

Consider, for example, how, without striking a blow, some Glasgow adolescents use remarks, songs, and gestures to infuse a mean spirit into everyday public scenes. The following was reported by a school teacher, who conducted participant observations in the early 1970s:

Back at the corner, we passed the time by criticizing everybody and anybody who passed by. Typical of the comments was a remark shouted to young girls walking in the street: "Hi! Sexy drawers! Ah want ma hole." Or again, to girls and, surprisingly to boys: "Ah'll kick yir cunt in." As darkness came down, their daring increased. The Young Trio broke into song, the melody being "The Auld Orange Flute" with the words rewritten by themselves:

I went to a party one Friday night,
The Tongs were there and wanted to fight,
I drew my blade out, quick as a flash,
And shouted 'Young Team, Young Team, Ya Bass.'
The first one that came was five foot four,
I lifted my boot and he fell to the floor.
The cunt was in agony, The cunt was in pain,
So I lifted my boot and I fucked him again. . . .

One gesture in particular, made from the top of buses and from the other side of streets, will be difficult to capture in words. I would call it the "Come oan, then" gesticulation. To the accompaniment of these words, the hands were outstretched, palm upwards, and the fingers moved up and down as if beckoning the opposition to approach. The final stage of the hand movement came when the boy drew his two index fingers across his cheeks in imitation of slashing razors. Two "Mars Bars" were being wished on the adversary's face.[102]

The involving potential of parading may be elaborated in various ways. The original skinheads used petty theft to spice up the process:

> Biggest laugh, loads of things really . . . there was so many things 'appening. . . . You go to a hot-dog stall and someone nicks one and then the geezer comes out after you, it just all 'appened.[103]

These incidents do not reflect the experience of "going on a (criminal) job" or of responding to "peer pressures." Rather, they illustrate the delight in discovering the spiritual power of a collective posturing as deviant: how, once the group is constituted, a coherent line of action can spring spontaneously from chaos. The very unpredicability of actions and reactions makes "being with the mob" predictably exciting. Otherwise unimaginable, transcendent possibilities are now sensed as real, as this account reveals:

> Yeah, they all want to fight when they're in the mob, it's like the pack qualities in the wolf. A wolf on its own will only attack small creatures. Once skinheads get together they think they're tough, they would attack something, anything. . . . It's like a copper, you get some kids jumping on coppers but they wouldn't do it on their own.[104]

Parading on foot, or in cars as a collective "cruising," is seductive as a way of injecting self-confident expressions into the consciousnesses of a mass of observers.[105] It follows that the mass media's coverage of "gang activities" is a powerful stimulus to members' involvement.[106] Note that what is involved in this acquisition of a "reputation" is not simply what sociologists call "prestige" or "peer acceptance." There is a transcendent, sensual quality to the experience that often shows up as hubris:

> We was saying that we going to make the name Mighty Vice Lords go down in history some day. We had so much confidence in ourselves that we felt we could do this here. Actually we was obligated to do it. This was our supreme purpose—to be known, to gain this certain respect. . . . It was at the meeting, and Count said, "One day the Mighty Vice Lord name will go out to history, and we'll be known nation wide. Everybody will remember the Mighty Vice Lords."
> Those were his exact words. And we tried to make it so.[107]

THE TRANSCENDENCE OF MUNDANE AUTHORITY

Relations with school authorities provide many opportunities for elaborating the transcendent significance of the group. In this regard it is useful to imagine a fourfold table constructed by two distinctions, one contrasting *individual and collective* forms of deviant response to school authority and the other contrasting an *oppositional and a transcendent* posture of deviance.

The commonest and mildest acts are *individual* acts that use sensual involvements to contest the demand by school authorities for intellectual attention: chewing gum, conversing with another, distributing food, sleeping, reading comic books, and the like. A further elaboration of deviant opposition is accomplished when students *collectively* elaborate a world of hedonism in the interstices of official oversight on school grounds.

The second distinction refers to the spiritual reach of the deviant project. Across all social classes and ethnic groups, adolescents enjoy *battles* with teachers and administrators on the official moral grounds of school authority—*rationality,* by exploiting gaps between rules and practice and between formal rules and institutional purposes, inconsistencies in the relations among rules, and the normatively ambiguous areas that are slightly beyond the school's jurisdiction. One widely popular tactic, for example, is to follow the rules so strictly that one undermines the authority they are intended to serve. When conducted before other students, the spirit raised in the audience makes the ploy an act of collective rebellion. Ruth Horowitz gave this example from one of the barrios that produce Chicago's Mexican-American "gang" problem:

> Rosita explained how she reacts without explicitly violating any rule when a teacher demeans her publicly in class. "When a teacher tells you to sit, you do, no matter where you are—on a desk, the floor, or a dude's lap. When she says take your gum out of your mouth and throw it away—take it out with your fingers and throw—particularly at someone you know will scream."[108]

Another collectively arranged ploy played off the gap between the wishes of authority and the formal boundaries of its jurisdiction:

> The students were required to wear uniforms to enter the [parochial] school building. In order to protest, they started changing into their uniforms in the street. That ended that rule.[109]

With such tactics, students may assume a momentary dominance over school officials, but all remain players within the same *moral framework.* The means of opposition is also a method of celebrating one's command of the very competence to which the institution is committed. The students triumph by demonstrating a superior ability to manipulate the institution of rational authority.[110]

A contrasting posture is that of transcendent superiority in which students treat the concerns of the school authorities as wholly alien, part of a world that is at an unbridgeable distance from their subjective reality—a moral sensibility to which they need not respond. Among black adolescents, a favorite way of signaling a transcendent superiority to mundane authorities is to refer to the authorities' normative demands as intractable nonsense: "noise," "beating his mouth," "talking shit." The following excerpts are from two of Carl Werthman's interviews with gang members in San Francisco:

> That Math teacher, I know he don't like us. He don't like me anyway. When I come to class, he always say something smart. Like "Don't talk."[111]

> I say, "I'll talk as loud as I want!" He want us to be silent all the time in class! . . . the teacher said he kicked me out cause I, you know, upset the class. And I just got in the class! He just don't like me reading comic books while he up there beating his mouth.[112]

Alternatively, one may dramatize that one's intractability to rational authority is constitutional, as when an administrator's inquiries are said to make one "sick," as this account illustrates:

> I don't hardly get along with no teacher. I just get in there and do what I got to do. Claudette and me used to go out to lunch. And when we come back, we be all late and stuff. Mr. Chasworth be breaking, "Where's our late passes?" and stuff. He used to get me sick. Always asking for a late pass. . . . And then we have to get one. Me and Claudette we used to try and get high.[113]

Membership in a physically intimidating street group is not necessary for presenting oneself as intractable to rational authority but it can help in several ways. Minimally, the group provides a chorus that can chant in the background and preserve especially daring dramatizations as legends. Ex-skinheads from London's East End recalled a memorable demonstration of the claim that students' sensual involvements—this time sex, not drugs—represent a subjectivity that the teacher's authority dare not reach.

> Oh Dave used to be really filthy like in school, he used to start singing, "We caught you rubbing off" and you get these right shy teachers and they get all red . . . "David, I'll tell the headmaster" . . . "We caught you rubbing off" and all this and 'e used to drive 'er mad, or 'e used to get it out, and he used to get it out on the desk and "AYYYYYEEEE,

AYYYYYEEEE" and all the girls used to scream like and shoot off out like and all the class would go wild.[114]

Cutting class is an effective way of demonstrating independence as an individual, but when the street group is used to organize a mass "ditching" or "blowout," absence from school takes on the additional significance of indicating who and what form of authority really "runs" the school. In the South Bronx in the 1970s, gangs made cutting class especially attractive by organizing "hooky parties" during school hours in abandoned buildings that directly faced the school.[115]

Just as effectively, students can demonstrate to their clear satisfaction who "runs" the school by remaining within school, structuring relations among students to fit the deviant norms of the street group, and ridiculing the inferiority of the school authority as a power for controlling their world. Horowitz reported that while a member of the Lions in Chicago was given (in absentia) an award at graduation as the best dressed student, he was celebrating the school's ignorance by "drinking wine with the boys out back."[116] As an example of how his "homies" ran the school and controlled the teachers, Tomas, a student in an Orange County continuation school, related how he and friends knifed a boy in shop class and then produced the story that the victim accidentally slipped. Tomas recalled with delight how the teacher, "this fucken' bitch," "fell for the soca."[117]

We are trying to understand the emotional process through which members make their involvement in physically threatening street elites compellingly seductive. No doubt, adolescents often join gangs for the same garden variety of uninspiring motives as do members of conventional groups: a fear of isolation, a desire for status in the eyes of one's peers, boredom, and so forth. But if what we want to explain is the special quality of deviance enacted by physically threatening young street elites, we should look for a correspondingly special charm that mobilizes involvement. The question is not what draws young men to hang out together, but how they draw themselves up into the posture of a street elite. I suggest that the special attraction is not in entering the worlds of formally rational authority and emerging superior on its terms but in a transcendent project. One expression of this project is the fantastic dream of capturing the mundane authority in the world of the street elite and proving it to be absurd and pathetic. In virtually all close ethnographies and detailed autobiographies of the worlds of proudly dreadful adolescent street elites, there is a version of a fantastic dream in which students, through uprisings, kidnappings, or other devices, utilize the collective deviance of the street to humiliate school officials. As Patrick noted:

At the time, Tim was fourteen. He had been expelled by the headmaster, an action which he still resented almost two years later. Tim, however, had struck back: he waited for the man to leave the school one evening, and then, surrounded by his team, had followed him along the road, cursing and swearing at him.[118]

The finest hour of Robby Wideman, a young black who was subsequently imprisoned for participating in a felony murder, came in 1968, when, wielding the symbols of "black power" with a physically threatening militant flourish, he led an assembly of students in the humiliation of the school administrators.[119] And from his high school days in East Los Angeles in the early 1970s, Gus Frias depicted what ensued when Lil Crow, who "proudly wore a blue head-band, a white T-shirt and grey khaki pants low-riding to the floor," walked into class late one day after "toking-up on a Oaxacan marihuana cigarrete [sic] on his way to school" and was ordered to the principal's office by the teacher:

> Very calmly, with a very accentured voice, he replied, "Say listen lady, don't make a big thing out of nothing, just mark me late and that's it. O.K.?" This strong response really infuriated the teacher as she said, "God damn! Nobody is going to answer me that way, your lack of respect condemns you to expulsion, young man!" Lil Crow with a sarcastic laugh and with an angry attitude threw his books to the floor and concluded by saying, "You know what lady? I've had enough with you!" He took out a .38 automatic and pointed it at the teacher. This really tripped everyone out. . . . Paul, in the background, jokingly said to Lil Crow, "Go ahead, Homeboy, be a little crazy, shoot her!!" This phrase was also repeated by another student, everyone in the class was in suspense. . . .[120]

The Transcendent Fascinations of Street Life

All the emotionally compelling activities examined thus far—battles and reviews of strategic intelligence, parading, strategies for expressing an inviolable superiority over mundane authorities—seduce their adherents with a common emotional logic. All are ways of enacting the transcendent superiority of what is subjectively "here"—a local neighborhood, a group of intimate friends, a sensual involvement—over what is encountered "there," at a distance, as anonymous strangers—those who live in other neighborhoods, passersby on the street, school officials who may not even be known as "teacher" but as "lady," whose normative world may be appreciated only as incomprehensible "noise" produced by a "flapping mouth." But even considered cumulatively, overt battles, parades, and acts of rebellion in the face of mundane authority still are relatively rare moments; by themselves, they are insufficient to sustain an involvement in the deviant spirit of an elitist street group.

"Street life" is the indispensably rich font for making participation in an intimidating elite an everyday experience. While in school, the adolescent may employ sartorial devices that constantly and subtly strike up an essential affiliation with street life. On the East Coast in the 1950s and 1960s, adolescents reproduced the sound of the streets in high school corridors by wearing metal taps on the soles of their shoes. Hats—bowler types for American black youths in the 1960s, furled knit caps among Mexican-Americans, and Rastafarian knit caps among London-born blacks—have also been popular for indicating that one's relationship to an enclosing institution is, at most, a temporary pause in a transcendent journey conducted outside.

"Streets," referred to with no further particularization, are generic devices for going from "here," an established, immediately familiar starting point, to "there," an initially removed destination that can be occupied and possessed as "here" only in the future and with effort. Adolescents—even those who "got a good brain," get high marks, and do not cut class—generally revel in "street life"; the phrase evokes a romantically mysteri- ous, independent place, where dangerous, vaguely evil, downright sexy events transpire.[121] "Street walkers" and "girls of the street" are prosti- tutes; runaways "live on the streets," and, although all cars are literally machines for transportation over streets, "street machines" are especially designed for the challenges of drag racing and are figuratively "bad." Members of fighting youth groups are fascinated with being *street* groups. They celebrate the transcendent accomplishment of treating as their emo- tionally natural home what is treated conventionally only as a means of passing from "here" to "there."

Consider the conversational terms that have a special charm in street talk. Adolescents who have known each other for years may refer to each other as "man" to begin turns in a conversation and then to punctuate their speech with the flavor of street life. "Man" may be attractive for its elevation to maturity of males who might well be seen as boys, but the age reference is not essential to the charm. "Dude," rendered as *vato* in South- western hispanic communities, often substitutes for "man." It is not age emphatic; it has a respectful overtone in that it identifies the other as someone surviving out in the world, like a nineteenth-century cowboy from the Wild West who was also slick or learned in the ways of the city. "Jack," long popular in black street talk, can accomplish a similar effect even though it could as easily be applied to a child as to a man. As with "man," "dude," or "vato," with "Jack" the speaker can transform a famil- iar friend into an anonymous other, thereby lending to whatever ensues the significance of affairs conducted not on the safe turf of home but out there in the world, among adult strangers, where one encounters unfamil- iar challenges.[122]

Another theme from street life is the attempt by one acquaintance to con another. The best ethnographic material for examining such tactics comes from black street life (although it certainly is not limited to the black culture), where the process has been known as, among other things, putting on a "front." Keiser presented a rich example from the Vice Lords. Tico asked Goliath for twenty-five cents to buy wine and Goliath replied, "I'll take care of you"; but he made no move to provide the money.

[Tico:] Shit man, we Vice Lords. We supposed to be brothers. Come on, Jack, I gotta get me a taste.
[Goliath:] I'll take care of you. You know that. Now I need forty for a Polish [sausage], twenty-five for carfare, fifty to get my baby some milk . . . shit! I'm fifteen cents short. Say man, can you loan me fifteen cents?
Tico shook his head, and walked away in disgust.

Keiser added that Goliath had ten dollars in his pocket and that Tico also had sufficient money that he did not need the loan.[123]

Note how devious wit transcends the potential humiliation of poverty. Disingenuously, Goliath exploited a lack of funds—a powerful sign of vulnerability and dependence—as an interactional resource for a dramatic personal triumph. Poverty became relatively insignificant in contrast to a capacity to move gracefully in a potentially humiliating social world out "there." Tico and Goliath knew each other well; to conduct their example of "whuffing the game," they had to pose as strangers to each other, each presenting to the other an artificial, potentially subordinating line of action, each testing the other's ability to see through a foreign guise and recognize a familiar, and then no longer threatening, ploy. In the end, Goliath triumphed, not by convincing Tico that he did not have the money but through showing Tico that he knew this ploy (or "play"). His triumph was transcendent in a double sense; he emerged a master not a victim of artificial style, and he showed that he had no emotional need for Tico's affections. For in this setting, to satisfy Tico's request would be a humiliating demonstration of gullible naivete, of a fear of being out in the world without the support of friends, or both.

The same testing of a graceful personal competence to transcend potentially humiliating foreign challenges can be seen in the "mock" fighting in which young males of all ethnicities engage on street corners in low-income urban areas.[124] In this interaction, friends square off in boxing stances and conduct something more unique than a fight or a mock fight. Each does not go all out to beat up the other. The challenge is not simply physical dominance; it is essential to retain some semblance of an institutionally regulated boxing style, even if the style is unconventional and includes, for example, some karate-like leg kicks. But neither do the participants simply cooperate in a dramatization of the maneuvers of a real fight.

The challenge is not simply to enact a fighting form, as in a cooperative dance.

The mock fight is a more interesting, uncertain process in which one or both play with the mock or serious character of the blows thrown. This puts meanness specifically at issue. Some blows will be thrown to raise the questions, Does the other mean it? Has this become a real fight? Can I hold my own in this interaction *both* in the physical sense of not being beaten up and in the moral sense of not breaking form and sacrificing dignity to effect a successful defense? As in intergroup battles, the outcome may be decided clearly when one side breaks style and runs off a little way from the battle scene.

The essential fascination of the street elite is as an outpost of spiritual creativity—a collective base located beyond the member's primary home from which he can work up an arrogant posture directed toward potential threats of humiliation emanating from some socially distant "there." Many studies have found that the status of group leader (whether formal, as in white, black, and Puerto Rican groups, or informal, as in Mexican-American barrios) does not depend on physical, athletic, or fighting prowess. Esthetic leadership appears to be the key. Depending on the ethnic setting, this type of leadership may involve a striking elegance in dancing:

> [Duke, despite being small in stature, was leader of the "King Rattlers," a black gang in Chicago in the late 1950s. Duke was not only] fearless and effective. . . . he could dance well enough to "turn out" most anyone in the neighborhood—other dancers typically cleared an area for him and his partner.[125]

Or it may require an everyday demeanor in which a laconic toughness is combined with an aristocratic, well-traveled air:

> [Dick, known as "the King" of one of the fighting teams in Glasgow, maintained an exceptionally elegant appearance. Entering a local bar, he would make a round, shaking hands like a visiting dignitary, looking] for all the world like the Duke of Edinburgh.[126]

Such leadership may also call for the mastery of street talk that the leader uses not so much to put down other members as to sustain the group's legends and the personal myths of members. Among London's skinheads, Dave had an admired reputation for patter such as, Who the 'am spam do you think you am, you think you're body everyself, pick on somebody your own long enough, if you get the opportunity rub off."[127] Carlos Parkin, aka Frijole, aka Bean, displayed the street poetry that helped sustain his informal leadership of the Sesentas, a combative barrio group from Oakland, in the following poetic resolve concerning outside youths:

They fuck around, they lay around.
They play they pay
They do they through.[128]

Krisberg, commenting on his observations and extensive interviews with black gang leaders in Philadelphia, was especially struck by the leaders' esthetic burdens:

> The gang leader possessed a keen insight into the personal myths of each of his gang fellows. . . . Past activities were glorified and portrayed as dramatic events. . . . buttressing self-images and attenuating self-doubts. [Explained one leader] "You know, Barry, the most important thing in the world to a dude is recognition. Pay attention to them, man, and they'll do anything you want." Another . . . explained: "I know that shit I say to them guys is bullshit—but they did [*sic*] it, man and they dig me."[129]

In effect, the leader's task is to charm his fellows into a faith that, as members of the group, they can go into that world beyond their primary home where one meets anonymous, potentially humiliating strangers and retain their pride. Leaders must exhibit a special charm, literally a saving grace, when they go out onto the streets. Bloch and Niederhoffer observed, among white street gang leaders in New York City in the 1950s,

> the spectacle of a young hoodlum, known to be a terror in gang fights, an expert burglar, and an accomplished ladies' man, to boot, who suddenly stops to use a store window for a mirror, takes out a comb, and carefully pats a wave in his beautifully set pompadour.[130]

The whole group, as well as the leader, provides analogous support for the street lives of the members. The transcendent significance of the group is recreated constantly in the routine conversational juxtaposition of demeaning personal names and inspiring collective titles. The nicknames of individual members are often denigrating: "two boys in our Los Angeles gangs with severe skin problems were known as 'Cornflakes' and 'Potato Face,' a boy with glasses was called 'Goggles,' and a Mexican boy given a mascot role in a Negro gang was called 'Taco' ";[131] Espestoso (Stinky), Flaco (Skinny), Fool, and Fat Rolls are not uncommon. But the group's name is never demeaning, and often it is glorious. The essence of the group's appeal is indicated by the poetic labels given to intergroup violence. Terms are drawn from music, as in "bopping" or "diddy bopping" (be-bop in jazz); from literature, as in "humbugs" (Scrooge's memorable phrase of disgust); and from dance, as in "jitterbugging." They all indicate a soaring delight in the violence that others regard as horrifying.[132]

On a daily basis, group support for the members' glorious transcendence from a familiar "here" to the larger world of anonymous strangers out "there" may include the provision of a refuge from "the streets" in the form of a "corner" (a clubhouse or store) that the group is known to dominate and within which members can relax and from which members can prepare a proud demeanor for excursions through the streets. From his observations in San Francisco in the early 1960s, Werthman described the demeanor of black and Mexican-American gang members on their group's corner:

> A noticeable relaxation of physical posture. Shoulders slump, shirt tails appear, and greetings are exchanged with an abandon. . . .
> As soon as the boys leave the street corner, however, they become self-consciously absorbed in the demands of public role. Careful attention is paid to uniform—either carelessly immaculate ("looking sharp") or meticulously dishevelled ("looking bad")—and the territory is covered in the characteristic hiking style ("walking pimp").[133]

The transcendent significance of the street elite for members is nowhere more concrete than in the practice of what might be called urban camping out. At one time or another, many members will "live in the streets": sleeping in cars, sheds, stores, and abandoned apartments or with friends; drinking wine, using drugs, shooting craps; "hustling," a form of urban hunting in which one seeks money and food through theft, petty extortion, and conning "loans"; and moving around the neighborhood independent of school and workday schedules. For living on the streets, the street elite is a significant source of assistance for locating food and temporary residences and a locally recognizable symbol useful for extorting money from younger or independent youths. Perhaps more important, the street elite supports members through its role as an audience that is uniquely well situated to appreciate one's mysterious comings and goings. While maintaining a discreet distance from his parents, the street hustler can demonstrate to his observant peers that he is "out there," "making it" on his own.[134]

Phenomenal Foreground and Structural Background

The recipe for the creation of a street elite is one part exotic status pretensions; some ingredients of dread, including at least enough violence to counter attacks that ridicule the elite pretensions; and stirring esthetics that promise the glorious mastery of a larger, anonymous, morally threatening social world that is vaguely apprehended out there. Each pattern may exist independent of the street elite but when combined they bring it to life.

But what social conditions lie behind the experience of becoming involved in a street elite? How do these processes relate to biographical and ecological dimensions, such as age, urban setting, social class, and ethnicity? If the preceding analysis accurately explains the foreground of constructing the world of the street elite, what is the background to which members respond when they assume the elitist posture, implement it in public through an aura of dread, and stir themselves to its distinctive transcendent project?

CIRCULAR REASONING IN THE TRADITIONAL APPROACH

It has been traditional in American sociology to define the problematic phenomenon as that of the gang and to look for ultimate causes in the conditions of urban, minority group, adolescent poverty. But the guiding definition of the "gang" is not only somehow uncomfortable for its subjects; the concept is a fateful step in a process of circular social analysis. As long as we define the problem to be explained as that of the "gang," we tend to seek relevant data only in the adolescent segment of ghetto society. We then find that key background factors lie in the struggles of adolescence, the pressures of urban life, the bitterness of poverty in an affluent society, the resentment of ethnically oppressed populations, and so forth. After over fifty years of work, the now dogged-edged sociological explanation of the gang has not yet broken out of this circular pattern; the appreciation of the phenomenon still chases its explanatory tail.

One route of escape is to look as closely at the experience of the subjects as qualitative data, in the most widespread and rich forms available, will allow. Immediately, we run into difficulties for some of the standard background explanations. In Great Britain—East London, Glasgow, and Northern Ireland—there are prominent examples of gangs that are dedicated to intergroup violence, the members of which often commit burglaries and occasionally attack adults.[135] British theorists cannot point convincingly to minority ethnic status for explanations; instead, they emphasize the tensions of class inequality. In the United States, recent research on Mexican-American neighborhood group fighters, many of whom have substantial criminal records for burglary and assault, has presented problems when explanations emphasize class oppositions. In their studies of the 32nd Street community in Chicago, Ruth Horowitz and Gary Schwartz discounted the explanatory value of social incompetence and frustration of material aspirations:

On the whole, the members of this community meet the basic require ments for inclusion in what mainstream America views as the socially respectable and politically significant segments of the working class. Mexican-Americans hold steady jobs and make a decent living. Very few intact families are on welfare. . . . The majority of young people in this community speak English fluently and command the verbal skills necessary to negotiate their way through urban institutions. . . . gang members have not opted out of the American dream.[136]

Not finding a basis to emphasize the causal relevance of economic inequality, the authors must emphasize the status of their subjects as ethnic aliens ("Mexican-Americans are outsiders in the urban community").[137]

If sociological theorizing looks just across the edge of adolescence, it runs into the disturbing phenomenon of motorcycle clubs like the Hell's Angels. The collective raison d'être of these groups of white, ethnic-majority young men of working-class backgrounds, from large and from small cities, was originally the dreadful practice of parading over highways and the conduct of battles, not with the police or the innocent folk portrayed as choice victims in media accounts, but with other proud, terrifying motorcycle clubs.[138]

The social distribution of street elites cannot be universally related to minority ethnic status, consistently attributed to class tensions, or empirically limited to the stresses of adolescence. Indeed, as I will suggest later, the phenomena to be explained are not even necessarily urban. Yet, class, ethnic, age, and urban factors are not randomly represented in the background of street elites. As I detailed in the first section of this chapter, if we compare ghetto and middle-class forms of collective, youthful deviance in the West since the end of World War II, we find the characteristic structure of street elites clearly concentrated in urban ghettoes.

We can make sense of this complex of patterns in two steps. First, we may note that deviant adolescent cultures include a shared moral concern, with transcendence expressed in a spatial metaphor. Across social classes and ethnic groups, adolescents in the modern West have developed forms of deviance in response to sensed challenges for moving from local environments to an anonymous, strange world out "there." Second, I suggest that deviant projects of transcendence differ when the local environment differs. In particular, Western adolescents have developed collective forms of deviance that embrace the fears or powers that haunt and intimidate their elders. In the recent history of the West, these lines of anxiety and apprehension have differed by social class and ethnicity and, therefore, so has the social distribution of street elites. In other times and places, the background of humiliation to which street elites have formed a transcendent response has not been concentrated in the urban, adolescent, ethnic-minority and lower-class sections of society.

SPATIAL MOBILITY AND COLLECTIVE DELINQUENCY

The distinctive adolescent celebrations of deviance that have flourished in the modern West, at least since the Second World War, display innumerable metaphors of spatial mobility. Thus, in numerous American and British cities, adolescent men have dressed themselves up in symbols of high-risk movement, donning costumes of motorcycle jackets, boots, and gloves, and viciously attacked other, similarly dressed adolescents, over "turf" boundaries. That the combatants may have no motorcycles, and that the territorial "control" they seek may have no economic or material significance, gives them no necessary pause.

Generally, the names of street elites give the identities of members a geographic significance.[139] When names of streets of neighborhoods are not incorporated, adolescent ghetto fighting groups may take titles that boast more generalized geographic powers. Like totemic tribes, they imagine themselves animals that range widely and freely: Eagles, Lions, and Sharks. Or they recall distant, ancient, obscure images of forceful or heroic Rangers, Crusaders, Marathons, Nomads, and Barbarians. Lords, Barons, and Dukes are common, but names that would place members at the top of powerful, wealthy, or prestigious hierarchies without suggesting that their dominance also has a geographic dimension—CEO, Millionaire, or Champion—are rare.[140]

The placement of graffiti similarly reflects a special sensitivity to the movements of people from "here" to "there." In New York City, graffiti writers run substantial physical and legal risks to "write" (spray paint) names, slogans, and images, some of them emphatically threatening, on subway trains. They have not developed a similar attraction to sites that dominate purely through vertical ascendence, such as the top stories of prominent buildings. Notably, New York graffiti writing became known on the streets as "getting up" only in the mid-1970s, when graphic forms of graffiti began to attract conventional indicia of success (art school scholarships, university classes, museum shows, and intellectual commentaries). Originally, the "writers" produced a simple combination of their name and street number (for example, Pete 188 was Pete from 188th Street) and talked about their activity as "getting around, getting over, and getting the name out."[141] In East Los Angeles, buses and highway overpasses are favored sites for graffiti (and sometimes the legend, "Sal si puedes"); alleys, fences, garages, and walls of buildings that form borders between barrios are the targets of the most challenging and threatening graffiti.[142]

As was already noted, "streets" share only the feature of facilitating movement from here to there, and across the country, as well as across youth subcultures, "street life" and "street people" conjure up an aura of deviance.[143] In black and Hispanic ghettoes, the position that sociologists often label "gang leader" may more commonly be referred to by members as the "runner." Often it is difficult to discern from interviews with street gang adolescents the legal forms of the deviance with which they so proudly associate because they prefer to express themselves in the rich metaphor of spatial mobility:

My life ain't been no playtoy. I mean, I had to really get out there and get it myself. Cause, like, I was traveling so fast like, it was a hell of a thing.[144]

If these examples point to a natural experience among ghetto youths of deviant freedom and power as a matter of spatial mobility, this adolescent fascination is not limited by ethnic and class lines. In the 1970s, Chicanos and Anglos in a suburban high school east of Los Angeles related to each other in threatening postures as "low riders" relating to "surfers."[145] In the rest of the country, "surfer" may provoke memories of peachy-cheeked, benignly smiling Beach Boys, but in adolescent circles on the east and west sides of Los Angeles, "surfer" frequently suggests an ill-shaven, overly physical, and vaguely threatening young man.

Adolescents are even likely to package activities with powerful hedonistic attractions in a spatial metaphor to enhance the pleasure of consuming deviance. Affluent adolescents have long concentrated their nonviolent deviant pleasures on cars and vans. Thus, an observational study in a Los Angeles suburb in the early 1960s found that deviance essentially consisted of presumptively enjoying the hedonistic privileges of adult status, of which the car was literally and figuratively the vehicle. A mobile parlor, bedroom, clubhouse, and bar, the car "was at once the setting and symbol of much of adolescent deviant . . . sociality and sexuality."[146]

A few years later, youths from the same backgrounds were elaborating a fascination with spatial mobility through the hippie movement. As an English observer noted:

There was a concern both with travelling, often to the East in Europe, and across the United States in America, or to South America. This was seen both as a geographical and a symbolic journey. It was also felt that one should move oneself, by drug use, mysticism, religion or by self-exploration. Any journey was then both physical and existential.[147]

The quintessential hippie experience was the "trip."

THE MORAL DIALECTICS OF YOUTHS AND ELDERS

If there is a cross-class adolescent fascination with deviance as a matter of spatial mobility, the vertical dimension of mobility is given radically different meaning in the class-specific forms of collective youth deviance. Middle-class, ethnic majoritarian adolescents oppose convention as if from below, whereas lower-class, ethnic-minority youths strut above the social order. Tying both forms together is the logic of generating a powerful presence by embracing the fears of the older generation, which vary by class and ethnicity.

It is crucial to appreciate that the thrust of collective violence between youth groups is defined less through adolescents' independent orientation to what may lie "out there" beyond local worlds (such as, their apprehensions about their economic futures) than as their moral transcendence of the social order with which they are intimately familiar. There are indications that involvement in street elites is inversely related to a direct focus by members on their disadvantaged class or ethnic status in the larger society. For example, Krisberg was struck by the distance of members of black gangs in Philadelphia in the 1960s from the emergence of civil rights consciousness within the black community as a whole. He noted that members had to be instructed repeatedly that it was no longer acceptable to use "colored folks," especially before whites.[148] And in a study of Mexican-American gang activity in Los Angeles, Howard Erlanger examined historical trends in incidents of intergroup violence and found evidence to suggest that the emergence of an ethnic civil rights self-consciousness in the early 1970s was responsible for a decrease in warfare in the barrio.[149]

The natural history of membership in adolescent street elites also suggests that involvement is inversely related to a focus on the relationship between the ghetto and conventional life outside. Although the age of desistance varies from one setting to the next, everywhere the most fanatical recruits enter at the earlier ages, and attrition accelerates toward the end of adolescence. From 18 to 22 or so, as members become more practically attentive to their place in the larger social order, membership becomes less attractive.

Just as youthful middle-class white beats, hippies, and punks have drawn disgust and a moral horror from their elders by mapping out various lines of their parents' moral fears, so do lower-class, ethnic-minority street fighting groups dramatically embrace forms of social power to which their elders have shown moral horror.[150] The tensions in collective youth deviance are shaped in dialectical relationship to the unspeakable fears in their elders' lives. Thus, middle-class youths represent dirt, the violation of all neat boundaries, lower-class rebellion, insidious esthetic attacks on the conventions of bourgeois, rule-manipulating, rationality-celebrating classes. In contrast, working-class youths embrace fascist forms that give a surreal, lock-step representation to the mechanical institutional disciplines that threaten to constrain their parents;[151] and ethnic-minority lower-class youths strut in the style of aristocratic authority, acting out a version of historical caste sentiments of humility and indignation that remain vivid for their elders.[152]

In the generational or social ecological background of U.S. ghetto gangs has been one or another recent immigration in which the moral feelings and symbolic systems of peasants, tenant farmers, sharecroppers, and migrant laborers have been kept alive. Behind the New York City gangs of the 1880s described by Asbury was the massive immigration of impoverished, rural Irish people. Behind the extraordinary variety of Chicago's

Southern and Eastern European youth gangs of the 1920s, as described by Thrasher, was the Polish peasant, the Italian peasant, and so on.[153] After the legal shutdown of massive immigration of foreign poor people to the United States, the ethnic character of the gang problem became black in the North and Midwest as poor blacks abandoned family histories of tenant farming and sharecropping to move north in the 1950s and 1960s. Behind the 1960s' British "rude boy," with a crop of hair plaited in "the ubiquitous natty or knotty style" and "wardrobe of sinister guerilla chic," was a wave of politically and socially conservative West Indian immigrants in the 1950s.[154] Behind much of contemporary urban American gang fighting is the uniquely continuing access to the United States of impoverished people from rural areas and small towns in Mexico and Puerto Rico.[155]

In England, the skinheads' famous proclivity for "Paki" bashing, carried to the point of unprovoked murder, was part of a broader racism that attacked hippies; the Jews who had been moving up and out of East London; and the colored immigrants from East Asia and the West Indies, who came in large numbers in the 1960s. Most directly, the antagonism is to groups that may be treated as inferiors in a caste-ordered society, not to more affluent classes. This hostility is vividly expressed in the following excerpt:

> We've still got the yids, Pakis, wogs, 'ippies on our backs. They use us and live off us. . . . We're in the middle, ain't we, and what can we do? I'll tell you what we fucking do, we go Paki-bashing and 'ippie-bashing. . . . Why should we be tolerant to people that they have invited into the country? We didn't invite them.[156]

In American materials, a similar downward prejudice is found, and not only among protofascist whites. The following dialogue occurred among members of the Sex Boys and Sex Girls, a Puerto Rican (and substantially black) street elite of the 1970s from Essex Street in Brooklyn:

> America really doesn't want foreigners like me coming in, but right now Puerto Rico isn't foreign.
>   Yeah, Dominican. Cuban. All those kind of people.
>   They can come on a boat. They can come on a boat from Santa Domingo to Puerto Rico. A lot of them get caught though, but a lot of them get in. And that's what fucks up the country.[157]

Ethnographies and unedited firsthand accounts from Mexican-American fighting barrios show an ironic hostility toward poor, *campesino*-styled Mexicans. In recalling his days as a barrio warrior in East Los Angeles, Gus Frias did not retouch the ugly prejudice that his U.S.-born homeboys enacted toward "wetbacks" or *mojados,* the recently arrived Mexican immigrants whose Indian appearance and rural ways have frequently subjected them to ridicule by U.S.-born, adolescent Mexican-Americans. He recounted

> an incident in which a wetback, a name we gave to those individuals that did not know how to speak the English language, decided to give a hard time to one of the homeboys whom we called "Chito." This homeboy, in a demanding tone of voice, asked the wetback for a dime. The wetback stubbornly refused, and in return pushed Chito to the ground. . . . [later] around thirty homeboys headed toward the wetbacks' special hang-out. . . .[158]

This was not an isolated incident. In Chicago, American-born Mexican-origin youths use "brazer" (from *bracero*) to disparage "newly arrived Mexicans" who "dress in straight-legged pants, cowboy boots, and hats . . . speak only Spanish . . . [and are] not too smart."[159] In a description of two East Los Angeles high schools, a student researcher quoted Rosie B:

> Students at ["Evergreen"] High School respect the Mexican from Mexico in a awful manner, they push him around, call him names, make fun of the way he dresses, make fun of his family.

From the other side, a recent arrival from Mexico, Mario A, wrote for the same report that "the problem between Mexicans and Chicanos are that the Chicanos think they are bad."[160]

Today, barrio warriors are likely to be surrounded by neighbors or by older relatives who, as children, worked as poorly paid, stoop farm laborers and who did not dare raise a note of protest in public, much less adopt the demeanor of superiority. The prejudice they generate toward mojados was in many cases suffered not long ago by their kinsmen. Despite the long history of the Mexican-origin population in the United States, immigration policies and market pressures have made the contemporary Mexican-American population in California overwhelmingly either Mexican-born or the U.S.-born children of Mexican-born parents.[161] In Chicago, Horowitz and Schwartz wrote, the Mexican-American youths living around 32nd Street seemed to be in constant contact with relatives moving up from the world still referred to as that of the bracero; when they got in trouble with the police in Chicago, they often escaped temporarily to agricultural valleys in Texas.[162] Many turf fighters display a dutiful respect for parents who sacrificed dearly to move the family from northern Mexico or from an agricultural valley in the Southwest to the big city of Chicago, Los Angeles, or Oakland, California.[163]

Members of the two major, mutually hostile street gangs in the densely black ghetto of south central Los Angeles are now a generation or two away from southern migrant roots. But they have kept alive the symbolic lines of racial oppression with a neat symbolic scheme. The Bloods, identifying with red, and the Crips, with blue, can and regularly do attack each other simply and specifically on the basis of color.

Within the social worlds of black ghetto street elites, caste sensitivities remain vivid in the sensual realms of taste and distaste. A young black woman from southeast Brooklyn recalled from her early teenage days in the Puma Crew, a shoplifting group of friends that was part of the local intergroup street fighting scene, why she broke off her relationship with Sam, a thief who had given her money liberally:

To a degree I wanted to have sex with Sam and stuff, you know, but he turned me off.

[Researcher:] Why? Not good-looking?

He is very good-looking.

[Researcher:] So why did he turn you off?

Because it's the way he talk.

[Researcher:] His whole attitude?

Yeah. The way he talked. Stupid. Don't make no damn sense. I tell him everything. Take him to the store, you got to tell him to buy. . . . He heard me talking about him like this, he'd want to kick my ass.

[Researcher:] But he was good-looking, gave you stuff, thought you were great. Why didn't you like him?

'Cos he gave me everything. A man can't give you everything. 'Cos he spoiled me, that's why. I kicked him in his ass, shit.

[Researcher:] So he wasn't much of a man?

No. Down south. Don't even know how to speak proper English, you know? Don't even know how to read, write. Naive motherfucker.[164]

Being "Down south" and a "Naive motherfucker" go together. Rural naivete means humiliating subordination; anyone who is more urbane, even a woman, can kick your ass. These moral concerns are more important than the unusual amount of money Sam provided. As in the gaming interaction between Tico and Goliath reviewed earlier, for the speaker here, poverty is less humiliating than being a fool. Black street culture keeps alive the feel of the naive country "down south" in the figure of that eternal premodern figure, the fool. Adolescent street elites will make sense in black ghettoes where Suttles' observations of twenty years ago continue to hold true: "Among the Negroes in the Addams area, the major identities that have to be avoided are those denoted by the labels 'country,' 'savage,' 'nigger,' and 'Uncle Tom.' "[165]

Consider whether the following features of street elites point to conditions of poverty, adolescence, minority group status, urban location, and so forth, or to historically recurrent forms of authority for lording power over the rural masses of an agrarian society and over the working class in a fascist social order.

Right-Wing Militarism.   Street elites often sport swastikas and German crosses. Some black and Puerto Rican adolescents in New York City enjoy calling themselves the Gestapo, and others adopt the imagery of the Chinese warlord and the Japanese samurai. Yet long, scraggly beards that are reminiscent of Marx and Castro never seem to come into fashion, despite their value for indicating masculine maturity. Members are not comrades; their militaristic parading does not celebrate the washed-out sartorial banality of peasant armies. The hammer and sickle are not worn on motorcycle jackets,[166] despite the wonderful outrage and fear that would be produced. When inducted into a Polish-Hungarian-German-Italian gang in 1950s Brooklyn, Ellison recalled being asked, "Are you a Jew or a nigger or a communist?", but not whether he was a fascist.[167]

Aristocratic Status.   Like members of high society, in a tradition now going back at least thirty years, Southern European, black, and Hispanic male street elites have recognized their female counterparts as "debs" or "debutantes." In Chicago, Mexican-American society around 32nd Street celebrates the Catholic confirmation of girls at age 15 with elaborate parties called cotillions, which members of fighting gangs attend in the dress and demeanor of *galanes* from traditional Mexican society. Some leaders of the Blackstone Rangers favored wide-brimmed southern planter's hats and riding crops. The nicknames that are almost universal in street elites reflect the same celebration of status as do the informal names by which members of High Society recognize each other: a delight in signifying that one's essential identity is not really known or controlled by birth certificates or the other bureaucratic instruments of the modern, rational-legal social order.

Physiocracy.   Violence is concentrated in public spaces, such as parks, and tensions recurrently focus on the control of "turf." Instead of simply robbing victims, street elites manifest their collective elite status by exacting tribute. Like urban physiocrats, street elites act as if all social respect ultimately comes from the control of landmarks, homelands, and residential territory. Like idle lords and barons who manifest the privileges of their status by not rationally organizing their holdings, members of street elites make taken-for-granted references to "running" a school, "owning" a movie theater, or "controlling" a neighborhood, although they do not exact tribute systematically, collect the revenues from a theater, or attempt to control much of anything that goes on behind the private doors of their neighborhood.

Collected across their various ethnic and historical versions, street elites make for extraordinarily bizarre populations. Considering the foreground themes of street elites, the search for causally essential background conditions does not stop with poverty, ethnic-minority status, adolescence, or even urban location, but reaches to the press of peasantlike populations to enter the modern world. From there, it extends to an ironically incompatible set of analytic bedfellows: postadolescent members of white working-class motorcycle clubs; Ku Klux Klanners, outfitted like ghosts and ritually stratified, bent on terrifying poor blacks into a symbolic acknowledgment of white territorial rule; demogogic juntas that rule by martialing terror in the streets of Latin America; and the historical mythologies of European and Asian fascism.

Of course, modern English and American urban adolescent street elites have no practical function in forcefully oppressing the peasant masses. They must deign themselves Lords and Emperors because, even though they act like samurai or knights, no land baron keeps them on a retainer. In effect, "gangs" are primarily an urban, minority-group, adolescent phenomena in North American and British cities because the ways of street elites have not found broader economic or political markets for their services. When street elites have found such markets, such as the Calabrian and Sicilian mafiosi in Southern Italy, an analogous aggressive/elite culture has not been primarily an urban phenomenon. In Japan, the *yakuza* organize corrupt labor relations for bosses, most famously in the entertainment industry, and make secretive alliances with extreme right-wing political movements. Like the American street elites, the yakuza tend to come from ethnically disadvantaged populations—*sangokujin* (or "third country" Korean and Chinese) and *eta*, a feudal class of untouchables whose family lines have not been forgotten in modern Japan—and they are mostly *burakumin* (or ghetto dwellers). Unlike American "gangs," however, they organize a collective social world that governs not just adolescence but the whole lifespan.[168]

I am suggesting that the longstanding association in the United States of street elites with urban, ethnic-minority, adolescent poverty groups is causally spurious. None of these social conditions, alone or in combination, is necessary for the social construction of the phenomenon. What is essential is the existence, in the generational background, of a culture humbled at the prospect of entering modern, rationalized society. In the United States, this culture has been constituted recurrently by masses of recently arrived, previously rural, and initially deferential poor people and continuously by the caste-segregation of blacks. In the experience of the would-be terrifying elite, this humbled background, by way of juxtaposition, elicits and makes sense of the postures of arrogant domination.

CHAPTER 5

Doing Stickup

There is a central paradox in the contemporary social reality of robbery. Many of the "heaviest" robbers—those who commit dozens of offenses over a period of years in a self-consciously shaped criminal career—create elaborate symbols and practical patterns that attest to a rational, utilitarian justification for being "professionals." Yet they shape their lives in ways that make it reasonable to expect that they will spend many years of their youth in prison. What are they trying to do?

If robbers are just trying to get money the best way they know how, why don't they focus more on the money they might get? Street robberies or muggings are almost by necessity spur-of-the-moment affairs, but even commercial robberies commonly develop out of quickly made plans. And there appears to be little increase in the sophistication of planning with age and experience.[1] The legal penalty for robbery does not depend on the amount taken, but even "career" robbers usually do not try to ascertain that there will be substantial money on hand when they strike. Despite their old image as jobs for "professionals," even bank robberies are "basically hit and run affairs with minimal 'casing' of the bank or banking practices. As a result, the amount of money obtained in a bank robbery [is] largely the result of chance."[2]

How much do they get? According to national samples of victims, the losses were as much as $250 or more in only 25 percent of the noncommercial robberies in 1985.[3] According to national police statistics, the average taken in 1986 during robberies of gas or service stations was $303.[4] Ethnographic evidence indicates that burglary and robbery, the most lucrative non-drug crimes, average only about $80.[5]

Bank robbers initially do much better. For 1986, their average take was $2,664.[6] But they do much worse at getting away. The "clearance" rates for robbery are notoriously suspect, but the common estimates are that the police at least think they know who did the crime in 10–20 percent of the reported cases. Statistical information on bank robberies is much more reliable; it shows that about 80 percent of the bank robberies are solved.[7]

It is possible to work toward a cost-benefit analysis of robbery by multiplying the figures for average "takes" against "get-away-with-it" percentages. If we do, we find that robbers appear to get away with many offenses, but their self-reports indicate that they face arrest about one in five to ten offenses.[8] And arrests for robbery lead to convictions and imprisonment in a high percentage of cases.[9] But such calculations are beset by tricky assumptions and the haunting possibility that there is a small set of skilled and exceptionally successful offenders who escape the averages.

More convincing are life histories, which indicate that however many offenses robbers may get away with, to persist in robbery for several years, they must anticipate a break in their career for a long term of incarceration. In the many excellent contemporary biographies and autobiographies, there are not even any legends, much less firsthand accounts, of robbers whose careers were unblemished by prison terms. In England, where prison terms are generally much shorter than in the United States, Laurie Taylor reported, from his recent travels in the London underworld: "I could not find a single example of a robber who had not at some time in his career served a sentence of at least eight years."[10]

In any case, we need not worry that a set of successful robbers will pop up to undermine the image of substantial imprisonment as an anticipated cost of robbers' careers. "Hardcore predatory felons" in a recent large-scale, broad based study of prisoners, averaged 10 prior arrests and 3 prior imprisonments.[11] Even if *some* robbers always get away with it, a substantial part of the contemporary problem of robbery obviously consists of offenders who persist, knowing that they have not.[12] What are *they* trying to do?

Perhaps persistence is simply an indication of how limited are the offenders' alternative ways of making money. By all measures—police reports, arrests, and convictions; surveys of victims; self-reports obtained from prisoners; the autobiographical and informant contents of life histories—robberies are overwhelmingly committed by men who are poor and, in recent U.S. history, black. To many commentators, the contemporary problem of robbery is easily understood as a way in which people with unusually limited means obtain what the commercial culture encourages everyone to need. Or, if poverty and the lack of economic opportunity do not themselves direct men toward robbery, they are often thought to create a range of associated social problems, such as drug addiction, which regularly do.

But if persistent robbers do not have attractive legal means for making money, many have alternative illegal means. Several studies have identified a small group of persistent offenders, variously labeled "violent predators," "heavies," "habitual felons," and "career criminals," who are responsible for a disproportionate number of the most serious crimes, including robbery. But they are generally not crime specialists who trade exclusively in robbery. They also deal in illegal drugs and commit various other property offenses, as well as personal assault offenses, at unusually high rates.[13]

Consider, as perhaps the best-documented case in point, the criminal career of John Allen, a persistent stickup man from an impoverished black section of Washington, D.C.:

> For a man, pimping is a good way of making money, but the fastest way is narcotics, and the safest and best way of all is numbers. Even though my whores were making a lot of money [he had a "stable" of five at one point], I just didn't like pimping that much. It ain't my style. . . . I missed stickup quite a bit. . . . What I really missed was the excitement of sticking up and the planning and the getting away with it. . . . [As to numbers] I didn't really get into it, just like I didn't like pimping—there wasn't enough excitement to it. . . . [At one point, as a drug dealer] I was doing something like a grand worth of heroin business a day. . . . I was rolling in drugs and rolling good. I'm well off. I'm dressing nice and keeping a knot in my pocket. I've got a nice ride. I've got me a stable of broads, so I'm cool.[14]

But pimping was a twenty-four-hour-a-day job, and "that sex thing was taking a terrible toll on me." The numbers business had a long career ladder that one had to work one's way up through steady service. Drugs became too tempting: Allen got hooked. So, at a time when his pimping business was going well and JoJo, an old friend, jumped bail and came to see him, Allen's response was not to weigh the costs and profitability of alternative opportunities, whether legal or illegal:

> Now, JoJo don't do a whole lot of talking. . . . I dug that he was the kind of dude that I wouldn't mind being with—real quiet but double danger-ous. . . . I said, "What you gonna do now?" And he said, "Well, man, what you gonna do?" I told him, "Well, I really don't dig what I'm doing now." So we both decided that what we wanted to do was hook back up. . . . We began to check out different things, little joints, and we doing a few little robbery-type things. We was just getting by.[15]

By the time he wrote his autobiography, John Allen was 34 years old and had spent about fourteen years in confinement. He was crippled from a police shooting. He was separated from his wife and was depressed. But he was still not sure that he wanted to abandon robbery. Indeed, he was arrested for a robbery committed after he was confined for life to a wheel-chair.

There is now too much evidence to remain complacent with the view that offenders, even persistent and presumably "professional" offenders, approach robbery in the calculating spirit of a money-making opportunity.

The Rand Corporation survey of 2,200 prison inmates, which identified the subgroup of "violent predators" referred to earlier, asked the respondents whether "committing crime against an armed victim is an exciting challenge." Three-quarters of the whole sample said no, but 40 percent of the "predators" agreed. "For a substantial minority of the Predators, in other words, the thrill of confrontation with an armed victim appears to be part of the positive motivation to commit crime."[16]

The characterization that robbers are trying to get money is obviously true in the narrow sense that money is what they demand. But perhaps we have seen enough to open up the seemingly simple question, Just what is it that robbers are trying to do?

When I tried to clarify a criminal project, in the previous chapters, I found it repeatedly necessary to address a line of action substantially different from those formally defined by the criminal law. But unlike most other crimes, the legal prohibition itself is often explicitly embraced by robbers as a definition of what they are doing. Impassioned murderers make sense of their violence as resurrecting the Good; sneak thieves seek to hide the immoral character of their project from their victims; and "warring" adolescent groups deny they are "gangs," often claiming that they are just "kick-back" guys who must, from time to time, avenge the irrational attacks of crazies from other neighborhoods. But robbers, to accomplish the act, find it useful to say, literally, "This is a robbery." Somewhat more commonly, and in a term more evocative for explanatory purposes, they say, "This is a stickup." In either case, they discipline their actions to convey to the victim the commonsense legal definition of the offense: that they are trying to take property by force or the threat of force.

So stickup or, more precisely, the maintenance of a persistent commitment to stickup, will define the problem. I first examine the situationally specific requirements of this form of criminal "career." Chapter 6 addresses the requirements for persisting in the stickup career that are moral in the sense that they are necessary to convince the offender that stickup is something he not only *can* do but *should* do. In chapter 7, I consider the relation of commonly associated background factors to robbery. There is no denying the contemporary correlations with male gender, poverty, and American black ethnic identity. We can best understand these background statistics if we first try to specify just what the project of robbery means to offenders.

We can distinguish three recurrent stages in the practice of doing a stickup. Commonly differentiated as phases in the offender's experience, these are sets of contingencies that may interrupt the completion of any given offense. The experience of repeatedly confronting these problems leads frequent offenders to develop customary styles of attack and a particular understanding of self.

1. *Subjective Moral Advantage.* In one phase, the would-be robber attains a private sense of moral competence to control the situation. This stage often, although not necessarily, comes first. The sense of moral advantage is commonly accomplished through a secret strategem, edge, or "angle" on the scene.

2. *Declaration.* Even after achieving a subjective sense of advantage, the prospective robber may still abandon the project. He appreciates that he must also commit himself wholeheartedly. Unlike the burglar, con man, or sneak thief, if the robber is to succeed he must announce publicly and clearly that he is trying to commit a crime.

3. *Sticking beyond Reason with Stickup.* Whether it fails or is successful, a stickup has the potential of transcendent significance for the offender. The robber may be killed, permanently injured, or captured, or he may take the event to demonstrate publicly the indomitability of his subjectivity. Although most instances have little consequence for either the offender or the victims, offenders soon learn that as much as they might like to, they cannot control their fate. Sometimes the uncertainties appear overwhelming, and offenders truncate the crime or refrain from repeatedly taking on its risks. If they are to persist, stickup men must adopt a characteristic hardness of will and insist on being criminal, regardless of the dictates of moral reason or instrumental considerations for disciplining their violence. In a phrase, they must become fascinated with the project of being a "hardman."

The best data on robbery as a situational practice consist of narrative accounts of particular events by witnesses, victims, offenders, and co-offenders. Franklin Zimring and James Zuehl constructed such a data set from police records on several types of robberies that occurred in Chicago between September 1982 and October 1983.[17] For robberies resulting in homicides and for homicides that the police categorized as "motive unknown," they also conducted interviews with investigating police. Robberies resulting in nonfatal injuries to victims were sampled by taking the first 30 appearing in police records each month. Working with the Zimring-Zuehl narratives, I came up with a set of 105 robbery-homicides. In passages below, these are identified by a number in the 10,000s. The cases of robbery with non-fatal injuries are identified by numbers in the 40,000s. In the last section of this chapter, I will also refer to a set of 85 cases, identified by numbers in a 20,000 series, which were motive-unknown homicides. These killings were apparently neither robberies nor conflicts within domestic or romantic relationships. For robbery killings and motive unknown killings, my counts differ slightly from those in the Zimring-Zuehl research paper because information about a few cases was either lost or appeared to me too ambiguous to analyze. In the original and in the current analysis, the unit of data is the robbery event, not victimization; in the rare case, there is more than one fatality or injury, but I will be counting such cases as one event. Where relevant and to provide an indication of reliability, I compare the counts which resulted from my codings with those reached by the original research team.[18]

Constructing Subjective Moral Dominance

In virtually all robberies, the offender discovers, fantasizes or manufactures *an angle of moral superiority* over the intended victim.[19] The stickup man knows that dominance requires a more sophisticated competence than the application of brute force alone.

Perhaps because more than physical superiority is at issue, autobiographies indicate that young men often work up to the moral competence necessary for robbery through a period of practicing muggings, purse snatchings, or "yokings."[20] Muggers seek to acquire the victim's valuables before the victim becomes aware that a crime is occurring. When they spot a target from behind and rush up, grab some valuables, and run off, muggers may get away without leaving the victim with enough information even to describe them in a sketchy way. Thus, they are not quite committing stickups because in stickups, the offender, as well as the victim, is held up; to obtain the victim's cooperation, the stickup man must visibly embrace a criminal identity and then, at least momentarily, pause in his progress. Relative to the stickup man, the mugger and the purse snatcher demonstrate a lack of faith that they can sustain an edge through this pause, when it must rest solely on their effective manipulation of the symbols of superiority.

The cost-benefit tradeoff of ease in getting away versus the likelihood of getting away without much, makes muggings especially appealing to the young and especially disdained by "heavy," self-conscious, "career" robbers. What also influences their differential appeal to offenders of different ages is that blind-side muggings, like takeout tackles and blocks in contact sports, put a special premium not solely on bulk or strength but on physical speed and agility.

A short step up from muggings in cognitive complexity is a strategy that combines blind-side mugging and the face-to-face confrontation characteristic of stickups, as this case illustrates:

[40228] A 44-year-old man, walking on the street in the late afternoon, is "accosted" by a young male who demands his wallet. Two other

young men grab him from behind; while the one in front strikes the
victim in the face, the one in back grabs his wallet. Then all flee.

Here the offenders posit their superior ability to control the robbery not
only on their *superior number* and force, but on a bit of *street smarts.* Note that
the offenders enact a "cold" (arrogant) dominance; they overwhelm the
victim by generating an experience of surprise from manipulating his
expectations. First, they make him believe the event is a stickup; then they
add an element of mugging from behind.

Analytically also a small step away from blind-side mugging is the
practice of victimizing the intoxicated. Once known as "jackrolling,"[21] the
selection of drunk victims appears to be eternally and ubiquitously attractive to young robbers. Of the 332 cases of robberies with nonfatal injury
in the Chicago data set, 59 (18 percent) had victims who were described
not only as having been drinking but as intoxicated, often as too intoxicated to identify their attackers. Again, like in blind-side muggings, the
robber has reason to feel secure that he will not be well identified and also
has grounds for anticipating that his take will be minimal. But now his
immunity comes not just from physical power and dexterity but from
superior perceptual competence; as the colloquialism has it, the drunken
victim is already "blind."

To commit a stickup in which sober victims are to be confronted face
to face, the would-be offender needs other grounds to presume a superior
competence to control the interaction. Age may offer the advantage. In the
Chicago data as elsewhere, robbers are overwhelmingly young men; in
national data on arrests, the age distribution peaks between 18 and 20,[22]
and robberies *by* people over age 50 are rare. But the *victimization* of people
over age 60 is common. In the Chicago set of robberies with nonfatal
injuries to victims, not counting the intoxicated victims, thirty were over
age 60.[23] Thus, fully 27 percent of the cases were against victims whose
physical status would provide all but the occasional stickup man with
grounds for increased self-confidence.

Note that the construction of a sense of advantage that is sufficient to
begin a robbery does not require a conviction that the offense will proceed
smoothly. In neighborhoods where robbery is common, stories often circu-
late about victims, including aged victims, who successfully resisted. The
essential sense of initial advantage is more narrowly the anticipation that
one will not have the tables turned on him. The intoxicated and the aged
may fight back and force the offender's flight, but they are much less likely
to "take him out," physically incapacitating him or holding him for the
police.

When victims are not physically weak, would-be offenders may take
encouragement from *contextual weaknesses.* One-third of the Chicago robberies with nonfatal injuries occurred between midnight and 5 A.M.; excluding
cases against aged or intoxicated victims, these constituted another 27

percent of the set. The relationship between stickup and late-night life is, as I will argue later, deeper than the attractiveness of isolation to would-be stickup men. But many of the narratives detail this theme. For example, two Hispanic musicians, smoking marijuana in their van in the parking lot of a nursing home at 5 A.M. after finishing work for the evening, are not likely to be disturbed by anyone other than stickup men [10810]. Many of the late-night robberies also are related to moral weakness in the form of the victim's disinclination to make public his presence in the setting that becomes the robbery context.

The classic strategy known as the Murphy game takes advantage of a moral weakness built on the victim's physical needs.[24] As a prostitute guides a customer to a private place, he is assaulted by a stickup man while she mysteriously vanishes; his prospects of pleasure abruptly fold up and disappear, like a Murphy bed. The victim is doubly disabled, by the isolation he sought and by the illicit nature of the scene, which will often inhibit his complaint. The stickup man simultaneously rips off and ridicules the victim.

A variation on the Murphy game uses the lure of drug sales instead of sex [10406]. Sometimes stickups emerge only over the course of an evening, after several indications of the victim's weakness have materialized:

[11202] The victim is a male Hispanic, aged 51, who meets a female Hispanic in a bar. He is with his son. They go to her place where they meet another male and, in a while, two other women. After some hours of partying, the son leaves. The victim, who has been drinking heavily, is drugged by his hostess, who lures him into her bedroom, where her male friend waits to help her go through his clothes for valuables.

It might be thought that offenders with guns need not first convince themselves that the status of the victim or the state of the scene facilitates their dominance. There may be some truth to the movie line that guns are "equalizers," but it is not just *equality* that stickup men require to begin the offense. Perhaps this is why it is so rare for robbers to break or sneak into homes and attack strangers. In the 437 cases of violent robbery in the Chicago set, no more than a handful might fit this nightmarish image.[25] Although the citizen who is sleeping at home is especially unable to resist a sneak attack, the robber who would break into a home to attack and steal cannot know precisely what to expect before putting himself at risk.

Thus, before they commit themselves overtly to attack, even armed robbers virtually always insist on satisfying themselves, through some form of situational strategy, however flimsy, that they have an "angle" or moral advantage over the victim. The times and places of robberies are not random; their selection frequently shows an effort to undermine the other's expectations. Stickup men may lie in wait to seize on the suddenly apparent weakness of a store owner in the moment he bends over to open his shop early in the morning [11104], a tavern owner and a barmaid as they lock up at a late hour on an abandoned street [10204], or motorists who split from the traffic flow and pull over to use a roadside emergency telephone [11105]. In such instances, the offenders seize on the general public's definition of the time as too early or too late for much business or on the state's considerate dedication of a site for one kind of emergency to manufacture another kind.

Whatever the effect on the victim, offenders who lay in wait can generate a sense of moral advantage by observing victims acting as unwitting pawns in their plans. Offenders in big cities turn vestibules [10405, 10709] and elevators [10304, 41907] into architectural colleagues by strategically timing the stickup to begin the moment after elevator doors close or, even more precisely, the moment after the outer vestibule door closes and before the inner one opens.[26] An offender who has been silently praying as a prospective victim enters a vestibule or elevator, "Come on, come on, get in already!" will often experience the victim as tacitly cooperating with his plan ("You can do it, that's it, good boy!").

The offenders' moral delight with victims' playing into their hands was especially dramatic in the case of four teenagers who ordered a pizza so they could rob the delivery man [11203]. This is a delight full of arrogant joy. When you want some money, call up and order a victim. They'll come to you! (Robberies of taxi drivers often have a similar theme.) The stickup becomes the end result of "running a game" on "some sucker."

In commercial robberies, the offender's initial movement to a position of moral superiority is often accomplished by "looking around." There is little evidence in either the cases or the autobiographies to indicate that those who stick up retail stores are looking to find or to rule out anything in particular. The applicable metaphor for their "casing" is not that of the prudent investor assessing whether to take a risk, but that of the sports player, reading the lay of the land and the opposition's defensive setup before determining just how to execute a play that will probably, but not inevitably, be brought off.

But if a stickup is gamelike behavior, it is surely unsportsmanlike conduct. The offender cannot enter to examine the field honorably as an adversary; he must pass as some sort of legitimately motivated member of the scene. This practical task deepens the experience of morally superior competence.

Hence, before committing the serious crime of robbery, the offender will often commit the simply civil offense of falsely pretending to be a morally respectful member of the scene. It is awkward to the point of being counterproductive to enter and look around like an inspector. Retail stores are, first of all, places of business, and the injunction to be about the business at hand holds for the customers as well as the owners and employees. Unless they are previously acquainted with employees, outsiders entering bars, liquor stores, quick-stop markets, and the like must usually manifest an interest in doing business to avoid special attention or suspicion. Thus, before robbing retail stores, stickup men may:

- Ask the tavern owner for a bag of potato chips [11003].
- Order meat and wait as one of the two workers in the grocery store goes to the end of the counter to fill the order [10209].
- First ask that the gas station attendant fill up a container they are carrying [10504].

Then, without further discussion, they pull out guns and begin stickups, apparently carrying out a plan.

Such strategies are not only intelligence-gathering operations (who is where, how many are they, how might they be approached); they are also, morally, warm-ups. In a way, the would-be offender knows that only he knows that he has already taken control of the significance of the situation; the victims are already serving his purposes against their will, simply by showing their qualities as potential victims. Before the offender begins to publicize the stickup, he already has gotten away with his immoral purpose privately.

Street robberies take off from analogous maneuvers, but street tactics are often more specifically perverse. They commonly exploit two moral elements in the social order of urban street life.

First, moral respectability on the streets has long had a positive association with spatial movement. Until recently, for example, "loitering" was a criminal offense. And we still sense deviant undertones when we talk about people "hanging out." For street robbers, "winos" are especially vulnerable, morally as well as physically, because they are classic loiterers who habitually hang out on street corners and around bars. But more profitable victims are likely to be on the move, respectably "going about their business."

From the robber's perspective, retail stores offer the practical advantage over street scenes in that other people—owners and customers—have already done the work of ordering, and incurred the costs of paying, prospective victims to remain more or less stationary. One can sit down in a bar or restaurant, walk around a convenience or liquor store, or pump gas into one's own car at a station, all the while watching the relatively circumscribed movements of a clerk, because the clerk goes about an essential part of his business simply by staying there. But to rob people on the street, you often must first stop the victim; if you run up from a distance with a gun waving, the problem of holding victims to a holdup scene may be exacerbated.

Second, robbers pay special attention to the moral theme of the injunction toward a modicum of altruistic accessibility. Street life is accurately termed public or communal life in the minimal sense that pedestrians risk giving offense if they are not open to strangers, at least enough to give them the time of day, change, or help with directions. Not to respond is to refuse to respect the moral existence of the other: his need to order himself in time and space and his social need to act as a dutifully paying customer. For reasons that need not concern us here, people in public places ubiquitously sense a moral pressure to act as if these requests are legitimate, even if they strongly suspect that they are not. If the person who makes these simple requests looks like he might be a stickup man, denying his humanity may seem all the more risky.

Not everyone who is approached will stop to give the assistance that is requested—that the sense of moral pressure is ubiquitous does not mean that it is determinative—but enough do that such setups are part of the stock-in-trade of street robbers. Asking for the time [40420, 40102], for directions, [40423], for a cigarette light, and for change all share the two advantages of holding the victim stationary and permitting a scan of his possible weaknesses and strengths without warranting overtly defensive maneuvers. The victim may be seriously worried, but, without more, it would often be "crazy" simply to run away. For the stickup man, a great deal may be accomplished by even a momentary stop. By walking up to the victim, the would-be robber can ascertain exactly who is bigger than whom—a fact that may not be obvious from a distance. By asking a brief question and watching who does and who does not stop, the offender can establish who is "with" whom—another relevant fact that can easily be mistakenly assumed in distant observations of street life.

Each of the common civic requests has its unique advantage for the offender. By asking the hour, the offender can learn, before the action starts and time for investigating such things becomes precious, whether the victim has a watch, where it is, whether it seems worth the bother, and, perhaps, whether the victim is right handed or left handed. The request for directions can be exploited to assess whether the victim is indigenous or a stranger to the scene. And asking for change of a large bill, say a twenty, is widely appreciated by street robbers as a ploy that may show where and how much of a roll the victim is carrying.[27]

Subjectively, the special values of these civil requests is not only that they gather practically useful information or begin to construct the power asymmetry—the direction of who serves whom—that would characterize a stickup. They carry the further value of launching the *moral perversion* of the offense. In a stickup, the offender will declare himself clearly to be "bad." Through the use of common civil requests, he establishes that the bad he will be, will overcome and be against a victim who, by stopping and responding to a simple request that a stranger's human needs be respected, has shown himself to be at least a minimally decent person. Even before he launches the offense, the would-be stickup man has succeeded in making a fool of his victim.

Many robbers are obviously not deterred by the unusually high risks of subsequent identification and arrest or retribution when they target acquaintances. Of the 105 robbery-homicides I analyzed from the Chicago data set, almost 40 percent involved earlier relationships between the offenders and the victims, and in another 29 percent, the information was insufficient to determine the issue.[28] In a sample of 360 nonlethal Chicago robberies drawn from the same calendar period, Zimring and Zuehl found that the victim and offender were not strangers in 10 percent of the cases.[29]

In the details of these events, we can often appreciate an offsetting, powerfully seductive, appeal to offenders in the opportunities afforded by the prior relationship for constructing a position of dominance before the stickup begins. Thus, a woman who had done cleaning for her victim, a 70-year-old man, brought along a male friend one day for a robbery [11108], and a young man arranged with his friends to rob the novelty store owned by his aged boss [11101]. The insider-offender will typically know the setting, the victim's habits, and the potential loot far more intimately than he would if the target were a stranger. If he can arrange a way to avoid being identified with the event (for example, by unlocking the door and then waiting outside), he may build the confidence to go ahead. In effect, the robbery seizes on the preceding sense of trust, retrospectively defining the relationship as a con scheme.

In the Chicago data, robbery-killings that occur in residences are about twice as likely to be characterized by previous relationships between the victim and the offender.[30] Many of these crimes target victims who run vice activities from residential locations. Would-be stickup men sometimes use the simple ploy of posing as customers to gain entry and secretly assess the potential and problems for a stickup, returning when prepared to commit the crime.[31] In one case [11206] the offender made explicit that his *pride* as well as profit was at stake in this robbery, which was also a murder. When he returned, just before opening fire, he shouted, "So you're Jean Washington. I've been wanting to meet you for a long time."

Masks are useful for reducing the chance of being identified by victims, but using a mask is inconsistent with gaining an opportunity for a close-up inspection of the target before committing oneself to the crime. Offenders who would use masks must usually devise elaborate strategies to construct a confident sense of initial advantage. The robbery of a monthly crap game in a Chicago Housing Authority project demonstrated one solution:

[11001] Three offenders planned the stickup. Two entered and viewed the game with some twenty or thirty other bettors. After about twenty minutes, one of the conspirators left. A while later, the remaining offender opened the door for the other two, and they entered wearing ski masks and waving handguns.

That these offenders enjoyed being *cunning* as well as cold was suggested by the disguise worn by one of the shooting offenders to aid his getaway.

When arrested in a Peoria, Illinois, Greyhound station, he was wearing a dress, ladies underwear, makeup, and a wig. In another, similarly structured robbery-homicide attack on a public housing crap game [11205], the masked offender opened his assault with the gratuitous, wry declaration: "You'll [presumably the folksy Southern "you-all"] having a party without me?" These offenders are not just trying to get away with something; they are also "getting over" on their victims.

Declaring the Crime

More clearly than is the case in perhaps any other common crime, stickups become objectified in a definitive moment of commitment. There is typically a moment of declaration that a robbery has begun: a widely used, literal and simple, "This is a stickup"; the currently popular, "Give it up," which is often emphasized through repetition; or a physical attack aimed at stunning or disabling, followed by the question, "Where is it?", an order, "Hand it over," or a simple grab at the victim's possessions. Whether the offender uses a verbal form of declaration, he concentrates on making the criminal nature of his project clearly visible to the victim.

Nonviolent thieves—shoplifters, pickpockets, burglars, and con men—may commit their crimes in face-to-face (or face-to-back or under-the-nose of) interaction with victims, and they seek to end up with someone else's property, much like the robber. But, unlike the robber, professional nonviolent thieves are well aware that they can begin the offense, get close to completing it, and then change their minds and walk off without any risk of culpability. Chic Conwell, sociology's original professional thief-autobiographer, gave the example of a booster who, left alone in the fur department when a sales person was called to the phone, decided to leave empty handed just because it all seemed too easy; he feared he had been set up by store guards.[32] Hotel burglars are prepared to dramatize confusion to convince would-be victims that they are in the "wrong room" because of an honest mistake.[33] And Henry Williamson, the "hustler" who was a thief-generalist in the heart of black Chicago in the fifties, had a variety of strategies for backing out of nonviolent offenses when they turned sour. Caught in the victim's car after cutting off the registration sticker, for example, he might feign illness or intoxication.[34]

Stickup men, however, seek to dramatize with unarguable clarity that the situation has been suddenly and irreversibly transformed into a crime. Toward this end, they sometimes take extra risks, such as vaulting a counter after pulling out a gun. When guns are displayed to victims who are unfamiliar with weapons, the result is typically effective; yet, many gun robbers further emphasize the moral transformation of the scene by striking or kicking the victim.

Armed robbers are pressed to make explicit their criminal definition of the scene not because their display of a gun is too silent but because it is too loud. They know that the sight of a gun stuns the victim, immediately generating a wild array of fearful imaginings. The declaration, "This is a stickup," or "give it up," is necessary to ensure their cognitive control of the event; it serves to move the victim from shock to a disciplined definition of the situation, and to avoid potential misinterpretations of the event as a rape, a kidnapping, or the act of a madman.

A stickup is a forced contractual interaction with three essential parts, any one of which, made explicit, can successfully bring the crime into undisputed existence, with the other two elements implicitly trailing along. One element is the designation of what the offender wants from the victim. Some stickups are perceived to exist when offenders demand something they have no right to possess; "Gimme that bike," said by one adolescent to another, may work this way. Or the offender may make apparent that he and the victim are in a stickup by announcing the illegal consideration in the relationship. Such a statement includes not what he is demanding, but his offer not to harm the victim, as in "Don't make this a murder," while displaying a gun. And third, unlike legitimate contracts that outline an offer that has yet to be accepted, the robber must make clear, even as he makes the victim aware of the contractual framework, that both parties already are committed to it. That the offender intends the contract to govern the interaction whether or not the victim would agree is often accomplished by an explicit characterization of the criminal nature of the interaction or by the revelation of a weapon.

Stickup men use expressive economy to introduce the contractual framework. Rarely do they articulate all three elements: (1) "Gimme that." (2) "Do what I say and you won't be hurt." (3) "This is a stickup—See, here's my gun." Operative phrases are notably succinct, and demonstrative motions are quick and brief. The robber must, after all, convince the victim that the offender's understanding *must* govern; if they labor too sensitively to ensure that the victim understands just what is expected of him, offenders risk showing an illogical deference to the victim's sensibility.

Stickups may fail, but once launched, they virtually never fail to become publicly recognized or objectified as at least unsuccessful stickups. One can imagine circumstances in which the forms for committing a stickup are engaged but the offense is not socially accepted as a committed offense, but these imaginings tend to be absurd and, therefore, especially instructive about the common-sense basis of doing stickups. In *Take the Money and Run,* Woody Allen represented himself as a would-be bank robber whose handwriting was so poor and whose presence so unintimidating, that tellers would labor seriously and unsuccessfully to read the demand note. And

Erving Goffman analyzed the situational troubles of a robber who, while masked and dressed in a green GI uniform, barged into a comedic night club show, fired into the ceiling, and was greeted by a roar of laughter from the audience.[35]

Failed attempts to commit oneself to robbery are rare for reasons that Goffman's work on behavior in public places makes clear: modern social life is elaborately laced by ubiquitous expectations that one display a decent moral sensibility. As I argued in chapter 3, one can create an intimidating presence by the solely negative achievement of holding back the deferential postures and gestures that assure others that one is sensitively respectful. Because people routinely read social interactions for indications that others are morally decent folk—because so much of the culture of public behavior is already dedicated to warding off interpretations that a malevolent spirit is present—it is remarkably easy to signal effectively that a stickup has begun.

Sticking Beyond Reason with Stickup

As the metaphors of "heart" and "guts" suggest, continuing with any given stickup, much less persisting with stickups as an ongoing criminal involvement, often requires commitments that are experienced as transcending rational considerations. The practice of stickup requires the achievement of a distinctive moral incompetence: the construction of indifference to the mundane consequences of the crime to oneself and, therefore, to others.

In interviews with researchers, robbers have contradicted this analysis. Here is John Allen's explanation:

Robbing is an art, and the whole art of robbing is fear, and the main reason for robbing is to get what you came after—the money—and get away. You don't go there to hurt people. Sometimes you have to . . . [but] most good hustling dudes, especially with robbing experience, they never go out to hurt people . . . Occasionally somebody say, "I ain't giving up nothing." But you can change his tune easy. You ain't got to kill him. Smack him with the gun or shoot him in the foot or kneecap, he give it right up. Knock his big toe off with one of them .45's, he give it up . . . . I know that I done a lot of cruel things, but it was something that I had to do at that particular moment for one reason or another. I have never did something unnecessary, especially when it comes to violence.[36]

Such statements, together with various situational patterns of violence in robbery and contrasts with other crimes, are the basis for the currently dominant view that robbers are essentially rational in their crimes, and sometimes by implication, in their commitments to their careers. I will address these patterns as a first step toward conveying the more fundamental truth, that the commitment of the persistent robber must transcend rational considerations.

RATIONALITY IN ROBBERY

Researchers have argued that robbers' working perspective is rational by contrasting the social characteristics of robbery with criminal violence in nonpredatory assaults. In contrast to assaults, robberies are much more often performed by people younger than the victim, against strangers, and against victims of a different race.[37] These demographic and relational differences suggest that violence has a different attraction to the offender in the two crimes, an expressive value in assault and an instrumental value in robbery.

Correlations between the offender's use of violence and the weapons he does or does not carry, the characteristics of the victim, and whether the victim resists, all indicate a rational perspective among robbers. Ironically, the more lethal the weapon the offender carries, the less likely he will be to use violence. Victims are less likely to be injured when robbers use guns than when they use, in descending order, knives, clubs, or no weapon. If you consider robbery from an instrumental perspective, this makes sense. The robber with a gun typically can intimidate his victim without using the weapon, while the unarmed robber anticipates that he may have to strike the victim to convey a threat successfully.[38]

Reflecting this logic, muggers state that they are more likely to use force against able-bodied men than against women, elderly victims, or "lames"—that is, against the weak in general.[39] For a similar reason, although only a few robberies are by women (10 percent in most studies), one Canadian study found that almost all women who committed robberies did so with a gun, compared to one-third of the male robbers.[40] Furthermore, in robberies of strangers, the victims are much more likely to be injured when they are men and the robbers are women than vice versa— whether or not the robbers have guns.[41]

A number of studies have related evidence of actual resistance by victims to the injury rate in robberies. "Resistance" sometimes includes physical resistance, as well as attempted flight and calls for help; sometimes the two forms of resistance have been separately measured. In either case, virtually all studies show a higher rate of injury when the victims resist.

In general, the injury rate for robbery victims is about 5 percent.[42] It should be noted, however, that, according to a common estimate, at least

20 percent of robberies are not reported, especially when there is no injury; thus, the actual rate of physical injury is probably overstated by official statistics. Be that as it may, studies using various methodologies have indicated that the rate of injury to victims is substantially greater for those victims who used a physical force, self-protective measure than for those victims who did not.[43] In a study of robbery events reflected in Texas police records, David Luckenbill found that if the victim resisted robber, the robber was as likely to abandon the scene without further action as to apply force.[44] In a study conducted in Northern California in the late 1960s, victims were interviewed about their own conduct. It was concluded that the more resistance, the more injury (but yelling alone was not related to a higher harm rate).[45] In Conklin's pioneering Boston study, the gun robber's use of force increased from 14 to 38 percent of the time, depending on whether the victim resisted.[46] In a study of over 1,000 robberies described in Chicago police records, Block found that the injury rate was 15 percent when victims did not resist and 50 percent when they did.[47]

By their cumulative effect, these studies have produced an overblown impression that rationality guides the robber's situated use of violence. Philip Cook recently reemphasized the caveat that correlation should not be taken for causation by describing a number of small samples of victims' reports, police cases, and prosecutors' files, which indicate that victims resisted in response to their perception that offenders were nonrationally bent on violence or, what is more important, in which the analyst could not clearly determine the causal direction in the relationship.[48] Zimring and Zuehl, although maintaining that victims should not resist lest they increase the risk of being injured, described a cloudier picture than the usual sharp contrast between nonrational assault among acquaintances and rationally controlled violence by a robber against a stranger. They found that offenders and victims are frequently acquainted in violent robberies and concluded that

> a category such as "recreational violence" seems to us not only evocative but descriptive of a large number of violent events—including those that produce homicide—that span robbery and nonrobbery events.[49]

The contrasting characterizations of homicides as impassioned acts among acquaintances and violent robberies as coldly instrumental acts against strangers has been exaggerated because of methodological limitations with the data. In police statistical categories, robbery-homicides are thrown in with the homicides; thus, "robbery" statistics artificially underrepresent the extent of prior acquaintance and presumably related passions between robbers and their victims. And victimization studies, which miss homicides altogether, disproportionately fail to detect nonfatal robberies against acquaintances.[50] Hence, acquaintance-victims are more likely to show up in police cases when they cannot help it, that is, when they are killed or seriously injured, than when they are victims of noninjury robberies. As a result of these biases, samples of noninjury robbery cases that are drawn from police files and samples of robbery victims in general are likely to understate the situationally irrational or nonrational themes that may be implicated when offenders victimize acquaintances.

Now, we need not throw out the instrumental framework for beginning our inquiry, but the more closely we examine violent interactions in robbery, the more we will appreciate that situational rationality will not do for the final analysis. Let us, then, sift several times through the 437 Chicago cases of robbery with fatal or nonfatal injuries.[51] On the first pass through, I will show that the violence of offenders is even *more* rational than previous studies detected. On the second pass, I will clarify the *nonrational commitment* that underlies the careers of persistent offenders.

SITUATIONAL AND TRANSSITUATIONAL RATIONALITY IN STICKUPS

At first glance, the Chicago robbery killings appear to follow the themes stated in autobiographies and the patterns found in previous studies of the relationship between violence in robberies and the resistance of victims: fatal violence by offenders in robberies is closely related to resistance by victims. Of the 105 robbery killings in the Chicago data set, it is clear that the fatal attack was *not* a response to resistance by the victim in only 23 cases. Put in other words, an offender's use of seemingly "irrational" violence is indicated in only about 20 percent of the set.

Reading the data directly, in 42 of the 105 cases the victim resisted the robbery at some point in the interaction and in some way. In 39 of the cases, there is insufficient information to determine the issue. Given this seemingly unavoidable measure of uncertainty, one tack by which to gain some further headway is to examine more closely the cases that initially appear to indicate irrational violence. We should not too quickly impute "irrationality" or "expressive motives" or "gratuitous violence" even to the 23 cases in which the robber's homicidal violence clearly was *not* a response to the victim's resistance.

For one thing, in six of the twenty-three cases, the victims were occupied with deviant activity when they were attacked. When we look at the process through which the violence developed, we find that the deviant character of the setting indicates why the offenders may have launched the fatal violence. The following case may serve as an example:

[11001] Three men conspired to rob a monthly dice game held in a Chicago public housing project. Two of the three entered the scene as observers. One subsequently left and, about half an hour later, the one who remained let the other two in when they appeared at the door, dressed in ski masks and waving hanguns. One announced: "Give it up, don't nobody move. Don't nobody be a hero." While one cleared money

from the dice tables, two held weapons pointed at the group and then, apparently to secure their exit, began spraying the room with gunfire. One of the victimized players pulled out his own gun and began firing at the offenders, two of whom turned on him, one fatally. Four others were injured in the gunfire.

If the act of spraying the room with gunfire is understood as a show of force not specifically intended to injure, then the fatal shooting might be understood as a response to a victim's resistance. But it is not clear that the resisting victim understood the initial shots this way. Nor would it be unreasonable for a victim to anticipate that even if the sole purpose of the offenders was to intimidate, bullets bouncing around a room might not respect that nicety. The spray of gunfire is at least reckless, from the victim's perspective.

Yet, from the offenders' perspective, the strategy of a spray of gunfire might be reasonably cautious. It is not unreasonable to anticipate, if one is going to try to stick up such a group, that one of the victims might pull a weapon to resist, not just to avoid injury but to refuse to give up big winnings. That one victim did pull out a gun and begin firing indicates that gamblers come to this setting materially and psychologically prepared for trouble. In the end, the deviant character of the scene makes the argument about the anticipatory use of potentially fatal violence at least reasonable.[52] In another case, the offender's use of fatal violence, without any evidence of physical opposition by the victims, was, on several grounds, in reasonable anticipation of a violent response by the victim:

[11905] Two men sat in the back seat of a car with a drug dealer and shot him and his girlfriend to death, subsequently taking money and drugs from them. One of the offenders had owed money to the male victim, and the latter, on a round of collections earlier that evening, had threatened the offender if he did not pay.

In four other cases in which the robbers used fatal violence before the victims resisted, the victims were either playing craps or had reputations as drug dealers and were attacked specifically because of their deviant activity. In this subset of six cases, then, the offenders had reason to anticipate that if the victims remained alive after the robbery, they might be murdered by the victims, both because the victims could not easily let the event pass and stay in business and because the victims either already knew the offenders' identities or might discover them.[53]

At this point in our countdown of all robbery killings that occurred in a recent year in Chicago, we are left with seventeen cases in which we have a detailed narrative on the interaction between the victims and offenders and in which the fatal violence appears to have been unjustified on instrumental grounds. In ten of these seventeen cases, at least one offender knew at least one victim personally.[54] Here the vulnerability of the offender to identification by the victim gives his violence an instrumental basis, even in the absence of situational resistance.

As soon as we abandon the narrow confines of the robbery situation and consider the meaning of the event as a moment in the ongoing life of the offender, we discover numerous additional themes that may make the offender's violence reasonable. In addition to the offender's reasonable basis for being concerned about revenge by victims who could later identify him, we must appreciate the instrumental value to the robber of "gratuitous" violence against victims for shaping relations with his peers. As I will discuss more fully later, the victim's reaction is not the only and sometimes not the most important practical concern that the offender has about those who are present. What his peers will do, on the scene and later, can be a more pressing matter.

At this point, we are left with seven cases of seemingly noninstrumental robbery-homicide, five of which had multiple offenders. In this respect, these few cases are not unlike the typical robbery, which is found to be the work of several offenders more often than a solo act.[55] If relations among offenders are significant in the development of violence in robberies, we should not expect to find much evidence of the fact in the offense itself because relations among offenders transcend the robbery scene.

After the offender's concern with overcoming the victim's resistance to theft, his next-most-immediate concern is to keep or get a decent part of what has been taken. It appears that the division of the take is rarely the subject of explicit discussion beforehand, and, in any case, talk of contractual commitment would not necessarily govern what transpires after the event. Henry Williamson, who participated in numerous stickups, acknowledged: "Everybody I hustled with I took from!"[56]

Even when the offenders articulate how the take is to be divided, the process of settling up is often impeded by the multiple roles that may be combined in robberies (some wait outside while others operate inside), by the cooperative combination of heavies who enact the stickup and insider/tipsters who finish their contribution before the robbery scene develops, and by the haste in which valuables are often taken from victims and escapes are accomplished. Clearly, a reputation for violence, perhaps sustained by "irrational" brutality against the robbery victim, could be valuable for offenders who are interested in not becoming their colleagues' secondary victims.

In many of the autobiographies of stickup men, the protagonists label some of their associates as having reputations for being particularly dangerous, the sort of person one would not want to cross. Malcolm X wrote of "West Indian Archie" in this vein, and himself enacted a (fraudulent) Russian roulette drama to demonstrate his "heart" to colleagues before beginning a series of burglaries with them.[57] David, the main character in

Dietz's study of robbery homicide in Detroit, described Donald as especially "mean" with victims and liable to threaten (or become "valiant
with") David at any time.[58] John Allen was attracted to work with Bones
in part because of, in part despite his reputation for "crazy" violence.[59]
Henry Williamson would try to "beat" all his colleagues in crime, except
for Benny:

> Benny was the kind that wanted to whup everyone to death that he
> robbed! That's the type of guy he was. When he'd rob somebody, he just
> wasn't satisfied with takin' his money, he actually wanted to whup him
> to death! He always had two pistols, and the pistols was almost as big
> as he was![60]

A reputation for "irrational" violence may be useful not only to ensure a
fair division of the take with such people, but to decrease the chances of
being victimized directly by them in some later, unrelated circumstance.

Although rarely visible in overt statements, this pressure to demonstrate
that one is not to be trifled with is not an abstract concern, ungrounded
in the situational events of robbery. Dietz found evidence in police files
on robbery-homicides that "group members often say, 'Go ahead, shoot'
to another member who has a weapon." In one instance, one robber tells
another, "Off all of them. I don't want no shit behind this." Whether said
to establish the inferior commitment of the other or to get the victim killed,
such a remark occasions a moment of "awe-full" truth with consequential
overtones for subsequent relations among offenders.[61]

If we broaden our sights on robber violence from interaction with victims to include interaction with associates and then lift our sights to grasp
the transsituational meaning of robbery events, we can appreciate further
dimensions of instrumentality in offenders' situationally "irrational" violence toward robbery victims. For the career or "heavy" stickup man,
peremptory and excessive violence may be instrumental for marketing his
reputation as a "badass." In effect, offenders in robberies can use "irrational" violence against victims as a resource for building their careers as
immoral entrepreneurs.[62]

In vice markets, pimps and drug dealers, cut off from legitimate enforcement powers, may at times use violent robbery to recapture or protect from
theft property that might be taken by prostitutes, other drug traffickers,
and miscellaneous thieves. The Chicago cases are rich in such incidents, as
are the Detroit cases analyzed by Dietz. Dietz noted that drug dealers, even
when resolute in killing people who stole from them, hesitate to kill
"innocent" bystanders, despite the risk that surviving witnesses would
identify the assailants.[63] In one incident, assailants killed two, paralyzed
a third, and let go a fourth—an uninvolved witness—only to return to
attempt his murder (unsuccessfully). Dietz commented:

This discrimination and hesitation to kill "innocent" people occurs frequently in both amateur and professional cases and is a key factor indicating the rationality, control and decision making in felony homicide cases.[64]

Attacks may appear to be unprovoked assault when seen in isolation from their meaning as responses to being "ripped off" by competitors or of being "lipped off" by subordinates, which poses an equivalent business threat.

The instrumental value of seemingly "irrational" violence by robbers who are attempting to bootstrap their way into immoral careers is more difficult to appreciate. Several of the most strikingly "irrational" cases of robbery-killings in the Chicago set were accomplished by entrepreneurial adolescents. In one especially well-detailed case [11206, discussed earlier], the leader of a local street gang shot a drug dealer known as "The Ts and Blues Queen of the South Side" in her apartment, when approximately eighteen of her relatives were present. She was a new resident in the area, and he had previously demanded "protection money" from her, which she had refused. The day of the killing, he entered her apartment in the guise of a drug buyer, left under the pretense that he had forgotten to bring sufficient money, and returned with a gasoline-filled coffee can, which he used to ignite the apartment after the shooting. Some hours later, he was heard to brag on the street, "When I do a murder, I do it right."

VIOLENCE BEYOND REASON: THE EMERGENCE OF THE HARDMAN

Fatal violence in robberies appears increasingly rational the more we expand our appreciation of the meaning of the event to the offender beyond the situational contingencies of the victim's resistance. In the end, we are left with few cases of killings during robberies in which the offender's violence does not appear instrumental. But the more we grasp the meaning of violence in robberies within transsituational relations between offenders and victims and within the lives of men who would make ongoing commitments to stickups, the closer the analysis comes to the point at which it turns back on itself and attacks the characterization of the offender's perspective as rational. If we are to consider the rationality of the offender's violence not just in relation to the compliance or resistance of victims to situated demands but within perspectives that transcend the robbery situation, why not ask, Why should offenders, faced with resisting victims, not simply abandon the situation and seek another, more compliant target? As we have seen, the typical robbery, street or commercial, is not the result of extensive planning; little preparatory investment would be sacrificed by a decision to cut and run.

Indeed, the resistance of victims is a rational basis for killing them during robberies only when victims threaten to harm offenders or block their escape.[65] When I reanalyzed the 105 robbery killings in the Chicago series on this issue, the results were that it was reasonable for the robber-killer to use fatal violence to protect himself physically or to ensure his escape in only 11 of the cases.[66] In 4 other cases, the offender appeared to kill in a "panic" after the victim resisted in some manner that did not physically endanger the offender and then abandoned the robbery in order to escape. What is usually coded as the resistance of victims in analyses that conclude that the violence of robbers is predominately rational is a range of behavior by victims, short of blocking escape routes, that make the robber's work more troublesome or perilous, such as claims by the victim that he has no money, cries for help, weak forms of physical counterattack, and attempts to flee.

This form of resistance by victims occurred before the fatal attack in twenty-seven of the Chicago robbery-killings on which there was sufficient information to permit coding on the question. The following are representative of the nine cases in this subset in which there was no evidence of a previous relationship between the offender and victim or any evidence that the victim was occupied in a vice activity.

[10801] Two young men entered a small grocery store–meat market on a Monday afternoon. They opened by firing a warning shot into a wall. When the 72-year-old owner, Michael Przybycien, began throwing things at them and then slipped, the offenders went around the back of the counter and shot him once while he was on the floor. His wallet was taken, but the offenders fled without removing all the cash from the store's register.

[11203] Four teenagers planned to rob a pizza delivery man. They called in an order, and when the delivery man reached their area, the youngest of the group, a 14 year old, approached him on foot and declared, "This is a stickup, don't make it a murder." The victim, 55 years old, threw up his hands and dropped the money he was holding. The 14 year old then asked, "Where is the rest of the money, man?" The victim ran to his car, got inside, and started it, but the two of them jumped in and began to struggle with him. Then one pulled a shotgun from his overcoat and shot the victim in the throat and chest. The four split with $27 to divide.

[11103] Levin was in Cruz's bar, collecting receipts from the jukeboxes and pinball machines. A young man ordered a beer, then pulled out a gun and announced a stickup. Levin tried to escape. The offender shot Levin once in the chest, directed Cruz to lay on the ground, took $97 from Cruz's wallet and Levin's change bag, containing $190 in quarters, ordered both victims into the bathroom, jammed the door shut, and ran off, leaving Cruz unharmed.

Overwhelmingly, robbery killings are acts in which offenders, in the face of situational opposition or in anticipation of revenge, insist that they will not bend from their initial definition of the situation as a stickup. When there is no reason to anticipate revenge or any resistance by victims, robbers only rarely kill. But when they do kill, it is not often because of the need to defend themselves. They might, in the first instance, have selected strangers instead of acquaintances as targets, for then, if the victims resisted, they could leave in search of a less troublesome opportunity. In the final analysis, the commitment according to which violence within robberies makes sense to the offenders is the commitment to be a hard man—a person whose will, once manifested, must prevail, regardless of practical calculations of physical self-interest. Fatal violence in robberies is far less often a reaction of panic or a rationally self-serving act than a commitment to the transcendence of a hard will.

UNCERTAINTY IN STICKUPS

To understand the necessity of becoming hardheaded to persist in robbery, we must try to appreciate the crime's existential difficulties. Once he has declared the stickup, the offender enters a state of suspense. Stickup men may begin the offense by being preoccupied with the material rewards that wait at its imagined ending, and they may open with a fearsome show of will designed to put victims into a state of suspense while the offenders remain the only moving and the solely determinative part. Thus, the display of a handgun and an utterance in the form, "Don't nobody move" [11001] or "hold it" [10208], or an order for the victims to "freeze" or lie down on the floor, is not an uncommon beginning tactic. But no matter how forcefully he may seek to manifest that all that transpires next will be under his control, the stickup man always knows it may not.

The ubiquity of suspense in stickups is, in a general sense, the product of the extraordinarily destructive consequences that rarely but always might occur. In more specific, experiential terms, it is a product of the number of alien systems that the offender may realize he has joined. First, there is the offender's uncertainty about how much he will have to pressure the victim before he succeeds. When he victimizes strangers, he comes suddenly and intimately into a subjective world that he knows he does not know well. And when his victims are acquaintances, the stickup man can anticipate the possibility of a response shaped by extraneous emotional themes. Applying to the Chicago data a broad definition of resistance by victims, which includes physical counterattacks as well as refusals to comply with orders and calls for help, I found that of the 105 robbery-homicides, 34 involved a form of resistance; and in the 332 robbery-nonfatal injury cases, 116 showed evidence of resistance.[67]

By using guns, robbers may minimize but they surely do not avoid suspense about their victims' resistance. A victim survey in Chicago found that victims resisted in 24 percent of the robbery attempts in which a gun was used.[68] Nor can robbers reasonably expect to eliminate the risk of the victims' resistance by attacking the aged or the intoxicated. Considering the Chicago data set, in the 89 robberies with nonfatal injuries in which the victims were either over age 60 or intoxicated, the rate of resistance was over 25 percent. Although especially weak or vulnerable victims may not usually resist, men who persist in doing robberies quickly learn that it is always reasonable to anticipate problems from victims. John Allen showed that he learned this lesson early in his career as a stickup man:

> One day . . . my cousin Frog . . . said there was an old man with a cane walking down Stanton Road who had a lot of money on him. So we decided to go after him. I would yoke the man, Snap would hit him, and Frog would be taking everything he could get—shoes, rings, money, and anything else.
>
> Well, that old man fooled the hell out of us—he was like a bull. When I came up behind him and put my arm around his neck, he throw me on top of Snap and we both hit the ground. Then he takes his cane and come down with it on Frog's back, and Frog ran like hell. . . . We started to run off, but the old man was too much for us. We started to run, but the old bull was right behind us.[69]

The offender's suspense about whether the victim will resist goes far beyond the level of resistance reported in statistical counts of police reports or surveys of victims. For one thing, information that is necessary to code the presence or absence of such resistance is often unavailable to the researcher. Second, and more significant, crucial information that is sufficient to judge whether a victim will resist is often unavailable to the offender. If we include passive resistance in the concept, we can appreciate that offenders may never be sure that victims are *not* holding something back.

Put another way, an essential uncertainty that contributes to the offender's experience of a stickup is the question, How much might be discovered if the victim is pushed further or the scene is searched longer? The level of statistically reported resistance by victims in robberies obscures the rapid, subtle negotiations in which the offender and the victim sometimes work out just how much pressure the offender will apply and just how much of value the victim will give up, as in the following account:

> [40106] A male offender demands money from a 28-year-old female, on the street, at night. She refuses. He picks up a broken bottle and cuts her hand and knocks her down with blows to the face. She agrees to give him the money if he will stop hitting her. She gives him $50 and he flees.

In commercial robberies, offenders have reason to suspect that managers of retail locations lie when they say they cannot open the safe, as this case illustrates:

> [40823] The offender enters the office of the gas station's manager, initially asking to buy cigarettes. As the victim turns to get the cigarettes, the offender pulls out a gun and demands that the safe be opened. The victim says he does not have the keys. The offender shoots once, the victim opens the safe, and the offender gets away with $3,000.

Stickup men know they do not know what victims might be induced to disclose. A cunning robber might try to trick victims into disclosure. For example, a masked offender who is engaged in the stickup of a bar, after ordering everyone present to get down on the floor, might call the barmaid by her first name, thus suggesting familiarity with the location, and demand "the gun which was usually kept" in the tavern [40107]. Whether the offender had knowledge of a gun, it is likely that a gun would be present. Therefore, a bluff—reinforced, after an initial denial, by throwing a bar stool at the victim and then by hitting her on the head with a half-gallon liquor bottle—could make sense.

For both the offender *and* the victim, the perception of whether the victim is resisting or not, is not as clear-cut as researchers often assume. The resistance of victims is a relative idea, one that depends on the offender's demands. In the quickly forced contractual interaction of the stickup, the offender may not articulate his demands with legalistic precision. Sometimes the offender's use of force and his expression of demands fuse so completely that the victim may only realize he had been resisting after his understanding is overcome. The following case is an example:

> [40427] A 33-year-old male is sitting in his car when he is approached by a male of about 25, who opens the car door, displays a handgun, and demands money. The victim gives all his money. The offender then begins hitting the victim, requesting more money. The victim gives his wallet to the offender, who then runs off.

The scope of the offender's objective is inherently open ended when the interaction of a robbery begins. What seems to be a stickup at the start, may start to seem like something else as well when the offender demands that the victim take off his clothes [40322]. The stickup may turn into a rape or a kidnapping [40419, 40220], and the robbery situation may move from the street back to the victim's home [40122, 40321]. Or the stickup may be mixed with gratuitous assault into a unique concoction of vicious will, with the offenders allowing fate to terminate the event, as in this case:

[41202] A 31-year-old man and some friends are in the bar of a motorcycle club when three or four males come up to the victim and suddenly
hit him in the face with a broken beer bottle. They continue the assault,
spreading it to the victim's friends and using folding chairs as weapons.
They forcibly take the victim's coat, wallet, and car keys. Then they tell
the victim they are going to shoot him. While the offenders are discussing this project, the victims escape and call the police.

Such elaborations and extensions of the stickup are relatively rare, but
their possibility is not. In the time it takes for the interaction to determine
that the typical stickup will be only short lived and only a stickup, the
offender, as well as the victim, is in suspense.

Robbers often run off when there is opposition. In only 4 of the 105
robbery killings in the data set did offenders abandon the efforts without
successfully completing the robbery, but robbery-homicides are probably
biased to overrepresent offenders who will not quit. In the sample of 332
Chicago robberies in which the victims were injured, the offenders fled in
58, or approximately 17 percent of the cases.[70] The following case is one
example:

[40426] A male Hispanic, judged by the victims to be between 18 and
22 years old, entered a variety store after closing on a Friday night and
ordered three females, aged 27, 33, and 39, to lie on the floor. He "then
told them that he 'was a mean, mother-fucker, and would shoot the head
off of anyone who attempted to move.'" But one of the women fought
back, striking and kicking him. He used the gun, but only as a club,
hitting her with the butt, and then ran off.

Even where the victims do not resist in any way, the offenders must
determine how long to keep taking. To take a victim's cash is relatively
quick. To take his food stamps as well may take a moment longer. To take
his jacket may also be attractive, but doing so requires that the offenders
remain exposed as being engaged in a stickup for yet another moment. And
to take his shirt is a bit more time consuming and more complex to negotiate [40925]. The next case, in its unusual character, indicates how much
robbers typically do *not* do, that they often *might* do.

[41915] Two males, estimated to be between 25 and 30, confront a man
and wife who are out for a mid-afternoon walk in their neighborhood.
One displays a knife and demands her money. As she fumbles to hand
over the $3 she then possesses, the offenders notice that she has gold-
filled dentures. Before fleeing, they forcibly extract her bridgework,
remove her diamond wedding band, and take $6 from her husband.

The longer the offender can keep the victims in suspense, the more opportunity he will have to exploit the potential for gain. As intimidating as guns may seem to victims, offenders do not act as if they have great faith in the power of their weapons to make them invulnerable. If they are to sustain the event for more than a few moments, they are likely to employ some additional strategy to maintain a state of suspense. They may join with other offenders in specialized roles, either to shorten the time required to complete the robbery—sending one to explore the back rooms while another cleans out the cash register and a third takes valuables directly from the victim—or to freeze the scene, as when one stands guard at the door and another holds the victims at bay.

If the victims' experience of suspense in a stickup is often harrowing, the offender's experience is often unnerving. The structure that offenders give to the interaction in robberies seems to have metaphorically reassuring, as well as utilitarian, values for them. Robbers call the event, most commonly, a stickup and less commonly, a holdup. Experienced stickup men are aware of the risks of having victims actually stick up their hands. As Henry Williamson warned, "Now you never allow a man to put his hands up in a robbery. That's just televisin' what you're doin'."[71] "Stickup" and "holdup" are specifically appealing for their metaphoric significance. Both terms have strikingly phallic overtones, but they also suggest victims with hands held up high, as if suspended or hung by invisible ropes.[72] Orders that victims should not move or that they should lie down serve to dramatize a corpselike state; in one case, three victims were ordered to lie one on top of the other, forming a stack reminiscent of a death-camp scene. The result is valuable to the offenders because the beginnings of resistance by the victims are more readily detectable in the context of a "frozen" scene. But they also reassure the offenders that they can control the situation, since they dramatize a background in which the possibility of opposition has already been killed off.

Through his sharp attentions to the possibilities of resistance by victims, outside intervention, and undisclosed loot, the stickup man, like the victim, moves into the suspense of existing in alien worlds. If he unites with co-offenders, the better to manage the uncertainties of the victim's and outside response, he subjects his fate to uncertainties in still other alien worlds.

Colleagues in a stickup may not do enough to dominate their assigned part of the interaction or, what is perhaps more disconcerting, they may do too much. When police question multiple offenders after robbery-homicides, it is customary for each suspect to allege that the other was the one who went beyond the collective understanding of the project. Although obviously self-serving, such accounts seem to be accurate at times, as in the following case:

[11209] While out walking, a middle-aged man was confronted by three teenage males. Offender 1 revealed a handgun and demanded money.

When the victim replied he had none to give, offender 1 began screaming
that he was lying and shot the victim in the left side. At this point,
offender 2 attempted to grab offender 1, while offender 3 tried to push
the victim out of the shooting range. They were unsuccessful. Offender
1 shot three more times before they all fled.[73]

The irrational inclinations of co-offenders increase the uncertainties not
only in amateurish or adolescent stickups. Even among "career" robbers,
a collective stickup operation makes possible risk-enhancing actions that
would be unlikely or impossible in a solo operation. When an adolescent
James Carr was taken by Willie Ransom, a supposedly sophisticated, older
associate, to a Mexican market in Pico Gardens in Los Angeles for his first
commercial stickup, Ransom put a gun into the clerk's face, and then, as
Ransom picked up bottles of port wine and lemon juice, Carr found himself "sweatin' blood behind the Wonder Bread, nervous as hell at doing
my first job like this, and fucking Willie's doing his shopping!"[74] During
the mature stage of his career as an armed robber, at age 28, John Allen,
using a "good stickup crew" that included his brother, Nut, robbed a
Washington, D.C., bar frequented by "sophisticated sissies." Their getaway was stalled by Nut's delay in surfacing from behind the bar. On the
way home, Nut explained that he interrupted his assigned task, which was
to get the money behind the bar, to rape one of the waitresses.[75]

In addition to the suspense that arises from the inevitable unknowns
about the reactions of victims and co-offenders, the offender is in suspense
most profoundly about himself. The ferocity and the tenacity of the claim
to be "bad" have no necessary relationship. The stickup is a process in
which one's *own* capacities and inclinations may become features of an
alien system. Henry Williamson was surprised at his reaction to resistance
by an aged victim in a "semi-drugstore" he was robbing:

> I was actually pullin' the trigger, and at that range I couldn't a missed!
> But I just caught myself, and stopped! See, it wasn't in my mind to kill
> him. I was doin' it without thinkin'!. . . . I was kinda shook up at myself
> for comin' so close.[76]

Even when the victim does not resist, the stickup man must feel sufficiently comfortable with his own actions so that he does not take flight.
In the Chicago data set, there were several instances in which the offender,
even without confronting resisting victims, appeared to abandon the crime
out of shock at what he had become.

> [41217] A 29-year-old man is confronted on the street on a Friday
> evening by a male who, in a robbery attempt, stabs him in the hand with
> a knife and flees without taking anything of value.
> [41218] In the early hours of a Saturday morning, the victim has just left

his car to enter a neighborhood tavern when two males approach. One reveals a handgun and demands the victim's money. As the victim turns to face the offender, the offender shoots him once in the abdomen. Both offenders then flee without taking anything.

Nor, again, is this aspect of the suspense in a stickup limited to the young or amateurish. There are always open-ended questions about features of the externals of stickups, such as How much might the victims be holding back? How long can they be controlled? Has the situation become so vulnerable to outside intervention that it should be abandoned? In response, there are always internal questions about "guts" or "heart"—about whether the offender can sustain for another moment the suspense of being in a stickup and becoming the person he must be to succeed.

Consider, finally, what the resistance of victims puts at stake for one who entertains robbery as a more or less regular practice. The most troublesome consequence that emerges when victims resist is not the difficulty in going on with the current offense, but the uncertainties that one's own response may create for going on to the next. Running off when victims resist to find other, easier, equally promising victims, would be the rational course, if one could enter robberies knowing that one will run off if the victims resist. The problem is to steel yourself to begin a robbery if you anticipate taking flight in the event of opposition.

In stickups, as in other fields in which a difficult spiritual commitment must be made, many are called but few are chosen. A large number of adolescents in low-income ghettoes try stickups, doing one or a few and then stopping; only a small percentage continue into their late twenties and thirties, becoming the relatively few heavies who commit scores or even hundreds of robberies for each year they spend out of jail. Whatever the influences of arrest and limited profitability that shape this pattern of desistance, the young, would-be heavy or career stickup man must struggle with the uncertainties of interaction in robberies as one of the major barriers to going on.

Put another way, the practical constraints on making a career of stickups are such that one *cannot* simply adopt violence as an instrumental device, to be enacted or dropped as situational contingencies dictate. It is practically impossible to make a career of stickups just by making a calculated show of a disposition to be "bad"; you must live the commitment to deviance. You must really mean it.

The crucial dangers for a career in stickups are not those posed by the failure to attend closely, within the quickly evolving dynamics of robbery scenes, to when and how much force must be applied to overcome victims. Rather, they are in attending too deliberately, even before entering the scene, to what victims are likely to do, to what you, in turn, may be required to do to succeed, and to the costs and benefits of the resulting fate. In every robbery, the offender's specific claim to take possession of the victim's valuables and the offender's general claim to possess a competent immorality to pull off such acts are simultaneously at risk. The ultimate challenge for the would-be stickup man is to convince *himself* not to "give it up."

That a distinctive morally insensitive will, a true hardheadedness, is essential to stick with stickup has not been appreciated in the study of robbery, which has emphasized numerous striking patterns depicting offenders as flexibly rational. These patterns are not false or artificial, but they do not warrant the characterization of offenders as simply instrumental, morally sensitive, and basically rational in their use of violence. Now, with an appreciation of the hardheadedness and moral meanness that are required by the situational practicalities of the offense to make sense of persisting in a stickup, we may turn to examine the peculiar project in which a career as a pointedly hard and publicly "bad" man makes sense.

CHAPTER 6

Action, Chaos, and Control: Persisting with Stickup

Our focus on stickups to this point has been on their situationally specific contingencies. If we wish to understand how men manage to experience stickups as persistently attractive, we must look more broadly into their lives. The major studies that have attempted to provide systematic data on career robbers have agreed on two relevant findings. One is that there *is* a distinguishable group of persistent criminals—"heavy," "professional," "serious," "hardened," or "intensive"—who commit a disproportionate percentage of robberies. The other is that these career criminals commit a *variety* of opportunistic crimes, not just robbery, and their predatory crimes are not done just to meet financial needs or to support an addiction, but to sustain what most studies dub a "hedonistic" lifestyle.[1]

A study of 500 bank robbers who were convicted in the federal Eastern District of New York (Brooklyn, Queens, Long Island, and Staten Island) between 1964 and 1976 identified a group of heavy or career robbers whom the author, James Haran, characterized as dedicated to hedonism. On the basis of official records, especially presentence reports, Haran found that the heavy-career criminal makes "his living primarily from a variety of illegal activity, including robbery, but not just bank robbery," and tends to repeat a type of crime but is not a specialist. On occasions when he got away from a bank robbery, the "loot was itself quickly dissipated on high living: women, travel, drugs and sometimes big cars."[2]

A famous Rand Corporation study, headed by Jan and Marcia Chaiken, gathered self-reports of criminal histories from 2,200 inmates in California, Michigan, and Texas. Sorting out numerous career lines, they isolated the "violent predator" who, compared to other offenders, distinctively begins his criminal career before age 16; frequently commits violent and property crimes before age 18; and, over his career, commits three or more types of crimes, particularly robbery, drug dealing, and assault, at high rates. Chaiken and Chaiken found that 10 percent of the violent predators re-

ported committing, in the period preceding confinement, robberies at the
rate of 135 per year. Unmarried, with few family obligations; not employed
steadily or for long stretches; frequently using hard drugs, including multiple combinations (heroin and barbiturates, barbiturates and alcohol, am-
phetamines and alcohol), these "violent predators [became] entrenched in
a highly deviant life-style while they [were] very young."[3]

James Wright and Peter Rossi's recent questionnaire survey of 1,874
inmates of 11 prisons in 10 states found that "the average respondent . . .
was 'into' sex, drugs, guns, and crime before he was even legally eligible to
drive in most states." Within this large set, the researchers identified about 5
percent of the sample, or 90 men, who did "more than a few" drug deals,
robberies, and assaults; they accounted for almost 20 percent of all the
crimes reported by the sample. These especially "heavy" criminals were not
criminal specialists but "omnibus felons"—"criminal 'opportunists' . . .
prone to commit virtually any kind of crime . . . in the environment."[4]

These studies support the thrust of the available life-history data that,
as a general rule, robbery is sufficiently attractive to make sense as a
sustained commitment only when it is part of a larger lifestyle of deviance.
Concretely, this means that one who would continue doing stickups must
(1) combine stickup with other activities that contribute to a life that is
diffusely characterized by illicit action and (2) elaborate throughout personal relations, as well as criminal practice, the transcendent significance
of being a hardman.

Action and Stickup

The question, "Where's the action?,"[5] could be asked by drug users looking for a score, hedonists looking for a party with an ambience of sexual
promiscuity, gamblers in search of a game, and professional thieves hunting up colleagues to join in a theft. These various forms of "action" share
three initially notable aspects. Each is either formally deviant or at least
conducted with an aura of the illicit.

Each is also a form of play: people may try to "score" not only by making
soccer goals, touchdowns, and baseball runs, but by "copping" illegal
drugs, "sticking up" a bank, or getting "laid." Like games, the outcome of
action is uncertain but, unlike most social relations outside games, in
action, there will be a clearly defined outcome, a measure of success given
in a zero-sum form.[6] Thus, in casual sexual encounters, one either does or
does not "make it," but when discussing a troubled marriage, spouses can
have long arguments in which one says, this is a failure, and the other
earnestly protests, no, it's not.

Furthermore, each of the forms of action share a promise of experience that is spiritually profound and existentially fundamental. In sex, white people "go down," black people "get down," and both progress toward a "come"; craps shooters try to "make" a point "come"; and drug users "get down" and drug deals, as well as stickups, "go down." If the terminology is not completely substitutable across the forms of action—one can "get off" on drugs or through sex but "get away" with crimes—the various forms of action share an everyday vocabulary of metaphysical transcendence, indicating the operation of a common seductive process.

The relevance of other forms of action to robbery is occasionally revealed in the situational specifics of the crime. In the following case (taken from the Chicago data set introduced in chapter 5), note the importance to the offender of signifying that various discrete forms of action were involved:

> [40220] A male, thought by victims to be in his mid-twenties, pulls a gun on four women who are in a car in a parking lot. He forces one to perform oral sex in the front seat, then robs two gold chains, and then says, "This is a regular robbery—bitch—hands up and heads down—take off all your clothes." As he leaves the car, he tells them not to look out for 15 minutes or he'll "blow your heads off." Then he strikes the face of the woman he raped, six times.

More commonly, stickup is combined with various other forms of action in a way that victims cannot know, as one stage in an ongoing episode of action. Robbery offenders sometimes work up their drive toward stickups with drugs and liquor in earlier episodes that victims have not witnessed and that the police, even when aware of the larger process, are not likely to describe in their official reports. But in the rare instance that a robbery ends in death, the police make extraordinary efforts to document the crime; then their reports indicate a variegated deviant lifestyle. For example:

> [11204] The four offenders, ranging in age from 18 to 22, had been smoking marijuana and drinking. One suggested they "rip off" someone. Another nominated as an easy "victim" a drug dealer he knew from previous buys. After the stickup, which resulted in murder and the robbery of cash, two revolvers, and two cannisters of "happysticks," they sped away in stolen vehicles. When stopped by the police for speeding, the offenders were tied to the murder through quickly circulated police identifications of the victim's weapons.

In exceptional instances, police reports on particular stickups capture so many intensely lived themes of illicit action that they depict a process of rampage:

[10201] A 59-year-old man was walking near his home at 8 P.M. when he was "accosted" by two males, aged 16 and 19, who had been driving when one observed that "old people get their checks today." Earlier, they had stolen the car at gunpoint, stopped a couple on the street, and robbed the man and raped the woman.

They drove past the victim, then backed up, and ran out of the car toward him, saying, "Freeze or I will blow your head off." The victim was a security guard carrying a holster gun. After his gun was spotted, and possibly after some resistance, he was shot. The offenders fled on foot, then stole another car and raped its female driver.

In their autobiographies, career robbers decry such events as amateurish, adolescent, or crazy. But if robbers who like to refer to themselves as "professionals" and who are regarded by the police as "heavies" conduct stickups in a more routine, businesslike manner, it is not because their attraction to the crime is unrelated to the seductive quality of action. Notwithstanding their affection for the rhetoric of "professionalism," experienced robbers differ from amateurs not so much because of a practical work attitude toward the crime as because they have had the time and have made the connections to build lives in which the action of stickups has become continuous with more diffusely established themes of action. In effect, "kids" and "crazies" are attempting to experience in one short-lived social situation the richness of action that career robbers have managed to institutionalize throughout their lives. Maturity for robbers does not mean an end to action in stickups as much as the routine integration of illicit sex, use of intoxicating substances, and high-risk methods of committing a variety of property crimes in an overall way of life. It is specifically the *connections* among the various forms of illicit action—the possibility of constructing a *transcendent* way of life around action—that sustains the motivation to do stickups.

We can isolate three ways in which career stickup men construct lives with this seductive appeal. One is to engage in sex, drug use, crime, and gambling in a particular *temporal form:* spontaneously started, open ended, and episodic. The second is to conduct these activities in a particular *social relational* form: within networks that are both crosscutting and accessible to strangers. The third is to juxtapose *irrationality in consumption* against any rationality accomplished in the commission of crimes.

In the following analysis, I will draw on fifteen life histories, ethnographies, and autobiographies that document the lives of men in stickups. These works cover a range of over fifty years and a diversity of regions and ethnicities: a young Polish "jackroller," who was active in Chicago in the 1920s; a white Canadian, who stole from warehouses, dealt drugs, and committed robberies in Toronto and Windsor in the 1950s; black "hustlers," who were active in Detroit, Los Angeles, Chicago, New York, and Washington, D.C., some in the 1950s, 1960s, and 1970s; recently retired robbers, who were interviewed in the early 1980s in the London "underworld"; Puerto Ricans from fighting street groups in the 1960s who moved into drug dealing and robbery outside Spanish Harlem; and the recent, vivid biography of a half-Irish, half-Sicilian, "wiseguy," connected to organized crime, who was active in New York until 1980. Running across the personal, class, ethnic, geographic, and historical variations in these lives is a common commitment to stickup (notably, the term itself is natural to all these settings) and a broader effort to sustain a life characterized by action through the use of intoxicating or euphoric substances, illicit sex, gambling, and participation in various forms of criminality other than robbery.[7]

As they construct lives characterized by transcendent themes of action, these men differ greatly in their skills, status, and style. They also differ enormously in the extent to which they succeed, not only in material terms but existentially, in the degree to which they infuse their lives with action. On the one hand, many run-of-the-mill professional criminals sleep a lot, not only during stretches in prison but also during the many boring afternoons they spend in cheap motel rooms between "jobs."[8] In a sense, so as not to be out of the action, they choose not to be, or at least not to be aware of their existence. On the other hand, well-connected wiseguys and locally celebrated "bad niggers" may, for years, early morning after early morning, regularly fall asleep on a different bed or couch, exhausted by the action of the day.[9] These variations make all the more convincing the centrality to the motivation of the persistent stickup man of the same temporal, social relational, and spending patterns.

TEMPORAL STRUCTURE IN THE LIFE OF DEVIANT ACTION

Not all who gamble, or are active in illicit sexual relations, or use illegal drugs, or commit stickups, are equally into the action. The extent of involvement is related to the temporal structure of participation. For example, one of the distinctions that is significant in the legal casinos in Gardena (a small city next to Los Angeles) is whether a player routinizes the beginning and end of given periods of play. As a recent participant-observer noted, those who are into the action play poker in an open-ended form, often for twenty or thirty hours straight, to the point of exhaustion.[10] For those who come to play between 8 P.M. and 10 P.M. each Tuesday and Thursday, the experience is a different matter. Similarly, a "party" may or may not have any action. "Party" recently took on an illicit overtone in American culture, as signaled by the emergence of the verb form "to party." Parents, using the traditional noun on behalf of young children, issue invitations to a "party" that prescribe the temporal limits of the event, say between 3 P.M. and 5 P.M. "Let's party" or "we were really partying" uses a verbal, temporally open form that acknowledges personal autonomy, which, in turn, entails a competence to act in morally deviant ways and that touches the provocative by suggesting that the collective activity has an unbounded character. When people party all night or for days on end, they don't have fun, as they might at a children's party; they are into the action.

If participants can be more into or less into the action, in a related way, the forms of action may be more diffused or less diffused in their lives. Those who would construct lives that are dominated by action structure their participation in episodic, cyclical forms, so that they can get into the action more or less spontaneously and with an air of an indefinitely extended commitment. Engaged in, in this temporal style, illicit sex, heavy drinking and illegal drug use, property crimes, and gambling carry an aura of special significance for characterizing one's life. And even without a substantive engagement, there is a constant possibility of involvement, which lends an aura of action to long stretches of what otherwise would be conventional life.

Sex.   Statistical descriptions of career robbers reveal that they are rarely married and usually have offspring whom they do not regularly support.[11] What such data mean from the inside, of course, is not self-evident. One can readily find claims in the autobiographies of professional criminals that their sexual experiences are sensually superior to those of respectable married men. Still we have no grounds to assess such claims.

But what is more important, neither do they. Such claims indicate a readily verifiable, gamelike character in the framework of sexual experience. The best available life histories of career stickup men usually describe a series of illicit sexual relationships. For low-level career criminals, these relationships often involve liaisons with prostitutes and for higher-level criminals, a succession of mistresses.[12] Somewhere in between might fit the relations with "club girls," the waitresses and hostesses in West End clubs who, Laurie Taylor reported, provide members of the London underworld with regular sexual services.[13] In all of these forms, sex is experienced in social relationships that are entered and renewed in an open-ended, quickly or constantly negotiated, fashion.

Career criminals who are married may routinize escapes from marital ties for episodic adventures with extramarital partners. Karen, the wife of Henry Hill (the wiseguy), recalled that her husband would often stay out all night and be absent for several days; "card-playing" was his excuse for not being home on Friday nights:

> Later I found out that it was also the girl friend night. Everybody who had a girl friend took her out on Friday night. Nobody took his wife out on Friday night. The wives went out on Saturday night. That way there were no accidents of running into somebody's wife when they were with their girl friends.[14]

Such illicit relations are abiding resources for action not simply because they are unconventional, but because they indicate an ongoing, gaming theme in sexual life. The wiseguy institution of seeing the girlfriend on Friday nights did not insulate Henry from the "constant battle" of maintaining his dual relationships, which required perhaps as many quick-thinking tactics and tricky maneuvers as did his criminal activities. His biographer treats us to accounts from both sides when Henry's wife is banging on the mistress's door for a confrontation; and later we see Henry sobering up in bed as he realizes that his wife is straddling him with a loaded gun aimed between his eyes.[15]

Henry Hill might be horrified by the comparison, but the gaming action in the social relationships in which his sexual life was embedded was similar to the following account by Billie Miller, who grew up in Hamilton, Canada, and pursued a varied but always cheap criminal career in several Canadian cities in the 1950s and 1960s:

> I had a lot of opportunities going, but I just couldn't dig it. I did, but I didn't. Like I'm staying with one chick, and I might have another one working out of there, and she won't know about the other, or else she's trying to move in with me. Like when I was with Donna, Holy Christ, it was ridiculous, some of the fucking things I used to go through with some of the broads down on the corners. It was a change. I used to duck out and do things and play all kinds of games, but I'd always end up with Donna because she was the main chick with me as far as I was concerned.[16]

The life histories of black stickup men represent other variations on the theme of sexual action. Henry Williamson, a street robber-hustler who was active in Chicago in the 1950s, reported, again and again, being approached by women who would invite him up for drinks, knock on his door, or simply ask him for sex, after which they might make his continued access to "free pussy" dependent on a more permanent commitment, which he would occasionally make but would never honor for long.[17] For many black hustlers, "the corner" is a place for picking up sex as well as other sorts of action; the "corner" symbolizes the conjunction of lines of action that begin to move toward each other unwittingly, eventually crossing in an unpredictable encounter.

Jones, a half-Italian, half-black mugger who was active on New York's Lower East Side in the early 1970s, when James Willwerth observed him, moved between his parents' house and the apartment of his black girlfriend, who was pregnant with his child, while maintaining a relationship with a white girlfriend who was also pregnant with his child.[18] For Jones, as for Henry Hill, the scheming that was necessary to maintain access to two women who knew of each other, frequently threatened to turn the relationships from provocative action into soap opera bathos.

James Carr, a black stickup man who was active in Los Angeles in the late 1950s and early 1960s, repeatedly used gaming or conning techniques to turn chance encounters into rape, first of women and then of men in prison. A frequent device was to obtain the victim's acquiescence as the cost of protection against the aggressions of others and then to delight in a second level of meaning for the screwing by turning the victim over to those others. Carr's arrangement of gang rapes, or "trains," kept action in sex by ensuring that relations would be short lived. As Carr explained:

> Sex was a very minute thing. It didn't have to make any sense. It was for the minute. You did it for a while, then it became natural. Everything we did was like that—unquestioning and explosive. You can only do crazy shit when it's your routine. With sex it was the game that was routine: nearly every train started and ended with the same moves. On the street it was more the attitude—looking for openings to fuck around or fuck somebody up—so the actions themselves were more diverse and spontaneous. Like the time, a couple of months after hooking up with the Farmers, when I was just walking around down on 103rd Street with four brothers. We'd been smoking some weed and were really broke and hungry when we walked by this Mexican bakery. There were all kinds of pastries and cakes in the window, just sitting there. We didn't hesitate.[19]

Stickups.   As Carr's stream of consciousness indicates, the structures of action in the social organization of sex and property crime were continuous for him. The distinctive temporal qualities that frequently characterized his sexual relations—capable of being initiated at virtually any time, not involving permanent commitments, and episodic in the sense of being recurrent or extended but not uniformly ending—also characterizes the career criminal's experience of stickup. Robberies are committed repeatedly, but not at any scheduled time, and will often be done in an open-ended series.

Persistent thieves work in units that are more accurately described as cycles, rather than as individual acts. For a short, indefinite period—until investigative or security systems shut down the opportunity—one attempts to convert a batch of counterfeit money or forged traveler's checks, make purchases on one or more stolen credit cards, or use stolen or false identification papers to pass bad personal checks.

An episodic quality of participation in crime develops smoothly for the mature stickup man out of forms of criminal activity that are widely popular among adolescents. As a teenager, Claude Brown would leave his Harlem home for several days of "catting," "knowing that I was going to get caught sooner or later, but I just didn't want to get caught before I had stolen a new suit."[20] Being "on the cat" entailed a combination of urban camping and urban poaching: an outing in which one had to arrange all the fundamentals of survival on one's own, without relying exclusively on conventional resources. An informant from East Los Angeles related that a common cue among his buddies for launching a series of sneak thefts and stickups would be the phrase, "Let's go on a run and pull some jales [ha-lays]." The "run" stands for the extended time for the adventure; "pull" and "jale" is a redundancy that plays off an old colloquialism for robbery, "to pull a job."

A cyclical form for committing crime has also been documented among middle-class white adolescents. A set of well-to-do, respectable adolescents observed by William Chambliss concentrated their acts of vandalism, con scheming, and petty theft on auto trips to nearby communities where their reputation as "saints" would not be affected.[21] They would go out, not to commit a discrete offense, but to exploit the opportunities that might arise during the ride.

Hustling also signifies a generalized search for criminal opportunities. One goes "on the hustle" not at appointed, routinized times and not for a particular stickup. When spontaneous opportunities would arise in a series, Henry Williamson would do a series of stickups. More systematically, he would go out at times specifically to do stickups in serial form, as this account indicates:

> At this time in that neighborhood they had a special type of hustlin' called "draggin'." That mean, we'd go a certain distance out of the neighborhood and we'd rob everybody we'd meet. Now we may pass up some people, but we don't pass up many.[22]

As a practical matter, men who stick up retail stores often learn quickly the value of getting away in a car that cannot be traced to them. Stolen cars are a common solution. Having successfully stolen a car, it is prudent to commit a series of stickups in a short period, before the car is likely to be placed on police lists, rather than to commit only one stickup per each car theft.

Well-connected criminals may commit bigger robberies with more planning, but their criminal involvement also tends to be episodic. Sophisticated hijackers may await notice of the arrival of trucks or ships carrying items for which they have requests from fences or buyers. The uncertainties of schedules in freight businesses lend an unpredictable, cyclical quality to their criminal activities.

When an especially big stickup is accomplished, for example, Henry Hill's involvement in the $480,000 Air France or the $6 million Lufthansa robberies, the execution of the robbery is short-lived and tightly bounded, but the event is extended as an organizing theme by elaborate planning and, even more so, by the repercussions of success. The wake of a big robbery brings massive investigative pressures and, from inside criminal networks, complex negotiations or a series of battles to distribute the take.

Small-time criminals like Billie Miller often exploit a variety of opportunities that arise from short-term acquaintances and living arrangements.

On one occasion, shortly after his release from prison, Billie, who was in a bar in Windsor with a fellow he recently met, was open to whatever might seduce him: the romantic attentions of the sister of his newfound friend, who was also the bar's owner and who ran numbers in the territory; drug connections through new acquaintances; and the entreaties of two burglars who needed help breaking into a safe. In effect, Billie's project became the exploitation of the possibilities for illicit action in a particular site—a project with its own rhythm and uncertain course.

On a more profitable level, a wiseguy may develop a criminal project through "muscling in" on a business: he obtains a partnership in a small business in settlement for a high-interest loan made to cover a gambling debt, puts several associates in no-show jobs on the payroll, arranges for the hijacking of shipments, and finally "busts out" or "milks" the business to bankruptcy by ordering large volumes of supplies on credit and reselling them without a concern for paying the creditors. Although more deliberate and systematic than the street robber's style, the wiseguy's methodology also structures his criminal involvement into the temporal form of episodes.

Some of the crimes involved would be big, some small. As Henry Hill recounted, major figures in organized crime are not necessarily averse to petty criminality. Paul Vario was chief of the first group of wiseguys with whom Henry worked:

> When I was doing pretty well in the stolen credit-card business, Paulie was always asking me for stolen credit cards whenever he and his wife, Phyllis, were going out for the night. Paulie called stolen cards "Muldoons," and he always said that liquor tastes better on a Muldoon. . . . if you knew wiseguys you would know right away that the best part of the night for Paulie came from the fact that he was getting over on somebody.[23]

The image of big-time robbers who take carefully isolated risks only when the stakes are high and avoid episodic involvement in little crimes appears to be mythical. As Laurie Taylor concluded, after interviews with a variety of English criminals:

> It isn't a case of two kinds of professional criminals—the small-time and the big-time. Only the opportunities which are available fit into these two categories. The criminals move between them.[24]

Heavy Drug and Alcohol Use.   There is a close association between the use of illicit drugs and robbery. Most of the life histories of persistent or "heavy" robbers reveal that they were also drug dealers and heavy users of heroin or cocaine. But a close look at their lives shows a relationship much more complex than is suggested by theories of the criminogenic powers of addiction.

• Piri Thomas moved along a well-trodden path, from "being a careful snorter, content to take my kicks of sniffing through my nose, to a not-so-careful skin-popper, and now was [*sic*] full-grown careless mainliner" of heroin in Spanish Harlem. He stole, dealt drugs, and fenced stolen goods to support his habit. But he began his serious robbing only *after* kicking his habit and as an alternative to dealing, specifically because "[I] can't trust myself to even get near that shit in no way."[25]

• Malcolm X recalled that at the time he "pulled" his "first robberies and stick-ups," his drug use was closely related to the practice of the crimes. But the robberies were not supporting his drug use; on the contrary, drug use, initially, was supporting his robberies: "As the pros did, I would key myself to pull these jobs by my first use of hard dope [sniffing cocaine]. Between jobs, staying high on narcotics kept me from getting nervous."[26]

• Contrary to their chief's injunctions, Henry Hill and some fellow wise-guys dealt drugs and used cocaine, but were hardly hijacking trucks to support an addiction.[27]

• Manny Torres developed what he described as a "love sickness" for heroin and later committed robberies partly to buy drugs. But he began using heroin, not out of low self-esteem or in frustration at an inability to escape poverty, but at a time when he was riding high as a numbers runner and gambler, as another step up in a life *already committed* to the pursuit of action.[28]

• Henry Williamson enjoyed dope, but it appears that in the black heroin market of Chicago in the 1950s, he did not have to steal much to be a user:

> Now back in those times dope was good, and you didn't have to spend no great deal of money for it. It cost a dollar and a half a cap. We could buy a cap, and just four of us all could sit down and snort it, and all of us would be messed up.[29]

He robbed and used the proceeds to buy drugs and other pleasures for years before he discovered, in jail and after a fellow inmate identified his "symptoms" for him, that he was addicted.[30] For a long time, even after he had developed a physical dependence, heroin meant freedom, not enslavement or necessity. Heroin use was not the organizing theme in his life; it was only one of several seductive ways of staying in the action.

• At different phases of his varied criminal career as a drug dealer, pimp, numbers runner, and stickup man, John Allen had different relationships to drug use. His phases of most intense heroin use were not necessarily his phases of most intense involvement in stickups. It was natural for John Allen to become involved in a stickup from the context of casual hedonism, while "we was doing our usual thing—drinking wine and smoking a little herb."[31] Like many others in this set, he became self-consciously addicted relatively late in his career, at age 27, long after he was a heavy stickup man.

• Jones bought and used cocaine often, much as he often bought and used marijuana and wine. The occasion for its use was sometimes a moment of irritation, but not always, and his irritation was not the dope fiend's desperation to "get well."

• Robby Wideman had been a desperate dope fiend, disgracing himself by such acts as arranging for the theft of his family's television set to support his habit, years before he participated in the robbery/homicide that lead to his life sentence. And when that critical stickup developed, it was not to buy drugs to satisfy a craving. Rather, it was in response to an arrest that had busted his effort to move up the drug-distribution ladder and as part of a cunning strategy to trick and rob a fence so he could, once again, finance his ascension to "Superfly," dealer—not user—status.[32] After the fatal robbery, he immediately used the proceeds not to consume drugs but to enter other forms of action:

> Two double hits of gin at the Hurricane and I'm cool. . . . we in business again. Everything gon be alright. Got some dough. . . . We got our shit together and we know people is watching us. We clean. We cool. They gon hear more about us. We headed for the big time. Number one. People's eyes on us and we ready to party party. Party hearty.[33]

Even for men who organize their days significantly around the maintenance of a heroin habit and who rob to support the habit, the practical requirements are not necessarily experienced as inconsistent with other themes of action, such as drudgery, monotony, or tiresome necessity. Heroin use, even when it responds to self-conscious physical dependence, does not condemn one to a discipline akin to that governing a menial working-class job. A recent study, involving in-depth interviews in the black ghettoes of Chicago, New York, Washington, D.C., and Philadelphia with 124 men who had used heroin daily for eight days before the interview and who had avoided arrest and treatment, found that

> users regard it with a sense of pride and dignity, that they stand tall in "the hustler's limelight" as one said. Hustling is a daily test of purpose and resourcefulness, even of stamina.[34]

Most of the men avoided violence in their hustling (only 18 percent had engaged in armed robbery or stickups) and, indeed, many hustled without committing crimes.[35] Those who did rob, however, seemed to appreciate the adventure they faced; as one said, "I like to stick-up. I like to take the risk," much as do stickup men who are not maintaining opiate habits.[36] Thus, even the hustling heroin addict may experience his drug use as part of a larger fascination to test his mettle.

More typically, heavy stickup men use "heavy" drugs in the gaps between other adventures. Alcohol, heroin, cocaine, marijuana, speed, and other pills are handy, transportable adventure kits—ideally suited for diffusing action throughout one's life. Indeed, because of the value of opiates for sustaining action, it seems that heroin use is more likely to be the proximate result than the immediate cause of stickups. From Chicago, Jug, who became a daily user, reported that his first experience came after "a couple of my partners went down and they pulled a stick-up and they had plenty of money, so they came back after buying dope for everybody."[37]

Gambling. Goffman saw gambling as the prototype of action; Becker noted the use by prostitutes and professional thieves of the vocabulary of action to refer to places where they could find abundant opportunities to work.[38] Many of the distinctive terms in the lingo of criminals draw on the symbolic structure of gambling to articulate a subtle sense of everyday action: to "go bust," "get busted," or "bust out" is to run out of wagering money, be arrested, or commit a bankruptcy fraud; "high play" is big betting and ostentatious spending; one may "fade," or avoid costs risked by, an arrest or a point in craps; to "shoot out" is to throw dice or to recruit a woman to prostitution; and one may try "to make it" and then have "made" a point in craps, a woman, or a safe.[39]

When stickup men recall the early phases of their lives, they often give an especially significant place to gambling men. Billie Miller remembered his home in Hamilton, Canada, in the 1940s as "a slum in a middle-class area," and his father, an elevator operator, as a "kind of a hustling type. . . . People used to come to the house all the time for card games."[40] As a young boy living in the Chicago black belt, Henry Williamson worshipped his father, whom he thought was "a pretty good gambler":

> I never went to no ball games with him or nothin' like that. We used to sit down and he'd teach me all the tricks of cards. There ain't too many games he taught me, but he did teach me how to play poker, coon cane, and he taught me one more game, blackjack. He taught me how to shoot dice too. Now he didn't teach me to gamble, but he taught me the games. I didn't gamble 'til he died.[41]

Robby Wideman's maternal grandfather, John French, was, to some neighbors,

> this crazy daddy who wore a big brown country hat and gambled and drank wine and once ran a man out of town, ran him away without ever laying a hand on him or making a bad-mouthed threat, just cut his eyes a certain way when he said the man's name and the word went out and the man who had cheated a drunk John French with loaded dice was gone.[42]

Gambling is a common form of entry into the general world of action. For some, gambling provided their first criminal work, even before gambling became a personal avocation. Many of the biographies of black, Puerto Rican, and Italian men from urban areas on the East Coast who became specialists in stickups describe boyhood periods as numbers runners. Others entered action through the consumer or user side of gambling. Stanley, in 1920s Chicago, quit his job, took his pay, met a friend from a juvenile detention facility (where he had been incarcerated essentially because he was a runaway), and

> . . . started to blow it in. I was lord of all for a few days. We had our "wild women," went to movies, and had plenty to eat. We also shot crap . . . and in a few days the dough was gone. This little spurt of fortune and adventure had turned my head. Now I wanted a good time.[43]

His career as a robber then developed when his friend instructed him in the ways of "jackrolling." Malcolm X was in his late adolescence in the early 1940s in Boston. In a short while, he would be a traveling marijuana dealer, a burglar, and then a stickup man. But in the early 1940s, he was a countrified boy from a small town in Michigan, and his initial experiences with illicit action were with a mix of traditional vices, of which gambling was an inseparable part.

> The first liquor I drank, my first cigarettes, even my first reefers, I can't specifically remember. But I know they were all mixed together with my first shooting craps, playing cards, and betting my dollar a day on the numbers, as I started hanging out at night with Shorty and his friends.[44]

For some stickup men, gambling is never particularly important, except as an underlying metaphor for their risk-taking career as a whole. For others, intense gambling characterizes a given phase of their career. The same could be said about the other forms of action, dope use, in particular. But for men who would construct a long-term career that is organized around the pursuit of illicit action, gambling is an especially elastic resource. Joe T., a "lowball" player at legal casinos, was aware of this advantage of gambling over other forms of action:

> I probably gambled more in high school than anything else. Back then there used to be only one thing better I liked to do than play poker. I think they call it s-s-sex. But I like poker a lot better now. You know why? With sex, one shot and you're through. Here I can keep it up all day.[45]

Others might not accept the "one-shot" characterization, but it is clear that, compared to sex, stickup, or even dope use, gambling is an especially useful existential filler. From the London underworld, Laurie Taylor reported:

> Professional criminals gambled heavily, some did little else between jobs, staying up at clubs . . . for sessions lasting up to 48 hours and casually losing several thousand pounds.[46]

Henry Hill provided the definition that "hanging around and hustling means gambling. A day doesn't go by without bets going down on this or that. When I had it, I'd bet a thousand dollars on the point spread of a basketball game."[47]

In addition to its temporal elasticity, gambling invites an elastic development of the depth of action. Bets can be made on multiple games, or one can have stakes in different "plays," each with a different duration. Gambling thus provides for an overlapping of action, a metaphysical structure that is especially seductive to the person who wants to have "something going" all the time.

THE SOCIAL NETWORKS OF ILLICIT ACTION

Who is not seduced by the attractions of one or another form of action at some time? What is relatively unusual about heavy career offenders is not their substantive involvements, considered one by one, but how pervasively they diffuse varieties of illicit action through their lives. Yet even for the most persistent, heavy criminals, the emotionally intense experiences at the center of stickups, sex, drug use, and gambling are relatively rare moments. To make action one's guiding spirit, one must temporally extend its substantive forms into vast stretches of an otherwise innocent life. Any moment may be charged with deviant significance if it is treated as a preparation for illicit action or its result. Thus, such an everyday habit as adjusting the rear-view mirror of a car may be given a touch of the illicit, simply by anticipating a police presence (as Paul Vario said to Henry Hill, "It'll help you make tails"),[48] and the most mundane purchases may take on undertones of deviance if they are bought with once-dirty money.

In addition to the maintenance of an open-ended temporal structure for illicit action, persistent offenders are organized by a social structure that interlocks their separate lines of action. Apparently, there are a few persistent robbers who keep their private hedonistic relationships independent of their episodic involvement in criminal work. Bruce Jackson was personally acquainted with one such exceptional case, "the Bobbsey twins," "two California robbers . . . who had in one eighteen-month period committed nearly two hundred robberies in the Los Angeles area." According to these two partners,

> if we had gone to the first places we hung out, the cocktail lounges and places like that where we went when we were making a hundred a week, if we started going in there in a $500 suit, wearing tailor-made clothes, monogrammed silk shirts, right away you get raised eyebrows. Somebody says, 'Hmmm, what's going on here?' So you got to drop your friends, too.
>
> We *never* associated with thieves or anything like that. If we *had* to have anything to do with them, we did it and that was it. But we never ran around with them.[49]

Although some studies have found a small percentage of robbers who live otherwise conventional lives, this exceptional type of robber is typically "naive" or robs as a "fling."[50] Among persistent robbers, the Bobbsey twins appear to be rare exceptions to the social network rule.

That rule has two characteristic parts. First, there are overlaps or closely mediated ties between the sets of people with whom the offender persistently robs and commits other crimes, gambles, does drugs, has sexual relations, and parties. Second, the stickup man is frequently open to participate in one or another line of action with people who are bare acquaintances.

Cross-cutting Networks. Statistics on the careers of heavy offenders, violent predators, or habitual criminals show that those who commit a disproportionate percentage of robberies also commit a variety of other crimes, including drug dealing; "assault," which covers a variety of extortionate offenses as well as personal fights; and nonviolent property theft and fencing. One way in which persistent stickup men construct social relations that cut across various lines of illicit action is simply to commit a variety of offenses. Malcolm X's varied career in deviance—as a pimp, drug dealer, fence, gambler, burglar, stickup man, and con man—is not atypical.

An offender may geometrically increase the action in his life by exploiting his social relations in one form of action to promote another. After he escaped from a boy's home, James Carr lived with Esther,

> a big woman about twenty-five, a divorcee with a bunch of kids and a big welfare check she spent most of on me. Me and this other dude were both living there, fucking Esther, eating her food, and lying around playing records.[51]

Another fellow who hung out there was Willie Ransom, and Willie was always talking about "how easy it was to pull a job, how he hadn't worked a day since he'd discovered divorcees and armed robbery."[52] Carr's sexual action with Esther gave him the tie to Ransom, who instructed him in armed robbery.

Having worked in the numbers racket, John Allen knew of "backers" who would be deep-pocket targets for stickups. Through his connections with bookies, Henry Hill was tipped on the Lufthansa robbery, which began when an airport employee was searching for a way to pay off a big gambling debt. Girlfriends and wives are commonly used to hide guns, to provide alibis, and to sell dope—up and down the criminal stratification system, from the relatively fancy criminal echelons of professional criminals who frequent posh gambling clubs in London to the black street hustlers who struggle each day to "get over."

Not only does the offender frequently exploit the possibilities of using the social relations around one line of action to promote another but the others with whom he conducts each form of action are, at times, attracted to him specifically for his ability to tie them into more distant lines. A pimp, for example, may be recruited by a lover-prostitute who is seeking the protection of a man with a locally fearsome reputation. Or a pimp may become a lover, a drug dealer, and a fearsomely violent figure to satisfy the demands of his "stable." Apparently, sexual relations often come to stickup men because women appreciate their hard tough-guy reputations. John Allen could keep his women in line with a reminder of his value as a bridge to street action: "I had a little thing I used to say, 'I don't need you bitch. Just like I made you a star, I can make somebody else a star.'"[53] Karen, a "Jewish princess" who married the wiseguy, Henry Hill, recalled her reaction when Henry put a gun into the mouth of a neighbor who had mistreated her and then, with the police coming, asked her to hide the weapon.

> "Get lost!" That's what a lot of girls, a lot of my own girl friends would have said the minute some guy put a gun in their hands. But I've got to admit the truth—it turned me on.[54]

Open-ended Networks. Criminals are properly called "professionals" when they do their criminal work from within widespread and multilayered social networks of illicit action. Many who like to refer to themselves as professional criminals seem at first glance to be mislabeling what are essentially working-class skills: the safecracker's expertise copies that of a locksmith, the robber's strong arm is usually a nighttime variation of the strengths of the day laborer, and the pickpocket's and the booster's manual dexterity does not rise above levels that are customary in traditional crafts and on many assembly lines. But professional criminals share with legitimate professionals who work on their own or in small partnerships, a social network-context for their work that distinguishes them from industrial employees, white-collar workers, and bureaucrats.

Like those of legitimate professionals, the "business opportunities" of professional criminals depend on personal reputation, often on acquaintanceships that appear to be casually made. One "case," legal or illegal, often leads by word of mouth to the next; contacts made in distant cities, whether at conferences or in the prison yard, may be recalled years later and exploited to open up new ventures. The everyday lives of professional criminals show less clearly the levels of material affluence that are associated with legitimate professionals—even wiseguys like Henry Hill often live in drab working-class settings, not to mention the poverty status of the more typical, black ghetto offender—than they do the more abstract occupational richness of continually negotiated, cumulatively relevant social relationships.

In any case, persistent offenders often take a great delight in developing the social networks within which they pursue deviant action. Their social networks have a permeable character in that they show an openness, to an extent prudent outsiders might find surprising, to bring people they barely know intimately into their lives. "Vouching" is often sufficient proof of acquaintance for partnerships in crime and may be accomplished with no more than a nod. Even offenders who work together for some time may not know much about each other's lives outside their present involvements. The tough, badass, or hardman style that is distinctively functional for doing stickups does not encourage intimate inquiry, even from colleagues. Thus, it was not at all unusual for Henry Williamson to note the following about a phase of his life: "I had started hustlin' with Oscar. I never did know his last name. He called me 'little bro' and I called him the same thing."[55]

Novices in stickup have special reasons for developing incriminating collegial relations with strangers. When faced with an opportunity to "pull a job" with someone they barely know, novices may self-consciously take the other's perspective and regard *themselves* as the unproved commodity. Piri Thomas recounted his concern, during his initiation into stickups, about showing stranger-offenders that they should extend their criminal networks to include him. His friend, Luis, knew two white men from New Jersey whose credentials consisted of the fact that they have been in state prison. Luis told Piri: "I can vouch for Danny and Danny vouches for Billy." Rather than question the basis of Luis's confidence, Piri was preoccupied with their doubts about him. He ran in to rob a candy store, with Luis, to show "heart" to Danny and Billy, who waited outside.[56]

Conversely, novices in stickups may have so much self-confidence that they can successfully con more experienced offenders to enter criminal combinations with them. Badass young men often parade a bravado before other offenders, some of whom, to their surprise, take them seriously. For example, James Carr at age 16 figured he could outmaneuver an old hand. He came across Slick, whom he knew "by sight and by reputation, since I was a kid" and who "was still pulling robberies at forty and not getting caught." Slick had little basis for judging Carr's qualifications for doing stickups. "Slick wanted to pull a liquor store job in West L.A. 'Naw,' I told him, 'those liquor stores are no good any more. I got a better idea.' " The better idea was a supermarket he pretended to know well but did not. Carr fabricated a potential take of $2,000 and went in with Slick, not even knowing who the manager was, an important issue, he soon realized, if he was to control the large space and the many people present.[57]

If novices and even experienced street-level robbers are quick to form criminal alliances with people they barely know, surely the most sophisticated stickup men in organized crime play it closer to the chest. Henry Hill explained that to protect themselves against appearing to be cooperating with the authorities if they are questioned later, colleagues in elaborate robberies often do not attempt to learn the identities of all the members of the operation, such as the persons who provide inside tips and transportation, the businessman who will do the fencing, and all the local power holders who will be paid at least tokens of respect for working in their territory.

Even at this rarefied level of robbery, however, offenders promote illicit action by expanding criminal networks to include others they barely know. Jimmy Burke, Hill's long-time associate and a man with an especially brutal reputation, shrewdly turned hijackings from stickups to "give ups" by taking truckers' licenses at gunpoint, pretending to write down their addresses, and adding a $50 bill before returning their wallets. As Henry commented:

> I can't tell you how many friends he made out at the airport because of that. People loved him. Drivers used to tip off his people about rich loads.[58]

The result of this maneuver was not necessarily to reduce the risk, since drivers were not hauling their own property anyway; the crime was made a give up only *after* the interaction had passed the danger point of showing force, and the subsequent value of the bribe to Burke for obtaining tips depended on stimulating interest in his identity. But the bribe increased the action in several senses: by leading to inside tips, which in effect recruited new members to Burke's criminal networks; by corrupting the system, a joy in its own right; and, most significantly, by creating a dynamic presence for Burke at the airport. If wiseguys do not expand their social networks by making quick alliances with unknown street criminals, they diffuse illicit action throughout their lives in an even more pervasive way, by creating an awesome, deviant presence where they do their hijackings, where they eat, where they take their wives and mistresses for entertainment and shopping, and so on.

Persistent stickup men develop permeable, overlapping networks to keep themselves in criminal action, whether they are poor street hustlers or established wiseguys, and whether they are itinerant or resident offenders. The older life-history accounts feature white career offenders who often moved from city to city, some making contacts with a hobo, drifter, or grifter population on the way and some establishing ties in local underworlds soon after their arrival in a new town.[59] The new arrival did not dutifully make the rounds and work up contacts during a preliminary investigative and calculating period, only then getting into criminal projects. He got into the action as opportunities arose. As a result, he often did not know who he was getting into action with or exactly what he was getting into.

Recent life histories of stickup men describe lives that have been led within narrow, fixed ethnic-minority-ghetto boundaries: a particular part of Harlem, the Homewood section of Pittsburgh, or Southeast in Washington, D.C. Having grown up in the area, the offenders carry around an ever-changing mental map of social relations in deviance networks. They have myriad possibilities for making "connections" for one form of illicit action or another. When they are not themselves active in action, they are close to someone who is. In effect, they position themselves to be seduced into action time and again, over against their own better, more prudent judgment.

John Allen's criminal record consists of many offenses that he entered in this manner. Late in his career, he was riding around with five others, including Raymond, whom he did not really know. As he recalled:

> [Lee] wanted to rob a gas station. Robbing a gas station is not my idea of a good robbery. There's no real money in it, and it's too complicated. People get hurt unnecessarily.[60]

John would not go in, but he did not leave, either. Two went in; one was shot dead and the other shot a victim dead and was then shot in the head by a man who worked in a gas station across the street. With the police on the way, John drove the group away. Later, Raymond was arrested and he involved John, who was arrested. On another occasion, JoJo tried to convince John to trust a tip on the stickup of a liquor store. John disapproved of this type of target on general considerations, and he specifically did not trust the source of the tip. He noted:

> Liquor stores are pretty dangerous. There's always guns, and you're more apt to get hurt or hurt someone and not get a substantial amount of money. . . . So this dude telling JoJo, "Yeah, man, they cash checks every Friday, and they have a large amount of money there, anywhere from three to four grand, maybe five." All he wanted for this information was a hundred dollars. JoJo tell me the dude pretty reliable, but I didn't like the idea.[61]

But John did the stickup with JoJo, and they netted something like $106. John was "very, very mad." By buying the tip from JoJo's friend, who, it seems, was running a con on them, John eventually got a sentence of "three to nine years four times running concurrently with a five-to-fifteen year sentence."[62] Again and again, Allen's fate was decided by his extension of his social networks a bit too far to stay in or close to the action.

Earning and Burning Money

Billie Miller's statement of what happens after a big take is representative: "And then you partied for the next week or two. Or paid your bills or bought a new car or something. Or went downtown and got a new girl."[63] Spending is fast and it is not limited by some objective level of need. The Bobbsey twins, the exceptionally calculating armed robbers known by Bruce Jackson, found that their sense of minimal acceptable living standards increased as their criminal objectives increased, over a series of plateaus, with no outside limit:

> When you first start off, you're a working man and you're acustomed to the $70- or $100-a-week paycheck [in the early 1970s], and when you get the extra amount to where you can afford to spend $200 a week, you're way up. But it don't last long. Maybe six weeks or two months. And then you get accustomed to this, and then you start looking for something a little bigger and better to hit. Which you do. And then you move up into the $300-a-week spending bracket. And this continues; there's no stoppage. It's a plane that just keeps advancing. And as you advance, your mode of living, your clothes, change in accordance. Your apartment changes. You can't go back.[64]

The pattern of superfast spending runs over the stickup stratification system. Jones, a street mugger living at a welfare–poverty level, said that after a rare, thousand-dollar rip-off:

> I go through it in three or four days. I buy clothes, I go out, I get high. I get shoes, or a knit, or slacks—I get a lot of things I don't need. You just live while the money's there; that's the rule of the street. That's one thing dope did—it made me live for the day. When I've got money, I don't sleep for three or four days—you're just *buying* something all the time.[65]

Nicholas Pileggi, Henry Hill's biographer, commented about Henry at age 22:

> He enjoyed the continuous action. Hustling and schemes took up every waking hour. They were the currency of all conversation and they fired

the day's excitement. In Henry's world, to hustle and score was to be alive. And yet Henry never bothered to accumulate money. . . . Within hours Henry's financial state would shift dramatically from black to red. . . . The speed with which he and most of his friends were able to dissipate capital was dazzling. Henry simply gave money away.[66]

Robby Wideman recalled, from his high times in Pittsburgh's black ghetto,

everybody trying to get over in a hurry. Here today and gone tomorrow. Ain't nothing to it, really. It ain't the money or the cars or the women. It's about all that but that ain't what it's deep down about. Cats blow a thousand a night when they on top. The money ain't nothing. You just use the money to make your play. To show people you the best.[67]

My overall objective in this book is to demonstrate that the causes of crime are constructed by the offenders themselves, but the causes they construct are lures and pressures that they experience as independently moving them toward crime. By dissipating the proceeds of their crimes, stickup men, regardless of the social position from which they start, create an environment of pressures that guide them back toward crime. As Malcolm X remembered from his days as a hustler: "I kept 'cased' in my head vulnerable places and situations and I would perform the next job only when my bankroll in my pocket began to get too low."[68] James Carr noted an interactive causal relationship between high spending, poverty, and stickup. That is, high living would produce poverty and the need to rob; at the same time, an inclination toward spontaneous robberies underlay fast spending, which would produce dire need, which would produce stickups:

Since we were spending money so fast we had to pull jobs at least once a week. We'd spend two hundred dollars a day buying everything we wanted. You spend money like this because in the back of your mind you know that you can always get more just by pulling another job. When we bought wine we'd get six or seven half gallons for the winos and get drunk with them on the street corner.[69]

The causal relationship through which high spending produces economic pressures that produce stickups is lived by persistent offenders in the details of various lines of illicit action. High living is done in particular ways, with particular others, and it creates social expectations that then propel the offender back toward crime. At age 26, Henry Hill had fifteen Brioni suits at a cost (ten or more years ago) of about $1,000 each. This sartorial display was part of an action-filled social life that featured costly mistresses. As Pileggi observed:

> For most wiseguys, having a steady girl was not unusual. You didn't
> leave a wife or abandon a family for one, but you did swank them
> around. . . . Having a steady girl was considered a sign of success, like
> a thoroughbred or a powerboat but better: a girl friend was the ultimate
> luxury purchase.[70]

The economic pressures of such a lifestyle were multiple: requirements to
show up socially in proper style, the material demands of a mistress, the
demands of a wife who might become aware of the mistress and want
material assurance of her position, and so forth. This complex of economic
pressures itself promoted and was promoted by other lines of illicit action,
gambling in particular.

Heavy drug users may create a personal material cause for continued
crime in the physiological symptoms of withdrawal. But the daily costs of
opiate drug use (recently estimated in research on inner-city blacks as less
than $25)[71] are made more pressing by offenders' pursuits of various other
forms of action. On a day when Jones, working with a partner, had earned
$337 from muggings, "Anything above the price of a day's habit would be
spent blindingly fast." Jones's biographer, James Willwerth, estimated that
Jones's income averaged about $100 per day in the early 1970s, far more
than his drug habit required. Willwerth continued:

> Yet Jones is constantly broke. He takes money from his women, borrows
> from his parents, and hits me up practically every time we get together
> (and always pays me back). He dresses well and uses expensive drugs—
> but they can't possibly account for all the money he spends. Yet beyond
> the drugs and clothes, he lives like a welfare recipient.[72]

Jones's fast spending produced poverty more consistently and diffusely in
his life than his drug use alone could accomplish.

Economic pressures toward crime emerge, not as the direct result of
particular substantive needs as much as through the pressure of obligations
accumulated in social networks. Borrowing and credit relations among
offenders form a subtle, elaborate institution. There are constant ambigui-
ties about just what may be owed to a female roommate from whom one
has "borrowed" money found in her purse or how much is due each of the
various participants in a stickup and when it will be paid. The measure and
timing of obligations incurred are also unclear when one becomes the
beneficiary of another's criminal success and free spending; when one must
make good one's gambling accounts, given that bets with bookies usually
do not follow the requirement in legal betting of up-front wagering; and
just when and with how much interest one must pay back "loans" that
associates in one line of action may supply so one can meet the obligations
of another line of action.

In one sense, then, high living indicates that the threat of impoverishment, or economic determinism more generally, is never the cause of persistence in stickups. But given the diffuse and relatively constant economic pressures created by his diverse debts to a cross-cutting extensive social network, the persistent offender's stickups are always a response to economic pressure.

Chaos and Control: Hardmen in Stickups

In proposing a theory of the causal conditions of careers in stickup, I have covered, in chapter 5, the contingencies specific to its situated practice and, thus far in this chapter, the ways in which the professional criminal may shape his social life so that he experiences ubiquitous provocations to engage in stickups as one of various seductive forms of illicit action. Now I have almost argued too much. Why, in particular, should anyone who would pursue action be inclined toward stickups? We have just seen that heavy stickup men are not specialists; if they do not have legitimate opportunities, frequently they do not lack for illegitimate alternatives. And we know from various autobiographies that many other offenders pursue lives of illicit action by combining partying, contraband drug use, gambling, and various forms of "professional" crime (as boosters, safecrackers, con men, and the like), while specifically avoiding violent crime.[73] What, then, are the distinctively compelling attractions of sustaining a criminal career specifically characterized by robbery?

The last requirement for being a heavy in stickup is to become a hardman, one who will appear ready to back his intentions violently and remorselessly, outside and independent of the situated interaction of robbery.

For many years, robbers' proclamations that they adopt violence from a solely instrumental perspective helped obscure the broader fascination that is characteristic of contemporary career robbers. About fifteen years ago, cohort and career criminal studies began reshaping the empirically documented image of the heavy criminal.[74] The Rand Corporation's small, provocative study, based on the self-reports and official records of 49 inmates in California prisons, announced in 1977 that

> 50 percent of the intensive offenders and 18 percent of the intermittent offenders either injured a victim seriously or said that, in at least two of their career periods, they would have injured a victim if it had been necessary to complete the crime. This finding counters the frequently expressed view that the more experienced an offender is the more con-

trolled he is in committing a crime and the less likely he is to injure the victim.[75]

The subsequent large-scale study by the Rand Corporation, which used the self-reports and official records of a national sample of inmates, found that violent predators had a commitment to violence that was not simply symbolic. According to the self-reports, 30 percent of the violent predators and 33 percent of the robber-assaulters had committed homicide in the measurement period, a relatively short span of up to two years before the current confinement.[76]

James Wright and Peter Rossi's large-scale survey of incarcerated offenders, which was addressed to issues of gun possession and use, adds a novel touch to the research collage. From self-reports of criminal histories, Wright and Rossi isolated a group of intensive offenders, whom they dubbed "handgun predators," who indicated that "the single most important reason to carry a gun was that 'when you have a gun, you are prepared for anything that might happen.' "[77] Almost three-quarters of the handgun predators reported that they carried a handgun most or all the time. Among these heavy offenders, gun possession is intimate as well as ubiquitous. Over 90 percent carried their handgun on their person, rather than in a car or elsewhere; 62 percent, in a belt or pocket; 23 percent, in a shoulder holster; and 10 percent, in a hip holster. Those who said they carried a gun outside the home often put it under a pillow or on a bedside table when it was not "on their person." Wright and Rossi observed:

> When these men told us that they carried a gun "all the time," we can apparently take the response quite literally. Even while sleeping, many of them kept their handgun within easy reach.[78]

In conjunction with these survey findings, the thrust of life-history evidence is that the construction of a career as a heavy in stickups requires living as a hardman—a person who anticipates mobilizing violence at any moment. The way of the hardman is a distinctive response to the chaos faced by virtually all who persist in common crimes. All career criminals, whether their MO is violent or nonviolent, recurrently face the threat that victims, their personal associates in various forms of illicit action, or law enforcement agents will suddenly seize control of their lives. In some times and places, career criminals have avoided the chaos that generally haunts them by a combined strategy of corrupting local officials, maintaining an itinerant lifestyle, and treating imprisonment as a time for hibernation.[79] Perhaps more commonly today, career criminals succumb to chaos, moving from addiction to petty hustle to abused status in prison, and being identified as some subtype of "loser" by the law enforcement, street, and prison communities alike. Only the hardman's response embraces rather than avoids or succumbs to chaos; the hardman seizes on chaos as a provocation to manifest transcendent powers of control. This way of appreciating chaos dialectically, as a motivational resource rather than as a barrier to a criminal career, is not adopted equally or consistently by career robbers, but it is, I submit, the distinctive project that they struggle to mount as long as it makes sense to them to stick with stickup.

BACKGROUND CHAOS

To appreciate how being a hardman can have a transcendent appeal, we must first appreciate the chaos that it promises to overcome. Henry Williamson, a low-level street criminal, was threatened by chaos because he did not know how given stickups would evolve. His accounts of robberies are rich with stories that illustrate how often the crimes threatened to escape his control. One petty purse snatching, for example, soon had him tumbling down the stairs of an apartment building with a resisting, elderly woman. The threat of chaos was characteristic of Henry's stickups, not only because he could not know what the victims would do, but because of his spur-of-the-moment method of beginning the crimes and because of his lack of knowledge of his colleagues—just because of the temporal and social-network characteristics that enabled the action of stickups to become diffused in his life. And the forms of action he favored created a great risk of chaos in the robberies themselves.

> The guys used to call me "lost weekend," I'd drink just this much! I would drink, and I wouldn't know what I had did, or where I had been. This is true![80]

He might realize in the middle of a stickup that he did not know how it began or even if he had yet taken the victim's money.

Henry Hill's life as a wiseguy at the top of the socioeconomic order of stickup men was no less chaotic. Henry and his wiseguy friends planned their hijackings, robberies, and other crimes, often in multiple sessions at a favorite restaurant and often in great detail, and they enjoyed whatever protection and security "organized crime" could provide. Occasionally, they worked with black-ghetto street hustlers, but always from a position of marked dominance and social distance. Yet

> to wiseguys, "working guys" were already dead. Henry and his pals had long ago dismissed the idea of security and the relative tranquillity that went with obeying the law. They exulted in the pleasures that came from breaking it. Life was lived without a safety net.[81]

Despite media images of loyal ties to organized crime, when a wiseguy could no longer put up a credible threat of mobilizing physical force, as happened when he was imprisoned, his social relations provided little security. As Pileggi stated:

> When a wiseguy went away he stopped earning. It was a fact. All bets and debts were off. No matter what it said in the movies, a wiseguy's friends, former partners, debtors, and ex-victims whined, lied, cheated, and hid rather than pay money owed to a man behind bars, much less to his wife.[82]

Cutting across all social distinctions among these career criminals is the status of a "regular suspect."[83] Henry Hill and his friends were "always under suspicion, arrest, or indictment for one crime or another."[84] John Allen's career is surely more representative of the career stickup man. Allen was well aware that he was one of those whom the police might look for when they began an investigation. "No matter what happened. If somebody got their pocketbook snatched. . . . If somebody got killed up the street . . . if a store got broke into," he knew the police would be after him.[85] And even though the crime might not be within his known style, the police were still well advised to question him; with his contacts on the street, he would likely know something of value, and with his extensive involvement in crime, he should appreciate friendly relations with the police.

It is thus reasonable for John Allen to have felt that he was virtually haunted by the police. If he was in his favorite "carryout" and "rollers" (mobile policemen) came up, he assumed, at times erroneously, that they were looking for him. When he returned home one day and found the police raiding his apartment, he was not sure what they were looking for, since he was "into" so much. Whenever the police stopped his car, he took for granted that he must lie in some manner because he always had something to hide, if only the failure to comply with antipollution requirements. In an attempt to purchase a small insurance policy for the life he led, he gave his family money to use at unspecified, future times, to bail him out.

The chaos threatening Allen's life was as pervasive as the illicit action that was diffused in his everyday experience. Because he could anticipate police intervention at any time, no social situations were immune from criminal significance. At an innocent party, the routine entrance of a maintenance man to work on the plumbing became a matter of comment, since it reflected on his involvement in a criminal subculture. The maintenance man entered through an open door, and this indicated, Allen remarked, how easily the FBI could have entered! Although not as a matter of law, phenomenologically, John Allen was always "on escape" by the time he was in his mid-twenties.

In reporting the lives of heavy career criminals, it is possible that the reporters, who are always middle-class and almost always white, exaggerate the sense of risk and conjure up an artificial sense of threatening chaos. James Willwerth, the biographer of Jones, the mugger from New York's Lower East Side, characterized Jones's world as one of "tense friendships, family problems, small-change business deals, people without last names—and sudden violence." Willwerth was impressed with *"how casually he lives with criminality.* Cocaine in his pocket . . . a rifle in the suitcase . . . joints in his coat."[86] But, notwithstanding the reporters' class anxieties, it is clear that the criminals themselves experience their lives on the border of chaos. In Jones's words:

> Don't ask me about my doubts. That will only hang me up. If I'm gonna survive—a motherfuckin' outlaw, man!—I have to be cool. I could die tomorrow. Can you dig that? Could you handle it? I've gotta live fast. If I make it through, I will *really* have gotten over; I'll be right up there with the Rockefellers! . . . I have to tell you, I am almost afraid to stop. I mean, the shit I got with me now—I can't hardly afford to let it catch up![87]

Jones's casual perspective is a contingent achievement in the face of chaos. Sometimes careers in stickup are washed out, at least temporarily, by a flood of anxiety. Jones's friend and ex-colleague in burglary, mugging, and dope trafficking, JC, "got off the streets" when " 'it was like getting ulcers—having to look over my back all the time.' "[88] Malcolm X reported that when he was finally arrested, it was almost a relief:

> The hustler's every waking hour is lived with both the practical and the sub-conscious knowledge that if he ever relaxes, if he ever slows down, the other hungry, restless foxes, ferrets, wolves, and vultures out there with him won't hesitate to make him their prey.[89]
>
> Everything was building up, closing in on me. I was trapped in so many cross turns. West Indian Archie gunning for me. The Italians who thought I'd stuck up their crap game after me. The scared kid hustler I'd hit. The cops. For four years, up to that point, I'd been lucky enough, or slick enough, to escape jail, or even getting arrested. Or any *serious* trouble. But I knew that any minute now something had to give.[90]
>
> If I hadn't been arrested right when I was, I could have been dead another way. Sophia's husband's friend had told her husband about me.[91]

Persistent criminals are officially linked to crimes primarily as a result of the chaos of their lives, either by their capture by patrolling police at the scene of a botched crime, by identifications made by victims, through the recognition by the police of an MO that leads directly to the suspect or to a mug shot that a victim identifies, or through their confessions when they are in custody for another charge or through the information supplied to the police by other criminals. Statistically, detective work plays an insignificant role in the capture of robbers.[92]

Thus, the chief threat to the freedom of hardened stickup men is themselves or, more precisely, the chaotic situations they create within crimes and within their lives. The patterns in social relations that provide the career stickup man with a pervasive and recurrent provocation to illicit action cause the chaos. Henry Williamson was liable to be arrested whenever the police happened to stop him:

> What I did, I got arrested. This was just a general pickup. I was in the poolroom. In my neighborhood then when they came to get you they ain't lookin' for no one guy in particular, they just come to raid the poolroom.[93]

Henry had dope tracks on his arms and a pistol in his pocket. Piri Thomas was caught when he and two others attempted an unusually big stickup, in a downtown disco. The hundreds of victims who made the crime a thrilling prospect were too many to control; the scene became chaotic.[94] At age 20, Manny Torres began a three-year sentence at Sing Sing on a weapons possession charge that came as a complete surprise, both to him and, apparently, to the police, who had come to arrest him on a robbery charge.[95] When Robby Wideman found the police at his door and was arrested on a drug charge, he first thought they must be acting on a tip supplied by a junkie he took along on a drug-purchasing trip to Detroit, but later he believed that the "roommate of one of my old girl friends dropped a dime on me." He recalled that he "had to put her down [the girlfriend] and after that she's always bad-mouthing me." He figured that someone else told her roommate he was in Detroit and she figured out why and then called the police.[96]

Jealousies and tensions growing out of relations with girlfriends or mistresses haunt the range of stickup men. Luis Santos began running numbers in Harlem at age 17 and was "getting into dope" and "rumbles" with friends. They developed a plan to buy and sell marijuana and they needed cash to start up, "so we mugged, robbed and burgled like hell. I was doing numbers again just to keep eating but my eyes were on the pot deal."[97] After a run of successful drug trafficking, Luis began living high, partying, flashing money, using drugs, and developing a relationship with Yvette, an older, more sophisticated woman. This lead to a fight with a man who claimed to be Yvette's husband, and then jail on a homicide charge. He was released, but later, after partying in a stolen car, a spurned Yvette turned him in.

Toward the end of his criminal career, Henry Hill was snorting "about a gram of coke just to keep all the insanity together." Part of the "insanity" was the need to keep his drug trafficking a secret from his organized crime superior, Paul Vario. Another part was his awareness of intense police surveillance focused on his drug trafficking or the $6 million Lufthansa robbery in which he participated (he was not sure which). His wife, Karen, frequently helped him by hiding guns and drugs. Meanwhile his girlfriend, Robin, was helping him sell and cut dope, but she was also using drugs. Robin would not wash dishes, even though washing was essential to remove incriminating traces of their drug business and even though Henry, knowing of her reluctance to wash dishes, bought her a dishwasher just for the purpose. Her refusal to wash dishes seems to have been related to her protests over her status as mistress. Henry would press her to clean up better, but "every time I went over there she wanted to have a talk about the relationship."[98]

On the day that he was arrested, knowing for hours that he was being followed by a helicopter, Henry carried guns to Jimmy Burke, who had silencers and wanted guns to fit, and stopped at the home of Robert Germaine, a robber "on the lam," where he snorted cocaine and picked up a shipment of heroin. Germaine's son dealt drugs; when caught, he gave up Henry and eventually his own father. The Lufthansa employee, Werner, who promoted the robbery to settle a debt with connected bookies, told a friend, Fischetti, about the robbery in a discussion of plans to invest the proceeds. Fischetti was having an affair with Werner's wife, which he had kept secret from his own wife. Fischetti's cooperation was crucial to the FBI investigation; one of his inducements to cooperate was to avoid being interviewed in his home, so he could keep his wife from knowing about his affair.

The chaos that Hill experienced as "insanity" ("I was under so much pressure that the day I got pinched almost came as a relief") is traceable to the intertwining of the major forms of illicit action that dominate the lives of heavy criminals: gambling, mistresses, drug use and drug trafficking, committing robberies, and associating with robbers. The overlapping social networks that he had used to build up a life of action now conspired to bring him down.

Speaking from his observational standpoint in the London underworld, Laurie Taylor extends our theme to another cultural context, where chaos seems almost a cultivated feature in the career criminal's everyday life.

There is something resembling a death wish among some such villains. Not just in the lack of care they take to cover their tracks, or in the reckless way in which "profits" are gambled away, but in the self-dramatizing which they bring to their roles. . . . actual robbers and con men and gangsters appear to go out of their way to increase their own visibility, and thus their likelihood of detection, by trying to live up to [mass media images of criminals.] . . . After a very short time, I found them instantly recognizable in straight clubs and restaurants; as though they were acting out a little stage version of the "underworld" for the benefit of the patrons at adjoining tables.[99]

CHAOS AND CONTROL

The chaos in the life of action lends a distinctive significance to those who respond by imposing a disciplined control through the force of their personality. This is the final, compelling appeal of the hardman—that he alone, in the face of chaos, embodies transcendence by sticking up for himself, literally and figuratively.

Consider the causal order that governs the following incident from John Allen's autobiography. Allen was initially a bystander to this one. However, its mixture of chaos and control is common in his life history; in the aftermath, he was arrested for assaulting a police officer. At about age 20, Allen was hanging around one night with friends at a carry-out restaurant. Three of the "younger dudes" entered an all-night drugstore.

> From what I understand from them, they didn't go in there with the intent to rob or beat anybody up or anything. I think they only really wanted to buy some gum and cigarettes, but by being drunk, they was talking pretty tough, and so the lady behind the counter automatically get scared. . . . The druggist . . . got a little pushy or ordered them out of the store, and by them being all fired up, naturally the next thing they did was jump on him.
>
> So now what do you have? You've got a drugstore. You've got a scared lady in the corner somewhere with her hands over her face. You've got a beat-up druggist laying on the floor. You've got three dudes that came in for chewing gum and cigarettes, but now they got two cash registers. So what do they do? They takes the cash. Wasn't nothing to stop them, and it was there. Why would they leave it? They're thieves anyway and supposed to be hustlers. . . . There wasn't nothing to stop them, so they just took the money.[100]

They entered as badasses, delighting in their play with symbols of evil and attitudes of defiance. The druggist challenged them, so to maintain their commitment to being bad, they had to beat him up. Now the cash register was available to them. If they did not take the money, what were they? "They're thieves anyway and supposed to be hustlers. . . ." They had to take the money or else, rather than transcend the chaos of the scene, it would define them; they would emerge as fools, punks, or crazies, not hustlers.

In countless stickups, the primary causal process is the project of being a "badass" or a "bad nigger," which brings on chaotic situations that then are transformed into courses of action that make self-respecting sense through the imposition of the form and discipline of a stickup. By carrying out the robbery in the face of chaos, John Allen and his friends imposed a transcendent control, emerging in the guise they used on entering the scene, reconfirmed as triumphant hardmen.

Consider next an incident from Laurie Taylor's account of professional British bank robbers. Phil is recounting his management of some less daring associates:

> I knew they'd get on the plot [the scene of the action] and find all sorts of clues to swallow it. "Oh, look at this and that." But they'd do it in such a way that nobody could accuse them of bottling out when we got back. I knew this. *I knew it.* And I thought, right, I'm going to force you bastards into that bank when we arrive.
>
> And when we got on the plot, and they were working up some excuses to pull off, I just went in. I went in, and they had to follow me. They *had* to come in. . . . otherwise their lives would have been destroyed. . . . The *stigma* of course. *Rats . . .* They're no longer bank robbers if they didn't come in that bank.[101]

Phil, who emphasized a businesslike attitude toward robbery, consciously took on associates whose known weaknesses made robberies especially risky and occasions for dramatizing the superior firmness of his will. Haran found a similar pattern in Brooklyn and Queens among predominately black, heavy bank robbers; working teams were often composed of experienced stickup men and "losers," whose drug involvements and previous records suggested that they would be relatively flaky colleagues.[102] The castelike division of labor in such robberies draws out and acknowledges the transcendent discipline that the hardman must impose.

If this seems too romanticized, sensational, or abstract a formulation, if this is mythology, it is a mythology vividly embraced in the detailed doings of stickups. Here is college professor–novelist John Wideman's impassioned but careful recreation from his brother Robby's accounts, of the crucial dynamics that led to Robby's life sentence for participating in a felony murder. In Pittsburgh on November 15, 1975, Robby Wideman, Michael Dukes, and Cecil Rice, three young black friends, posed as thieves to rob a fence; they planned to use the proceeds to finance a move to a higher position in the heroin-distribution hierarchy. They arrived with a truck that was supposed to contain a load of Sony color television sets but that really contained Cecil and a shotgun. But the fence, Stavros, assisted by two Kramer brothers who would help unload, was conning them as well; he did not have the money he promised. At the scene, each side wanted the other to deliver first. Dukes, a basketball player, handled the negotiations for the blacks:

> Mike got this way of staring down at people. Intimidation is what it's about. Don't matter how tall a dude be, Mike can stare down at him. Get that hard look in his eyes and stand still as a statue. Nothing moving like he's froze or something. Just staring down at you and letting you know he owns you. Letting you know he could set up on you and squash

you like a bug and ain't nothing you could do about it. So they hit it back and forth a couple times like it's Ping-Pong. Money—TVs—Money—TVs. Then Stavros sees Mike ain't up for no game. He's dealing with one them hardhead, hard-leg niggers and ain't no win.

As with John Allen and his friends in the drug store, the causal process in this decisive event in Robby Wideman's life displays, first, a general project of becoming Superfly, the transcendent pest, a "bad nigger" celebrated as a star in a social world of illicit action; next, a predatory act that flirts with chaos; next, an attempt to overcome chaos with the disciplined control of the "hardhead, hard-leg nigger"; and, finally, pathos on all sides. Stavros took out some money and the truck was opened, revealing Cecil and his sawed-off shotgun. Stavros dropped some "chump change" and started to run off. Money was blowing around, and Robby yelled *"Get 'em,"* perhaps meaning the flying bills. A shot rang out, and Stavros was hit. His running opened the wound, and he died.[103] The mythological symbolism of the transcendent hardman may seem bizarre and sensational to outsiders, but it is essential to the causal process.

Given the uncertainties involved, one must, as a practical matter, become a hardman to make sense of repeatedly attempting to commit robbery. But being a hardman is not simply lived as a dispensable tool; rather, it is an organizing theme in the lives of those who stick with stickup. Heavy stickup men generally respond to the chaos that recurs in their personal lives in the same hardened, dramatically evil spirit that they mobilize when robberies threaten to go out of control.

Just as black stickup men embrace the "hard-leg," formally evil identity of "bad nigger" in ghetto social life generally, so Mexican Americans adopt the negative *cholo* stereotype when they wish to convey an intimidating spirit in everyday life, and Sicilian Americans may proudly assume a wiseguy identity with which they threaten, like an irritated parent, to "whack" anyone who even mildly disturbs them. Henry Hill described Jimmy Burke, an Irishman who worked with Sicilian crime groups, who had a remarkable passion for hijacking; his fascination with the "outlaw" metaphor led him to name his sons, Frank James Burke and Jesse James Burke:

[Jimmy] had a broken nose and he had a lot of hands. If there was just the littlest amount of trouble, he'd be all over you in a second. He'd grab a guy's tie and slam his chin into the table before the guy knew he was in a war. If the guy was lucky, Jimmy would let him live. Jimmy had a reputation for being wild. He'd whack you. There was no question—Jimmy could plant you just as fast as shake your hand. . . . He was very scary and he scared some very scary fellows.[104]

Obviously, Henry's wiseguy world does not require daily murders, but, apparently, the symbolic invocation of murderous intent was an everyday matter. When, as a boy, Henry's hanging out with wiseguys first brought complaints of truancy to his parents' attentions, his friends solved the problem by kidnapping the mailman and instructing him to deliver correspondence from the school to the pizza parlor. When a wiseguy took a partnership in a restaurant, Henry explained:

> He gets his money, no matter what. You got no business? Fuck you, pay me. You had a fire? Fuck you, pay me. The place got hit by lightning and World War Three started in the lounge? Fuck you, pay me.[105]

When Henry and Paul Vario's son irritated Vario by chasing off the cook and walking off their jobs in a Lucchese-controlled restaurant, Vario "put a hit on his own kid's car"; he had Henry burn it.

The biographies of stickup men are rich with evidence of a gut-deep desire to impose this hard control on close personal relationships. As John Allen related:

> I done had quite a few women. . . . there's been several times when I've been deeply involved with this person. Then it really hurts when they cross me. And when I'm hurt, I strike out. Always.[106]

Allen was not confessing to a regretted psychological weakness; he was articulating his hardman philosophy of life, which transcends any situational provocation or instrumentality:

> Just today I told my son on the phone, "When I see you, I'm gonna hit you in your chest." He said, "For what? I ain't did nothing." I told him, "'Cause I feel like it." And I probably will. . . . but he know that this won't be no beating or no hitting on him. This is a part of him growing up and a part of me that's coming out and that I want him to inherit from me.[107]

The point is not that one must regularly beat up one's lover and children to make sense of persisting in stickups. It is that persisting in stickup seems to make sense only as part of a larger project of transcending chaos in general, virtually wherever it may appear in one's life, through imposing a cold, hard, violent discipline. For many, it means the humiliation and often the physical abuse of women. In London, Laurie Taylor described the "tragic chronology" of the lives of most underworld women: "At first innocent girl-friend—the object of sentimental adoration; and then their gradual transformation over the years into disturbed, demented, even suicidal, spouses."[108]

The biographies of contemporary American stickup men from the ghetto are full of the abuse of women:

• Malcolm X punched the girlfriend of his colleague, Sammy ("Not able to figure out why Sammy didn't shut her up, I did"), and described how he controlled his white girlfriend:

> Even when I had hundreds of dollars in my pocket, when she came to Harlem I would take everything she had short of her train fare back to Boston. It seems that some women love to be exploited. . . . Always, every now and then, I had given her a hard time, just to keep her in line. Every once in a while a woman seems to need, in fact *wants* this, too. But now, I would feel evil and slap her around worse than ever.[109]

• Jones, sitting around his girlfriend, Carol's apartment, heard the doorbell ring, and told Carol to open it. She did not move, and his biographer recorded his yell:

> *"Bitch, there's someone at the door! . . . Get it!"* Suddenly his voice conveys violence; the rumble is frightening. . . . He turns to me. "During a mugging, things like that make you hurt people." He points at her, nodding his finger, "You tell people to do something and they don't go along with the program—and that makes you *mad.*"[110]

When Ritchie, Carol's toddler-child by an ex-boyfriend, accidently bumped into Jones, he was told: "You hit me again, Ritchie, and I'll break your motherfucking jaw."[111]

• Claude Brown recalled that when he was age 13, the "slickest nigger" in Harlem was Johnny D. "Everybody respected him, the whole neighborhood." A con man, pimp, and pusher, Johnny D was also a celebrated hardman. "He was the first cat I ever saw hit a guy and knock him out with one punch, just like in the movies." He was also a model of how a hardman should control women:

> Johnny was always telling us about bitches. To Johnny, every chick was a bitch. Even mothers were bitches. Of course, there were some nice bitches, but they were still bitches. And a man had to be a dog in order to handle a bitch.[112]

• Henry Williamson recounted with evident pride how he handled the potential changes in his life when Callie, his girlfriend, announced she was pregnant. First, "I said, 'We ain't able to take care of no crumbs around here!'" When he told her he was leaving because she would not have an abortion, she picked up a dagger and he hit her hard enough to provoke a miscarriage. Callie's mother then found him in a poolroom and, at gunpoint, brought him back while the miscarriage was in progress. When he was told to fill a prescription for Callie's recovery, he protested:

"I ain't got no money to fill this thing with!" He [the doctor] had told me it would cost seven or eight dollars. So her mother came up with the money. The old lady's got it too, and her mother gave it to me, and gave me the key to the car. Now I was suppose to go to Fifty-eight and Indiana to get this filled. . . . I just kept goin'![113]

Because the threat of chaos is ubiquitous in the life of illicit action, so is the transcendent project of the hardman. There is the constant threat that the criminal justice system will suddenly wrench control of one's life. Here the biographical sources are less than satisfactory because the evidence appears to be too strong. With the exception of Henry Hill, who became a government witness, these stickup men show no evidence of cooperating with the police or of acting as informants, and that is not a credible picture. Still, three patterns of conduct in relation to the criminal justice system are notable.

One theme is the defiant attitude with which youthful offenders respond to arrest and punishment. For example, when Claude Brown was ordered to a training school by a judge who labeled him a chronic liar, his response, which shocked his mother, was sarcasm: "I asked him if he wanted me to thank him." He insisted on his moral superiority—looking down on the judge in ridicule—even as control over his life was being wrested from him. At his first conviction for a shooting crime, John Allen was at a loss for dealing with the system. In an effort to stay above the confusing scene and the undercurrents of fear he was experiencing, he played right into official hands:

They tried to make me sign some old thing. I said, "Man, I can't read or write." So the dude say, "Just sign right here. You can write you name, can't you?" I said, "No. I can't write, man." Because I knew I wasn't supposed to say nothing. I wasn't supposed to sign nothing. But I think that I was so mad and confused that I just didn't care what I said. At that particular moment it didn't make no difference. It was just, "Yeah, I shot him. So what?"[114]

A second theme is the remarkable ability of career stickup men to find triumph in the face of apparent defeat. At the end of his autobiography, we find Allen crippled, indigent, and isolated. He has spent fourteen of his first thirty-one years locked up. He acknowledges that he has not, overall, made much money through crime. But he still senses the romance of being the bad nigger:

Bad breaks. I catch a lot of that. But I can honestly say that I got away with much more than what I ever got caught and convicted for, so in the long run that made it worthwhile.[115]

In his *moral* accounting book—one that measures "got away with its" against "got caughts"—one in which the forces of evil are metaphysically arrayed against the forces of good, Allen is a winner.

Even when concretely losing control over their lives, experienced stickup men find spiritually inspiring evidence of their superior ability to transcend the controls of the system. Upon his arrest, John Allen recalled the respectful awe expressed by the policeman who was tracking the chase with pins on a map. John McVicar, finally succumbing to Laurie Taylor's ceaseless proddings to reveal what he found most attractive in his robbery career, reported:

> Well it wasn't the money, Laurie. Not money. I'll tell you, I used to get a kick . . . especially when I was on the run . . . I used to get a buzz out of being wanted and outwitting them.[116]

Similarly, a heavy stickup man can experience confinement in prison not as a time out from the joys of street life but as an opportunity to beat the system from within, even while it is pressing down with its most minute controls. In the underground prison economy, in the corruption of the guards, and in the maintenance of the ghetto street culture in rural penitentiaries, there are infinite daily opportunities to ridicule, to corrupt, and to control the most powerful forces of social control. The prison environment, which seems to outsiders to be an overwhelming spiritually deadening world, can provoke and seduce hardened inmates to keep intensely alive the ways of the badass. So intimately and authentically do stickup men embody the hardman's project of transcendence that they appear, with some regularity, to be able to make a smooth transition from being heterosexual "motherfuckers" on the streets to homosexual dominants on the inside.[117]

The Transcendence of the Hardman

Of the many strategies for "getting over" or transcending the everyday challenges of living a life of illicit action, being a hardman is surely not universally regarded as the most attractive. Among career criminals, violent predators and robber-assaulters are a distinct minority. Con men, pimps, drug dealers, and nonviolent professional thieves often look down on robbers as living a brutish, more insecure, and materially less rewarding life.

But stickup men find local audiences who enthusiastically celebrate the hardman's identity. As they perceive it, communal celebration may come in the form "people on the street" who "want to pry."

> People on the street want to pry. They think: how has he stayed alive? . . . They think I'm crazy, but they look up to me because I dress good, I keep cash, I've got women, and I don't work.[118]

John Allen recognized his community's embrace of his reputation as a "star," that extra-terrestrial entity shining over everyone at night. He manipulated his street-earned status to intimidate challengers and debtors, to attract offers of criminal employment, and to promote his sex life. Being with him could enhance a woman's reputation on the streets—make her "a star."[119]

We are perhaps most familiar today with the celebration of the hard-man's transcendent status in black ghettoes, in the versions of "Superfly" and "bad niggers." But, wherever their lives have been closely examined, something similar appears to have supported robbers' careers. In Chicago in the 1920s, Stanley, the Polish "Jackroller," reported: "The older guys did big jobs like stick-up, burglary, and stealing autos. The little fellows admired the 'big shots' and longed for the day when they could get into the racket."[120] And in the London underworld, Laurie Taylor

> noticed in clubs . . . that all other professional criminals deferred to the successful robber. A great deal of this status obviously derived from the independence and spontaneity of the activity. . . . Out in the open. Exposed. . . . These were the reasons, rather than anything about the intrinsic activity itself—firing guns, driving fast cars—which made robbery an acknowledged breeding-ground for those values which other professional criminals liked to cite as their own. Ideas about how a robber would behave in a dangerous situation—how he would face up to trouble, spend his money, share out his loot, serve his "time," dispatch his enemies, treat his women, look after his friends—were guides for every career-criminal, from the pickpocket on the Central Line to gentlemen fraudsters hard at work in the bowels of the city.[121]

If we stop here and regard the attractions of being a hardman simply as striving for status or other directed, we will miss the deeper internal meaning and beg the question of the more universal appeal of the project. It is not only ghetto-bound residents who find the hardman fascinating. The hardmen's middle-class biographers often fall under the spell. Although Billie Miller is described as a pathetic loser, penniless, lonely, and begging old acquaintances for small favors, at the end of his biography, the academic who wrote the volume initially appreciated his subject in a heroic vein when he met him in prison:

> He was a fine example of young manhood—tall, agile, brave, keen, and full of nerve. I could vision him "sticking-up" a man without flinching. I could see him in the midst of a robbery, with the police closing in on him, and with his pals frantic and unnerved, yet Billy would be cool and self-possessed. In fact, I thought he could face death without a quiver or qualm.[122]

The black version of the hardman, the bad nigger, has long had an appeal far beyond the ghetto.[123] When politicized, the uncompromising, hardheaded posture of bad niggers has generated an appeal that goes beyond racial tensions. Malcolm X, the first and most famous of the modern series of urban ghetto outlaws who developed national followings, was admired by many middle-class blacks and whites not only for the truth they found in his ideology but for the fierce honesty of conviction he projected. Malcolm knew that he inspired respect from others just because, as Ossie Davis put it, he "kept snatching our lies away. . . . And he wouldn't stop for love nor money."[124]

From the outside, the hardman may be admired as a "real man" or as "courageous," but from the inside, such recognition is tangential and secondary. It is also based on a limited picture of the hardman's life. Malcolm X's account of his criminal life showed little gratuitous cruelty, except for his relationships with women. There is an undeniable charm in Henry Williamson's autobiography, related to his honesty about his immorality. With boyish innocence, he is often declaring:

> I guess I really just liked to be goin' out and doin' wrong. That's all it were. I would be gettin' more enjoyment out of that then [*sic*] sittin' up in the show. Now I wouldn't get no enjoyment out of doin' wrong until after I had did it. I liked to just sit back and think about what I had did.[125]

But we stop smiling when he takes off from the scene of the miscarriage/abortion with the prescription money. James Carr, a prison associate of George Jackson, is admirable for saying before we can, "Right from the start I guess I was a bad motherfucker."[126] We may even empathize when, slighted by the coach at age 9, he burned down his elementary school, but we're taken aback when, at age 10, in the park on Easter Sunday, he asked another kid for his fishing rod and when the kid said no, he stabbed him with a hunting knife.

In his everyday doings, the hardman transcends the difference between how he and others experience everyday situations by insisting that his subjectivity remains firm as he moves into and out of others' worlds. In street language, the challenge arises when others try to take him through "too many changes." When it rains, Jones finds "it fucks with my mind. Maybe I'll have to change to my dungarees, and that messes with my head. . . ." The project is to move, without being visibly impressed, emotionally affected, or spiritually swayed, between "here" (wherever you are "at" at the moment) and "there" (all situations defined by others). This, rather than sadistic pleasure, is what Jones meant when, while watching a soap opera that depicted a woman crying and yelling at her lover, he remarked, "He should knock that lamb out. She is takin' him through too many changes."[127]

We first examined the everyday project of the hardman in an adolescent form, in the ways of the badass. For the badass, transcendence is essentially a *presence;* the badass strives to be so intimidating that he becomes virtually any situation he is in. All eye movements are either toward or away from him. For everyone, his identity becomes what the moment is about.

For the adolescent, being a hardman, a bad man, or a "stone gangster," is often initially a role taken on at a distance and portrayed with a playful attitude. As Robby Wideman recalled:

> That's the way we was. Stone Gangsters. Robbing people. Waving guns in people's face. Serious Shit. But it was like playing too. A game. A big game and we was just big kids having fun.[128]

In a way that becomes increasingly serious over the lifecourse, the hardman lives a moral mandate to move continuously between "crib" and "street" life without "going through changes." On those rare occasions when hardmen come to the attentions of hostile audiences who are usually beyond their reach, their struggle not to go through changes becomes particularly pressed, setting off sparks that, if we look quickly enough, allow us to glimpse what is most fundamentally at stake in the posture. Such a moment of truth occurred when Malcolm X made his famous Los Angeles statement, "I've just heard some good news!" after learning of an airplane crash in Paris that had killed thirty-odd whites, many from Atlanta. It was a moment, pure and simple, of delicious meanness: pure because it was not confused with anger, delicious because it was spiced with the ridicule of conventional restraint, and simple in its meanness because of its air of limitless moral indifference.

At times, Malcolm seemed to feel required to express aspects of racial tensions that others would often feel, less often think, but never express— like a perverse delight in hearing news reports of the accidental death of some of "them." Even if he quickly recognized that the thought was indefensible, once he had thought the thought, *not* to express it, much less publicly to recant its expression later, would have been to undermine the very source of his distinctive appeal. Of course, if he had not expressed the obnoxious thought, no one else would have known he had it. But it was as if he understood that reticence could cost him not simply some measure of popular appeal, but something more fundamental—his ability to go with his gut reactions and his direct touch with the source he drew on to know what he was to do, in a word, his soul.

To the hardman, what is most precious in transcending reason is not the occasional admiring response or sadistic pleasure, but a more constant reward, *the ability always to know what to do.* This is what he achieves by transcending the protests of reason, whether the protests come from a victim in a stickup or from the implications of capture and punishment.

Nietzsche, calling for a renewal of moral strength, wrote of a time when "doubt was the will to self." In the modern world that the hardman will not enter, one who is in doubt should ask forgiveness, be soft, and adopt a malleable self. The hardman can entertain reason about his career in the form of strategic planning on "how to" do stickup and other forms of action, but to ask "why" he does it is artificial; for him to provoke reasoned doubt over his motivation is inconsistent with the very foundation of his life, which is a matter of faith laid over the ever-threatening world of chaos he has so elaborately constructed. The hardman is one version of the hustler, who is constantly strategizing, sometimes negotiating, but never debating—a man who always uses reason but never lets it use him. If Malcolm X had listened to his reason, it would have spoken of death threats, cautioning him to compromise. If John Allen had listened to his reason, he would not have gone into the liquor store. He would have gotten out of the car before his friends reached the gas station. He would not have picked up whores and driven the car to make a drug connection right after the messy getaway from the stickup. And, most of all, he would not have been John Allen. The hardman triumphs, after all, by inducing others to calculate the costs and benefits.

Seen in the form of snapshots taken from the outside, the hardman seems to be a collection of impulsive outpourings of hostile feelings—anger, aggressive instincts, and sadistic inclinations. But after a series of frustrated robberies, lost fights, betrayals by intimates, arrests, and prison sentences, one always has a multitude of reasons for *not* responding from the guts. Just because they are done against the background of reasonable grounds for deterrence, the hardman's aggressive moves carry, in their sensual vibrance—in the heavy awe and felt charge they bring to scenes—the ringing significance of their transcendent project.

Finally, we can appreciate just how the hardman's gratuitous little cruelties in everyday life—the whacks and insults delivered to friends and lovers, as well as to strangers—are fundamentally related to his persistence in stickups. Now we can specify why one must be a hardman to make sense of sticking with stickup. Those who would celebrate a negative transcendence—as bad niggers, punks, wiseguys, cholos, and so on—have a devil of a time with reason. They often acknowledge the seductions of reason by playing with "professional," "business," and "accounting" metaphors to interpret their affairs; not only the sensual pulse of illicit action but also the framework of rational accounting has its temptations. In recurrently assaulting others' sensibilities, even when no economic motive is present, the stickup man performs rituals to sustain the faith that is essential if he is not to give in to his reason.

CHAPTER 7

Of Hardmen and 'Bad Niggers': Gender and Ethnicity in the Background of Stickup

In examining stickups, I have sought materials from a variety of times, places, and ethnic groups to isolate the common elements in situational and "career" experiences. Despite my attempt to cover the widest range, I have not been able to present much data on female robbers, and to avoid suggesting that stickups are somehow committed only by blacks, I have had to reach for Canadian and English sources, a sixty-year-old life story of a Polish American, and the biography of an exceptional Irish-Sicilian "wiseguy." In fact, the contemporary relations between stickups and gender and ethnicity are profound, and a naturalistic inquiry need not ignore them.

With reference to gender, the statistical description of the relationship generally cites a ratio of 10–15 robberies by men for each robbery by a woman.[1] When compared to sex ratios for other forms of crime, the dimensions of gender involved in robbery appear more complex and interesting than might be suggested by ideas of male superiority in the physical requirements, interactional experience, or social expectations for performing violent acts. As might be expected, the participation of females is higher in various forms of nonviolent sneak theft, most famously, shoplifting. But for crimes in which there is personal contact with victims but no assault or robbery (auto theft, burglary, and household larceny in which the victim saw the offender), victims' reports show almost the same enormous overrepresentation of males that they do for robbery or theft with assault.[2] Thus, it is not clear that positing a female incompetence or distaste for violence is *necessary* to explain the overrepresentation of males in robbery.

Moreover, although *assaults,* or fights without the objective of theft, display a disproportionate involvement of males in police or victimization data, they show a much *lower* level of gender imbalance than do robberies—at about 3 or 4 to 1.[3] Much assault involves intrasex conduct and thus would not necessarily model the confrontation to be anticipated by robbers, but cross-sex domestic homicide also shows a much lower sex imbalance than does robbery. As was noted in chapter 1, in many major American cities, women are almost as likely to kill as to be killed by their mates. Positing a female incompetence or distaste for violence is not *sufficient* to explain the overrepresentation of males in robbery.

One way to try to make theoretical sense of the sex ratios in robbery is to use ideas that suggest some preexisting, generalized differences between men and women. The sex ratio in robbery seems naturally to invite causal rhetoric on the order of "men tend to" or "it is more probable that men will," which, in turn, invites implications of generalized differences between men and women. In this perspective, the relation between background (sex) and act (robbery) is explained by "characteristics," "motives," "inclinations," or "predispositions" that are supposedly true of all those in the background category, but that are manifest only under certain conditions. Thus, the distinctive relationship between men and robbery may be taken to reveal some truth about the male identity, at least in a given culture or historical period. Within this determinist or positivist explanatory perspective, the problem of sex ratios in robbery is an especially nice one because correlation does not leave one confused about the causal direction. Differences in the background factor of gender must explain gender differences in robbery rates, not the other way around.

Consider how disastrous this course of interpretation would be for analyzing relationships between robbery and race! Despite the centrality of the relationship between race and robbery in modern criminology, the academic community is particularly reluctant to address the matter.[4] I would suggest that this reluctance is due, in part, to the fact that the conventional perspective, by imputing explanatory forces diffusely to all who fit the correlated causal categories, inevitably leads to highly offensive ideas about what blacks or black men "tend to" or "are likely" to do.[5] It is essential, for pursuing the relationship of both sex and race to robbery, that we turn the issue around and ask, first, not what robbery patterns reveal about sex or race, but *what the sex and race patterns reveal about robbery,* that is, about what people are trying to do when they do stickup.

The relationship between robbery and sex, although not grounded in any predisposition of men, whether biological or socially acquired, is not spurious. Within the experience of the act, doing a stickup enacts and extends a particular version of being male. The construction of maleness in a stickup, which I have been implicitly addressing as the way of being a "hardman" and that I addressed more directly in chapter 3 as the phallic metaphor embodied in the ways of the badass, makes compelling sense to relatively few men and to virtually no women.

Similarly, for the relationship of race and robbery, we need not impute any general racial tendencies, not even any general inclinations among "ghetto blacks," to appreciate that for some urban, black ghetto-located young men, the stickup is particularly attractive as a distinctive way of being black.

To avoid acknowledging a true empirical relationship between robbery and the contemporary black identity, two lines of argument have often been pressed. One argument is that when national police statistics on arrests for robberies are compared to national population percentages, the enormous overrepresentation of blacks versus whites among arrestees, of over 5 to 1, is due to the bias of the police in making arrests or in hearing victims complain. Michael Hindelang responded effectively to this argument when he found that the ratio is virtually identical when victims of robbery, located through random telephone surveys, identify offenders.[6]

The second argument is to attribute the relationship between race and robbery to underlying economic differences. There is, of course, a strong relationship between low-income status and robbery. It would not appear to make sense to commit robbery unless one is close to poverty, for two reasons. One is the rational advantage of alternative pursuits, licit or illicit, with respect to payoff and risk. The other reason is that a person with a respectable, middle-income occupation would be more likely to construct, through a mugging or a convenience store robbery, a social identity, not as a hardman, but as pathetic and perhaps crazy. In any case, when socioeconomic information has been obtained on robbers, it appears that they are lower class in education, income, and occupational skill.[7]

But the overrepresentation of blacks in robbery statistics cannot be explained by their overrepresentation in low-income groups. Two forms of evidence make the point. One comes from comparing the representation of different ethnic groups in *different offenses.* In national U.S. data, the overrepresentation of blacks is much greater with respect to robbery than to either violent nonproperty offenses (simple assaults and aggravated assaults)[8] or nonviolent property offenses (burglary).[9] Neither theories of a "subculture of violence" nor ideas about greater economic need appear to explain the distinctive overrepresentation of blacks in robbery.

The issue may also be examined by comparing the rates of blacks with those of similar low-income groups.[10] In the Chicago data from the early 1980s that was analyzed in chapter 5, for robbery-homicides, the ethnicity of the offender was identified in 88 of the 105 cases of robbery-homicide; of these 88 offenders, 79, or 90 percent, were black, and 5, or 6 percent were Hispanic.[11] Although we do not have data describing the economic status of Chicago's robbery offenders, if we assume that they are overwhelmingly poor, the economic differences between Chicago's black and Hispanic populations would not appear large enough to explain the large difference in robbery rates. In the 1980 census, the percentages of persons below the poverty level in Chicago were 11 percent for whites, 32 percent for blacks, and 24 percent for "Spanish origin."[12]

California's population, in which the Hispanic group is overwhelmingly of one national origin and has virtually no overlap with the black category in census counts, provides a strategic contrast.[13] If, for Los Angeles County, we use just the poverty populations for comparison, the robbery rate for blacks is over four times that for the Hispanics, while the black rate for other major crimes is about twice the Hispanic rate (see table 7.1).

It is possible to hypothesize additional economically relevant ways in which young male urban poverty-level blacks differ from young male urban poverty-level Hispanics or whites: unemployment levels, type of employment experience or occupational skills, immigration status, and so forth. It seems unwise to push the discussion much further, however, because the data on offenders do not describe their standing on these dimensions and so we risk imputing to the offenders group differences that misrepresent their personal characteristics. But whatever the precise relation between income and robbery, the interethnic, intercrime comparison makes it unreasonable to discount the overrepresentation of blacks in robbery, either by reference to a culture of violence or by attributions of economic causes or pressures. Why should the overrepresentation of blacks be so much greater in robbery than in violent offenses without property-acquisition objectives *and* in property-acquisition offenses without violence (burglary)?

Putting aside the quantified data, the relevance of black ethnic identity to robbery can be documented from the ethnographic and biographical materials on robbery. Even if, in more refined statistics, blacks would not be overrepresented in robbery, it would still be essential to appreciate how robbery is significantly attractive for black robbers as an extension of a way of being black. The thrust of this chapter implies that if the qualitative materials were available, persistent Hispanic and white robbers would also

TABLE 7.1

Arrest Rates in Los Angeles County,
by Type of Offense and Race/Ethnicity,
per 10,000 Persons below Poverty (1984)

Type of Offense	White	Hispanic	Black
Homicide	7	17	38
Assault	89	149	308
Burglary	162	253	464
Robbery	35	81	356

SOURCES: Bureau of Criminal Statistics and Special Services, *Criminal Justice Profile: Los Angeles County, 1984* (Sacramento: State of California Department of Justice, 1985); "Characteristics of the Population: General Social and Economic Characteristics," *1980 Census of the Population,* vol. 1, chap. C, part 6 (Washington, D.C.: U.S. Government Printing Office, 1983), table 59, p. 57.

be revealed as being seduced by the attractions of robbery for constructing what they experience as their castelike, moralized, ethnic or subculture identities.

I analyze the overrepresentation of blacks in robbery along three lines. A disproportionately high percentage of young black men are involved in social worlds of illicit action and thus, as a practical matter, are closer to the seductions of stickup. Second, the social appearance of the violent black hardman has been uniquely shaped into the narrow role of the street robber, compared to the more diffuse, ambiguous, and hidden forms given the role of violent hardman in the historical experience of other urban ethnic low-income groups. Third, on the emotional level, within the modern poor black urban community, the seduction is provoked by the existential attractions of being "bad" as a collectively celebrated way of being that transcends good and evil.

Gender and Stickup

Perhaps the most common explanation of gender differences in robbery rates is that women are less practiced in or capable of enacting the physical aggression that is necessary to dominate interaction in robbery. Indeed, in biographical accounts, stickup men begin robbing without guns, often with "yokings" (throwing an arm lock around the victim's neck from the rear and pulling the victim sharply back).[14] We should expect such moves to be more inviting to those for whom wrestling seems natural. But, again, the much lower male/female ratio for assault than for robbery raises doubts about how much work this argument can be asked to perform. For example, victimization data on offenders identified as black adolescents show about one assault by females for every three assaults by males, compared to one robbery by females for every fifteen robberies by males.[15] We might also bear in mind that guns minimize the relevance of physical differences for planned robberies.

More significantly, patterns of criminal involvement do not fit the stereotype of men as self-confident loners and women as dependent on others for support in risk-taking activity. In fact, women commit their high-frequency offenses—shoplifting, prostitution, and petty theft without contact—often without co-offenders and, in the case of prostitution, they run substantial physical risks.[16] Robbery, however, is more often conducted jointly rather than singly. If anything, it appears to be more difficult for male street criminals than for female street criminals to sustain autonomously a line of criminal action.[17]

The group character of robbery should not be taken to reflect a sensed need by men for help in controlling victims, any more than the absence of women from robbery statistics should be taken to reflect a sense of physical inadequacy. Rather, the group character of robbery indicates the presence of an aura of illicit action, which sustains a braggadocio, badass posturing and gamelike or conlike playing, which, in turn, easily move into the beginnings of stickups.

As we saw in chapter 5, the initial moves made to assume a posture of domination in stickups are not necessarily physical moves; for street robberies, they may involve the appreciation of a potential victim as particularly defenseless—drunk, aged, burdened with packages, and thus unable to guard against a purse snatching—and little cons or "games" of feigning a need for change, directions, or the time. Inquiry into gender differences in stickups more fruitfully begins at this *seductive edge* of interpersonal dynamics for achieving *moral superiority,* where the temptation and the challenge to self-confidence concern not simply what may be taken but the prospect of "taking" or making a fool of the victim.

So, the first step back from the foreground experience of stickups toward an understanding of background gender differences takes us to patterns of involvement in illicit action. Women are not commonly found in ghetto poolrooms or in crap games held in alleys and hallways.[18] As Edith Folb noted, drawing on years of data she collected on the everyday adolescent street culture of the black ghetto of south-central Los Angeles, "many young women are not especially familiar with, interested in, or privy to certain 'male' activities—such as low riding, gambling, gang banging, sports, or certain specific street hustles or activities."[19] Although I know of no census on the question, ethnographic accounts describe those who hang out on ghetto corners, with the ambience of anything can happen, as overwhelmingly male.[20] It is not uncommon for robberies to emerge casually out of corner-group drinking situations.[21] The stickup is a form of illicit action that some men and few women find seductive—the kind of illicit action that may be represented equally by activities like low riding, gang banging, and sports that have no monetary overlay and by those like street hustles and gambling that do.

A second step is to specify what in illicit action is distinctively attractive to men. Gambling is a useful focus. In national surveys, women report that they gamble at high rates and at levels only slightly lower than those that men report.[22] But not all types of gambling structure risk in the same form. Playing the numbers, betting on a horse, pulling the arm of a one-arm bandit, and wagering on board games like bingo can all be easily managed so that the "action" is diffused over and limited by the passage of time. It is possible, of course, to risk everything on one horse race or on a particular day's number, but that is personal decision.[23] One can easily stay in these forms of action for extended periods by limiting one's bets; Mah-Jongg can delay the determination of winners and losers for hours, and one may have to struggle to exhaustion to succeed in losing everything through pulls on slot-machine arms. In contrast are games in which another participant may suddenly issue a challenge to put everything at stake or get out of the action. Craps, often through progressive betting, and poker, through sudden raises, are well suited for dramatic tests of who can handle the action.

Thus, although it is absurd to ask the typical numbers, bingo, or even horse player whether he or she has "heart," this issue is alive both in "gang banging" and in poker playing. In the report of his study of "professional" poker players in the legalized casinos in Gardena, California, David Hayano presented the following commentary about "heart" and its close metaphoric companion, "balls":

> He probably knows more about the game than anybody else. . . . But he's got no balls. He's got a heart this big [measures a half inch with his fingers]. If he doesn't have the nuts he's not going to be in the hand. . . . You see all those crying calls he made with the best hand? No balls and no heart.[24]

Predictably, this masculine metaphor for celebrating one's readiness to take action is contrasted with the pathetic, feminine image of losing self-control as "opening up," which is something done to you by others; "Being 'opened up' feeds on itself . . . often creates a chain reaction that results in further losses."[25]

If robbery is distinctively, if not exclusively, male, prostitution may be its inverse analogy. Although prostitution is a form of illicit action for the "Johns," for prostitutes, a key objective is to minimize risks. Sometimes prostitutes bear the costs of exploitative pimps for this purpose. Reducing risks is one of several reasons why prostitutes treasure relations with steady, predictable clients. As Marsha Rosenbaum noted with regard to male and female heroin addicts:

> Men and women differ in their attitude toward risk. For male addicts, particularly at the beginning of their career with heroin or at the beginning of each new run, the daily overcoming of risk and chaos makes this life exciting and alluring . . . heroin is deemed a rewarding feeling for a hard half-day's work . . . on a subjective level, women disdain the riskiness of the heroin lifestyle. It is not suprising that women derive no positive status from engaging in risk.[26]

A similar gender difference was documented in Terry Williams and William Kornblum's study of adolescents' participation in the "underground economy," or illicit money-making activities, in a wide range of low-income communities: the "depressed blue-collar" community of Greenpoint, Brooklyn; a Puerto Rican section of Williamsburg, Brooklyn; a black section of Harlem; the black Hough ghetto in Cleveland; a group

of poor blacks in Meridian, Mississippi; and low-income blacks living in
Louisville. They found that "in all the cities [they] studied, prostitution is
the main occupation for girls in the underground economy"; boys hustle
in pool rooms and discos, peddle marijuana, pimp their girlfriends, bur-
glarize, perform small cons, and rob.[27] Sally Engle Merry's interviews with
George, a young pimp in a northeastern city, illustrated that the strategy
of the young pimp in recruiting adolescent girls into prostitution specifically plays up a contrast between the male as socially adventuresome and
the girl as tied to the home, envious, and feeling incompetent to risk entry
into a bigger, classier world without the security of her pimp-guide. As
George stated:

> Give a pimp a young girl, she lives in a real tacky apartment somewhere,
> with four or five brothers and sisters, and she's dying to get out. . . . So
> they go to this big restaurant, and he make sure she doesn't know what
> to order, makes sure she has never been there before. "How do you like
> it?" he asks, and she says, "Oh, I've been places like this before." And
> the music's nice. And if he knows how to speak a little French or
> something, that'll freak her right off. If he orders in French, it'll kill
> her.[28]

We have left robbery's arena of physical challenge to begin specifying
what it is about illicit action that some males but apparently very few
females find fascinating. It is something about the possibility of losing
everything that develops when the stakes suddenly rise, and it is something about pretensions, whether in the form of a pimp's social pretentiousness, a poker player's bluff, or the strutting braggadocio of a badass.
The essential challenge is moral rather than physical. This challenge may
be clarified if we take another look at combative physical interaction on
the streetcorner.

On the streetcorners at the site of Elijah Anderson's research on the near
Southside of Chicago, the "play" fighting that may readily be observed on
low-income streetcorners anywhere was frequently on display. Anderson
described a typical set of "play-acting of physical violence toward others"
in this way:

> It is not unusual to see two men "punch each other out" for a few
> minutes, looking as though they were seriously involved during the
> whole encounter. When such a play contest is going on, it may be hard
> for a passerby to tell that the men are "just playing." The participants
> themselves may not know for sure until the activity is over. At times,
> for example, one person will take out his knife and "go after" another,
> putting the dull side of the blade against the other man's skin or cloth-
> ing. The person "attacked" usually stands still and tolerates the game for
> fear of accidentally being cut "for real." Such unpredictable physical

play has plenty of chance to go amiss. For instance, even the slight appearance of the "attacker" getting the best of the "victim" may be just enough to violate the delicate boundary between play abuse and real fighting.[29]

Not all males find such "mock" fighting fascinating, and females sometimes fight for real, sometimes with knives. But mock fighting among friends appears to be almost exclusively a male fascination.[30]

"Mock" fighting is not a test of physical prowess; a real fight would be more to that point. Nor is the issue simply the "dramatization" of a tough self, since at any moment, the play may become real fighting. It is the tension and uncertainty that makes mock fighting literally full of wonder for its afficionados. At play in mock fighting is the moral metaphysical question, Are you for real or are you bluffing? The kindred phenomena consist not just of risk taking in betting but of the possibility of bluffing that can make for big action, whether in poker, con games, or stickups.

What action brings alive is not pretentiousness but play with pretentiousness: the recurring issue of whether one "means it" or is "for real." Now we can take another step back toward the roots of gender differences in stickups. A self-consciousness about whether one's apparent intentions are "real" purposes or just "fake" moves also distinguishes casual forms of interaction among girls and boys. In a detailed study of white middle-class fifth-grade schoolchildren in spontaneous interaction, Janet Lever found that "sixty-five percent of boys' activities were competitive games compared to only 37% of girls' activities. In other words, *girls played more* while *boys gamed more.*"[31] The distinction, Lever was careful to note, is not between physically strenuous forms and more abstract forms. The girls played at jump rope and hopscotch while the boys might game at chess or racing toy cars. Girls' play was characterized by a structure of "coaction rather than interaction"; frequently, one girl performed at the center of attention while a circle of others formed a supportive context. The girls' play was physical and challenging, but the challenge was more typically against the self rather than against others. Boys' games, in contrast, were structured more often into competitive sides, whether one-on-one or team against team. Here, interactional strategy becomes relevant in the specific sense of bluffing. Boys' games do not necessarily require greater physical strength or agility than do girls' forms of play, but they more commonly feature bravado and faking out. No move in jump rope can become a "fake out"; no move in basketball cannot.[32]

Put in other words, boys' games constantly raise the issue of whether one will follow through on the apparent intent. With this conceptual edge, we can make one last move away from stickups toward broader but continuously connected gender differences. "Throwing like a girl" becomes apparent by age 5. As Iris Marion Young indicated, "throwing like a girl" means throwing with the arm and not the body:

Not only is there a typical style of throwing like a girl, but there is a more or less typical style of running like a girl, climbing like a girl, swinging like a girl, hitting like a girl. They have in common, first, that the whole body is not put into fluid and directed motion, but rather, in swinging and hitting, for example, the motion is concentrated in one body part; and second, that the woman's motin [sic] tends not to reach, extend, lean, stretch, and follow through in the direction of her intention.[33]

Throwing like a girl creates a dialectic of self in which the throw simultaneously throws itself off from the self: the self that throws is at once abandoned; one takes distance from the role even as one enacts it. Thus, the center of the body or the essence of the self remains back, uncommitted to the assertion or projection of self into the world. "Throwing like a boy" mobilizes an inverse dialectic of self, in which every projection of self into the world is followed by a meta-statement that the essence or center of the self is, in some way or degree, implicated in the apparent action. Each presentation of self immediately raises a challenge of moral metaphysics, Is that purpose for real or a pretense, to what degree, and with just what humor or emotional accent? Throwing like a boy is no less dialectical and sets up no less a moral question than does throwing like a girl, but the issues have their own forms of moral doubt and sensual wonder.

Young noted that the difference between throwing "like a girl" and "like a boy" is a gender distinction with its own empirically varying relations to sex (some boys throw more like a girl, and vice versa), and its immediate background in corporeal development may be traced to Ray Birdwhistell's classic claims of a male pelvis rolled slightly back in contrast with a female pelvis rolled forward, a difference he documented in a film of a 15-month-old child and a 22-month-old child.[34] Whether these rolls are roles, that is, socially learned or biologically rooted, the difference indicates how thoroughly embodied and deeply based in everyday sensuality are the inverse dialectics that characterize throwing like a boy and like a girl. A forward roll of the pelvis holds the trunk of the body back as the arm is projected out, setting up the female dialectic without the necessity of any specific reason or decision on the matter; the converse is true for boys.

But I risk taking the argument too far. It would be a fundamental misreading of the linkages drawn here to read different "inclinations" to commit robbery into gender differences in the ways toddlers toddle. There is nothing in the male's cocked pelvis, in boys' fake-out moves in childhood sports, in the mock fighting of streetcorner men, or in the bluffing and testing of "heart" and "balls" in big-action gambling that makes males more likely than females to engage in stickups. Most males are no more likely than are females to do stickups; there is no evidence of subconscious motivation or widespread male fascination with the project of robbery.

Yet, we should now be able to appreciate why street robbery, which makes little rational sense as a way of making money, would be an almost exclusively male activity. Unless it is given sense as a way of elaborating, perhaps celebrating, distinctively male forms of action and ways of being, such as collective drinking and gambling on street corners, interpersonal physical challenges and moral tests, cocky posturing and arrogant claims to back up "tough" fronts, stickup has almost no appeal at all.

Black Ethnicity and Stickup

Our focus on the seductions of crime suggests three interrelated dimensions that may explain the overrepresentation of blacks in robbery. One is the much higher percentage of the population of poor blacks that is "at risk" to commit stickups, compared to other contemporary poverty populations, in the sense of young males generally involved in a life of illicit action. As a practical matter, the step into robbery is shorter for a higher percentage of young black males than it is for young males of other ethnic groups. The second is the distinctive shape given to the social role of criminal hardman in American black ghettoes, compared to the shaping of that role in the historical experience of other ethnic groups. And third is the emotionally powerful attraction of the "bad-nigger" identity as a transcendent response to the racial humiliation of ghetto blacks by ghetto blacks.

YOUNG GHETTO BLACKS IN ACTION

Two demographic patterns indicate that young black urban males are involved in lifestyles of illicit action far more often than are their white or Mexican-origin counterparts. One is the rate at which young males disappear from census counts. Consider table 7.2, which shows the excess or deficit of males relative to females, for three age and three ethnic categories in Chicago in 1980. The direction and the magnitude of the sex differential for blacks suggest that a large percentage of young male blacks are, at the time of census counts, incarcerated[35] or "underground," either having no fixed address or maintaining relations with householders who do not declare their presence to official record keepers.[36]

This interpretation is supported by several dimensions of family structure on which white and Mexican-origin families share a sharp contrast to black families. Considering only households with at least one child present, both husband and wife are present in 86 percent of the white households and 80 percent of the Mexican-origin units, but in only 56 percent of the black households.[37]

The point is not to resurrect arguments that the black family is responsi-

TABLE 7.2

*Number of Men per 100 Women in Three
Age Groups, Chicago, 1980*

Age Groups	White	Black	Spanish Origin[a]
15–19	102.7	96.5	106.6
20–24	101.0	80.8	114.9
25–34	104.9	75.5[b]	113.3

SOURCE: U.S. Bureau of the Census, *1980 Census of Population and Housing* (Washington, D.C.: U.S. Government Printing Office, May 1983).
[a]In Chicago, "Spanish origin" means about 60 percent Mexican origin and 30 percent Puerto Rican.
[b]For blacks in the oldest age group, the "deficit" was 25,705.

ble for crime.[38] I offer these data simply as indicators of the much greater extent to which poor young black men, compared with economically analogous ethnic subgroups, go "underground" in lifestyles of illicit action.[39] Why this should be the case is a historical question that is properly beyond the scope of this work.

THE COMMUNAL SHAPING OF THE CRIMINAL HARDMAN

Many American urban poor ethnic communities have featured what might generically be termed a role for criminal hardmen—a significant number of young men who recurrently use criminal violence to make money. But the form of this role has varied greatly. The criminal hardman systematically takes his shape in relation to the social structure of his ethnic community.

Black Stickup Men as Parasites. Read properly, cross-race statistics on robbery can help us assess the extent to which the current black ghetto stickup man practices his criminality in close relation to the shape of his community. Two patterns are frequently cited. First, cases of whites robbing blacks are quite rare, but in national victimization surveys, more than half the victims of black robbers are white.[40] Second, despite this cross-race pattern, because there are many more whites than blacks in the population, blacks are still more than twice as likely as whites to be victims of robbery.[41]

Some interpret the cross-race patterns as suggesting that black robbers are racist. But compared to what population proportions would predict—that about 88 percent of black robbers' victims should be white—only 64 percent (according to recent victimization surveys) are white.[42] And differences in the economic statuses of potential white victims and black victims would give rational, racially indifferent black robbers far *more* than a 64 percent preference for white victims.

Cross-race statistical patterns and intrarace victimization rates are too simplistic and contradictory to assess whether black robbery is parasitical, notably animated by racism, or otherwise motivationally related to the victims' ethnic-group ties.[43] Is it any more logical to consider that the imbalance in cross-race patterns indicates racist motivations by black robbers than to attribute the relatively infrequent selection by white robbers of black victims to pro-black sentiments?

Qualitative evidence on stickups indicates that black robbers are fundamentally parasitic in their criminality on several grounds that victimization statistics cannot appreciate. First, life histories show robberies by blacks emerging from conflict among blacks. Early experiences in robbery often do not look like "robbery" at all, but like "gang fights" and personal bullying or assaults on schoolmates or neighborhood acquaintances and, particularly, "winos." Attacks outside the familiar social contours of ghetto life, when they come at all, typically are made after experience is acquired in shaking down, yoking, and "jumping and taking off" peers and especially vulnerable ghetto residents. Thus, in the personal-history sense, the shaping of the motivation of black stickup men occurs in their community.

Second, both arrest and victimization data are biased against representing a significant form of robbery—the use of violence to extort money from peers and others engaged in the various worlds of illicit action. Countless robberies are committed against victims who do not wish to call themselves to the attention of the police and who are unlikely to wish to discuss the matter with telephone interviewers who are conducting victimization surveys. Such victims include prostitutes, drug dealers, participants in crap games, and legitimate patrons of bars and other action scenes who, in their social and sexual practices, have reasons to avoid a public disclosure of the circumstances of their victimization.

At least equally important, robbery attacks against victims who are mirror images of the offenders are especially unlikely to be picked up by the police or in victimization surveys. Are we to assume that men who are intensely involved in violent criminal lifestyles are as likely to be reached by victimization surveyors as anyone else and if they are, that they are as willing to report the times they were "taken"?[44] In addition, robberies among inmates of jails and prisons systematically escape the attentions of police and victim survey data, but the prison literature indicates that such robberies are hardly rare events.[45]

One way to get a sense of how much like-on-like robbery may be missing from official data on robberies is to examine robbery-homicide cases for themes of deviance other than the robbery-homicide itself. When they become homicides, robberies are less likely to escape official recording than when they do not have fatal results. And apart from their value for assessing the overrepresentation of robberies by blacks against whites in police and victimization data, robbery-homicides show stickup men operating close to their own routines of illicit action.

The evidence of deviant context in robbery-homicide is remarkably strong, at least in the Chicago data.[46] Two patterns noted by Zimring and Zuehl give an initial indication of how much more closely hewed to lives of illicit action are robbery-homicides than are police cases of robberies in general. Robbery-homicides more often occur in residences (36 percent) than on the street (19 percent); inversely, robberies in general more often occur on the street than in residences (51 percent and 8 percent, respectively). Robbery-homicides, compared to robberies in general, are committed less often against strangers (53 percent versus 87 percent).[47]

The qualitative content of the cases shows in detail just how closely tied the black stickup is to its local sociocultural base. First, we may examine cases of robbery-homicide for indications that they occur within the contours of the life of illicit action. In 29 of the 105 cases in the Chicago data set, deviant institutions or ghetto "street culture" apparently was significant to the offender when he constructed the attack. These 29 cases featured 16 drug dealers attacked; 2 crap games raided; 3 winos rolled; and 8 miscellaneous events, including these:

[10503] A young male black who was carrying his new portable radio/ cassette player, presumably appreciated as a "ghetto blaster," was coerced by a group of adolescents he encountered on the street and was "rescued" by the intervention of an older, larger black man, apparently a stranger. He was then approached by a young black male who had been observing and who shot the radio owner after a testing of wills that provoked the original rescuer to flight and that had the victim hanging onto his radio right to the end.

[11002] The supervisor of a construction site was attacked on payday by three offenders. The leader of the attack remarked, in the pre-attack discussions, "I'll kill this nigger 'cause I know he gots the money"; their homes were close enough that they could return to the scene within minutes with guns. Two of the offenders recruited the third, an acquaintance, on the way to the attack, shouting to him, "Do you want to make some easy money?" to which he responded, "I'm in."

[10301] A mile from his house, a young man entered a bus and, to recruit a colleague to rob the passengers, flashed a "gang" sign to a young male passenger. The latter "responded that he didn't not have time for that," ran off, and eventually was shot.

In five other cases, the victim was a drug dealer, but the evidence does not establish that this fact was known or relevant to the offender, who, in most of these cases, was not identified. In twenty-two additional cases, the victims were either seeking action or were situated in times or at places where others customarily seek action. Most of these cases occurred either in the early morning hours (between midnight and 5 A.M.) or around bars. A few showed deviant practices or contexts: picking up strangers in gay bars; a double-legged amputee, confined to a wheelchair, hanging around with the offenders and others in the early morning hours, apparently in an atmosphere inspired by drinking and smoking dope; and sleeping on a salt box on the El platform at Congress and Kedzie at 3 A.M.

To this point, we have indications from fifty-four of the robbery/homicides, not necessarily that the victims invited risk—our focus is on the *offenders'* perspectives—but that the offenders committed the crimes within the contours of lives of illicit action, coming across victims within the offenders' or the victims' partying, bar-centered, vice-oriented, drug-dealing, early-morning pursuits of action. In an additional fifteen cases, the offender and victim had been acquainted. In thirteen additional cases, the offender was not identified and there was insufficient evidence to characterize their previous relationship or the situation immediately antecedent to the crime. Thus, in sixty-nine of the ninety-two robbery-homicides for which details are available with which to address the issue, or *in 75 percent of the cases,* the offenders appeared to be acting within social lines of illicit action.

Even the cross-race cases, when examined for qualitative detail, support a characterization of the offenders' perspectives as parasitic, rather than racist. In the Chicago data set, there were no cases of nonblacks victimizing blacks but eighteen cases in which black offenders robbed and killed whites (ten cases), Asians (three cases), or Hispanics (five cases). In ten of the eighteen cases, the victims were running retail stores or were otherwise commercially engaged—making a delivery, driving a taxi, trying to buy drugs, or tending bar—seven in black areas and three in Hispanic areas. The underrepresentation of blacks in small retail businesses, even in the black ghetto, is a long-standing pattern that indicates a practical, nonemotional, and non"racist" contribution to the imbalance between the victimization rates of black/white robberies and of white/black robberies. There are relatively few objective opportunities for either whites or blacks to rob black owners of neighborhood retail stores—a form of business that particularly favors the hiring, and thus victimization, of family members (nonblacks).[48]

Five of the remaining eight cases in the Chicago data set indicate other ways in which the figures for black offenders/nonblack victims can misleadingly suggest an effort by black robbers to victimize the ethnically different. Three of the five will serve as examples:

[11906] A middle-aged Asian instructor and graduate student was killed on the campus of the University of Illinois–Chicago by two offenders who had been acquainted in prison. One lived near the campus, and they walked to it to rob someone.

[10602] The victim, 72 years old, was attacked by an adolescent neighbor. He "was one of the last whites living in what had become an all-black neighborhood."

[10211] The victim, Paciejewski, a 42-year-old man, died from a blow to the head with a wooden table leg. He was attacked at about 3 A.M. after he had stopped in a bar to ask for directions back to his home in Indiana and was spotted, seemingly drunk, by two adolescents and one 20 year old, who robbed and beat him.

Now if we look at the qualitative details of the cases involving black offenders and black victims, we can appreciate even more vividly how statistics on cross-race robberies obscure the intense concentration of the nightmarish reality of contemporary urban robbery in black communities. In 38 of the 105 robbery-homicides in this set, blacks were killed in or while entering their homes. In all the 31 cases in which the offender was identified, the offender was identified as black. Many of these cases began with knocks on the door or ambushes in the hallway, the fatal, intimate invasions of home turf that provoke the profound anxiety that one has no safe place anywhere to exist. Not only in its spatial social distribution but in the depths of its horrors, black robbery-homicide is especially confined to the black ghetto community.[49]

A final source of evidence on how closely black stickup men adhere to their local social and moral worlds are the problems they experience in transcending these boundaries. Interviews with thirty-eight black and forty-five white property criminals (only twenty-four were robbers) in Oklahoma City indicated a sharp contrast not only in the areas of the city targeted for crime but in the criteria of a good target location. Blacks were concerned that they would "stand out" in white areas, and whites feared for their safety in black areas.[50]

Ethnographies of black street life have elaborated on this point. Members of black street "gangs" in the ghetto of San Francisco, whom Werthman and Piliavin studied in the 1960s, reported a more subtle discrimination by police than simple reactions to skin color out of residential place. They understood police to focus on the boundaries of neighborhoods and to be "very hard on 'suspicious looking' adolescents who have strayed from home territory":

Why do they pick us up? They don't pick everybody up. They just pick up on the ones with the hats on and trench coats and conks . . . They think you going to rob somebody. And don't have a head scarf on your head. They'll bust you for having a head scarf. . . . Don't try to walk pimp. Don't try to be cool . . . . like you got a boss high. Like you got a fix or something. Last night a cop picked me up for that. He told me I had a bad walk. He say, "You think you're bad."[51]

"Suspicious looking" is partly a matter of hardman or "bad" style, of symbols and movements that suggest toughness (trench coats), purposiveness (hats are worn by adults—serious people), and participation in forms of illicit action, such as pimping and drug use.

In effect, black ghetto street men face a tradeoff between the rational and the sensual attractions of crime. To approach the more prosperous targets, they must at least temporarily abandon the spiritual and symbolic embodiment of the spirit of illicit action that gives the project its emotional sense. Biographies of black stickup men indicate that the tradeoff is rarely accomplished. Robby Wideman's one attempt to "run a game" outside the ghetto ended in disaster for all involved because the fence who was to be conned, with a truck containing a "hard-assed nigger" and a shotgun rather than stolen television sets, was trying to con Robby and his friends. James Carr was aware that commercial targets on the prosperous west side of Los Angeles—a white area—had the advantage that the clerks were less wary of stickups: when he tried to exploit this advantage, however, he was caught "by chance in one of those 'field interrogations' the cops are always pulling."[52] John Allen, although stopped by the police when he would occasionally walk in affluent white areas of Washington, D.C., claimed that "I know more about their world than they know about mine."[53] But consider what happened when, toward the end of his reported criminal career, he carefully planned the robbery of a department store in the embassy area. This was to be "something really, really big, something that should've paid thirty or forty thousand dollars. This kind of big money we had never been into before." He had to abort the plan because unexpected traffic frustrated his arrival at the appointed time. "There's some *long* lines, everybody trying to get to work! So when we finally get there, it's too late." Angry and restless at the frustration, he and a friend attempted what he had long regarded as a foolishly dangerous crime, the robbery of a liquor store. They took $106 (he remembered the paltry sum well), and then were caught after a high-speed attempt to escape. He thought he had acted as a jerk.[54]

John Allen literally did not know what was involved in getting from "here" to "there." And this humiliation is precisely the challenge that the hardman is distinctively styled to overcome. His toughness claims he need never alter himself as he moves about; rather, scenes must alter to suit him. His hardness is a metaphor for uncompromising purposiveness. The hardman style works most reliably only when kept close to its community of origin.

The somewhat dramatic "parasite" image helps to offset powerful distortions that imagine racially motivated black crimes directed against whites. There is a great irony in the structure of the public's fear of crime: those who are most victimized—young black men—voice the least fear of crime when surveys manage to reach them, while the most fearful—elderly women, black or white—are the least victimized.[55] The predominant reality of black offenders brutally victimizing black ghetto residents is frequently displaced in the mass public eye, as well as in the most politically powerful eyes, by the isolated robbery-homicides by blacks of white victims in the victims' home preserves.

In the black community, robbery-homicide takes on dimensions that are virtually unknown in white middle-class areas. In the Chicago data set, there are a handful of cases in which young men posed as drug buyers to enter the ghetto homes of single women who raise numerous children without the regular presence of a man. The women apparently sell drugs as a sort of small business that, with its low storage and capital requirements, can be run conveniently from the home, while allowing them to care for small children more conveniently than if they engage in other forms of criminal enterprise.[56] The social characteristics of the men who con their way in to rob and kill the dealers—and sometimes the children who may be around—cannot be markedly different from the characteristics of the men who fathered the children or the men who supply the drugs that the women take risks to sell.

The intraghetto cases have another unique subset: late-night or early-morning attacks on blacks who are going to or returning from work, sometimes second jobs in which they guard or clean downtown institutions, essentially for whites.

When whites are fatally attacked by black robbers, they are almost always engaged in their own pursuit of action, if only in the form of returning home in the early morning after a night of partying. When attacked in their private lives outside the ghetto, whites are typically in their cars or in open public spaces. But black ghetto residents, as well as an occasional elderly, ethnically isolated white resident, are trapped by the architecture of their everyday lives in hallways and vestibules, imprisoned on buses, and locked in their homes with neighbors who came to do a favor or perform a service only to reveal malevolent plans.

As a result of the qualitative difference in black-white and black-black robbery-homicides, whites in middle-class areas can take comfort from the advice of the experts that they not resist attacks. Even if the advice does not work out well when put to the test, it is put to the test so rarely that it does a service by putting to rest some anxious imaginings. Many ghetto blacks, however, seem generally to understand that they face an almost systematic testing by neighborhood predators who, if not resisted, may return to exploit them as they exploit local winos, again and again.[57] Their decision about whether they should resist is not simply a matter of the relationship of resistance and injury in given situations, but a transcendent, ongoing issue.

The parasite image is useful to bring to the fore various qualitative dimensions of robbery that are often obscured by the statistical appearance of cross-race victimization in police or survey data. It is also especially useful as a reminder that in comparative analysis, the role of the contemporary black stickup man takes its shape from the social structure of the community to which it is fundamentally related.

Varieties of Predatory Hardmen. In chapter 6 I pressed Henry Hill into an analogous relationship to black and other stickup men. Now we can appreciate that when robbing cash deposits at Kennedy Airport, wiseguys operate as especially sophisticated stickup men. Their form of robbery is assisted by inside information supplied by employees who owe "connected" bookies and by logistical cooperation from "connected" airport unions. In hijacking trucks, wiseguys can convert "stickups" into "giveups," partly because hijacked drivers have reasons not to panic and resist; they know, from various signs of "connections" between criminals, unions, and employers, that they can calmly take bribes, since these will be especially "organized" robberies.

Malcolm X provides a revealing contrast. Having worked briefly as a railroad employee, he had a railroad employee's card that enabled him to ride free and provided a convenient cover for his movements. Using the railroad for his work as a traveling reefer salesman, he simultaneously cut business costs and minimized risks, since neither the police nor other black hardmen, who were a more apparent threat to ghetto-based dope dealers, had a hint of his modus operandi.[58] An enterprising black stickup man like Malcolm X will seize any slight advantage for improving his methods of committing crime, but the only entree he had to a legitimate employment context in white society that he could use as a cover was through the heavily black food-service crews on the railroads.

It has long been assumed that the extent to which an ethnic group establishes itself in the legitimate occupational order determines the extent to which its members will resort to crime, at least to violent street crime. The contrast of Malcolm X and Henry Hill indicates a qualitatively more complex pattern: that the extent and nature of an ethnic group's inroads into the legitimate occupational order shape that group's attendant criminal roles. Thus, in the 1980s, a Chicano used car dealer in the Southwest can report, "there isn't a day when someone doesn't come off the street asking me if I wanted to make a deal on hot TVs, stereos, tires, you name it, even drugs."[59] U.S. criminals of Mexican-origin can connect with fellow ethnics in the used car lot and auto repair shop to facilitate crimes to which their ethnic ties give them special access, such as the smuggling of aliens and the sale in Mexico of cars stolen in the United States.

As a result of differences in the way ethnic communities relate to the economy, some criminal hardmen will be more and some less apparent. For example, in New York in the late nineteenth century, the definition of arson, in the popular press, was "Jewish lightning." Although fed by anti-Semitism, the label also reflected a substantial reality: in the 1890s, Jews were tied to 44 percent of all arson cases described in the *New York*

Times.[60] Practiced as an instrument of insurance fraud, arson made sense only to the owners of insurable "constructed properties," a necessary condition that Jews disproportionately satisfied.

There is no evidence that blacks are less eager than are others to exploit the possibilities of making criminal connections in business. In Harlem in the 1970s, Francis Ianni traced the supportive interactions of a network composed of a black pimp, a black narcotics dealer, and a black owner of two types of businesses in which blacks historically have specialized—a night club and a dry cleaning store.[61] Professional thieves, working at times on special order, sold clothes at the dry cleaning store. The pimp bought clothes there and supplied prostitutes to the illegal after-hours night club. Some of the "Johns" wanted to buy drugs, so they were directed to the narcotics dealer, who had an interest in a boutique that, in turn, had a profitable association with the stolen clothes at the dry cleaning store. The network prospered on an integration of the distinctive culture of action and business in the black community.

Blacks are underrepresented in business entrepreneurship,[62] and this difference in the way in which blacks have participated in the economy helps explain why they have been overrepresented in street robbery. Other ethnic groups have produced varieties of violent predators—wiseguys, *shtarkers* (strong-arm men), gorillas, muscle, enforcers and executioners— who have abjured street robbery in favor of parasitical "racketeer" roles, developed especially in relation to co-ethnics in business.

Racketeers and Stickup Men. "Rackets" originated as a reference to a noisy dance or ball, the tickets to which local toughs would sell to shopkeepers in the early 1900s on the Lower East Side of New York.[63] The term has often conveyed an image of the ethnic hoodlum or gangster who extorts tribute by the threat of violence. Although not without documented instances, this image has been overplayed. If the relationship were so unilateral, it would be difficult to understand a series of anomalies: why businesses, in particular, would be selected for threats, rather than wealthy individuals; why "protection racketeers" would routinely collect from shopkeepers in a given area, rather than sporadically attack like contemporary street robbers; why the threat of violence would be veiled in a metaphor of a legitimate charitable contribution, rather than presented as a straightforward robbery; why the exploited businessmen, who would be taxed recurrently by the same individuals, could neither call in the law nor, if the legal system was corrupted, hire gunmen to make a "final offer" in response; and, perhaps what is most perplexing of all, why the racketeers would not simply take over the businesses completely and immediately if the owners were so defenseless in the face of the racketeers' threats.

If the threat of violence was all that the practical work of rackets required, bad niggers would have prospered in comparison with Jewish *schlammers* or *bolagulas*[64] and Sicilian wiseguys, at least in their own ghetto.

Comparative issues aside, surely black stickup men would have developed impressive dimensions of the institution by routinizing the victimization of white, and now Asian, shopkeepers in their neighborhoods.[65] But, the historical records indicate, the racketeer exploited resources other than violence, and his relationship with the businessman was not simply that of an enforcer of unilateral contracts.

Violent hardmen have recurrently exploited at least five points in the social organization of small businesses. First, they have protected owners from those who would be new entrants in the field. The more established and successful the businessman, the easier he could afford the criminal's tax and the more valuable the prohibitory consequences of demands for "key money."[66] By demanding key money from prospective competitors of his regular businessmen-clients in amounts that reflected the many payments that his regular clients had made over a long period, the racketeer might even induce old clients to become enthusiastic about their contributions.

Second, racketeers have served local businessmen as intermediaries with local political machines. John Landesco provides an invaluable, contemporaneous account of the intricate connections that existed in Chicago, primarily among the Irish and Italians, in the 1910s and 1920s.[67] The urban political party organization, or "machine," enjoyed the assistance of clubs of young men with reputations for wild partying and violence, who would marshall the residents to vote the right way. The clubs were accepted locally because they represented the toughness or masculinity of the local populace, for example, through their support of ethnic boxers and, occasionally but memorably, their rioting against blacks. Thus, payments made to local toughs were, in effect, contributions to the reigning political party, which, in turn, could provide a helpful "understanding" to local businesses in countless ways. One was in avoiding or reducing the costs to protected businesses from the enforcement of municipal regulations. Local government maintained the market value of favors early in the century by filing tens of thousands of criminal citations for such matters as commercial intrusion on pedestrian space and garbage disposal.

Third, violent ethnic toughs have often developed parasitic relationships with small businessmen of their ethnic groups through what outsiders call "loan sharking." Ethnic entrepreneurs of all varieties have depended on intragroup mechanisms for raising capital. For the Japanese, the Chinese, and the Koreans, these mechanisms have included the use of revolving credit associations maintained by ethnic societies that are rooted in extended kinship, religious, and old-country (regional) loyalties. Money is contributed by the general membership, the choice of beneficiary is sometimes made by lot, and the enforcement of repayment is handled informally but, because of the closed nature of the ethnic subgroup's social relations, with near-inescapable firmness.[68] Some Jewish congregations in urban working-class areas now simply have a standing offer of small, noninterest-bearing loans of $5,000–$10,000 that are available essentially as an incident of membership.

According to Francis Ianni's study of a Sicilian organized-crime family, loan sharking had analogous origins.[69] In the case he described in New York's "Little Italy," a relatively prosperous immigrant developed the type of extended family that was traditionally idealized but economically beyond common reach in Naples, Calabria, and Sicily. As with the Asian ethnic groups, loyalties ran not to "Italy" or even, in this case, to "Sicily," but to particular villages or subregions. The making of loans to kinsmen-countrymen was handled within the metaphoric structure of patriarchal family authority, which would readily make sense of informal financial terms, as well as a last resort to decisive and brutal enforcement methods. In Ianni's "Lupollo family," the aged head seemed to treasure the moral and social relational richness of the money-lending business so much that he persisted with it as one of the few remaining illegal arms of the economically diversified "family" business. With authority in such relations tied to age and a dense symbolism of deferential honor, enforcement tasks would naturally be handled not by the respected head but by specialists. Hence, a labor market for violent hardmen.

Fourth, labor-management and labor union–labor union relations have been fertile grounds for the development of parasitic connections for violent predators with previous experience in hijacking and other forms of robbery. A measure of the market that has existed for labor "muscle" is suggested by Alan Block's review of the areas of the New York economy that governmental investigations found to be subject to systematic extortion from 1930 to 1950:

> bead, cinder, cloth shrinking, clothing, construction, flower shops, Fulton market, funeral, fur dressing, grape, hod carriers, ice, Kosher butchers, laundry, leather, live poultry, master barbers, milk, millinery, musical, night patrol, neckwear, newsstand, operating engineers, overall, paper box, paper hangers, shirt makers, taxicabs and window cleaners.[70]

Not only were there many sites for employment, there was a lot to do. Muscle was useful in labor relations in a variety of roles: to "break heads" of strikers, to protect scabs from the retribution of striking workers, to intimidate those who would form or bring in a competing union, to forge corrupt connections with governmental officials, to convince workers and clients of other enterprises to respect secondary boycotts, to encourage workers to believe that they could join a union and not be abused by toughs who were associated with management or other unions, or simply—through physical imagery—to encourage workers to "stand up" and "be strong" in the face of hostile employers.

Fifth, racketeers have often developed parasitic roles in warehousing and delivery services. Congressional investigations and federal prosecutions since the Second World War have repeatedly drawn public attention to the sometimes violent racketeering on East Coast docks and, more generally, in the trucking industry. Before the First World War, New Yorkers were familiar with a now-outmoded form of organized criminal activity that exploited the dependence of many businesses on a delivery service that could be sabotaged easily and dramatically. Borrowing on the negative symbolism of other ethnic groups, a dozen Jews directed by "Yushke Nigger" and conducting public relations under the name, Yiddish Black Hand, built a significant extortion operation through poisoning delivery horses. In 1910, ice cream manufacturers, who had been losing one to five horses each while they attempted to respond to the problem through a self-insurance program, agreed to pay $1,000 for two years of security.[71]

One reason for the vulnerability of delivery and warehousing functions to exploitation by violent criminals is the frequent attention given by professional thieves to cargo-holding areas and methods of transportation. In many cities, young men who develop theft beyond its attractions for "sneaky thrills" into "serious" or "professional" thieving often focus on buglarizing warehouses and stealing from trucks. Typically from working-class backgrounds, "serious" young urban thieves often have contacts through personal networks to drivers and workers in warehouses and loading docks; they exploit these contacts by bribery or kickbacks to obtain inside information and to minimize the risk of arrest.[72] When the resulting thieves' culture is combined with the muscle involved in labor organizing, the market for violent hardmen is likely to expand.

The structure of black entrepreneurship has offered comparatively poor employment opportunities to black hardmen. Not only have blacks developed businesses in the United States at a rate lower than have other ethnic groups, but black businesses have been concentrated in personal service, solo proprietorships ("barbering and beauty shops, mortuaries, drayage, and various repair services"),[73] with relatively little stock on hand and relatively few employees. Compared to the social arrangements of retail stores and small manufacturers, the black small business has minimized its vulnerability to racketeering. Capital or financing requirements are relatively low; union organization is generally irrelevant; deliveries are on a scale that may be personally managed; and customers tend to have personal loyalties, which makes black-owned businesses less vulnerable to competition than those of other ethnic groups. The one point in the social organization of business at which black entrepreneurs may otherwise have enjoyed relations with organized criminals, through political influence on the enforcement of municipal regulations, was irrelevant, until recently, because of the exclusion of blacks from significant power in urban political machines.

The role of the violent predator can quickly become diverse and sophisticated when elaborated through ongoing ties to business. The language commonly used by outsiders to damn violent criminal roles in business—

"loan sharking," "extortion," "racketeering"—indicates a relatively subtle form of crime. These phrases fail to conjure up an image of situational behavior as specific as does "stickup." Bribery by businessmen and political corruption add to the confusion, often obscuring the correct identity of victims. Deprived of these subtleties, the black stickup man has been a historically unusual, institutionally independent, version of the criminally violent ethnic hardman. Thus, while the wiseguy, having "muscled in" to a business or labor organization seeks constantly to exploit new "angles," John Allen's ideal was "getting in, getting what you could, and getting out fast."[74]

Even in the vice industry, blacks have been underrepresented in organized forms for doing business. In the late nineteenth and early twentieth centuries, West Coast Chinatowns developed prostitution almost exclusively in the form of small businesses or brothels, which were controlled by Chinese social organizations (*tongs*) on the basis of kinship and regional (old-country) loyalties. Black prostitution, in contrast, has often taken the form of individual streetwalkers and a small number of women who work under black pimps; brothels, the more organizationally complex form of black prostitution, have often been controlled by whites. Ivan Light analyzed the consequences of different social organizational forms for the shape of prostitution-related violence:

> The black vice industry consisted of streetwalkers and pimps who settled quarrels with fights. The Chinese vice industry consisted of syndicated brothels which resolved severe business rivalries by gang wars, but adjudicated individual quarrels. . . . complex alliances knit the nation's fighting tongs together, [so] a purely local dispute could and often did precipitate a fight between affiliates and their allies in every U.S. Chinatown. . . . Black pimps relied upon their reputation for violent prowess to intimidate workers and rival pimps. Maintaining one's reputation required frequent dueling, and beatings or murders of prostitutes.[75]

The relations of clients to Chinese vice businesses, which included gambling houses and opium dens as well as brothels, were protected by disciplined community-based organizations. In contrast, black streetwalking and pimp-controlled prostitution created a relatively open market for street robberies of clients. In turn-of-the-century Philadelphia and on the East Coast in general, the contemporary phenomena of street armed robberies of strangers and retail stores were, according to Roger Lane, virtually unknown. But an early, primitive form developed in the victimization by blacks of the customers of street prostitutes in the most impoverished areas:

> "Panel thievery" was the name given to the version in which a man, perhaps hidden behind a panel, crept in to rifle pockets in pantaloons

not currently occupied by their owners. The "badger game" involved the sudden appearance of a large male confederate, the woman's alleged husband, in the middle of a tryst. The victim might then be blackmailed or simply forced to flee without his valuables. . . . The best brothels . . . worked hard to give their visitors a sense of comfort and security. . . . Badger theft was practiced [at] . . . hardcore slum addresses. . . . especially [against] those who were strangers to the community.[76]

The social stratification in the worlds of violent urban hardmen was reflected in the occupational status and ethnic distribution of victims of "professional" murderers in New York from 1930 through 1949. Alan Block counted a set of 242 "gangland slayings" that were described in governmental investigations and newspaper accounts.[77] About three-quarters of the victims were "professional" criminals; the median age of those victims whose age could be determined was 33. Italians and Jews constituted over 90 percent of the victims whose ethnicities could be identified, with Irish and Chinese victims about equally making up the rest. Blacks were apparently irrelevant in the tensions within the profitable organized vice (bootlegging, gambling) and labor-racketeering businesses that produced these killings.

With neither black businesses, black labor unions, nor formally organized black vice institutions to exploit, violent black predators have operated in a distinctively individualistic form. This form is reflected in the in-and-out structure of interaction in stickups, as well as in their cultural style. Working with organizations that are rooted in traditional kinship-regional associations, other varieties of violent ethnic hardmen have often fashioned themselves as extensions of socially and often politically conservative ethnic traditions. Thus, Sicilian wiseguys would understand themselves to be members of "families," the heads of which often have lived in modest middle-class settings. Violent agents of Chinese organizations would be members of tongs, a traditional form of association that only rarely developed criminal activities. Japanese *yakuza* have often been allied with fascist political organizations. And Jewish pimps in New York embraced the social welfare traditions of their community by forming associations that offered members the security of prepurchased funeral plots.[78]

In contrast are two themes in the ways of black hardmen. One is the celebration of "bad" individualism, which is most familiar to outsiders in the showy pimp style. The other, a general pattern in black ghetto street life, is a kinship ethos in which loyalties symbolically extend to all blacks through fictive "blood" or "cousin" relationships, not to a subethnic unit or to any intermediary "family" or regional-kinship association. Thus, from the adolescent pimp culture in South Central Los Angeles, Folb quoted the following:

Like you got your righteous kind—*for real* brothers and sisters . . . and den you got your play brothers and sisters. Like yo' partner, yo' *first* partner, yo' *best* partner, he be like a brother to you. Like he in d' family. You be sayin', "What it is, cuz."[79]

When black criminal hardmen develop collective associations, they usually do not extend preexisting legitimate communal units of association ("families" and other regional-kinship units), as have other ethnic hardmen. Instead, they attempt to construct and maintain collective associations in and through criminal activity. The black street gang may be seen as a sociologically thin attempt to create a unit of criminal association that is based on a region (neighborhood) and fictive-kinship ("brothers" or "cousins")—an association that is independent of other organizational forms in the black community. Membership in black gangs is tenuous on the streets in comparison to the intensity of affiliations in jails and prisons.[80]

The cultural individualism and structural atomization that distinguish the role of the black hardman indicate an extraordinarily chaotic street life in which trust among associates has little grounding in transcendent loyalties. As a result, blacks in the contemporary illegal drug world have the worst of both ends. At the street level, they are disproportionate among users. And at the higher, more organized, levels of distribution, they are underrepresented.[81]

Motivated by the exceptional image of a Nicky Barnes or another superstar black drug dealer, young black street dealers struggle against each other and against black stickup men in a high turnover occupation that promises quick, big rewards but that has no code of honor to suggest how one might retain them.

Among blacks who sell marijuana on the streets of the West Coast, whose work might be compared to that of the beer distributors during Prohibition, no organization guarantees their share of the market. According to one street dealer, "You got to be here regular. . . . If you ain't 'round, they just gonna say fuck that nigga and buy from the competition." The ethnographer Allen B. Fields observed: "When they are stationary for brief periods, dealers constantly glance around for possible sneak thieves." As a result, the otherwise ingratiating salesman's role must take on the aspect of the violent hardman: "You gotta be hard 'cause, if you ain't, niggas don't respect nothin' else."[82]

In Detroit, a group of heroin "runners," aged 18–21, make an average of $100 per day, but they apparently have short careers, partly because of the weak discipline in their working group, "Young Boys, Inc.," and partly because their work requires a measure of agility and endurance that becomes increasingly humiliating, if not physically difficult to perform, with age. Crew bosses hire men with especially "bad" reputations to serve as "guns," but runners are still vulnerable to stickup men (as well as to

.,ir own inclinations to rip off the bosses by falsely claiming to have been
(timized).[83]

In New York, Darryl, a young black from Harlem who was "among the
i'te" in drug sales and who claimed to have made more than $500,000 in
i ie year, went to the top of his distribution system to buy from Cubans,
/ho were governed by a tradition that combined honor with symbols of
nasculinity in a way he had never experienced. In Darryl's street life,
nasculinity meant don't trust anyone.

> I thought it was a sign of manhood to have the money for coke up front
> but every time I did that he would look at me funny but he would take
> the money. Then one day I heard him say in Spanish, "No tiene co-
> jones." I understood that to mean that I wasn't a man because I wouldn't
> accept the coke without paying for it. I didn't understand until then that
> only those who couldn't be trusted according to his code would bring
> money to cop.[84]

THE TRANSCENDENCE OF THE "BAD NIGGER"

Black hardmen, who parasitically stick up victims in or close to their
byways of action, are social worlds away from the white and Asian-
American violent hardmen who have historically exploited businesses,
unions, and vice institutions developed by their ethnic kinsmen. In part,
blacks have been historically overrepresented in robbery statistics because
robbery is the form that the structure of the black community has given
to its version of the violent hardman. "Robbery" statistics have given little
recognition to violent hardmen who have exploited, through corruption
and racketeering, different "angles" on the ways in which their ethnic
kinsmen participate in the economy. The racketeer's victim is less likely
to file complaints; corrupted criminal justice machines are less likely to
prosecute; and when prosecutions come, they are likely to take forms other
than robbery charges (such as perjury, intimidating witnesses, kidnapping,
conspiracy, bank fraud, and tax fraud).

Of course, blacks who do stickups are not acting out of comparative
sociological reflections. In their community, they pursue an attraction to
transcending a challenge that America's ghetto blacks have long found
especially compelling.

Insults and their Responses. The nature of this challenge is most succinctly
captured in the symbolism of the bad nigger. Many others have examined
the significance of the "bad nigger" in black poverty communities.[85] I risk
redundancy, as well as offense, to clarify the specifically existential challenge to which bad niggers respond. The risk of offense is related to the
shame that blacks commonly feel when they see whites witnessing blacks
who are engaged in "nigger" talk. Although unpleasant to address, the
very offensiveness risked by the analysis helps make its point. When

asserting either in play or with malevolence that another is a "nigger," blacks enact a white role, simultaneously pressing the other to establish his moral competence with a transcendent response and asserting that for both, a personal sense of moral competence is vulnerable to respectability as defined by white society. In this respect, "nigger" poses for blacks a moral challenge unequalled by intragroup conflict among other ethnics. The Yiddish terms *gonif* (thief) and *schmuck* (fool/prick), for example, have no reference to gentile society; *pendejo* (jerk), *cabrón* (prick/cunning devil), and *puto* (homosexual male prostitute) have as much or more force in Mexico City, where the *gringo* is the outcast, as they do in East Los Angeles.[86]

Just as "nigger" presupposes the historical oppression of blacks by white society, so "bad nigger" takes its particular resonance from a project of transcending a presumedly radical, racial distance. This resonance is apparent even in lives like John Allen's, in which direct personal contact with whites is so rare as to be irrelevant to the development of a taken-for-granted fascination with the ways of "bad niggers."[87] Men like John Allen are not historically aware or racially self-conscious in their use of "nigger." However, they register a sensual awareness that "nigger" essentially alleges what Erving Goffman called a "nonperson" status: a moral ontological negativity in which one does not exist as a competent human being.[88] They realize in overtones of pathos and ridicule the meaning of "nigger" as silly, childlike or animallike, and they experience in awe its transcended form, the "bad nigger," as a type of superman.

Although the literal use of "nigger" is only an indicator of a variety of racially formulated, black-mobilized pressures to humiliate blacks as nonpersons, literal usages are vividly evident in the following examples of ethnographies and biographies on black street criminals:

In John Allen's autobiography, which was drafted from tape-recorded interviews, Allen refers to the blacks he most respected, whether neighborhood toughs or teachers, as "bad niggers."

> In junior high, I was beginning to learn a little something 'cause I had a teacher named Mr. Samuels. And Mr. Samuels was a really, really rough dude. He drummed and he made you learn. It made it easier to learn 'cause Mr. Samuels was a big, black, bad nigger and was mean.[89]

In Lee Rainwater's writings, based on observational studies of the Pruitt-Igoe public housing projects in St. Louis, black residents defined the threats in amorous relations that they had to overcome as pressures posed by "niggers." Thus, a man might warn his woman, "Girl, I'm gonna hurt you if you keep on messin' around these other niggers."[90] In joking conversations, women assert their freedom in terms of independence from the demands on "niggers." Josephine, in a particularly outrageous conversation, proclaims her freedom by professing to be satisfied with masturbation, concluding, "I don't need no nigger to put a black ass dick in me."[91]

Darryl, the "elite" young drug dealer from Harlem, described in Williams and Kornblum's recent study of young people in several poverty communities, related the problems he faced in a drug transaction when "the nigger did not want to hear I lost the shit."[92] And Ray-Ray showed his understanding of the origins of his criminality in an effort to transcend his "nigger" occupational status:

> I got a job when I got out working at Morrison's [Restaurant] as a cook. But at $1.95 an hour, that's bullshit. At Morrison's they thought they had a real nigger working 'cause I really tried to keep that job. But that damn man [boss] was crazy. He started bitching with me. Now he knows a cook don't wash no damn dishes. I wouldn't do that shuffling routine, so I quit. I started stealing hams and making some money.[93]

Janet Mancini, whose unique study involved in-depth interviews with poor black youths at three stages over several years of their lives, described the family background of Leroy, who, among the five types of ghetto personalities (or personal "strategies") she traced, represented the violent street criminal. Leroy's mother was continuously denigrating him as an especially black "nigger." His father told the researchers:

> I get so sick and tired of her saying that word, "nigger." "Nigger," that's all I hear in the house, "nigger." It's got to be monotonous, you know? She'll turn around and ask them to do something, and they won't do it. Then she tells me, "Duncan, you better make that nigger do this!" I say "I'm not making him do nothing. You learn how to talk to them, they'll do what you want them to do."[94]

Mancini added that "especially in response to racial name-calling, he [his father] says Leroy gets 'pretty evil' and swears himself."[95]

Claude Brown indicated the way in which the challenge of transcending the "nigger" status took on overtones of Oedipal conflict for him. When his father punished him with beatings for truancy, the beatings would begin with the following announcement, "Nigger, you got a ass whippin' comin'."[96]

Of course, these correlations of verbal "nigger" challenges and violent black hardmen's careers only begin to suggest a causal relationship. Williams and Kornblum advanced the issue by comparing the forms of self-denigration they found practiced by black, Puerto Rican, and white youths who were involved in street crimes in poverty areas:

> The style and themes of their self-belittlement differ: black teenagers refer to each other as "nigger"; poor white teenagers drink themselves

into oblivion while blaming blacks and Hispanics for their fate; Hispanic teenagers retreat within the boundaries of their ethnic culture and question the desirability and possibility of ever becoming part of the mainstream.[97]

In this comparison, we can see how correlation can become causation. Both poor black and poor white youths use "nigger" to define the challenge they face. But in the rhetoric of white youths, "nigger" is an abstraction thrown out lightly among white peers, one that elicits no challenging response. MacLeod described white criminally involved youths in a public-subsidized housing project in Boston as having the same sour-grapes resentment as Williams and Kornblum found in Brooklyn. "Slick" claimed he dropped out of high school because "they favor all them fucking rich kids at that school. . . . [and] they baby all the fucking niggers up there."[98] No "niggers" hear this talk. Such claims made by whites typically justify inaction. But when blacks call other blacks "nigger," they immediately create a social pressure for some form of transcendence. In the rhetoric of whites, "nigger" is thrown into a social vacuum, into a spiritually vacant space; among blacks, "nigger" ubiquitously charges moments with existential significance, stimulating rather than deadening further interaction, and demands a spirited response.

The resulting challenge is elegantly clear in the frequently analyzed, ritually insulting, banter among black youths that has variously been labeled "the dozens," "signifying," "woofing," and "rapping." In substance, the distinctive black-youth tradition of trading insults mobilizes any moral incompetence the speakers can imagine. It might involve physical features denigrated in stereotypes of blacks (skin color, hair texture, the size or shape of lips, and so on) or poverty ("When I came across your house, a rat gave me a jay-walkin' ticket").[99] Or it might refer to a female relative's sexual promiscuity ("It takes twelve barrels of water to make a steamboat run; it takes an elephant's dick to make your Grandmammy come; she been elephant fucked, camel fucked and hit side the head with you Grandpappy's nuts"),[100] to incivility ("Your mama don't wear no drawers; She wash'm in alcohol; She put 'em on a clothesline, the sun refused to shine; She put 'm in a garbage can, they scared the garbage man."),[101] or to an unfashionable appearance ("Hey man, you look like a goddamn Christmas tree! You a regular caution sign. You righteously light up the whole street!").[102] The utterance of such insults, without more, predictably motivates the recipient to search for an inspired response.

Occasionally, the substance of insults directly speaks to the ontological charge that to be black is not to exist in any morally recognizable way. "You so black you drink white milk so you kin see yo' pee"[103] treats blackness as a lack of visible being, as does Ralph Ellison's powerful novel, *Invisible Man.*[104] More significantly, the process forcefully conveys the teaching that to exist in a morally self-respecting way, one must overcome insult with insult. A participant who becomes noticeably flustered and starts a physical attack may win the battle but loses the moral war, as "Rap" Brown noted:

> For dudes who couldn't [rap], it was like they were humiliated because they were born black and then they turned around and got humiliated by their own people, which was really all they had left. . . . Those that feel most humiliated humiliate others. The real aim of the dozens was to get a dude so mad that he'd cry or get mad enough to fight.[105]

More precisely, the process is premised on the understanding that moral incompetence may be transcended not simply by physical aggression but by mobilizing that most distinctly human capacity, esthetic creativity. Thus, such insults are far richer in their processual and structural aspects— as lyrical couplets and rhymes and by using assonance, alliteration, consonance, metaphors, hyperbole, and the like—than in their substantive range.[106]

In contrast, the forms of insults that ethnographers have documented among criminally active white street toughs in the United States and Great Britain emphasize, in substance, charges of homosexuality (which are strikingly underrepresented in the published data from black language studies) and brief comebacks or one-uppers that are taken for quick wit:

Shorty (*drunk*): Hey Steve, what are you doing tonight?
Steve: Nuttin'. Why?
Shorty: You wanna suck my dick?
Steve: You're the only gay motherfucker around here.
Shorty: Yeah? Ask your girlfriend if I'm gay.
Steve: Yeah, well, ask your mother if I'm gay.[107]

The familiar "Oh yeah, yours also" form does not attempt to transcend; rather, it specifically turns the charge around, remaining on the same moral and esthetic level and seeking only to defend a position already staked out and presumptively respectable.

It appears also that the work accomplished by "nigger" as used in the rapping of black youths, of repeatedly grounding interaction in a mood of ontological firmness, is accomplished in the street talk of white youths by the grammatical exploitation of "fuck." "Get your fucken' foot off my chair" and "Get your nigger ass out of my face" use "fuck" and "nigger" to make the message sensually more realized, but only "nigger" imputes personal incompetence to its target, as well as declaring the speaker's hostility. ("Fuck," of course, is also familiar in black street talk, but, notably, often through variations on the more specifically antisocial form, "motherfucker.")

Much of the emotional dynamics of "bad" youth culture play off routine practices of insult. In comparative analysis, we can see how the nature of an insult structures the meaning of a transcendent response. Homosexual charges in the white and Hispanic youth cultures—fag, *maricon*, punk, *puto*—emphasize masculinity by juxtaposition, but not necessarily any more universal human capacities, such as intelligence or personal grace. "Nigger" is a unique insult in the versatile juxtaposition it invites; virtually any and all bases of respect may serve for a transcendent response.

It is not clear that even if they wanted to, young Mexican-Americans, Appalachian whites, American-Italians, or members of other white ethnic groups could develop a culture of self-denigration that would convey the thoroughgoing existential assault with which young ghetto blacks challenge each other in an everyday, taken-for-granted manner. There appear to be empirical limits on substantive creativity within cultures of insult; the terms must have some historical basis to make sense. An important criterion for a group's generation of self-denigrating insults is the way the group has related to the means of production. Thus, "nigger" invokes the nonperson status of the slave and domestic servant, while "Jewing down" calls on images of shrewd marketplace activity, and "redneck" and, for Mexican-Americans, "Beaner," draw meaning from rural agricultural and migrant-labor work. No other ethnic insult appears to be as boundlessly negating as is "nigger." "White trash," from the American South, at once borrows and attenuates humiliating power from an implicit play off of "nigger": "white trash" is shockingly lower than a Caucasian ought to be, but someone who is white trash is still white. "Jewing down" someone, while selfish and tricky, acknowledges a form of intellectual capacity. "Beaner" has an occupational role reference, giving it a situationally specific narrowness and an acknowledgment of hard work that "nigger" does not convey. "Nigger work" is any work that no one else wants to do; "nigga bidness" is just foolishness.[108]

Running Games.   If, as I argued in chapter 5, the initial phase in doing stickups is to move into a position of moral superiority over the victim and if, as I contended in chapter 6, the deepest commitment in the career of persistent robbers is to sustain a generalized firmness of purpose in life, then we should expect the distinctive forms of moral pressure in poor black urban communities to make stickups especially attractive as a transcendent response. The link in street life between rituals of personal denigration and the practice of stickups is made, in part, by "running games."

"Games" that others may attempt to "run on" ghetto residents elaborate the moral challenge of the practice of insults. Ethnographers of life in the modern black ghetto have drawn powerful depictions of gaming as a routinely encountered risk. From Los Angeles in the 1970s, Cynthia stated her philosophy:

> Ain' nothin' happ'nin' 'cept a whole lotta frontin' and gamin' goin' on down here [in South Central]. The brothers—and d' sisters too—they be tryin' to keep on top, get over any way dey kin. Dey do you in a minute!—love wise, fightin' wise—or else jus' blow on you hard and heavy, fuck wi'chu mind. Gots to have your program together else some nigger gon' righteously do you. Like the Golden Rule say, "Do onto others like they do you" else "Do onto others *before* they do you"—da's my own version. Bertha [the speaker's sister] she got her own self sayin'—"Do onto others, den split!"[109]

From Northeastern ghettoes in the 1970s, John Langston Gwaltney described "a world where would-be burglars are posing as salesmen, repairmen and census takers, . . . where the ringing of the phone may be a prelude to breaking and entering."[110] From Boston in the 1970s, Janet Mancini quoted Hank, whom she typed as the "Cool Guy," on what he would expect if everyone became black: " 'You wouldn't have no house the next day, or anything else.' He seems to view blacks as irresponsible, an attitude that reflects his mother's feelings."[111] Lee Rainwater first developed this theme in his studies of Pruitt-Igoe in the 1960s, quoting a resident on the daily risk of being conned:

> You can't trust anybody here because everybody is always trying to beat you up, so you have to be on guard. . . . *it's not the stranger that you want to be afraid of. . . . Your friends are the ones that'll put you in the trick. . . . You know yourself, man, when you walk out in the streets you have got to be ready. Everybody walking out there is game on everybody else. If you don't watch what you're doing, before you know it you're going to be put in a trick bag.*
> [Interviewer:] Is that true only for Pruitt-Igoe?
> No, *it's true anywhere where the members [blacks] are found. Our people are always plotting and scheming.* I was talking to a cat yesterday who said this to me, "I can send you a letter without putting a stamp on it."[112]

The structuring of everyday reality in the form of games may be as simple as playing a practical joke on a stranger:

> Like I use to tell people, "It's a party on Vernon and Slauson." Now, Vernon and Slauson they both be runnin' the same way. "Al-right! Al-right!" "I don' know d' address, but you cain't miss it, 'cause music is *loud* an' d' people havin' fon." Send 'em on a stone trip! Righteous lame brain. Fool d' sucker![113]

Or games may take on multiple levels, ironic twists, and unexpected turn-abouts. For example, a man may win a momentary victory in the moral battle of humiliation with the welfare system by using his wife's name for his children on the original birth certificate, welfare records, and hospital records, as if he were not related to them, and later change their names to his. But, at times, the cooperation of others is necessary to win such games, and they may exploit their role in the welfare game by blackmail. Thus, Bettylou Valentine described Randy's decision to give up the money he was obtaining from defrauding welfare, which involved misrepresenting his address, when he began receiving humiliating demands for money from the legal resident at his official address who, for Randy's scheme to work, had to hold and turn over Randy's checks.[114]

In the adolescent culture of the black ghetto, gaming in sexual relations is widely celebrated by bragging about "pimping," a term given a broad meaning to cover any economic support received from a woman whom one sexually satisfies.[115] Actually, having such a relationship with a woman is not a necessary condition for participating in streetcorner bragging. Indeed, more constant than the reality of economically exploiting a woman is a mode of comportment on streetcorners that suggests that one is "constantly on the move, ducking and being searched for by one or another female, as [if] some aspect of the 'contracted' relationship was [being] . . . violated."[116]

And blacks may play games on blacks that are specifically related to the criminal justice system. Those who are socially close to people who are likely to be arrested and pressured by the police are often anxious about being implicated in crimes they did not commit. Edith Folb reported the poignant personal philosophy that one "loner" developed to minimize this risk, "I'ma tell you, I'ma *loner!* I'm by myself, so you cain't be tellin' shit on me—'cause I wadn't wi'cha!"[117]

Being by Being "Bad." Ubiquitous attempts by hustlers to run games on friend and stranger alike stimulate many young ghetto residents to rise to the challenge. Against this background of moral pressure, black street crime has taken on specifically transcendent meanings. Like those in criminal cultures in other ethnic settings, blacks who seek to exploit illicit opportunities are said to live the "fast life"—an image that suggests great fluidity in moving from one situation to the next, from "here" to "there." More distinctively, the black street criminal's project is one of "getting over." In the black urban poverty circles described in *Drylongso,* the "gitover boy" is a known type. Mr. Wilmot told the author, John Gwaltney, of a day when he was washing dishes at a small restaurant owned by two neighborhood women:

One of them git-over boys ate six thirds of one of Miz Hattie's fish dinna's and stone refused to pay and swore he would run if she called the man! Miz Hattie said, "Well, son, if you think you faster than this hot grease, run on." Jim, that dude paid and shook![118]

"Getting over" suggests not just material survival but spiritual integrity achieved through illicit means, such as through making a drug score or a street hustle. Here "survival" implies being deviant, and being deviant, or "bad," takes on the meaning of *being* in general. In the black ghetto street culture, being bad does not necessarily mean committing crimes or embracing any other, independently defined, version of the illicit; it may be achieved just by emphasizing one's moral existence. Thus, a stylish form of dress that might be said to be "sharp" in other cultures is referred to in the black ghetto culture alternatively as looking "clean" and as showing a "bad" style. This usage is strikingly paradoxical, but the seeming contradiction is resolved by the presupposition that one has been ordained not to exist morally. In the case of appearance, a nigger's proper "place" is in the dirt. Thus, a style of dress that draws attention to and thereby asserts one's competence to dress is defiant even while it is conforming. As Folb observed:

> Even among the hardheads—those who are into physical fireworks rather than costuming—there is a grudging recognition that to get clean and stay that way is an important mark of getting over in the world. "Dude dress nice, stay clean, brother maybe think twice 'fore he mess 'im up."[119]

Virtually any emphatically claimed moral competence can be bad, against this background understanding of an injunction not to exist as a morally competent being. A way of being becomes bad when it is understood to be daring and pretentious. Thus, a youngster who acts as if it is fitting for him to hang out with older males might be seen as "trying to be bad." Here the worldly knowledge that presumably attends age is the relevant moral competence, the pretensions to which earn the label "bad."[120]

Being bad is, fundamentally, *not* acting criminally or immorally, or even acting with physical aggression, but something that is more precisely defined with a morally charged, spatial metaphor: charting out a big space in public interactions and claiming to be able to fill it. Thus, John Allen could, without any sense of irony, speak of a good junior high school teacher who was seriously committed to teaching, as a "bad nigger." And Claudia Mitchell Kernan analyzed "loud talking" as a distinctive black sociolinguistic form of the style of being bad. Loud talking is a public event in which a somewhat shameful matter that one participant would prefer to handle privately is picked up by another participant and, with a flourish, made visible to all.

Creditor: Man, when yo gon pay me my five dollars?

Debtor: Soon as I get it.

Creditor: (to audience) Anybody want to buy a five dollar nigger? I got one to sell.

Debtor: Man, if I gave you your five dollars, you wouldn't have nothing to signify about.

Creditor: Nigger, long as you don't change, I'll always have me a subject.[121]

If being bad celebrates the maintenance of purpose in a morally challenging environment, we can understand how the project of being a bad nigger by committing stickups can be sustained even against the dictates of rationally assessed material benefit. Doing a stickup itself serves a larger, more widely embraced, fascination with the achievement of a morally competent existence.

GHETTO STICKUPS

I began this inquiry into background factors as a way of understanding the overrepresentation of blacks in robbery. For a final note, I wish to avoid two possible misreadings by returning to the foreground phenomena. The first misreading is that the relationship between the contemporary black ghetto and stickups depends on demographic comparisons. In case-by-case analyses over chapters 5 and 6 and this chapter, I have tried to make obvious how the participants themselves forge a relationship with their ethnic culture right in the process through which the crime emerges. These materials would be no less probative were blacks underrepresented in robbery statistics; they would continue to display robber-assailants constructing their attraction to the act in and through dynamics and significances distinctive to the black ghetto.

The second misreading I would like to discourage is that robberies committed by offenders other than blacks do *not* show comparably strong cultural relevance. When Jews were prominent among professionally criminal hardmen, their murders of other Jews in the process of collecting debts exhibited a mixture of material objective and ethnically relevant battles over personal dignity that are analogous to those I have reviewed here, although the ethnic terms differed.[122] Fragments from other contemporary ethnic settings likewise indicate that participation in robbery makes sense only as part of a larger ethnically or subculturally relevant project of being a hardman. For example, in Great Britain, as an extension of the subculture around gyms, where "Once money comes into it, the line between ordinary body builders, [sic] and criminals blurs in the bent gym into an area of semi-legal, semi-illegal activities. Strong men who are prepared to threaten or injure for money are drawn in willy-nilly by money and flattery."[123] In California, white and Hispanic offenders exploit "outlaw" and "lowrider" metaphors to give purpose and symbolic allure to their careers. Unlike the "bad-nigger" style, these avenues are not restricted to whites. John Irwin describes a South Pacific islander and a black, as well as a white and a Mexican American, in detailing these types.[124] Notably, some version of caste or castelike identity seems necessary to make the lifestyles of contemporary street criminals persistently attractive, whether the imagery is drawn from a racial culture or borrowed from Hollywood. Straightforward class imagery does not seem to work.

CHAPTER 8

Primordial Evil: Sense and Dynamic in Cold-Blooded, 'Senseless' Murder

> Thus speaks the red judge, "Why did this criminal murder?
> He wanted to rob." But I say unto you: his soul wanted blood,
> not robbery; he thirsted after the bliss of the knife. His poor
> reason, however, did not comprehend this madness and per-
> suaded him: "What matters blood?" it asked; "don't you
> want at least to commit a robbery with it? To take revenge?"
> And he listened to his poor reason: its speech lay upon him
> like lead; so he robbed when he murdered. He did not want
> to be ashamed of his madness.
>
> —FRIEDRICH NIETZSCHE,
> *On the Pale Criminal*[1]

Cold-blooded, "senseless" killings have several features that distinguish
them from other forms of violent crimes. Killings are generally *not* regarded
as cold-blooded in the following instances:

- When they are understood to grow suddenly from a situationally
  emergent rage, as in the cases of "righteous slaughter" that were
  examined in chapter 1.
- When the killer appears to have gone "berserk," for example, by
  climbing a tower or entering a restaurant and shooting at randomly
  available targets with no robbery objective and with no plan of
  escape.
- When the killings exhibit the sexual or sadistic practices common
  in serial murders.[2]
- When a robber's mortal violence appears to respond to a victim's
  resistance.

Multiple and serial murders are often presumed to be not so much
"senseless" as crazy—the work of mentally disturbed people. But when

violence develops in the context of a seemingly materialistic act like robbery and yet goes beyond the practical requirements for economically
measured success, it both evokes and strains a utilitarian understanding.
Thus, when little money is taken, robberies in which nonresisting victims
are murdered seem especially "senseless."[3]

In such cases, police spokesmen sometimes offer, as an alternative to the
"senseless" characterization, an especially "cold," narrowly utilitarian explanation: the killer was guided by a desire to leave no witnesses. But the
appeal of this account is often more to the public's fear than to its validity in
capturing the meaning of the event to the offender. Consider Gary Gilmore's robbery-murders in their context. In July 1976, after robbing a fully
compliant gas-station attendant, Gilmore shot him in the head, twice, at
close range; the next day, while robbing a motel, Gilmore executed the
manager in a similar way. The explanation that Gilmore was animated by a
desire to leave no witnesses is inconsistent with a variety of attendant facts.

- Gilmore committed the first murder while a mentally unstable, hal-
  lucinating young woman waited in the truck he had driven to the
  scene.
- The gas station attendant did not know him; a mask would have
  been a more prudent way of avoiding identification.
- Gilmore later ran out of gas and, after locating two strangers who
  would help him get fuel, he allowed them to see him recover from
  some bushes a gun, a coin changer, and a clip of bullets that he
  slammed into the gun.
- The next day, he made an unprecedented offer to his cousin of $50,
  which led her to question whether he had committed the already-
  infamous gas station crime.
- His second murder was committed close to his uncle's home, shortly
  after he had left the truck he was driving with an acquaintance who
  was at work in a repair shop and who was immediately able to link
  Gilmore to the crime.

The crime that Gilmore committed does not fit neatly either the motivation of robbery or of murder. It was a robbery, but one in which the
objective of violence clearly transcended the self-interested justifications
of material acquisition and the avoidance of legal culpability; it displayed
a murderous desire, but one that required the context of robbery to be
realized. Answering an interviewer's questions, Gilmore himself shows an
awareness of the mixed metaphors in the crime, and in words that could
speak for Nietzsche's pale criminal:

WHY DID YOU ROB BEFORE YOU KILLED—WHY NOT JUST KILL
OR JUST ROB? [Gary Gilmore's answer:] . . . That's a good question.
A valid question. I may as well have just killed—but I'm a thief. An

ex-con, a robber. I was reverting to habit—perhaps so that it made some sense to me.[4]

To explain acts such as Gilmore's, I will pursue three lines of inquiry: the self-definition that the offenders present to others, the emotional dynamic that the crimes complete, and the situational contingencies that catalyze the relevant emotional dynamic and make it practicable to present the desired self-image.

Image. With regard to self-image, it is useful to consider Paul Ricoeur's phenomenology of evil.[5] In primordial symbolism, the sacred makes its appearance in the form of dreadful devastations. To cold-blooded "senseless" killers, the senseless appearance of the events is not incidental but essential to the dread they seek to represent.

Emotion. The mixture of metaphors of robbery and murder in these crimes reflects the emotional dynamic that lies behind them. With unparalleled insight, David Matza captured this dynamic as a "dizzyness" that characterizes one type of committed career in deviance.[6] All the protagonists whose cold-blooded, senseless murders we will be examining had been shifting between a playful use of the symbolism of deviance, in which they explored its unique power in social interaction, and a paranoic shame in conformity. The confused, wavering meaning of the crimes—not straightforward robberies and not just murders—reflects the confused emotional process that carries the offenders to the act.

Practical Act. As we search for an explanation, we must keep in mind that a constant cannot explain a change. Whatever the appeal of appearing in the world as dreadfully evil and however intense the moral dizzyness, these aspects of image and emotion do not emerge for the first time in the fatal scene. These killings are rare events in society and in the lives of the offenders. We can throw up our hands at the challenge and pass them by as inexplicable, random events or we can try to understand them as the result of a unique moment in which long-standing potentials are realized and a sudden clarity of deadly intent fundamentally transforms the killer's life. If we take up the challenge of explanation, we will need to attend to the situational factors that relate the symbolism of evil and the dizzying emotions of deviance to each other and to the practical features of the killing scene.

The Cases

Just because they are deemed "senseless," robbery-murders like Gilmore's tap a deep curiosity for investigative, biographical reporting. As Truman Capote was the first to prove, public disquietude about such events creates fantastically lucrative opportunities for writers.[7] We can now develop a theory across a range of cases. In addition to Gilmore's history, the variety of facts in the following three cases—taken from *In Cold Blood, Victim,* and *The Onion Field*—help us avoid at least some of the dangers of overly broad generalization.[8] The varying quality of the reporting methods used in these cases also helps us remain sensitive to the inherent evidentiary risks.

'IN COLD BLOOD'

In November 1959, Perry Edward Smith, aged 31, and Richard Eugene (Dick) Hickock, aged 28, met about four months after their release from prison to carry out a plan Dick had devised. Neither had a criminal record for violent crime, but Dick, who had been a burglar and check fraud, believed Perry's prison reputation as a cold-hearted killer. On the basis of talk by another prisoner who once worked for a prosperous farmer named Clutter, Dick and Perry drove to Clutter's home to find a safe with a payroll of up to $10,000. They arrived at about midnight, after Mr. and Mrs. Clutter and their adolescent son and daughter were asleep. Waking Mr. Clutter, they demanded access to the safe but were told none existed there. All members of the family were tied up, and the two robbers searched for valuables. Dick had apparently told Perry many times before they arrived that they would kill the victims, no matter how many they found. Perry was the one who killed the first victim, Mr. Clutter; he began by slashing his throat with a knife and, after Dick opened the wound further and Mr. Clutter fought back, Perry ended the struggle with a close-range shotgun blast. According to both Perry and Dick, Perry also killed the son. Dick attributed all the shooting to Perry, who eventually agreed, but initially, Perry attributed the shooting of the women to Dick, perhaps from a sense that that part of the killing was unmanly and thus disgraceful.

Although the author, Truman Capote, claimed that Perry's assault was the result of a "mind explosion," neither the descriptions by the offenders nor the material evidence of the crimes suggest an act of passion.[9] The immediately antecedent experience was anything but emotional. They drove four hundred miles across Kansas in one day to arrive at the scene. Inside the Clutter's home, they were careful to cut the telephone lines and to bind and gag each family member securely. Ironically, Perry was particularly kind to the victims, making one comfortable with a pillow, bringing a mattress for another, blocking Dick's intention to rape the daughter, and respecting the son's request not to mar the newly varnished finish of a piece of furniture. There was neither open hostility nor provocation between Perry and the victims. Before the first attack, Perry and Dick dared each other to show the guts to kill. If Perry was anything more than mildly irritated at Dick during the first attack, the image of a mind explosion is inconsistent with the methodical, sustained, mutually cooperative nature of the offenders' attack as a whole, which ranged widely over the house and involved a careful recovery of the shotgun shells after each victim was murdered.

If the killings were cold-blooded, they were also senseless in that there was no resistance by the victims and no need to murder the victims to avoid identification (as Perry had urged Dick, they could have used masks). And if monetary reward could ever make such an act sensible, in this case, the offenders made off with $40–$50.

'VICTIM'

In April 1974, in Ogden, Utah, three soldiers from a nearby air force base conspired to rob a hi-fi store. They had cased the store some days before, noticing a basement where, on the day of the offense, they confined the two young employees, a young friend who came by, and then the father of one and the mother of another victim. Two victims survived but only one, the father, Mr. Walker, immediately had the capacity to recount his experience of the crime.

Initially, the offenders labored for a long time to remove stereo equipment from the store and load it in their van. Then two of the offenders, William Andrews and Dale Pierre, the latter aged 21, forced the victims to drink a liquid that they said would harmlessly knock them out but that was Drano. A few days earlier, Andrews and Pierre had seen a Clint Eastwood movie in which a pimp forced a prostitute to drink Drano, after which she quickly died. Here the victims gagged and writhed in pain.

The two then robbed the victims, taking their wallets and purses. After a discussion, Andrews said, "I can't do it, man! I'm scared!" and left the store. Pierre then shot each of the victims directly in the head, taking minutes between some of the shots, and raped the young woman before shooting her. Pierre shot Mr. Walker along with the others, but later felt his neck for a pulse and then hoisted him by the neck with a rope. After letting Mr. Walker down, Pierre placed a ballpoint pen in his ear and kicked it three times, the pen finally lodging in Mr. Walker's throat.

However impassioned the event appears because of the gruesome methods and the rape, the project as a whole is better understood as a cold-blooded offense. The rape emerged apparently as an afterthought or intermission in a calculated series of activities. The logistics of the crime were imposing. Before the robbery began, the offenders rented a storage facility to hide the take; it took almost two hours to load all the equipment; care was taken to wipe off fingerprints; the brutality did not begin wildly but only after the victims were tied up; wallets were taken and the offenders debated whether to remove the contents and leave the wallets; and the offense in the hi-fi shop lasted for over three hours, a period within which the mortal attacks were relatively brief. Moreover, the Drano, however bizarre, was administered by Andrews and Pierre together; perhaps they believed that, like in the movie, it would work quickly to silence the victims. This interpretation suggests that we make a crucial distinction between a sadistic and a ritualistic attraction for Pierre's various assaults. It does not appear that he attempted to prolong suffering to enjoy it. Since the Drano did not work as it had in the movie, gun shots to the head seem to have been designed to end the matter as quickly as possible. Pierre shot seven times but only hit victims five times. It was only the surprisingly vigorous survivor, Mr. Walker, who, after Pierre checked for his pulse, was hanged and then subjected to the kicks of the ball point pen.

As to whether this event was senseless, some readers might point to an apparent utilitarian justification of Pierre's inclination to kill: he and Andrews spoke on the scene of the fact that only Pierre had been "booked," and, indeed, Pierre was then on bail for three auto theft charges and had been accused by the local police of a recent murder. But whatever Pierre's special vulnerability to punishment had he been identified by surviving victims, ironically he had a long-standing, peculiar practice of making it obvious to authorities that he was responsible for his crimes. (I will detail this practice later.) And in a seemingly inconsistent, unguarded manner, he spoke with a child who appeared at the rear door, allowing her to hear his West Indian accent, a distinguishing feature in Ogden, Utah. Other readers will think of the event less as senseless than as wildly insane. Indeed, there is the form of "madness" here that Nietzsche had in mind, but it can best be comprehended if we stick with our challenge to make sense of the conduct before us. As with Nietzsche's pale criminal, Pierre was not so insane that he killed outside of contexts that suggested the motivation of revenge or robbery. At least up to the time of these killings, he had maintained a sufficient veneer of reasonableness that he could convince two associates to work with him.

'THE ONION FIELD'

On March 9, 1963, Gregory Powell and Jimmy Lee Smith were in their ninth day of a robbery partnership. Greg, aged 29, had been paroled in May; he had spent ten of the past thirteen years in penal institutions. Jimmy Lee, aged 32, had been paroled about two weeks earlier; he had been out of penal institutions for a total of about one year since he was 19 (as an adult, his longest stretch of freedom was five months).

On this Saturday night, while driving on Hollywood streets in search of a robbery target, Greg and Jimmy Lee were stopped by two Los Angeles policemen, Ian and Karl, who seized on a minor vehicle infraction—an inoperative light on the license plate—to investigate what they saw as almost a caricature of bad guys dressed in black leather caps and jackets. Aware that his possession of a gun was a parole violation, Jimmy Lee placed his gun on the floor and kicked it toward Greg. When he emerged from the car, Greg surprised the policemen, drawing a gun and ordering them into his car. The four then drove ninety miles over mountains to the San Joaquin valley, where they stopped at about midnight in an onion field.

Greg dominated the conversation en route and directed Ian, who was driving, where to stop the car. Greg and Jimmy Lee both held guns; Greg instructed everyone to get out, arranged a face-to-face, two-on-two confrontation at the side of the car with the unarmed policemen; and Greg then shot Ian in the mouth. At this point Karl ran off. Ian, now on the ground, was shot four times in the chest; bullets were also fired at Karl. Captured within hours, both Greg and Jimmy Lee gave several versions of the events to the police (Karl had observed only the first shot directly). From material evidence, we know that the first shot to hit Ian, from Greg, was from a .38-caliber gun, and so was the third. A .32-caliber gun was also fired.

There were no indications of passion or provocation. Greg's conversation en route had been amiable. Twice he made reference to a "Little Lindbergh Law," which he apparently understood as a statutory provision raising the penalty for kidnapping a policeman to the status of a capital offense. The killing was "senseless" not only because this understanding, if it animated Greg, was in error, but because the image of a disciplined, practical use of violence does not fit with the detailed experience of the shooting. Greg, and perhaps Jimmy Lee as well, repeated the attack on the defenseless Ian, while Karl, who might have been rendered helpless in any number of ways before the shooting began, was given the opportunity to escape. In any case, Greg's general criminal methodology, from the wearing of provocative symbols of deviance to a recurrent bravado about the risks of capture during robberies and in confrontations with law enforcement agents, belies any claim to his being a rational stickup man.

A Methodological Note

What are we to make of this body of material, created by novelists and journalists who can anticipate large, even huge, economic rewards, and who enigmatically claim to be guided by "the facts" while creating new literary forms which they dub with strange and seemingly self-contradictory rubrics, "nonfiction novel" and "true-life novel"? A genuine sociological consideration of the question of evidence insists on a comparative assessment. The issue is not whether a given research procedure or a given body of data is, somehow inherently, good or bad, but how it compares to other ways of learning about the phenomena. Academic social scientists will either learn how to think intelligently about using the genre of nonfiction novels about murders or they will leave this part of our social life, and whatever these crimes might reveal about us more generally, to journalists, politicians and literary critics. A hands-off attitude is disingenuous—the public's concern about "cold-blooded, senseless" murders is not unrelated to its support of academics who study crime—and it is unnecessary. If we cannot assess these materials by comparing them with what official statistics, survey questionnaires, or laboratory experiments tell us about cold-blooded senseless murders, we can get the necessary methodological angle by examining comparatively different books and different parts of the same book.

For starters, we can apply some of the evidentiary criteria developed for evaluating ethnographic research, such as assigning higher evidentiary value to (1) conduct reported versus thoughts imputed (by the author) to the killer, (2) individual acts by the killer that are recounted by many observers versus those recounted by one observer, and (3) a pattern of conduct reported by multiple observers, each observing a different time and situation versus an act reported once.[10] Mailer's subtle use of Gilmore's claim of having stabbed a "nigger" to death (and beyond) in prison—a claim he made on at least three different occasions to at least three different people and that he indirectly recanted in a postmurder interview—is a good example. (It also indicates that Mailer implicitly knows these rules; and that, conversely, the work of a sociological methodologist in this area is to explicate the "praxis" or tacit methodology of the virtuoso.) Using these criteria, we can distinguish more and less trustworthy pieces of a nonfiction novel, and we can judge that some of the works in this genre are too weak to use.[11]

In addition to methodological criteria that are generally useful for the assessment of qualitative data on social interaction, we should appreciate the constraints that are distinctive to the phenomena under study. Given that these events are exceptional in both statistical and moral senses, writers will almost invariably come to them after the fact. As a result, any interviews or observations of the killer that authors may obtain are almost inevitably subject to the distortions of retrospective, self-interested memory. In a way, it is more honest to write about dead subjects: you cannot presume to write from a unique opportunity for insight granted by the subject, and you are freed both from the confounding influence of your writing project on the killer's statements and from the distorting influence of your moral responsibility for influencing the killer's fate.

Compared to Capote's work, the fact that Mailer began his work after Gilmore's execution may have been an advantage.[12] A clearer advantage enjoyed by Mailer was that, in the three months between his release from prison and the murders he committed, Gilmore had a range of relations, from superficial to supremely intimate, with people who, without risking culpability for the crime, could recount their experiences with him in great detail. For reasons I will discuss at the end of this chapter, the works in this genre tend to cover isolated individuals; one must search for personal insight either far in the past, using the highly prejudicial guidance of (folk or formal) psychological theory, or in the protagonist's being-for-others, as represented by the recollections of those who had interacted with him shortly before the crime. The extraordinary excellence of Mailer's book is due mainly to his depiction, without artificially imposed consistency, of the lived reality of Gilmore as experienced in the everyday social interactions of a great number and variety of people.

The Appearance of Primordial Evil

That these events generate an extraordinary impression is appreciated by the offenders as well as by the public. These are not seasoned or "professional" killers. The path to the killing is traveled by some in fear and trembling: Perry (*In Cold Blood*) registered "bubbles in the blood" during the trip to the Clutter's home; even after he arrived at the scene, he turned away in anxious uncertainty. Like Perry, Gary Gilmore (*The Executioner's Song*) bragged about killing a "nigger," but both were lying. The importance they gave to this brag and its falsity indicate the profound leap that the killing was for both of them. Greg Powell (*The Onion Field*) misinterpreted the law but got right the understanding that to kill a policeman is an astonishingly deviant act. Dale Pierre's fascination (*Victim*) with mimicking the movie method of killing with Drano suggests purification; given to a prostitute, Drano burns a clean path through moral waste.

How shall we understand the attractions of producing such awe-full, dreadful acts? Paul Ricoeur shows the way: "Dread of the impure and rites of purification are in the background of all our feelings and all our behavior relating to fault."[13] Our original sense of deviance is through a nonreflective, sensual awareness of evil in the forms of dread, defilement, transgression, vengeance, sacrilege, sacrifice, and the like. In chapter 3, we encountered the sensibility of dread as it is sustained in contemporary street life by the ways of the badass. The protagonists in the four cases of modern murder in this chapter neither discovered nor uniquely carried this dramatization of evil, but it was essential to the compelling sense they constructed for their crimes.

'MAN ENTERS INTO THE ETHICAL WORLD THROUGH FEAR AND NOT THROUGH LOVE'[14]

In man's primordial awareness, the sacred transcends and is known through negativity. This awareness is constructed most fundamentally not through didactic teaching but through everyday routines that proscribe and limit human possibilities, all for no immediately visible practical reason. Dietary laws,[15] proscriptions on sex during specific phases of the menstrual cycle, customs of purification, speaking in hushed voices when approaching sacred places, and prohibitions on the use of totemic animals and plants—all these ethical injunctions create a ubiquitous presence for the sacred as a negativity, even without cataclysmic interventions.

So the badass constructs a presence far more generally than he overtly engages in crime. We acknowledge his dreadful stature by averting our glance, crossing to the other side of the street, and making sure that our suspicious looks remain covert. Whether we literally think about the danger the badass represents, much less publicly label him as deviant, we respect his awesome being by little acts of self-denial and self-limitation—by enacting a *negativity*.

Greg Powell constructed his intimidating aura not so much by embracing unusually "bad" symbols (black leather outfits are not rare in Hollywood), but by maintaining, in the days leading up to the murder, an everyday social environment that was populated by personalities like Jimmy Lee. Greg did not seek other badasses for his associates; his crime partners were petty, nonviolent thieves like Jimmy Lee and Billy Small. The latter, once a creeper thief, was now known on Hill Street as a "drunken shine stand proprietor." Billy would pretend to enter a store to rob according to Greg's instructions, but, once inside, he would invent an excuse not to go through with it. Jimmy Lee could not stop noticing each time Greg's pretentions were proved wrong: on the escape route from robberies, Greg would drive them into dead ends or he would have them lie in wait fruitlessly to rob a fellow who supposedly carried huge amounts of cash that he had collected from parking lots. And despite Greg's claim to be a captivating lover, Jimmy Lee easily managed a sexual liaison with Greg's woman. But at the same time, Jimmy Lee would not dare to depreciate Greg openly. His associates' deep disrespect ironically manifested to Greg an emphatic respect just because it was studiously kept private. Their silence was a measure of the intimidation or awe he inspired.

Dale Pierre was a loner; he had associates but no close friends. When, six months before the hi-fi murders, the police were investigating the murder of an air force sergeant who had accused Pierre of theft, they found that airmen, when questioned about Pierre, might begin to shake or answer tight lipped and in whispers, "as though no matter where they were Pierre could easily hear them."[16] The investigating officer recalled:

Of all the subjects I've ever interrogated, he was by far the toughest because of the way he looked back at you. I think Pierre could probably intimidate people just with that look. That look, that whole attitude, it was an eerie, eerie feeling that would emit from him. He could probably scare the daylights out of somebody.[17]

An airman who called the police soon after the hi-fi murders to identify Pierre and Andrews as the murderers, recalled a barracks conversation in which Andrews had spoken of a plan to rob a hi-fi shop and to kill anyone who became an obstacle. The informant had no direct information from Pierre. "I didn't know Pierre and I'm glad I didn't. I think everybody did what they could to stay away from him."[18]

Paroled to Provo, Utah, Gary Gilmore entered a conventional community that knew him to be a convict and whose members, no matter how helpful, were routinely sensitive to the subjects of discussion they should avoid. Aware of the fear and discomfort he represented for others, Gilmore often exploited his magical, invisible power to restrain others' expressions, stunning women with tales of cruelty in prison (for example, tattooing penises on the neck of an inmate who had been promised a snake design) and silently daring clerks to challenge him as he brazenly removed cases of beer from convenience stores. He soon lived in a social world that routinely acknowledged his presence by studiously limiting the expression of anxious and morally judgmental thought about him.

'THE SACRED REVEALS ITSELF AS SUPERHUMAN DESTRUCTION OF MAN'[19]

The primordial god may have created the world as a miracle at the mythological beginning of history, but when He has reappeared to work again on such a large scale, it has not been to create wondrously new forms of life but to destroy. He has sent a flood to destroy most of mankind and fires to destroy cities of defilement. And he helped a chosen people, not simply through positive miracles, such as transporting them to a newly minted land of milk and honey, but by sending plagues to its enemies.

The primitive god is an object of dread, known through the suffering of humanity and the evil in the world, approached only with ritual care and respected in everyday rites of purification. But the primitive god himself was not understood as evil or as "good" opposed to evil. If Hades ruled the underworld, he was not a devil; Zeus and other gods on Olympus more often threatened the well-being of human kind. The modern god is a savior, opposed by the devil in a battle for people's souls, but Yahweh may test man Himself and He does not wait for the devil to torture man in an afterlife. He responds to failures to sustain faith with exiles suffered here and now: "the threat of the 'Day of Yahweh,' terrible as it is, remains a threat internal to history; no trace of a 'hell' or 'eternal punishments,' outside historical time and geographical space."[20]

That primitive gods appear in the world as evil does not mean that they are evil. The Sacred exists for Itself beyond good and evil, not for people's understanding, but as a power that essentially overwhelms them. Given the difference in their natures, mortals cannot look at immortals without being damaged. Lot's wife turned to see the god's devastation and became a pillar of salt. The Greek gods had to approach their mortal lovers in disguised forms or with injunctions to avert their eyes; hopelessly curious mortal lovers were destroyed.

Note that there is no necessity for a discrete, lordly decision to bring about destruction. The gods could destroy human beings at will, but once a sacred warning was issued, transgression could lead to destruction with no specific decision by the gods. Thus, Zeus could regret the loss of a mortal lover who was consumed by fire when she glanced at him. The result was dictated by the nature of sacred being.

Physical signs of badass stature, like evil tattoos and "bad" clothing styles, manifest their warnings automatically, without requiring a repeated decision to do so. The automaticity of their message itself conveys another message—that destruction may follow without any deliberation by the badass, perhaps without any moral reflection at all, even impersonally. Hence, Perry could kill as if in a dream, simultaneously doing the deed and standing outside himself and watching the deed be done. Afterward, the tone of automaticity in the act might lead him, as well as a shocked public, to wonder about the moral status of the determinative power: "Know what I think? . . . I think there must be something wrong with us. To do what we did. . . . There's got to be something wrong with somebody who'd do a thing like that."[21]

The moral relations of our protagonists to the symbols of evil are dialectical. Tattoos of frightening forms—Perry was adorned with a snarling tiger on one bicep; a spitting snake, coiled around a dagger, running down his arm; a skull; a tombstone—are directed outward. In the first instance, they call others to enact deferential respect; they encourage the exercise of a restraint or caution in interaction that silently acknowledges the individual's inviolable core of being. But however vividly they portray evil on the outside, the badass's symbols of deviance do not so clearly reflect an evil identity within their bearer. Thus, it is understandable that Gary Gilmore's lover, Nicole, might ask him if he was the devil, and it is equally understandable that Gilmore might recall enigmatically that someone else once asked him that. And there is no contradiction between the incomprehensible evil wrought by Dale Pierre in the basement of the hi-fi shop and his background in apocalyptic religion or in his prison writings, which damn the corruption of the modern world and profess that despite the darkness his skin showed the world, in some inner, real sense he is white.

'THE INVINCIBLE BOND BETWEEN VENGEANCE AND DEFILEMENT IS ANTERIOR TO ANY INSTITUTION, ANY INTENTION, ANY DECREE'[22]

Additional features of primordial evil are revealed by the inconsistencies between the model of justice it invokes and the modern model of rational-legal justice. It has not been uncommon for the modern criminal statutes of the various states in the United States to specify penalties (so many years of imprisonment, a fine of a certain magnitude, execution to be conducted within this many days of judgment) for offenses that are simply labeled, not defined, in statutory language. Traditional understandings and the more mystically maintained understandings of the "common law" are left to hold the subtleties that define the substance of offenses. In primitive religious beliefs, there is an inverse relationship between the articulation of punishment and offense. There is a logical relationship—the gods are not unjust, much less are they crazy—but the punishment is not specified in advance as a particular penalty that will follow rule breaking, on a particular date, to endure for a set period of time, as calculable by mortals. Rather, the emphasis is on the commandment, on the deliverance of interdicts with "the shadow of vengeance."[23]

God's commandments emphasize that they command, sometimes by using the form, "Thou Shalt Not . . .": there may be no express statement of what will happen if people do what they should not. In contemporary street form, the interdict delivered by the badass conveys its promise of penalty with a cold stare, a pointed gun, and a shouted order to "Give it up!" The threat need not be made explicit to work. The manner of delivering the commandment is an express "Thou shall" or "Thou shalt not" underwritten implicitly by a style that conveys, "Or else."

Acting on this moral logic, our protagonists articulated, before the event, the style of the badass in the form of omens, as in Dick's repeated promise, on the way to the Clutter's home, that they would not pass over the victims but would "blast hair all over them walls."[24] Gary Gilmore intensified his ominous presence, astonishing acquaintances by pressing on them guns to stash. Greg Powell would practice his chilling look before a mirror, uttering the phrase, "Give me the goddamn money," while drawing and cocking his gun with a click—all to achieve the maximum shock.[25] Greg had also made frequent ominous threats about conventional legal authority. For example, he asserted that if Jimmy's parole officer gave him a hard time, he would shoot him right there.

'IMPURITY IS MEASURED NOT BY IMPUTATION TO A RESPONSIBLE AGENT BUT BY THE OBJECTIVE VIOLATION OF AN INTERDICT'[26]

In the modern understanding of authority and justice, there must be a reason for punishment, in the sense of both a preestablished rule defining the offense and an intentional act by the offender. It seems absurd or grossly unfair to punish the *actus reus* without the *mens rea:* if the shopper really forgot that he had that item in his hand when he walked out of the store, he's not guilty of theft. Thus, as Ricoeur writes:

We are astonished . . . when we see involuntary or unconscious human actions, the actions of animals, and even simple material events called defilements—the frog that leaps into the fire, the hyena that leaves its excrements in the neighborhood of a tent. Why are we astonished?

Because we do not find in these actions or events any point where we might insert a judgment of personal imputation, or even simply human imputation.[27]

Ritual prohibitions are ritual prohibitions; they admit no exceptions for a mistake or the lack of improper intent. According to Jewish ritual, if the dairy utensils were thoughtlessly used to eat meat, even if the violation was by "the *shiksa,*" they must be discarded or at least buried for the prescribed time before they will again be kosher.

As the mortal leader's sacrilege can disturb the heavens, bringing storms that spare him but kill many of the children of the realm, so could Gary Gilmore rumble with discontent because of the intolerable loss of faith represented by Nicole's desertion, and he could then coherently resurrect his sacred inviolability by "unnecessarily" killing compliant robbery victims. If it makes sense that the hyena's defilement can trigger a drought that punishes all humans for years, Dale Pierre could make sense of purging the sins of modern society by forcing a handful of robbery victims to ingest Drano. When the gods battle each other, they may use men as pawns, helping to defend some and to strike down others, forging enmities and alliances with mortals for Olympian reasons that are best reached by the warriors through prayer. Similarly, Perry may have shown that his moral sensibility was superior to Dick's, first by gratuitous acts of kindness to the victims, like putting a pillow under the head of Kenyon Clutter and blocking Dick's intention to rape Nancy Clutter, and then by demonstrating the superior strength of his will, when Dick declined to take the lead, by "senselessly" cutting Mr. Clutter's throat and blasting him with a shotgun.

Our reaction that these crimes are "senseless" reflects an identification with the impotence of the victims, who would give up whatever valuables they had, but who could not imagine the value of their death to the offenders. As they sought desperately to negotiate a relationship with the offenders, the victims suffered a compressed version of a dilemma that always challenges people before the sacred. At one level, piety requires a delicate attitude of care whenever any signs are used to address the sacred: a switch to the holy language that is reserved for prayer, a bow when approaching the alter, or a rite to cleanse the body before entering the temple. But although people must constantly and elaborately signify a pietistic awareness to keep the sacred intimate in their lives, they must never attempt too directly to touch or capture the essence of the sacred in their culture. For if our eyes, language, or esthetic artifacts are competent to comprehend the sacred fully—if we can raise our eyes to look at God or speak His name or model His figure, we risk the sacrilegious implication that we share a moral equality with Him, or worse, that we would control the sacred, disciplining Him to serve our culture. The sacred at once attracts and repels, demanding symbolic understanding and threatening attempts at rational control. So the badass simultaneously compels and wards off our attentions.

Among the infinite horrors in contemporary life that the modern public might address, the "senseless" sufferings created for the victims by merciless killers have an extraordinary symbolic power. They capture a haunting dilemma for which we lack alternative ways of focusing our reflections. For the offenders as well, the "senseless" nature of their killing creates a crisis of understanding. Thus, after the event, Perry pestered Dick with questions about their normalcy. More generally, when captured and brought into the institutions of modern justice, cold-blooded "senseless" murderers face the challenge that to explain their crimes within conventional terms and accept the assistance of psychiatrists or defense lawyers may require abandoning the position of privileged meaning they had given the act. Dale Pierre continued to deny he had anything to do with the hi-fi slayings. Gary Gilmore battled the interest groups that would exploit legalities and argue that he was insane to block his execution. The civil rights and anti-capital punishment groups only became interested in Gilmore after his conviction; they were not around to serve him at the trial, when he was looking for better-quality representation and when it still seemed that only *his* fate was at risk; they came in specifically to fight for the power to define the contingencies of his death. He would not permit them to subordinate the idiosyncratic meaning of his life to broader social concerns.

We must not go too far with this analysis and suggest a point-by-point analogy between primitive religious belief and the understandings of the protagonists in these murder cases. The killers, after all, only became killers in a moment of their lives; they could not be sure that they would do it until they did it, and they lived the primordial symbolism of evil inconsistently and in a compromised way. If their understanding were less confused, they either would not have killed as they robbed or they would not have robbed to kill.

But if the police enter scenes like the mass deaths in the basement of the hi-fi shop as if entering a negatively hallowed ground, using hushed tones, walking with a care inspired by dread as much as by a concern for preserving evidence,[28] they are not bringing a novel moral sensibility to the scene. Something ritualistic went on there. And if the victims in these murders are especially pure—the Clutters, a prosperous, hard-working, dutiful Methodist, close-knit farm family; or Max Jensen (Gilmore's first victim), a model young Mormon husband and father, working at the gas station to pay his way through law school—it is not insignificant that these sacrificial lambs are of excellent quality. It is one thing, Perry often noted when Dick pressed him about his claims of having killed before, to kill a "nigger"; it is another thing—something utterly transcendent—to kill the Clutters. Like the geographic distance they traveled, the social distance that Dick and Perry covered to reach these targets was so phenomenal that it gave their plan an unprecedented significance in their lives, and it gave them confidence that the crime could not be traced back to them. It is one thing to shoot a victim who resists a robbery but, as Greg Powell understood it, it is another to disarm two policeman and force them to drive away with you; that is such an extraordinary moral achievement, society has made the kidnapping itself a capital offense!

In primitive understanding, sacrificial practices are people's enactments of godly acts of destruction and thus are properly performed by priests, or at least with devotional care. As with the cataclysmic sufferings through which the sacred may appear in the world, sacrificial practices are not sadistic, they are existential prophylaxes, destroying flesh to restore the proper order of being. The objective of sacrificial violence is to avoid the greater violence or chaos that would develop if the sacrifice were not undertaken.[29] To understand this other, greater chaos that "senseless" violence anticipates and seeks to control, we must examine the dizziness that characterized the emotional dynamics of our protagonists.

The Dizziness of Deviance and Its Narrative Resolution

Again, Paul Ricoeur guides us into the relevant experience of evil:

> To avenge is not only to destroy, but by destroying to re-establish. Along with the dread of being stricken, annihilated, there is perception of the movement by which order—whatever order it may be—is restored. That which had been established and which has now been destroyed is re-established. By negation, order reaffirms itself.[30]

The destruction that the sacred brings constructs a narrative. *Suffering* develops as the third phase in a retrospectively understood narrative. It is the product of *vengeance* that, in turn, is the inevitable result of a *defilement* of the sacred. By reading the primordial symbolism of evil in physical suffering, one may discover a source of moral order.

PHYSICAL DESTRUCTION AND MORAL RECONSTRUCTION

Once a year, the currents are right and the boats can go out to the traditional fishing waters. The community must live for the rest of the year on whatever is brought back. Failure means that many will starve to death. When there has been a failure, nothing can be done to avoid the physical destruction that will follow; no magic or priest's ceremony can save those who will die.

But the certain effects of failure stir up anxieties about a new order of uncertainty. Are our priests and kings, who ceremonially declare the time to launch the annual fishing expedition, incompetent to rule? Is something wrong with their knowledge? Are the kinship principles for organizing labor in the cooperative fishing venture basically faulty? Are we, in effect, collectively in the right business?[31]

If any of these reasonable questions come to dominate public understanding, the moral integrity of the community will be shattered. Tradition and ideology, political leadership and social stratification, technology and the division of labor—all will be up for grabs. The people's collective institutions, the very essence of their competence to impose a humanly beneficial framework on nature, will be cast into doubt.

Here, the priests step in to make socially constructive sense of *suffering*. Perhaps this time they find an adulterer. Now all know why the expedition failed. There was a *defilement* of the sacred order. That brought on the disappearance of the fish as a superhuman *vengeance* and the suffering that will endure for the whole year to come, and perhaps beyond. Now everyone once again appreciates the need for the priests, the political leaders, and the traditional kinship system. Now the ordinary division of labor is more necessary than ever, for the gods must be propitiated with elaborate rituals that only the traditional order can quickly mobilize.

The physically destructive actions of the primordial gods construct an eternally significant meaning. Sacred devastation becomes the stuff of myths, of stories used throughout the community's history to explain the physical and social landscape. Future generations are encouraged to recall acts of defilement and sacrilege, and the transcendent ordering powers they violated, to explain why the snake must crawl on its belly, why women have menstrual pains, and why the volcano erupts.

The protagonists we have been examining reconstructed within the fatal scene a version of their lives. Essential to the motivation of these cold-blooded, "senseless" killers was a creative resolution of one of the many narrative possibilities they had been developing.

The formula—defilement brings vengeance, which imposes suffering—can be applied to the lives of our protagonists in either of two ways, depending on the denotation given the term of suffering. If it is the offenders who are suffering, then they suffer as pariahs who repulse and disgust the sacred core of the community. If, with a smile of bravado, they deny that they suffer and turn to the harm they impose, then the equation is reversed and their inviolable integrity is honored by avenging others' failures to pay them the respect they had been due. The key emotional dynamic on the path to these murders is a play with moral symbolics in which (1) the protagonist enters as a pariah, (2) soon becomes lost in the dizzying symbolics of deviance, and then (3) emerges to reverse the equation in a violent act of transcendence.

ACT I: PATHOS AND THE PARIAH

We pick up the biographies of our protagonists as they waver on the border between disadvantage and moral alienation. Disadvantage is empirically predictable, biographically explicable, remediable, and morally neutral. Moral alienation is expressed as a permanently damning outcast or pariah status that gives a "subterranean hue to . . . [all] thoughts and actions."[32]

The Executioner's Song: Gary Gilmore was released from prison in April and killed in July. Having spent about twenty of his thirty-five years in prison, it is not surprising that he faced a host of disadvantages as he moved into civilian statuses in Provo. In occupational skills, his background had prepared him well to break up a driveway with a sledgehammer, but given a wood drill, he might fail to realize that it is set to turn in reverse and so he might apply it endlessly without success. In routine social skills, he was also understandably deficient. Having been issued his clothes so long by prison authorities, he might have been unaware that a customer is allowed to try on garments in a department store before deciding whether to buy them. And in social graces, he was equally deficient; he was not likely to find that the stories of brutality and deceit with which he entertained inmates would be received delightfully in family gatherings and on first dates. Nor is it surprising that with the sexual experiences of his adult life limited to masturbation and homosexual opportunities, he might risk impotence in a relationship with a sexually experienced 19-year-old woman. It turned out that he was not even good in a fight, at least not when strength and skill determine the outcome.

But there is no evidence that Gilmore experienced his practical frustrations in these pathetic terms. From the start, his problems had a moralized dimension. He was aware, in his first job in a shoe repair shop, that it was wiser for him to work on shoes in the back than with customers up front; he was not sure he could tolerate rudeness. For him, occupational problems did not represent just the predictable barriers that anyone with his past might have to struggle to overcome; they also represented the risks of intolerable humiliation in conventional society.

Gilmore did not consider his status, that of a convict on parole, as simply a sad tale of disadvantage, nor did he perceive it as wholly negative. Perhaps, he reflected, his rightful place was not temporarily in the lower regions of straight society; rather, it was permanently and triumphantly as an outcast. In fact, his social manners, if crude in the society of his relatives, proved seductive to an attractive young woman who, as a young welfare mother of two, married three times by age 19, was also an outcast. And with her, his "half a hard-on" was not a shameful reason for self-doubt or for abandoning his ingestion of Fiorinal, but a cause for pressing her to "help him." If his circumstances suggested to some that he was pathetic, Gilmore would have prefered to appear in straight society as a pariah and to begin intimate relations with Nicole as someone he had already known "in the darkness."

Victim: Apart from his Caribbean birthplace, the outlines of Dale Pierre's biography read like an unexceptional record of American social disadvantage. Born and raised in a religious Seventh-Day Adventist family in Trinidad and Tobago, he left school at age 15 and was soon in and then dismissed from a local apprenticeship program with Texaco. At age 17, after a period in which he was out of school and unemployed in Trinidad, he moved with his family to New York City, where he had a succession of at least three unskilled-labor jobs, and entered the air force at age 20, coming to Hill Air Force Base in Utah about six months before the hi-fi killings in April 1974. Although Pierre had not been convicted of a crime, he was investigated in October for the murder of an air force sergeant; and in January, he was arrested on the first of three separate charges for auto theft.

Pierre was already regarded as a pariah by the local police, and officials at his base had been waiting for his conviction on auto-theft charges before they processed his separation from the service. Pierre had already judged himself an outsider. When he was released from jail, he filed to leave the air force as someone unable to adjust to military life. (Two days later, Andrews, Pierre's colleague inside the hi-fi shop, also resigned, and both were assigned to janitorial duties pending completion of the bureaucratic separation process.) And, what is more significant, the meaning of theft to Pierre had long become highly moralized.

Charges of theft had pursued him in his Caribbean childhood, in school, and on his first jobs (they were the precipitating cause of his dismissal from the apprenticeship program with Texaco). The author, Gary Kinder, interviewed relatives, neighbors, and school officials in Trinidad, and, although it is not uncommon to find retrospectively obvious signs of deviance described in post hoc interviews conducted with the early associates of infamous criminals, a peculiar theme reappeared in their recollections of Pierre's problems. He would express admiration for an object and, moments later, when its owner turned away, take it; then, when the predictable accusation came, he would deny, with forceful self-righteousness, ever having taken it. Or he might steal cash from one neighbor's house and the record collection from another's and then spend in a style and stash the records in a place that enabled others immediately to tie him to the crimes.

Poor, but no poorer than his neighbors, and with little education or occupational training, but no less prepared than many of his air force colleagues, Pierre lived more as a pariah than as a disadvantaged young man. He seemed so fascinated with the meaning of getting away with deviance that he would steal, not simply to acquire desired items, or simply to get away with a sneaky thrill. Nor would he steal as a masochist, just to be caught and punished. Rather, he would steal specifically to move above and beyond the conventional moral order, to create the challenge of moralized accusation and the consequent opportunity to prove his superior competence by transcending it.

The Onion Field: Given that, when paroled at age 28, Greg Powell had spent ten of the previous thirteen years in confinement, his relative social disadvantages were obviously severe. Along with the parolee's predictable economic problems, Greg soon faced extraordinary pressures from his family. Greg's sister introduced him to Maxine, a 26-year-old woman with three children, and by January, they were expecting a child.

But the objectively recognizable pathos of his situation was moralized into a potentially humiliating status in unique ways. Maxine was accused of writing an anonymous letter accusing Greg's sister of marital infidelities and incestuous relations with Greg. What bothered Greg about the family battle over the anonymous letter was not just the attack on his woman friend, but that the family went through his clothes to obtain a handwriting sample in notes written to him by Maxine. They were treating him like a child—a status his parole appeared to ordain but that challenged Greg's preferred posture as head of the family. Greg had assumed that posture years earlier when his mother became ill, and it had become a source of tension in the family ever since.

Greg made great use of the family metaphor, encompassing in it not only Maxine and his brother Douglas, with whom he conducted a series of robberies in the Las Vegas area in January, but also Jimmy Lee, Billy, and others who were to join his entourage in Los Angeles. In this "family," he was the patriarch; he acted as the chief authority in the house and took on the responsibility of leading the economic ventures of the group. But Greg was an especially dubious patriarch; his means of making money were limited to robbery, and his ability to retain the respect of his family members was limited by his previous homosexual lifestyle, which included a period of residence with a black queen. To Jimmy Lee, a 32-year-old black man, Greg, whom he had known for only a few days but who insisted on considering him part of his "family," was a "complete fucking fool." In any case, by embedding his efforts at robbery in so tenuous a "family" framework, Greg had invested great moral stakes in what was already a risky project.

In Cold Blood: Dick and Perry had both been released from prison four months before they killed the Clutter family. Dick, at age 28, had frequently been caught passing bad checks, which his family would often make good. Now he was paroled to his parents, who lived on a small farm in his hometown near Kansas City, where he had been married twice and had fathered three children, where he took a mechanic's job in an auto body shop, and where he still was trusted enough by some local people that he could pass bad checks. If Dick's family, occupational, and economic background was relatively conventional, Perry's was like a textbook case of pathology; his mother was a promiscuous alcoholic and his father a failed rodeo performer; his parents split during his childhood, and two of three siblings committed suicide. Perry was first arrested at age 8, at which point his schooling ended; he then spent time in a cruel orphanage and a children's shelter. For several years, he lived an unsettled life traveling with his father in a home-built "house car" and ended up in Alaska, where they would "scratch a living" each day.[33] He joined the Merchant Marine at age 16; and spent four years in the army, where he was court-martialed for violent attacks in Japan. After he left the army, he went to Alaska, where he lived in poverty and bitterly severed relations with his father. He then took odd jobs while drifting toward the East Coast, was convicted for a burglary in Kansas, escaped from jail, spent two weeks in jail on a vagrancy charge and was picked up by the FBI in New York City on the Kansas charges.

To speak of Perry as disadvantaged is important but insufficient, since it misses the distinctive quality of his life as a pariah. He was literally an outcast, with a Cherokee mother and an Irish father. When Perry came to Kansas to meet Dick, Dick was legally home, but Perry was once again out of place, entering Kansas in violation of a commitment he made to his parole board. Even at Dick's family home, Perry assumed he was unwelcome and regarded as a pariah. Indeed, Perry claimed that he went to Kansas not actually to take Dick up on the "score" he proposed, but to meet Willy-Jay, a prison inmate with whom he had developed a treasured relationship. Perry had kept a letter that Willy-Jay wrote him. It portrayed him romantically as a dangerous outcast: "You are a man of extreme passion. . . . You are strong but there is a flaw in your strength. . . . *Explosive emotional reaction out of all proportion to the occasion."* And Perry recalled a lecture from Willy-Jay: "You pursue the negative. You want not to give a damn, to exist without responsibility, without faith or friends or warmth."[34]

Apparently, Willy-Jay had left Kansas City just hours before Perry arrived. As he turned to accept Dick's offer, Perry was "dizzy with anger and disappointment."[35]

ACT II: DEVIANCE AND DIZZINESS

The killings we are examining were not simply the work of actors managing the impressions received by an audience. Mailer imagined that when Gilmore killed Max Jensen, he declared before each shot, respectively, "This one is for me. This one is for Nicole." No matter what Gilmore told the people who interviewed him, we cannot know what, if anything, he said as he shot. But that's the point: the meaning being constructed was ultimately a production for Gilmore—not for us, not for Nicole, and certainly not for Max Jensen. Our protagonists were taken up by an emotional dynamic, such that any communicative significance of their killings was in a conversation they were holding with themselves.

Jack Abbott's writings help us understand how this internal conversation can become a dizzying experience in which a man, no matter his intelligence or strength of will, spins wildly around the symbolics of deviance.[36] Abbott wrote as though he found each moment in confinement a fundamental challenge to his existence. He seemed at rest spiritually only when he was being tortured physically. Only then was he sure he was not consenting to his jailers' constraints.

Born on a military base, half-Irish and half-Chinese, Abbott began serving periods in juvenile detention quarters at age 9. He was sent to a reform school at age 12 and, besides nine months of freedom at age 19 (he was incarcerated on a bad-check charge) and a six-week escape from prison (during which he committed a bank robbery), Abbott remained confined up to the point of the publication of his book, at which time he was 37. He killed another inmate as a young man. Mailer helped Abbott get released from prison. Shortly after his parole, Abbott killed a waiter in a New York restaurant and was put back in prison.

Abbott described his response to confinement as a constant protest. As a result of aggressive action to preserve his self-respect in relations with other inmates and with guards, he served about twenty-four years in confinement between ages 12 and 37, and he estimated that of these years, fourteen or fifteen were passed in solitary. As a youngster, he made multiple escape attempts; regardless of the prospects of success and the extra confinement that might follow capture, he felt it was incumbent on him to attempt to escape if there was a chance to do so. He had "never gone a month in prison without incurring disciplinary action for violating 'rules.' Not in all these years."[37] Mandatory solitary confinement, starvation (at one point he was eating cockroaches for protein), and drug treatments temporarily disabled his mind, his sight, and his voice.

Why, we keep asking, could he not just go along, just long enough to get out? However long that takes, what could be worse than prolonging confinement as a result of one's own actions? But Abbott asked another question:

> How would you like to be forced all the days of your life to sit beside a stinking, stupid wino every morning at breakfast? Or for some loud fool in his infinite ignorance to be at any moment able to say (slur) "Gimme a cigarette, man!" And I just look into his sleazy eyes and want to kill his ass there in front of God and everyone.[38]

We cannot understand his self-destructive protest because we cannot imagine this environment "all the days of your life." But Abbott had little basis for a sense of himself outside confinement. So the issue for him could be, precisely stated, whether they will "take Jack Abbott away from Jack Abbott." He was willing to sacrifice his physical existence, faculty by faculty, because he understood that each moment of conformity to prison put his spiritual freedom at risk. Abbott saw the challenge of spiritual salvation posed constantly in crudely material forms:

> There is a boundary in each man. He can eat crow and brown-nose to an extent. He can shuck the man for a while, become a good "actor." But when a man goes beyond the last essential boundary, it alters his ontology, so to speak. It's like the small pebble that starts a landslide no one can stop. You can betray the pigs until, lo, you've betrayed yourself. You want to survive so badly, to be free of violence so terribly, you will literally do anything after you start across that boundary. You'll allow anyone to order you around. You'd let your ma, wife, kids die just to stay alive yourself. You'll wallow in the gutter of man's soul to live. You'll suck every cock in the cell house to "get along." There is nothing you won't do.[39]

The killings we are examining did not grow out of the protagonists' reflections on the pathos of their conditions; like Abbott, they do not kill because they suffer for *not* going straight, for *not* reaching conventional goals. They have lived too long with a moralized, pariah status for that superficial motivation to work. Their killings emerge from a *dizziness* in which *conformity* is the greatest spiritual challenge and *deviance* promises the peace of transcendent significance.

Abbott's spinning between paranoia in conformity and spiritual peace while oppressed as a deviant is a general dis-ease in advanced careers in deviance. David Matza helps us understand the deviant's dizziness by asking us to imagine an ex-con playing in a sandlot game.[40] The ball is hit to him; he picks it up and makes a successful throw to first. How should we describe what he is doing? It is a routine play, as long as we neglect the player's status as an ex-con. With that background in mind, we see him as "just playing baseball." The player's awareness of the second description can torture.

Others may enjoy the peace of playing baseball (or engaging in any other morally inconsequential pursuit) without "just playing baseball." But the person with an established reputation for deviance understands that his engagement in conventionally routine activities may be taken by any observer, at any moment, as evidence of his performance of the specifically moralized activity, "keeping his nose clean." In a moralized sense, when he is "just playing baseball," he is *never just* playing baseball; he is also, more fundamentally, doing what he is supposed to do, choosing not to be deviant, toeing the line, deferring to normative expectations.

Whether any onlookers communicate that reflection, the ex-con has reason to assume they might. And the movement from this reflection to a state of moral dis-ease can be a dizzyingly quick passage. "What sort of punk am I, that I have to prove my 'normality' in these childish social pursuits?" "in this cheap, stupid job?" "on this antiseptic date?" "Am I a coward, that I must keep my nose clean? Must I go about, just 'going-to-work'? just 'going-to-the-movies'? just 'playing baseball'?" Once this inquiry has begun, the ex-con cannot simply go along with a free spirit, following as the ball bounces. He is under what Matza called the "spell" of deviance.

He cannot use *reason* to stop the spinning. The ballplayer cannot break the spell by stopping in the middle of what seems, on the surface, to be a perfectly ordinary play on a perfectly ordinary day, to interrupt the observers' silence with the assertion, "Look, damn it! I'm not *just* playing baseball, I'm just playing baseball." No one, after all, dared voice the question to which this is a logical response. If he tries to attack the spell of deviance by addressing it logically and directly, he would confirm—not deny—his deviance. His exclamation, which after all is self-contradictory, would make no sense; he would again become "mad," although perhaps now with an image of insanity added to the suspicion of buried anger.

The deviant's dizzyness is a spinning around and between two poles. On the one side, the pariah cannot rest when he achieves conformity. His deepest fear is not failure in conventional terms, but that success means cowardice. On the other side, he discovers more in deviance than just a refuge. *Being deviant gives him an edge.* We have seen this edge before in milder forms of deviance. The shoplifter establishes her competence by appreciating that others cannot appreciate that her "ordinary behavior" is a cover. The badass appreciates that his mere gestures have the extraordinary power to make others step aside and turn away. As the deviant increasingly appreciates the moral dangers of conforming to conventional rules and reason, he may simultaneously appreciate the transcendent power he might attain through a "senseless" killing.

The Executioner's Song: Mailer lets us see in detail how powerful the spell of deviance was for Gary Gilmore. Gilmore took to wearing funny hats, like his uncle Vern's fishing hat or haberdashery that was too small for his head, and he would make a point of asking others for their approval, predictably putting them in an awkward position. Was he using hats *defensively* and *negatively,* as an anticipatory counter to the likelihood he would not fit in? His embrace of little everyday signs of deviance is not exhausted by this pathetic interpretation. The hats were *constructive* and *positive;* they gave him an edge. Similarly, he might put his feet up on the table when chatting with his boss's wife, revealing with a post hoc smile that he had anticipated her reprobation all along. Or, sitting in the dark of a movie theater, where he might easily have managed the issue of conformity without bothersome oversight, he might laugh at odd moments and comment loudly on the film. When it was especially easy *not* to draw moral suspicions to himself, *he went out of his way to make sure he did.* For Gilmore, the most profound danger was not others' judgments that he would *not* fit but his own view that he *would,* that he would "go straight" out of cowardice.

Gilmore fought in Provo along the lines Abbott recommended for killin in prison: attacking by surprise, using the rules of friendship or honor t get an edge on the adversary, with the understanding that conforming t the "rules" for fighting is just another disgraceful, fool's conformity; actua dominance is everything. Gilmore frequently seemed to go out of his wa to challenge authority (official discipline and conventional morality) t challenge him. He openly walked out of stores with water skis, eve though the market for selling them was not great in Provo. Chastized b the management of a drive-in movie for playfully running over the con crete bumps separating parking spaces, he ripped off speakers that he the hauled around in Nicole's car, without any real use for them. Soon afte his release from prison, he violated his parole by traveling out of state three hundred miles to Idaho, where he was caught by the police fc driving without a license, and called his relatives in Utah, claiming to b broke and asking to be picked up. His cousin, Brenda, berated him as fool. Mailer interpolated: "He seemed to think getting into the damnedes situations and finding a way out of them was common sense."[41]

The Onion Field: Greg Powell similarly flouted convention and playe with the liberating significance of deviance, until it trapped him into mur der. In the days before the onion-field killings, Greg was elaborately in volved in a symbolic play with authority. He fancied himself a maste criminal. He worked on a walk that, with a skip and a hop, would enabl him to move quickly away from a robbery scene but without appearin to flee. He had a costume of dark clothes, a hat and a trenchcoat, and h pointed with pride to a little mole with three hairs that he had drawn o his earlobe so witnesses might provide an erroneous identification. On th getaway from a market robbery, Greg directed Jimmy Lee, who was driv ing, into a dead end, and then, discovering he did not have his hat, tol Jimmy Lee to turn around and drive back so he could recover it (he sai it carried identifying writing).[42] Here his play with the symbols of devi ance almost trapped him into taking up a foolish, self-imposed challeng This time he was saved from himself when he found the hat in the ca But on their next trip to a stickup, when the policemen, Ian and Kar stopped Greg and Jimmy Lee because they were struck by their "bad uniform, the symbolism of evil that Greg had been so fascinated to pla with was out of his hands and playing with his fate.

In Cold Blood: On the one hand, Perry vividly sensed his pariah status a a half-breed and ex-con; and on the other hand, he played with sophis ticating his association with evil. The following were entries in a treasure notebook that he carried wherever he went:

Thanatoid = deathlike; . . . Amerce = punishment, amount fixed b court; . . . Facinorous = atrociously wicked; Hagiophobia = a morbi fear of holy places & things; Lapidicolous = living under stones . . . ; Dyspathy = lack of sympathy, fellow feeling; Psilopher = a fellow who fain would pass as a philosopher; Omophagia = eating raw flesh . . . ; Depredate = to pillage, rob, and prey upon; . . . Myrtophobia = fear of night and darkness.[43]

Perry's moral dizziness had him spinning between degradation in conformity and a tremulous flirting with an unimaginably "big score."

Victim: Dale Pierre's long-standing dizziness in deviance was exaggerated and intensified at his air force assignment in Utah. Shortly after he arrived, Pierre was investigated for the murder of a black air force sergeant, Jefferson. Pierre had been in Jefferson's apartment, taping music, when Jefferson's key ring disappeared. The next day, Pierre returned and suggested they search again for the keys, which he soon found. Jefferson regarded this suggestion as a transparent maneuver and accused Pierre of theft. Two days later, Jefferson was found dead on his couch from multiple bayonet thrusts through his face. Investigators found that the campus locksmith had been asked to duplicate Jefferson's keys by a person who signed a fictitious name. When asked to sign that name, Pierre produced a handwriting sample that experts declared was a match.

Besides the method of murder, the bizarre features of the crime were the use of the base locksmith to duplicate the keys—as if Pierre wanted to facilitate the investigation—and the gratuitous, transparent maneuver to return the keys the next day—as if Pierre did not so much want to cover his tracks as point to them. The methodology of his auto thefts further clarified that Pierre's overriding concern was not simply to accomplish evil but to establish his superiority to conventional authority. Pierre showed great interest in a particular car on a used-car lot, stole it that night, and returned the next day to dramatize righteous indignation because, now that he was ready to buy it, it was not there! The car dealer called the police. The police found that the car Pierre had used to drive to the lot was also a stolen car and that it held a loaded .45-caliber gun. When searched, Pierre was found to have three sets of car keys, one fitting the stolen car he was then driving and the others fitting two other stolen cars, including the car Pierre had come to demand, both of which were found at the air force base. In his own peculiar way, Pierre devised an analogy to Jack Abbott's spitting in the face of the guards and to Gary Gilmore's and Greg Powell's flaunting of their deviance.

Pierre is a documented variation on a stock character of crime's folk mythology—the criminal who, seduced against the dictates of reason to return to the scene of the crime, thereby gives himself away. In detective stories, the criminal unnecessarily tries to sneak back to remove identifying evidence because he is haunted by unconscious guilt. In Pierre's case, the return was not sneaky—for example, he might have replaced Jefferson's keys when Jefferson was absent. Rather, it was showy, as if he were so awed by the transcendent significance of his criminal triumph that he felt drawn to elaborate it through a celebration held in the face of the very people who might damn him. (Perhaps this was the attraction of destroying Jefferson's face and the mouth, tongue, and throats of the hi-fi victims.)

ACT III: RESOLUTION OF THE NARRATIVE

When robbers make their violence contingent on the victim's provocation, they share the responsibility for what unfolds and they confuse the drama. When they use violence only to ensure escape, they may leave without knowing whether their assault has been mortal. In effect, the typical robber, by acting "reasonably," sacrifices opportunities to construct the event with emphatic autobiographical significance. Cold-blooded, "senseless" robber-killers, in contrast, set up the scene of violence to make a point, often remaining longer than the robbery requires to ensure that their design has been properly executed.

When our protagonists approached the killing scenes, their dizzying relations with deviance had recently accelerated in intensity. Dale Pierre was out on bail, pursued by a variety of well-substantiated charges. Gary Gilmore's identification with the "darkness" proved inadequate to hold Nicole, and he had just made a seemingly impossible commitment to buy a fascinating white truck. Perry Smith missed a connection with his special friend, Willy-Jay, and turned to his prison acquaintance, Dick Hickock, who seized on the image Perry had cultivated to work up enthusiasm for a "perfect" crime. Greg Powell's "family" was placing new challenges on his patriarchal responsibilities; Maxine was two months from giving birth; Jimmy Lee, who had been Greg's partner only for a few days, was working on his courage to steal Greg's car and leave; and Greg, who was down to about $60, was committed to rob enough in one night in Los Angeles to finance a "family" trip to San Francisco.

In our set of "senseless" acts, the killers used cold-blooded methods against the moralized chaos in the immediate backgrounds of their lives. By way of juxtaposition, the dizziness they had been living put into relief the narrative accomplishments of their killings. For these killers, the dramaturgic aspects of the fatal scenes were specifically appealing.

Victim: If Dale Pierre's methods seem so horrifying to us that we imagine a man gone berserk, we are wrong. Pierre had to improvise when Mr. Walker unexpectedly escaped death, and he delayed the killing for a sexual interlude with one victim. But when Andrews showed uncertainty about what they were to do after the van was loaded, Pierre invoked a script, "What I told you we would do." He directed Andrews to get the bottle of liquid Drano, and when Andrews declared his lack of guts after assisting with this stage of the event and begged off, Pierre, knowing more or less what remained on the program, could tell him, "Give me half an hour."

In Cold Blood: If Dick ultimately did not have the stomach to commit Perry and himself to killing, he supplied important elements of dramatic flair. Beyond the material gains, there was a scene he wanted to design, with "hair on them walls." Even if he and Perry did not find the promised safe, the trip and killings had gone so neatly according to plan that it was a "perfect" crime; it fulfilled his fascination to conduct a purposive criminal undertaking like "a real pro would. Like a torpedo from Detroit or someplace. . . . I remember thinking, I wish I had worn a trench coat."[44]

The Onion Field: Greg Powell, who often did wear a trenchcoat as he went out into the Los Angeles sun in search of robbery targets, recalled a sense of doing "what had to be done" when shooting Ian. Cueing himself with a reference to the "Little Lindbergh Law," he knew the drama that should unfold; it was clear to him how he should bring this long drive with the kidnapped policemen to a close. His killing was an acting out of a quickly rehearsed role.

The Executioner's Song: We do not know what Gary Gilmore said or thought as he was shooting. The audio track that Mailer suggested he produced— "This one is for me [bang]. This one is for Nicole [bang]"—conveys an ambiguous double entendre. But the point of marching Max Jensen to the bathroom in the rear of the service station, ordering him to lay face down with his hands tucked under his body, and pulling the trigger twice at point-blank range, was to make a point. Gilmore had shaped a life that would support either, or more richly both, the revenge and the suicidal meanings of his putative speech. If Mailer got the phrases wrong, what he got right was the sense of denouement.

The resolve enacted in the lived emotions of these killings constructed a resolution of the moral uncertainty that had doggedly pursued the protagonists: in which direction should the explanatory causal formula, defilement-revenge-suffering, be applied? They had suffered disgust and moral exile as pariahs who defiled conventional society. Now, after years of playing with the symbolism of evil, *they* specifically imposed suffering, writing in their victims' blood the history of disrespect and lack of faith by which *others had defiled them.*

That these protagonists experienced an apotheosis is indicated by several details. Dick recalled, "At the time . . . I thought a person could get a lot of glory out of a killing. The world 'glory' seemed to keep going through my mind. . . . When you bump somebody off you are really in the big time."[45] Perry and Dick remembered laughing as they left the Clutter's home, apparently from a sense of absurd contrast between their brief actions and the irrevocable change they had created. They laughed as they contemplated how much work the morticians (who would have to deal with the mundane consequences of their act) would have, if they attempted to restore the victims' faces for a proper funeral: they had breached the order of the everyday moral world in a way that could not be patched up.

That these men were *becoming* "cold-blooded" through their killings is revealed by the temporal structure of the events in their biographies. Despite his bragging of having killed a "nigger," Perry had never killed before. But after the killings, he revised his autobiography and was ready to kill again, just a few weeks later when he and Dick, hitchhiking in Nebraska, were picked up by a traveling salesman—so close to Kansas, so soon after the murders of the Clutters, with the likelihood of so small a gain. The idea that having killed once they might as well kill again makes no utilitarian sense, but at that point such considerations no longer gave them much pause.

After the hi-fi murders, Dale Pierre reappeared to report an apotheosis. His colleagues in that crime were black, but afterward, he said:

> I often feel that I am white, but I don't feel bad being black. I consider myself superior to most blacks. I don't trust them. They're boisterous, not well-mannered, and they have habits like smoking and blaspheming that I was not brought up with.[46]

Despite his boasts of having killed a "nigger" in prison, it took Gilmore thirty-five years to work up to his first killing. But it took him only another day to get to the second. Already awakened to the narrative possibilities, after his capture and conviction he exploited his death to make himself the moral tale of the year.

Contingencies of Relevance

Thus far much that we have examined existed long before the killing scenes were constituted. If our protagonists used the form of primordial evil to make compelling sense of committing "senseless" murder, they had long been familiar with that form. Indeed, so have we all.

This familiarity develops naturally, not pathologically, through the child's experience of authority. Children may experience love before they experience the constraint of ethical injunctions, but that is another matter. As Ricoeur wrote, "Man enters into the ethical world [not the emotional world in general] through fear and not through love."[47] Parents do not have to engage in child abuse to convey moral limitations to small children through sudden physical intervention; they may do so simply by shouting and pulling a child from danger. If holy interdicts are delivered "with the shadow of vengeance," so are instructions like "Don't you dare!" which, through the tone of voice, forcefully, if implicitly, warn, "Or else!" If the countenance of the primordial god is unbearable to human beings, the downcast eyes of small children suggest the same awe-ful truth in their relations with an angry parent. The parent's presumption of an inherent superiority in moral competence makes sense of "senseless" prohibitions.

Some dangers will be put beyond the child's reach because comprehension of their danger is outside the child's grasp, and some orders will be justified by a rationally unsatisfactory but emotionally effective "Because I told you so!" And the child will also be trained to understand the moral formula that *sufferings* imposed on him or her proceed from *vengeance,* which is the result of *defilement* that *requires no intention* to pollute, and which punishment, although destructive to the child, somehow *reconstructs order and makes sense of the chaos* lived in the parents' world. Thus the child may suffer a beating (or just a shout, or just a temporary exile from a room), delivered with curses (or just a tone of irritation), as the result of something spilled (or a noise that became too loud), that was produced by an infant sibling (or perhaps the pet), and which punishment observably creates an emotionally effective, momentary resolution of tensions for the adults. Later, in adult understanding, the motivating tensions may be attributed to interparental conflicts (or culinary disasters, or bill collectors' pressures). But this last insight does not come through to the child's understanding, which remains focused on the primordial, moralized formula that causally relates defilement, suffering, chaos, and the transcendent restoration of order in the universe.

If creating the appearance of primordial evil is a necessary condition for committing a cold-blooded "senseless" murder, surely it is not a sufficient condition. Nor does the explanation become sufficient by adding the dizziness of deviance. Our protagonists may have been becoming more dizzy before entering the killing scene, but they had no monopoly on the experience.

As John Irwin documented twenty-eight years ago, "state-raised" youths—people like Gary Gilmore, Jack Abbott, and Greg Powell, who are confined for much of their adolescence in reform schools, who pass much of their adult lives in prison, and who shape much of their emotions in opposition to the all-encompassing oppression of incarcerative authority—generally anticipate, immediately on release, beginning "escapades" or frenetic involvements with deviance in which they will show scant concern for practical risks. Any of our protagonists might have uttered the quotation Irwin used to illustrate the "escapade" dream:

> Ya, baby, I'm laying to get out there and shoot me some of that good shit. I got a partner who's waiting for me. He's gonna have some stuff for me when I hit the bricks. We got some capers planned, he's just waiting for me to get out. I'm gonna hang that parole on the fence and make it. I figure I'll lay around and get high for a few days, rip off some pussy—my partner's got some little hot cocked bitches waiting—then we'll pull some scores and leave the state.[48]

But there are thousands of such men for every one who becomes a "cold-blooded" killer. If we have identified the symbolic form and the emotional process that are essential to this form of criminality, we still cannot predict its occurrence. A variety of situational contingencies determine whether the dizziness will be provoked, whether the metaphor of primordial evil will seem relevant and practicable, and whether both conditions will be precipitated at the same time. The details of our four cases enable us to make some progress in specifying these contingencies.

COSMOLOGICAL CONTROL

First, there is a cosmological contingency. The primitive god reigns as master of the universe, throwing thunderbolts from on high or speaking through the silence of the prophet's thoughts. When he sends a message, it will boom forth like thunder or stun a man's awareness, as might the sudden burning of a bush. Thus, if one is effectively to mobilize the form of primordial evil, he needs a situation structured for cosmological transcendence:

- Greg did not begin shooting until it was midnight and he was dominating his little group in an onion field, which he presumed (wrongly again) was otherwise uninhabited.
- If the image of Dick and Perry driving four hundred miles across Kansas to arrive at the Clutter's home, isolated in the fields at midnight, has great dramatic power over the reader and viewer, it was also dramatically significant to Dick and Perry. The next time they planned a cold-blooded murder was when they were hitchhiking in the Mojave desert; when they began executing the plan on a driver who picked them up in Nebraska, one hundred miles outside Omaha, this good samaritan was saved only because he stopped to pick up yet another hitchhiker.
- Gary Gilmore had Nicole's sister, April, in his truck when he drove to the gas station, but he parked the truck around the corner, leaving April in it, and walked in alone. Finding Max Jensen alone, he took him to a place of further isolation, in the back, and then further isolated his act by taking Max into the bathroom. He then further emphasized his domination over the scene by ordering Max down on the floor and only then shot.
- Dale Pierre committed his murders in the basement of the hi-fi store, with the doors locked, two hours after closing time, when the commercial neighborhood had finally quieted down. It seems that the isolated, underworld character of the scene was significant to him. At least, we know that he was observed in the hi-fi store two days before the killings, when he "walked back through the sound room to the back door, turned to his right, and peered down the stairs into the basement."[49]

The structural isolation of the scene makes it practical for the offender to endow the situation with a privileged meaning. In one respect, isolation facilitates the removal of witnesses, but killing robbery victims is hardly a course of action dictated by a desire to escape capture, given the greater investigative resources devoted by police to homicides and the alternative means by which offenders might avoid identification. "Eliminating witnesses" in robberies of this sort is another way of referring to the killer's objective of stamping the scene with an uncontroverted meaning. It is notable that these killers were more successful in temporarily defining the situation as one they dominated without opposition than in actually eliminating all the witnesses. Dale Pierre, with all his brutality, managed to kill only three of his five victims. Although he devoted an hour to terror, he failed even to disable one victim; Mr. Walker soon walked out and told the police what had just happened, with a pen wiggling in his ear as he spoke. Greg Powell arranged the shooting so ineptly that Karl had a chance to escape. Gary Gilmore terminated his attack in the motel after shooting the manager, although he knew that the manager's wife had seen him; he started toward her but then fled, apparently because he became aware that someone on the street also had been watching.

SITUATIONAL TENSIONS

However sensitive these men may have been to the primordial symbolics of evil, their murders depended on features of situational design that enabled them to move into and retain a posture of cosmological control. And however dizzy they may previously have become from alternately exploiting symbols of deviance for interpersonal dominance and experiencing conformity as a moral dis-ease, their move into murder came only when interpersonal dynamics translated their dizziness into situational tensions. In each of these cases, the movement of the protagonist into killing developed when actions by others brought into relief the question of whether the protagonist could sustain a posture of terrifying dominance.

Victim: Dale Pierre was out on bail on March 20, about a month before the hi-fi killings on April 22. (He saw the movie *Magnum Force* on April 2.) Pierre had previously stolen items that he had provided to Andrews; now both had filed to leave the service and this was to be a crime that started them on a new career. Andrews had a reputation as an unexceptional hedonist and as a person who was easily influenced by others. Pierre faced mounting, unprecedented police pressure and expectations from Andrews that he would engineer a big score. At the scene, Pierre's ability to maintain a terrifying domination was tested against the powers of eros as well as thanatos. After administering the Drano in cooperation with Pierre, Andrews expressly abandoned the scene because he had become "scared." After the rape, Pierre's victim tried to joke with him, commenting lightly about how much she had to urinate, and anxiously attempted to seduce him to take her with him.

The Executioner's Song: The relationship between Gary and Nicole often grew stronger when one or the other was treated as a pariah by conventional people. When Gary got into a fight with a fellow who had suggested to others that Gary might be seeking to molest a young girl, Nicole enthusiastically came to his aid, threatening the fellow that if he filed a police complaint about the fight, she would kill him if Gary did not. On July 4, two weeks before Gary murdered, Nicole attended a large family party with Gary, aware that even in her own family she was a pariah: the event had been planned for months but her invitation came at the last minute. When Gary pugnaciously provoked the male guests, Nicole felt a strong loyalty to him, and she was proud to neck openly with him in the midst of the gathering. But "she lost respect when he jumped so fast after Verna [her grandmother] said, 'Knock it off.' "[50]

Gary's identification with evil had brought them together and had repeatedly brought them closer. But Nicole became disenchanted with him. Gary's impotence remained a problem in their relationship. About a week before Gary murdered, he and Nicole broke up. She had secretly begun a new relationship with a businessman who wrote her an anonymous letter earlier, offering $50 if she would sleep with him. Gary, when shown the letter, threatened to kill the fellow. The day after they split, Gary was searching for her, repeatedly stopping at her mother's house to ask for her new address and to see if she had come by.

Gary's lost influence over Nicole was in the immediate background of his murders. The day before he killed Max Jensen, Nicole met him at the house they had shared and reconfirmed the breakup. When he held her as she tried to drive off, she pulled a gun he had given her and he told her to shoot. She declined; he could not keep her in his life and although it may have emerged as bravado, he found that he could not even order his own death.

Gary arranged a reminder of his failed relationship with Nicole in the immediate background as he drove to the gas station that he would rob. Previously, he had placed stolen guns with Nicole's mother, Kathryne, and with a friend, Craig; he had made their acceptance of his identification with deviance a test of their faith in him. That night, he picked up the gun he had stashed at Kathryne's, breaking that tie, and then picked up the gun he had left with Craig. But he simultaneously reconstructed a reminder of his loss of Nicole: he picked up Nicole's sister, April, supposedly to take her on a short errand; she remained in the truck, babbling incoherently, as he entered the gas station and confronted Max Jensen. His shooting was not only revenge or a symbolical suicide, it was a positive act of reclaiming his status as an awesome deviant.

In Cold Blood: In the Clutter killings, the interaction between the offenders mobilized dizzying moral emotions for the protagonists and made salient their transcendent capacities for evil. On the long drive across Kansas, Dick had been chiding Perry for indicating a limited ability to embrace their project in deviance. Perry wanted Dick to obtain black stockings so they might use masks, rather than face their victims openly; sitting in the car outside the house, Perry told Dick that he would have to do it alone; and inside the house, after they were told there was no safe and they searched a while, Perry indicated his opinion that there was no safe and he suggested that they leave.

All the while, it was Dick who maintained a posture of vicious domination, addressing Mr. Clutter roughly, scaring Mrs. Clutter so she turned to befriend Perry when she had a private moment with him, proposing to rape the daughter, and reminding Perry of their plan to kill everyone present.

Perry's perspective on Dick gave Perry's hesitations a double meaning. He might have been nervous, but he was also motivated to test Dick's presumptive status as the leader in the attack. For Perry, the problems they confronted were both practical obstacles and moral resources for demonstrating that Dick was a fraud. When Dick balked at beginning and then at finishing the initial assault on Mr. Clutter, Perry stepped in triumphantly, demonstrating, in what he would take to be a timelessly revealing moment, which of the two really had the primordial power.

The Onion Field: There is a parallel theme of assymetrical power and unidirectional criticism in the relationship between Greg and Jimmy Lee, but in this case, Jimmy Lee was the carping critic and Greg maintained an unbroken line of domination in their relationship, right through his initiation of the murderous attack. Jimmy Lee's criticisms were usually but not always silent, and they pushed Greg to ever-more-grandiose claims of deviant power. When Jimmy Lee complained about the small split Greg gave him from their market robberies, Greg brushed aside his complaint with talk of a $25,000 score. When Jimmy Lee complained, as they fled from a robbery, that Greg had led them to a dead end, Greg not only discounted Jimmy Lee's fear, he proposed that they return to the scene of the crime to retrieve his hat. And when, after they kidnapped the policemen, Jimmy Lee became irritated that Greg was using his name openly and that Greg was talking of their plans to return to a hideout, Greg was forming the plan to make those concerns irrelevant by killing the policemen.

Right at the start of the kidnapping, Jimmy Lee manifested a practical impotence that recast Greg as head of their "family": instructed by Greg to move the police car, Jimmy Lee could not figure out how to release the parking brake. But the salience to Greg of his claims to patriarchal status was also stimulated in his interaction with the policemen. The kidnapping began in Hollywood and ended on the other side of the mountains, and Greg had to rely on the policemen for directions. The policemen "cooperated" beyond Greg's explicit requests, holding their hands high over their heads when Greg initially got the drop on them, then suggesting that Greg and Jimmy Lee remove their notorious caps and that Greg stop drinking from a whiskey bottle, the better to avoid attracting the attentions of other police. The moral implications of this relationship stirred Greg's dizzying paranoia: conformity to conventional authority is a trap; perhaps they were trying to make a fool of him! He realized that they waved flashlights in the hands they held high over their heads; it was a trick. He asked for directions when he knew the correct route, checking the sincerity of their cooperation. And in several instances, he manufactured opportunities to celebrate his situational omnipotence: demonstrating munificence by offering to return their guns so they would not have to pay for new ones, challenging Ian to a shooting contest, proposing a wild idea to let the policemen free after capturing a new set of hostages in a passing family car, and finally showing that as a devil, his knowledge of the law, "the Little Lindbergh Law," could not be surpassed by the law's officers.

Almost consistently, Greg remained outwardly cool, dramatizing an emotional experience of the scene that emphasized his domination. Greg progressively got more and more into the transcendent project of reversing the relationship of domination with the police; and into reversing the moral equation of his life: instead of being a small-time "fucking fool" of a crook, he would emerge from the onion field as a fearless cop killer.

Foreground and Background

There is a double phenomenological validity to the labels that Capote and Mailer gave to this genre of "nonfiction" or "true-life" "novels." Not only does the narrative creativity belong in the first instance to the killers (if Capote was pretentious for laying claim to a genre, his rubric in this respect implied humility); what the protagonists wrote was itself fiction. In the first instance, the lie was the protagonists'—a lie about their own lives that portrayed glory, essential nature, and predestination or fate. As Nietzsche understood:

> Thought is one thing, the deed, is another, and the image of the deed still another: the wheel of causality does not roll between them.
> An image made this pale man pale. He was equal to his deed when he did it; but he could not bear its image after it was done. Now he always saw himself as the doer of one deed. Madness I call this: the exception now became the essence for him. A chalk streak stops a hen; the stroke that he himself struck stopped his poor reason: madness *after* the deed I call this.[51]

To believe, as we review them after the fact, that these acts were pre-ordained or that they revealed essential identity is to be, like Nietzsche's hen, a dumb cluck. The fiction that these killers constructed was that an act of such ferocious domination was always what they were headed toward. We should be especially cautious before we echo these overtones of predestination or essential revelation as we search for explanatory ideas. So, instead of ending with a claim to have discovered or confirmed the hidden, causally crucial factor in the backgrounds of cold-blooded "senseless" murder, I would emphasize a methodological caution.

All the killers in *Victim, In Cold Blood, The Onion Field,* and *The Executioner's Song* were isolated individuals before they killed. Given the public view of these events as "senseless" killings, it is a short jump from these narratives to a psychological theory of antisocial personality disorder or to a sociological theory that attributes deviance to a lack of social ties. But it may well be the social process of producing these texts that makes it likely that nonfiction novels of cold-blooded, senseless murder will exhibit that theme.

Because these killers were socially isolated men, the environment that the researchers-authors had to enter was relatively or even extremely benign: there were not many similarly dreadful deviants who were closely related to the authors' subjects. The fact that Dale Pierre, Gary Gilmore, Dick Hickock and Perry Smith, and Gregory Powell and Jimmy Lee Smith killed in the center of conventional morality made their killings infamous and made the research tasks relatively comfortable.

Consider the challenges of investigating "senseless" killings in inter-youth gang or intraghetto settings. The problem is not only that the researchers and authors tend to be white and middle class. I suggest that our image of the modern cold-blooded senseless killer tends to be a miscreant living without a sense of collective place because those with a strong sense of collective place are likely to have as their place a community that is an inhospitable, daunting research site for anyone. The image that it is socially isolated, cold-blooded men who commit "senseless" murders may be an artificial reflection of the relationship of authors to the social means of producing their books.

CHAPTER 9

Seductions and Repulsions
of Crime

In 1835, in a small French village, Pierre Rivière killed half his family: his mother, a sister, and a brother. After his arrest, he wrote a lengthy explanation to the effect that he had killed his mother to protect his father from her ceaseless cruelties, which had frequently become public humiliations, and he had killed two siblings who were living with her because they had sided with her in the family quarrels, either actively or simply through sustained love. In addition, Rivière explained that by killing his young brother, whom he knew his father to love, he would turn his father against him, thus making less burdensome to his father Rivière's legally mandated death, which he expected would result from his crimes.[1] A team of scholars, led by Michel Foucault, traced the ensuing conflicts among the various "discourses" engaged in by Rivière, the lawyers, doctors, the mayor, the priest, and the villagers, and they added their own.

Rivière wrote a carefully composed, emotionally compelling account of the background to his crime, recounting, as if reconstructing a contemporaneous journal, a long series of deceits and monetary exploitations by his mother against his father. But, although he entitled his account "Particulars and Explanation of the Occurrence," in the sixty-seven pages his "memoir" covers (in this translated reproduction), less than a sentence describes the "particulars of the occurrence." Rivière gave no specific significance to the aim or the force of the blows he struck with an axlike farm implement (he destroyed the vertebrae that had connected the head of his mother from her body, and he separated brain from skull, converting bone and muscle to mush); to the multiplicity of the blows, which extended far beyond what was necessary to accomplish death; to his mother's advanced state of pregnancy; or to details of the violence suffered by his brother and sister. Instead, he focused exclusively on the background of his family biography. Although Rivière's account was elaborately inculpating in substance, in style, it bespoke a sophisticated rationality, which in many eyes was exculpating. (Some even labeled it "beautiful.")

As an author, Pierre Rivière was primarily concerned with the moral power that the narrative could lend to his crime. By glossing over the homicidal event itself, he continued the attack on his mother before a new, larger audience. The state and lay professional interpreters of his crime followed his lead, relying largely on facts he had acknowledged and discounting the situational details in favor of biographical, historical, and social ecological factors. As Foucault suggested, the very barbarity of the attack made it an act of resistance against the forms of civility. But after the fact, Rivière and many powerful groups in his society literally rationalized the event, locating it as the logical outcome of an ongoing family injustice, a form of madness or mental illness, or (in the comments offered later in the book by some of Foucault's colleagues) of the historical and class position of French peasants.[2]

In short, many of the interpreters sought to exploit too much from the murder to dwell on its gruesome lived reality. Rivière was motivated to construct an account that would make his viciously cruel, extremely messy act neatly reappear as a self-sacrificial, efficient blow for justice. The other commentators had general theoretical perspectives at stake: medical-psychological ideology, institutions of religious understanding, and politically significant interpretations (including the emergence of a school of thought around Foucault himself). On all sides, modern forms of civility would govern the posthumous experience of the crime.

Today, the contemporary incarnations of professional, legal-scientific, and civil interpretive spirits are both stronger and more petty than they were 150 years ago. The effective political spectrum for debate still features a Right and a Left, but most of the intellectual action is within a small and relatively tame segment on the left side of the scale. The length of the scale is much narrower than when the Church and tradition, and occasionally even anarchist voices, were powerful in the debate. Now various disciplines in the social sciences have a go at it, but they go at each other more than at "lay" opinion, and what is at stake is less clearly the institutionalization of a field than the relative popularity of fads in research methodology.

If the preceding chapters contribute to the study of crime, it is only because the readily available, detailed meaning of common criminality has been systematically ruled out as ineligible for serious discussion in the conventions of modern sociological and political thought. Something important happened when it became obscenely sensational or damnably insensitive to track the lived experience of criminality in favor of imputing factors to the background of crime that are invisible in its situational manifestation. Somehow in the psychological and sociological disciplines, the lived mysticism and magic in the foreground of criminal experience became unseeable, while the abstractions hypothesized by "empirical theory" as the determining background causes, especially those conveniently quantified by state agencies, became the stuff of "scientific" thought and "rigorous" method.

Whatever the historical causes for treating background factors as the theoretical core for the empirical study of crime, the point of this volume is to demonstrate that it is not necessary to constitute the field back to front. We may begin with the foreground, attempting to discover common or homogeneous criminal projects and to test explanations of the necessary and sufficient steps through which people construct given forms of crime. If we take as our primary research commitment an exploration of the distinctive phenomena of crime, we may produce not just ad hoc bits of description or a collection of provocative anecdotes but a systematic empirical theory of crime—one that explains at the individual level the causal process of committing a crime and that accounts at the aggregate level for recurrently documented correlations with biographical and ecological background factors.

Moral Emotions and Crime

The closer one looks at crime, at least at the varieties examined here, the more vividly relevant become the moral emotions. Follow vandals and amateur shoplifters as they duck into alleys and dressing rooms and you will be moved by their delight in deviance; observe them under arrest and you may be stunned by their shame. Watch their strutting street display and you will be struck by the awesome fascination that symbols of evil hold for the young men who are linked in the groups we often call gangs. If we specify the opening moves in muggings and stickups, we describe an array of "games" or tricks that turn victims into fools before their pockets are turned out. The careers of persistent robbers show us, not the increasingly precise calculations and hedged risks of "professionals," but men for whom gambling and other vices are a way of life, who are "wise" in the cynical sense of the term, and who take pride in a defiant reputation as "bad." And if we examine the lived sensuality behind events of cold-blooded "senseless" murder, we are compelled to acknowledge the power that may still be created in the modern world through the sensualities of defilement, spiritual chaos, and the apprehension of vengeance.

Running across these experiences of criminality is a process juxtaposed in one manner or another against humiliation. In committing a righteous slaughter, the impassioned assailant takes humiliation and turns it into rage; through laying claim to a moral status of transcendent significance, he tries to burn humiliation up. The badass, with searing purposiveness, tries to scare humiliation off; as one ex-punk explained to me, after years of adolescent anxiety about the ugliness of his complexion and the stupidity of his every word, he found a wonderful calm in making "them" anxious about *his* perceptions and understandings. Young vandals and shoplifters innovate games with the risks of humiliation, running along the edge of shame for its exciting reverberations. Fashioned as street elites, young men square off against the increasingly humiliating social restrictions of childhood by mythologizing differences with other groups of young men who might be their mirror image. Against the historical background of a collective insistence on the moral nonexistence of their people, "bad niggers" exploit ethnically unique possibilities for celebrating assertive conduct as "bad."

What does the moral fascination in the foreground of criminal experience imply for background factors, particularly poverty and social class? Is crime only the most visible peak of a mountain of shame suffered at the bottom of the social order? Is the vulnerability to humiliation skewed in its distribution through the social structure? To address these questions, we should examine the incidence and motivational qualities of what is usually called "white-collar" crime. Perhaps we would find a greater level of involvement in criminality, even more closely linked to shameful motivations. But the study of white-collar crime has been largely a muckraking operation from the outside; despite isolated exceptions, we have no general empirical understanding of the incidence or internal feel of white-collar crime. This absence of data makes all the more remarkable the influence, within both academic and lay political thought on crime, of the assumption of materialist causation.

Sentimental Materialism

> But whatever the differential rates of deviant behavior in the several social strata, and we know from many sources that the official crime statistics uniformly showing higher rates in the lower strata are far from complete or reliable, it appears from our analysis that the greatest pressures toward deviation are exerted upon the lower strata.[3]

Just fifty years ago, Robert K. Merton published his "Social Structure and Anomie," an article once counted as the single most frequently cited and reprinted paper in the history of American sociology.[4] Arguing against Freud and psychological analysis in general, Merton attributed deviance to a contradiction in the structure of modern society: "Americans are bombarded on all sides" by the goal of monetary success, but the means or

opportunities for achieving it are not as uniformly distributed. A generation later, Richard Cloward and Lloyd Ohlin, with a revised version of
"opportunity" theory, hit perhaps the pinnacle of academic and political
success in the history of criminology, winning professional awards and
finding their work adopted by the Kennedy administration as part of the
intellectual foundations of what later became the War on Poverty.[5] After
a hiatus during much of the Republican 1970s and 1980s, materialist
theory—the Mertonian ideas now bolstered by rational-economic models
of social action that had become academically attractive in the interim—is
again promoting the lack of opportunity (unemployment, underemployment, and low "opportunity cost") to explain crime.[6]

That this materialist perspective is twentieth-century sentimentality
about crime is indicated by its overwhelming inadequacy for grasping the
experiential facts of crime. The "model" or "theory" is so persuasive that
the observable facts really do not matter, as Merton put it: "whatever the
differential rates of deviant behavior in the several social strata . . . it
appears from our analysis that the greatest pressures toward deviation are
exerted upon the lower strata."[7] Indeed, the Mertonian framework as
originally presented, as elaborated in the 1960s, and as recently paralleled
by the economist's perspective, should now be recognized as an institutionalized academic-political sensibility for systematically making literally
unthinkable the contemporary horrors of deviance and for sustaining a
quietist criminology.

Consider the many sensually explosive, diabolically creative, realities of
crime that the materialist sentiment cannot appreciate. Where is the materialism in the experience of the *barrio* "homeboy," the night before the first
day of high school?

> Although I was not going to be alone, I still felt insecure. . . . my mother,
> with an accentuated voice, ordered me to go to sleep. Nevertheless, my
> anxiety did not let my consciousness rest; instead, what I did was look
> in the mirror, and began practicing the traditional steps that would show
> my machismo. . . . Furthermore, I was nervously thinking about taking
> a weapon to the school grounds just to show Vatos from other barrios
> the answer of my holy clique. All kinds of evil thoughts were stirring
> in me.[8]

The problem for Merton and materialist theory is not simply with some
youthful "gang" activity. There is now strong evidence that a high proportion of those who go on to especially "serious," "heavy," "career" involvements in criminality start in early adolescence, long before job opportunities could or, in a free social order, should become meaningful
considerations.[9] Actually, when Albert Cohen pointed out, long ago, the
" 'versatility' and the 'zest' with which some boys are observed to pursue
their group-supported deviations," Merton was willing to concede that

much of youth crime was beyond his theory of deviance.[10] It was enough if, as Cohen had offered in a conciliatory gesture, Merton's materialism applied to "professional" or serious adult property criminals.

But if we look at persistent criminals, we see a life of action in which materialism is by no means the god. Instead, material goods are treated more like offerings to be burnt, quickly, lest retention become sacrilege. As suggested by "dead presidents," a black street term for U.S. cash, there is an aggressive attack on materialism as a potentially misleading, false deity. Robby Wideman seemed to have Merton in mind when he told his brother:

> Straight people don't understand. I mean, they think dudes is after the things straight people got. It ain't that at all. People in the life ain't looking for no home and grass in the yard and shit like that. We the show people. The glamour people. Come on the set with the finest car, the finest woman, the finest vines. Hear people talking about you. Hear the bar get quiet when you walk in the door. Throw down a yard and tell everybody drink up. . . . You make something out of nothing.[11]

The aspiration is not to what is advertised on television. Robby Wideman was not incapable of identifying what drove him; it was to be a star—something literally, distinctively transcendent. Street people are not inarticulate when they say that "the endgame is to *get over*, to *get across*, to *make it*, to *step fast*."[12] This language is only a "poetic" indirect reference to aspirations for material status if we refuse to recognize that it directly captures the objective of transcendence.[13]

So, a lot of juvenile forms of violent crime and an important segment of serious adult crime do not fit the sentimentality of materialism. Neither does the central thrust that guides men and women to righteous slaughters, nor the project of primordial evil that makes "senseless killings" compellingly sensible to their killers, nor the tactics and reverberations of sneaky thrills. None of these fits, in the Mertonian scheme, the actions of "innovators" who accept the conventional aims but use deviant means. The aims are specifically unconventional: to go beyond the established moral definitions of the situation as it visibly obtains here and now. Nor can we categorize these deviants as "retreatists" who reject conventional means and ends. For Merton, retreatists were a spiritually dead, socially isolated, lot of psychotics, drunkards, and vagrants; today's "bag ladies" would fit that category. And, surely, these deviants are not "rebels" with revolutionary ideas to implement new goals and means.

None of this argument denies the validity of the recurrent correlations between low socioeconomic status or relative lack of economic opportunity, on the one hand, and violent and personal property crime on the other. The issue is the causal significance of this background for deviance. A person's material background will not determine his intent to commit acquisitive crime, but a person, whether or not he is intent on acquisitive crime, is not likely to be unaware of his circumstances.

Instead of reading into ghetto poverty an unusually strong motivation to become deviant, we may understand the concentration of robbery among ghetto residents as being due to the fact that for people in economically more promising circumstances, it would literally make no sense—it would virtually be crazy—to commit robbery. Merton had no basis but the sentiments stirred by his theory to assume that crime, even materially acquisitive crime, was more common in the "lower strata." In part, the appeal of his theory was promoted by the obvious significance of material circumstance in the shaping of crime. We need fear only a few exceptions if we claim that lawyers will not stick up banks, "frequent-flyer" executives will not kill their spouses in passionate rages, and physicians will not punch out their colleagues or that the unemployed will not embezzle, the indigent will not fix prices, and the politically powerless will not commit perjury in congressional testimony. But this is a different matter from claiming that crime or deviance is distributed in the social structure according to the relative lack of opportunity for material gain.

It is not inconsequential that major forms of contemporary criminality cannot simply be fit within the dominant sentimentality for understanding deviance. If it were recognized that changes in material circumstance affect the form more than the drive toward deviance, it would be more difficult to promote publicly financed programs to increase benefits or opportunities where they are most lacking. A revision of the theory of materialism that would limit it to the explanation of the quality, rather than the quantity, of deviance, would be much less palatable across the political spectrum. Such an analytic framework would not serve those on the Right who point to the social distribution of common crime, along with other pathologies, to discount the moral claims of lower-class minorities for governmental outlays. But neither would a comparative theory of the qualities of crime serve well the social-class sympathies that have often been promoted by the study of white-collar crime. For muckrakers, it has been important to depict the prevalence of elite deviance to weaken the moral basis of corporate political power; often they have argued that white-collar crime is every bit as "real" and destructive a form of deviance as is street crime. But unless one agrees to reduce nonviolent crimes of deception to a less heinous status than violent personal crime, the comparative perspective will undercut traditional policies of social reform to aid the underprivileged. One has to promise more than a trade-off between street crime and administrative fraud to work up moral enthusiasm for job training programs.

More generally, from Marx through Durkheim and Freud to the contemporary sociological materialists, the hallmark of rhetorically successful theory has been its specification of the source of social evil.[14] Without the claim that background conditions breed the motivation to deviance, criminological theory would not serve the high priestly function of transforming diffuse anxiety about chaos into discrete problems that are confined to marginal segments of social life. Indeed, the research agenda implied by a theory that relates material conditions to the form or quality of deviance but not to its incidence or prevalence is profoundly disquieting.

Repulsions of Deviance

Whether their policy implications point toward increasing penalties to decrease crime or toward increasing legitimate opportunities or "opportunity costs" to decrease crime, modern causal theories have obliterated a natural fascination to follow in detail the lived contours of crime. Perhaps the indecisive battle among competing determinist theories of crime is itself an important aspect of their persistent popularity, inside academia, in columnists' opinions, and in political speech. Methodological innovations, policy experiments, and the latest wave of governmental statistics continually stimulate the ongoing dialogue, with no side ever gaining a decisive advantage but all sharing in an ideological structure that blocks unsettling encounters with the human experience of crime.

What would follow if we stuck with the research tactic of defining the form of deviance to be explained from the inside and searching for explanations by examining how people construct the experience at issue and then, only as a secondary matter, turned to trace connections from the phenomenal foreground to the generational and social ecological background? We would have to acknowledge that just because blacks have been denied fair opportunity for so long, and so often,[15] the criminality of ghetto blacks can no longer be explained by a lack of opportunity. Just because the critique of American racial injustice has been right for so long, as criminological explanation it now is wrong. Even accepting the Mertonian analysis as initially valid, for how many generations can a community maintain a moral independence of means and ends, innovating deviance only to reach conventional goals? How does a people restrict its economic participation only to the stunted spiritual engagement permitted over centuries of racism? By what anthropological theory can one hold his real self somehow outside the cynical hustles he devises day by day, his soul, untouched by a constant pursuit of illicit action, waiting with confident innocence in some purgatory to emerge when a fair opportunity materializes? The realities of ghetto crime are literally too "bad" to be confined to the role of "innovative means" for conventional ends. This is not to deny that the history of racial injustice makes a morally convincing case for increasing opportunities for the ghetto poor. It is to say that materialist theories refuse to confront the spiritual challenge represented by contemporary crime.

The profundity of the embrace of deviance in the black ghetto and the tensions that will emerge among us if we discuss the lived details of these phenomena form one set of the contemporary horrors our positivist theories help us avoid facing. Another blindness they sustain is to the lack of any intellectual or political leadership to confront the massive bloodletting of mate against mate and brother against brother that continues to be a daily reality in the inner city. Each time the sentimentality of materialism is trotted out to cover the void of empirically grounded ideas, it seems more transparent and less inspiring; each time the exhortation to positivism carries a more desperate sentiment that it *has* to be right. And, finally, there is the incalculable chaos that would break out if the institutions of social science were to apply the methods of investigation used here to deviance all across the social order.

Theories of background causes lead naturally to a reliance on the state's definition of deviance, especially as assembled in official crime statistics, and they make case studies virtually irrelevant. But the state will never supply data describing white-collar crime that are comparable to the data describing street or common crime. Politically, morally, and logically, it can't.

The problem is due not to political bias in the narrow sense, but to the dialectical character of white-collar crime as a form of deviance that necessarily exists in a moral metaphysical suspense. To assess the incidence and consequences of common crimes like robbery, one can survey victims and count arrests in a research operation that may be conducted independently of the conviction of the offenders. But individual victims generally cannot authoritatively assert the existence of tax cheating, consumer fraud, insider trading, price fixing, and political corruption; when prosecutions of such crimes fail, not only can the defendants protest their personal innocence, but they can deny that *any* crime occurred. We are on especially shaky grounds for asserting with methodological confidence that white-collar crimes exist before the state fully certifies the allegation through a conviction.

On the one hand, then, white-collar crime can exist as a researchable social problem only if the state officially warrants the problem; on the other hand, white-collar crimes will *not* exist if the state gets too serious about them. The existence of prohibitions against white-collar crimes distinctively depends on the prohibitions not being enforced. The strength of public and political support for robbery and murder prosecutions is not weakened with increased enforcement. But if the official system for prosecuting tax cheating, pollution violations, and even immigration fraud becomes too vigorous, pressure will build to reduce the prohibitory reach of the underlying laws.[16] At the extreme, any group that becomes subject to massive state treatment as criminally deviant is either not an elite or is a class engaged in civil war.

Explanatory social research relies on the state's definition of deviance when it statistically manipulates the demographic and ecological variables quantified by the state, rather than documents in detail the the experience and circumstances of the actual doings of deviance. So long as this reliance continues, we will be unable intellectually to constitute a field for the study of white-collar crime. Disparate, occasional studies of white-collar crime will continue to emerge from the margins of organization theory, from interests in equal justice that are sustained by the sociology of law, from studies of criminal justice agencies and of the professions, and from the atheoretical moral force generated by recurrent waves of scandal. But a reliance for explanation on background determinism has made twentieth-century social theory fundamentally incapable of comprehending the causation of white-collar crime.

Consider how the traditional boundaries of the field of criminology would break down if we were to extend to white-collar crime the strategy taken in this work to explain common crime. As we did in approaching criminal homicide, adolescent theft, gang delinquency, and other forms of violent or personal property crime, we would begin, not with the state's official accounting of crime but by looking for lines of action, distinctive to occupants of high social position, that are homogeneously understood by the offenders themselves to enact a variety of deviance. We would quickly arrive at a broad field with vague boundaries between forms of conduct regarded by the offenders as criminal, civilly liable, professionally unethical, and publicly unseemly. Simultaneously, we would follow the logic of analytic induction and search for negative cases, which means that evidence would take the form of qualitative case studies.

Now, where would we get the data? With white-collar crime, we have a special problem in locating facts to demonstrate the lived experience of deviance. Despite their presumably superior capacity to write books and the healthy markets that await their publication efforts, we have virtually no "how-I-did-it-and-how-it-felt-doing-it" autobiographies by corrupted politicians, convicted tax frauds, and chief executive officers who have been deposed by scandals over inside trading. This absence of naturalistic, autobiographical, participant-observational data is itself an important clue to the distinctive emotional quality of white-collar crime. Stickup men, safecrackers, fences, and drug dealers often wear the criminal label with pride, apparently relishing the opportunity to tell their criminal histories in colorful, intimate detail. But white-collar criminals, perhaps from shame or because the ties to those whom they would have to incriminate are so intimate a part of their own identities that they can *never* be broken, rarely publicly confess; when they do confess, they virtually never confess with the sustained attention to detail that characterizes, for example, almost any mugging related by an ordinary, semiliterate hustler like Henry Williamson.[17]

As a result, to obtain data, etiological theorists of white-collar crime would have to join forces with public and private investigators and with enemy constituencies of the elites under focus—hardly a promising tack for winning academic, much less governmental-institutional, support for developing a broad data base. Even more absurd is the suggestion that the researcher take up the data-generating task directly by working from readily accessible gossip and looking around one or another local corner. Depending on time and place, that might mean studying the chancellor's project to remodel his home; the law professor's marijuana smoking; the medical researcher's practice of putting his name on research papers, the data for which he has never seen; the alumni's means of supporting the football team; the professor's management of expenditures and accounting in research grants; the administrator's exploitation through real estate profiteering of inside information about the expansion of the university; the process of defaulting on student loans; and so on. By maintaining background determinism as the dominant framework for the study of crime, the social sciences leave the serious academic investigation of elite deviance to those proper intellectual folk, the ethical philosophers, who exploit qualitative case materials in the innocuous forms of delightful illustrations from literature, lively hypotheticals, and colorful histories documented by others. All who already have them retain their jobs and their sanity.

But is it so absurd to imagine a democratic society that would treat the arrogance, the public frauds, and the self-deceptions of its elites as a field that would be amenable to theoretically guided, empirical investigation? Is it obvious that institutionally supported social research on the etiology of deviance should seek causal drives more in the shame and impotence of poverty than in the hubris of affluence and power?

And we can go one step further. The fear of chaos that blocks a truly empirical study of crime is not just a repulsion for a disquieting process of investigation. There is also a substantive chaos—a crisis of meaning in collective identity—lurking more deeply behind the dogged appeal of traditions that intimidate the contemporary intellectual confrontation with the lived experience of deviance.

If we were to develop a comparative analysis of the crimes committed by ghetto residents and by occupants of high social positions, we would surely not be examining the identical qualities of experience. Where the ghetto resident may be proud of his reputation as a "bad nigger" at home and on the streets, the governmental leader is likely to be ashamed, at least in some family and community settings, of a breach in his pristine image. Although the stickup man focuses on the simple requirements for instantly and unambiguously conveying to victims the criminal intentions of his actions, organization men will tacitly work out a concerted ignorance that provides each with "deniability" while they arrange the most complex frauds.[18]

But considering the third causal condition that we have been tracing in the paths toward common crime—emotional processes that seduce people to deviance—it is much less clear that the quality of the dynamic differs by social position. Putting aside differences in the practical means that social position makes available and the different degrees and forms of moral stereotype and prejudice that are attached to social position, there may be a fundamental similarity in the dynamics that people create to seduce themselves toward deviance. Although the means differ, white middle-class youths may as self-destructively pursue spatial mobility, through reckless driving, as do ghetto youths in gang wars. The attractions of sneaky thrills may not disappear with age, but instead may migrate from shoplifting to adultery and embezzlement. And even the bump that the egocentric badass, strutting arrogantly outside his own neighborhood, arranges as an "accident" compelling him to battle, is not without its analogies to the incidents that have been arranged by ethnocentric nations, provocatively sailing in foreign waters, to escalate wars.[19]

It would appear that, with respect to the moral-emotional dynamics of deviance, we have grounds to pursue a parallel across the social hierarchy. Consider two strong candidates for the status of most awful street and white-collar crimes: the killing of defenseless victims to sustain a career of robberies and the deception of democratic publics to support government-sponsored killings of defenseless foreigners. In both the street and the high-government cases, both the Left and the Right have their favored materialist-background explanations and accusations: poverty and lack of economic opportunity versus a liberal judiciary, "handcuffed" police, and inadequate deterrents; the value to capitalists of maintaining power in foreign economic spheres versus the need to use military force against non-Russians to maintain a deterrent strength vis-à-vis the ever-menacing Soviet Union. For the most part, public discussion of both these lowly and exalted social problems proceeds as a ritualized exchange between two politically opposed materialist interpretations.

But in both forms of deviance the actors are engaged in a transcendent project to exploit the ultimate symbolic value of force to show that one "means it." Those who persist in stickups use violence when it is not justified on cost-benefit grounds because *not* to use violence would be to raise chaotic questions about their purpose in life. They understand that to limit their violence by materialist concerns would weaken them in conflicts with other hardmen and would raise a series of questions about their commitment to their careers that is more intimidating than is the prospect of prison. Just because materialist motivations do not control the drive toward doing stickups, the events are rife with foolish risks and fatal bungles.

It is a fair question whether the foreign exercises of Western governments in legally undeclared, surreptitiously instigated, and secretly aided military conflicts less often bungle into pathetic results—the shooting of innocent fisherman, the kidnapping of CIA chiefs, the mechanical surprises from helicopters and explosive devices, the failures to make "operational" defenses against sea mines and air attacks, the lapses in security that allow massive military casualties from terrorist tactics, and the like. What is more remarkable still, is that utilitarian evaluations of success and failure do not dominate the public discussions of such interventions, any more than they dominate the career considerations of persistent robbers. In public debates, symbolic displays of national will, like the cultural style of the hardman, give cost-benefit analysis a cowardly overtone.

This is not to suggest that some collective machismo is behind the conspiratorial deceptions of domestic publics undertaken to support state killings of foreigners. (At the time of writing, the fresh examples are "Contragate," the secret, illegal American government program for generating lies to promote the killing of Nicaraguans, and the French government's deceit over homicidal attacks on environmental activists.)[20] Postulated as a determining background factor, personality traits are no more convincing on the state level than on the individual street level. But in both arenas, the use of violence beyond its clear materialist justification is a powerful strategy for *constructing* purposiveness.

The case of Bernhard ("Bernie") Goetz provides us with a bridge between the street experience of the bad nigger and the collective moral perspective that state leaders may rely on in arranging their homicidal deceits. In 1984, Goetz, a white electrical engineer, shot four young "bad" blacks in a New York City subway train. Acquitted (of all but the weapons charges) in 1987, Goetz became a hero for large segments of the public,[21] essentially because he manipulated to his advantage a detailed understanding of the doings of stickups.

First, Goetz identified a typical opening strategem in street robberies— the use of civility to move into a position of moral dominance. One of his victims approached him and said,

> "How are you?" just, you know, "How are you?" . . . that's a meaningless thing, but in certain circumstances that can be, that can be a real threat. You see, there's an implication there. . . .[22]

Next followed a "request" for money, which Goetz (and one of the victims) recalled as, "Give me five dollars." Goetz recalled:

> I looked at his eyes and I looked at his face . . . his eyes were shiny. He was enjoying himself . . . had this big smile on his face. You know at that point, you're in a bad situation. . . . I know in my mind they wanted to play with me . . . like a cat plays with a mouse. . . . I know my situation. I knew my situation.[23]

Next Goetz seized on this opening ambiguity, which he understood the blacks had created not simply to further their robbery or assault but to ridicule him, as a pause in which he could draw out his gun unopposed.[24] Goetz likewise turned the tightly enclosed space of the subway car to his advantage; now the impossibility of escape was a problem for them, not for him. Goetz was aware of the fantastic moral reversal he had effected: "It was so crazy . . . because they had set a trap for me and only they were trapped. . . . I know this is disgusting to say—but it was so easy. I can't believe it."

As in many stickups, Goetz's violence was, to a significant degree if not completely, gratuitous within the situational context of his shooting. Since his victims did not have guns, just showing his gun probably would have been enough. Instead, his five shots continued after the end of any personal threat that may have been present; before the last shot, which was aimed at the fourth, as yet uninjured victim, he announced, "You seem to be all right; here's another." After the fact, he recalled, "My intention was to, to anything I could to hurt them. . . . to murder them, to hurt them, to make them suffer as much as possible."[25]

Overall, Goetz demonstrated the rational irrationality of violence that characterizes hardened stickup men. Earlier, and independent of this scene, he had arranged to have hollowed-out ("dum-dum") bullets in his gun to enhance destructive consequence should he fire his weapon. Having been victimized in muggings twice before, he found that a readiness to instigate violence had become especially relevant to him for making sense of continuing to travel the streets and subways of New York City. Like the stickup man who routinely keeps a weapon close at hand so he might exploit a fortuitous circumstance, Goetz would not have carried a gun to the scene had he not had this larger, transsituational project.

Beyond practical danger, Goetz was intent on not suffering further humiliation—not simply the humiliations that muggers could inflict, but the humiliation of his own fear, of continuing in the world with the common, cowardly wish to believe that such things would not happen to him. A similar project guides the career of the criminal hardman, whose violence may go beyond what the resistance of a victim may require because he must not only get out of *this* situation but stay "out there" and be ready to get into *the next.* An inquiry that is limited to the situational reasonableness of violence, which social scientists have often asked in relation to data on robberies in which the offenders harm the victims and that courts must ask of a defendant like Goetz, is, to a great degree, absurd. In both cases, the moral inquiry ignores the transcendent purpose of violent men. Put another way, whether violence was reasonably necessary to escape harm or capture in the situated interaction, the decision to *enter* the situation prepared for violence is not, in itself, a matter for reasonable calculations.

The celebrity that Goetz received was, in significant measure, a celebration by "good people" of his transcendent meanness. This same spirit more often wreaks devastation through the instrumentality of national foreign policy. Indeed, if youth "gangs" rely on military metaphors to organize their conflicts, the mobilization of military action in Western democracies also depends, through the chief executive's histrionics and the jingoism of the press, on fashioning international conflicts into dramaturgic lines of street-fighting tactics (showdowns and callings of bluff, ambushes and quick-draw contests, "bumps" and the issuance of dares to cross lines that have been artificially drawn over international waters).[26] Surely, there are fundamental differences between the processes of using violence to manifest meanness on city streets and to dramatize resolute purposiveness in relations with foreign states. But we will not know just what the spiritual-emotional-moral differences are until we use a comprehensive theoretical approach to analyze and compare the varieties of criminal experience across the social order, including the uses of deceit by elites for conduct they experience as morally significant.

So it is appropriate to begin a study of the seductions of crime with cases of the use of torture by the American military to interrogate Vietnamese peasants and to close this phase of the study by suggesting that, in the late twentieth century, the great powers of the West find themselves in one dubious foreign, militarized situation after another—promoting wars they cannot win, achieving victories that bring them only the prize of emotional domestic support, and entering battles they would lose for winning—all because, at least in the immediate calculations, not to use violence would signal a loss of meaning in national history. Like the bad nigger who, refusing to be a "chump" like others of his humbled class and ethnicity, draws innocent blood to construct a more self-respecting career that leads predictably to prison confinement, the Western democracies, still seduced by the colonial myth of omnipotence, must again and again strike down thousands so that when the inevitable retreat comes, it will lead over masses of corpses toward "peace with honor." Perhaps in the end, what we find so repulsive about studying the reality of crime—the reason we so insistently refuse to look closely at how street criminals destroy others and bungle their way into confinement to save their sense of purposive control over their lives—is the piercing reflection we catch when we steady our glance at those evil men.

NOTES

Introduction

1. The two prominent exceptions in the sociology of deviance are Howard S. Becker, "Becoming a Marihuana User," *American Journal of Sociology* 59 (November 1953): 235–42; and David Matza, *Becoming Deviant* (Englewood Cliffs, N.J.: Prentice-Hall, 1969), built directly on Becker's interactionist perspective, turning it in a more phenomenological direction but making a cautiously narrow concrete application only to the marijuana "high." Although these works have been widely respected by a generation of academic researchers on deviance, fields of substantive study have not taken off from them. But a number of recent studies may indicate that this situation is finally changing. See, for example, Trevor Bennett and Richard Wright, *Burglars on Burglary* (Aldershot, Hampshire, England: Gower, 1984); and Malin Åkerström, *Crooks and Squares* (New Brunswick, N.J.: Transaction Books, 1985).

2. M. Merleau-Ponty, *Phenomenology of Perception,* trans. Colin Smith (London: Routledge & Kegan Paul, 1962).

3. An exemplary study is David Sudnow, *Ways of the Hand* (Cambridge, Mass.: Harvard University Press, 1978).

4. Compare Elaine Scarry, *The Body in Pain* (New York: Oxford University Press, 1985).

5. James William Gibson, *The Perfect War* (New York: Atlantic Monthly Press, 1986), p. 184.

6. Ibid., p. 185.

7. Ibid., pp. 205–6.

8. Ibid., p. 205.

9. Matza, *Becoming Deviant.*

10. William James treated religious ecstasy, even the "supernatural," as authentic. He would grant ontological authenticity to "multiple" worlds. See *The Varieties of Religious Experience* (Cambridge, Mass.: Harvard University Press, 1985); and *A Pluralistic Universe* (Cambridge, Mass.: Harvard University Press, 1977). Merleau-Ponty did not use existentialist understandings of inescapable human freedom to deny the authentic terror in a madman's haunted consciousness. See *Phenomenology of Perception,* p. 125.

11. For more on this line of argument, see Jack Katz, "A Theory of Qualitative Methodology," in *Contemporary Field Research,* ed. R. Emerson (Boston: Little, Brown, 1983), pp. 127–48.

Chapter 1. Righteous Slaughter

1. In some American jurisdictions, the modal homicide has been a killing conducted in the course of other criminal activities, particularly drug marketing. Ronald Heffernan, John M. Martin, and Anne T. Romano, "Homicides Related to Drug Trafficking," *Federal Probation* 46 (September 1982): 3–7. At other exceptional times, "gang warfare" or vendettas have accounted for the single greatest number of criminal killings. It is not possible to state exactly what percentage of officially labeled criminal homicides are righteous slaughters, since such detailed information is not available. However, on the basis of a variety of indicators presented throughout this chapter, it appears that the characterization to follow describes the single most numerous (modal) type of criminal homicide. Insofar as criminal homicide can be identified as a homogeneous experience, this is what, in most times and places, it most often has been. In any case, the validity of the current explanation is independent of the relative frequency of righteous slaughters compared with other forms of homicide.

2. Note that there is no question here of "getting into the offender's mind." The key evidentiary facts are what was said and done, in what order, and what was not said and not done. Neither the evidence nor the theoretical focus is on what is "in the mind" of the subject.

3. David F. Luckenbill, "Criminal Homicide as a Situated Transaction," *Social Problems* 25 (December 1977): 180.

4. Indeed, some would question Luckenbill's gratuitous interpretation that the infant's crying may have been a protest against soiled diapers. It is not clear that 5-week-old infants are as sensitive to cleanliness, or "messes," as are adults.

5. David Kaplun and Robert Reich, "The Murdered Child and His Killers," *American Journal of Psychiatry* 133, no. 7 (July 1976): 810. See also Marvin E. Wolfgang and Margaret A. Zahn, "Homicide: Behavioral Aspects," in *Encyclopedia of Crime and Justice,* ed. Sanford H. Kadish (New York: Free Press, 1983), 2:853. (But Philip J. Resnick, "Child Murder by Parents," *American Journal of Psychiatry* 126 [September 1969]: 328, found that fathers used striking, squeezing, and stabbing, and mothers used drowning, suffocation, and gassing.) That infanticide is typically an extension of routine disciplinary attacks is all the more striking, given the frequency of parental attempts to shoot and stab children. See Murray Straus, Richard J. Gelles, and Suzanne K. Steinmetz, *Behind Closed Doors* (Garden City, N.Y.: Doubleday Anchor Press, 1980), pp. 61–62. See also Murray Straus and Richard J. Gelles, "Societal Change and Change in Family Violence from 1975 to 1985 as Revealed by Two National Surveys," *Journal of Marriage and the Family* 48 (August 1986): 465–80.

6. Henry P. Lundsgaarde, *Murder in Space City* (New York: Oxford University Press, 1977), pp. 107–8. See also, from the first great qualitative sociological study in the United States, the case of Krupka murdering his wife. William I. Thomas and Florian Znaniecki, *The Polish Peasant in Europe and America* (New York: Dover, 1958), 2:1770–71.

7. The significance of her case in the evolution of the feminist movement is traced in Ann Jones, *Women Who Kill* (New York: Holt, Rinehart & Winston, 1980), pp. 281–95.

8. Peter D. Chimbos, *Marital Violence: A Study of Interspouse Homicide* (San Francisco: R & E Research Associates, 1978), p. 64.

9. Lundsgaarde, *Murder in Space City,* p. 61.

10. Ibid., pp. 109–10. For a similar incident, see Howard Harlan, "Five Hundred Homicides," *Journal of Criminal Law and Criminology* 40 (March–April 1950): 751 (data from Birmingham, Alabama, 1937–44).

11. Lundsgaarde, *Murder in Space City,* p. 111. For a similar incident, see Robert C. Bensing and Oliver Schroeder, Jr., *Homicide in an Urban Community* (Springfield, Ill.: Charles C Thomas, 1960), pp. 72–73 (data from Cleveland).

12. Chimbos, *Marital Violence,* p. 47.

13. Lundsgaarde, *Murder in Space City,* p. 65.

14. Ibid., p. 60. For a similar incident, see Harlan, "Five Hundred Homicides," 746.

15. See, for example, Bensing and Schroeder, *Homicide in an Urban Community,* p. 13, n. 2; Lynn A. Curtis, *Criminal Violence* (Lexington, Mass.: Lexington Books, 1974) (10 percent sample of police offense and arrest reports for 1967 for each of four major crimes in each of the seventeen large U.S. urban areas); and Marvin E. Wolfgang, *Patterns in Criminal Homicide* (Philadelphia: University of Pennsylvania Press, 1958), pp. 289–90 (data from Philadelphia, 1948–52).

16. About 30 percent in Luckenbill's study, "Criminal Homicide as a Situated Transaction." Quantified data on this question have rarely been collected, but widespread qualitative accounts support an impression of generality.

17. Wolfgang, *Patterns in Criminal Homicide,* p. 295.

18. Ibid.

19. Luckenbill, "Criminal Homicide as a Situated Transaction."

20. Richard B. Felson and Henry J. Steadman, "Situational Factors in Disputes Leading to Criminal Violence," *Criminology* 21 (February 1983): 72.

21. For an early formulation of the phenomenon and summaries of ten incidents that parallel those quoted here, see Marvin E. Wolfgang, "Victim-Precipitated Criminal Homicide," *Journal of Criminal Law, Criminology and Police Science* 48 (June 1957): 1–11. See also Curtis, *Criminal Violence,* table 5.1, p. 82; and Harwin L. Voss and John R. Hepburn, "Patterns in Criminal Homicide in Chicago," *Journal of Criminal Law, Criminology and Police Science* 59 (December 1968): 499–508.

22. "Some of the victims so goaded their killers either by provocation in words or deeds,

or by incessant nagging that they directly precipitated their own deaths." Terence Morris and Louis Blom-Cooper, *A Calendar of Murder* (London: Michael Joseph, 1964), p. 322.

23. See also John M. Macdonald, *Homicidal Threats* (Springfield, Ill.: Charles C Thomas, 1968). For a broader analysis of the victim's role in killings, see Edwin S. Shneidman, *Deaths of Man* (New York: Jason Aronson, 1983).

24. Luckenbill, "Criminal Homicide as a Situated Transaction." It should be noted, however, that Felson and Steadman, "Situational Factors," 72, claimed that the role of third parties may be exaggerated, since incidents in which no witnesses are present were likely to be excluded.

25. Wolfgang, *Patterns in Criminal Homicide,* pp. 120–33; Luckenbill, "Criminal Homicide as a Situated Transaction"; Voss and Hepburn, "Patterns in Criminal Homicide in Chicago"; and Roger Lane, *Violent Death in the City: Suicide, Accident and Murder in Nineteenth-century Philadelphia* (Cambridge, Mass.: Harvard University Press, 1979).

26. Wolfgang and Zahn, "Homicide: Behavioral Aspects," 2:852.

27. Wolfgang, *Patterns in Criminal Homicide,* pp. 204–14; Voss and Hepburn, "Patterns in Criminal Homicide in Chicago," 505; Richard Block, *Violent Crime* (Lexington, Mass.: Lexington Books, 1977), p. 497 (data from Chicago, 1965–73); Alex D. Pokorny, "A Comparison of Homicide in Two Cities," *Journal of Criminal Law, Criminology and Police Science* 56 (December 1965): 479–87 (data from Houston, 1958–61); and Curtis, *Criminal Violence.* Early in the century the Chicago police counted "Polish warfare" to be their typical murder. These were killings occurring outside of known family or friendship relations, which suggested an "apparently unmotivated and therefore incomprehensible and incalculable aggressiveness" thought to be "a special characteristic of the Poles." Thomas and Znaniecki, *Polish Peasant,* 2:1772.

28. Marvin E. Wolfgang, "The Relationship Between Alcohol and Criminal Homicide," *Quarterly Journal of Studies in Alcohol* 17 (September 1956): 411–25. For confirmation of Wolfgang's findings in other times and places, see David J. Pittman and William Handy, "Patterns in Criminal Aggravated Assault," *Journal of Criminal Law, Criminology and Police Science* 55 (December 1964): 462–70; Bensing and Schroeder, *Homicide in an Urban Community,* pp. 8, 9, 11; Pokorny, "Comparison of Homicide"; and Harlan, "Five Hundred Homicides," 742.

29. Wolfgang, "Alcohol and Criminal Homicides." See also Franklin E. Zimring, "Is Gun Control Likely to Reduce Violent Killings?" *University of Chicago Law Review* 35 (Summer 1968): 723. It should be noted that earlier studies indicated the presence of alcohol in a higher percentage of incidents than did later studies, a difference that may be explained by the introduction into routine police work of technically precise methods of establishing intoxication. Note also that the finding is phrased as the presence of liquor in the situation, not necessarily in the killer. Liquor more consistently indicates the casual nature of the setting than a chemical influence on the killer.

30. An assertion that the moment of homicidal rage is a "myth" appears in a polemical work directed against gun control. See James D. Wright, Peter H. Rossi, and Kathleen Daly, *Under the Gun: Weapons, Crime and Violence in America* (Chicago: Aldine, 1983), pp. 18–19. No evidence of the emotional character of homicidal behavior is cited; rather, the authors contest the inferences about emotions that others have drawn from statistics on the prior relationship of victim and killer. The intimacy and the legal significance of the emotional experience of homicide systematically block the acquisition of statistically representative, high-quality evidence on the issue. Thus, those who wish to limit their understanding of human experience to what may be documented according to statistical conventions might contest as a myth *any* characterization of the emotional dimension of homicide. Given the indications of qualitative accounts, it is not clear why any serious investigator of the phenomenon would want to do so, outside the context of policy debate or adversarial advocacy. Perhaps part of the confusion is due to the fact that although rage quickly transforms the sense of a situation, that may happen many times in a relationship. Gary Kleck and David J. Bordua, "The Assumptions of Gun Control," in *Firearms and Violence,* ed. Don B. Kates (San Francisco: Ballinger, 1984), pp. 42–43. As a Canadian study of spousal homicide noted, "The lethal act was rarely 'sudden, explosive and unexpected.' " Yet, in each of six cases detailed in this research there is an indication of rage in the form of a "heated argument" or a "bitter quarrel." See Chimbos, *Marital Violence,* pp. 62–67. Like sexual experience, violence in a relationship may occur repeatedly yet develop in passion each time.

31. Harold Garfinkel, "Conditions of Successful Degradation Ceremonies," *American Journal of Sociology* 61 (March 1956): 420–24.

32. Humus then goes back further to a root in *Homo sapiens.* Like shame, whose German root

refers to the pubic region, the history of "humiliation" points to a morally sensitive fertility as basic to man's nature. See Eric Partridge, *A Short Etymological Dictionary of Modern English,* 4th ed. (London: Routledge & Kegan Paul, 1966), pp. 292–93.

33. L. Frank Baum, *The Wonderful Wizard of Oz* (Berkeley: University of California Press, 1986), p. 149.

34. People recall, within their experiences of shame, a search for a "hole to crawl into! Let me just cover myself up and nobody can see me." The wish is not exactly to die, but to be in a place where one can exist safely. Janice Lindsay-Hartz, "The Structures of Experience of Shame and Guilt," *American Behavioral Scientist* 27 (July–August 1984): 692.

35. Lewis Carroll, *Alice's Adventures in Wonderland,* in *The Annotated Alice,* introduction and notes by Martin Gardner (New York: Bramwell House, 1960), p. 51.

36. Block, *Violent Crime,* p. 88. See also Felson and Steadman, "Situational Factors."

37. Pittman and Handy, "Patterns in Criminal Aggravated Assault," 462.

38. Fatality rates from single shots to the head or chest were found to be 16 percent for .22-caliber guns and 55 percent for .38-caliber guns, in Franklin E. Zimring, "The Medium Is the Message: Firearm Caliber as a Determinant of Death from Assault," *Journal of Legal Studies* 1 (January 1972): 92–124.

39. Chimbos, *Marital Violence,* p. 71.

40. Philip J. Cook, "The Role of Firearms in Violent Crime," in *Criminal Violence,* ed. Marvin E. Wolfgang and Neil Alan Weiner (Beverly Hills, Calif.: Sage Publications, 1982), p. 249.

41. Straus, Gelles, and Steinmetz, *Behind Closed Doors,* pp. 32, 34 (emphasis in original).

42. Zimring, "Gun Control," 721–37. Of course, the fact that so many die with one shot might be interpreted as evidence that there was in fact a specific intention to kill—therefore, once death occurred there was no need for further shots. But many of the gun deaths occur after and outside the scene of the shooting, and even when death occurs in the same scene, there is no evidence in the research literature, qualitative or quantitative, that the killers inspect their victims for signs of life.

43. Cook, "Role of Firearms," p. 249.

44. Lonnie H. Athens, *Violent Criminal Acts and Actors* (Boston, London, and Henley: Routledge & Kegan Paul, 1980), pp. 46, 48.

45. Chimbos, *Marital Violence,* p. 67.

46. Michel Foucault, *Discipline and Punish* (New York: Vintage, 1979).

47. M. Goldstein, "When Did You Stop Beating Your Wife?" *Newsday, Long Island Magazine,* September 18, 1977, pp. 9–10, as quoted in Straus, Gelles, and Steinmetz, *Behind Closed Doors,* pp. 98, 99.

48. Faith McNulty, *The Burning Bed* (New York: Harcourt Brace Jovanovich, 1980), p. 169.

49. Ralph LaRossa, *Conflict and Power in Marriage* (Beverly Hills, Calif.: Sage, 1977), as quoted in Straus, Gelles, and Steinmetz, *Behind Closed Doors,* p. 42.

50. Many such recollections are given in Athens, *Violent Criminal Acts and Actors.* See also Richard J. Gelles, *The Violent Home* (Beverly Hills, Calif.: Sage Publications, 1972), p. 192.

51. For a discussion of these findings, see Kleck and Bordua, "Assumptions of Gun Control," pp. 42–43.

52. Ronald K. Breedlove, John W. Kennish, Donald M. Sandker, and Robert K. Sawtell, "Domestic Violence and the Police: Kansas City," in Police Foundation, *Domestic Violence and the Police* (Washington, D.C.: National Institute of Justice, 1977), p. 23.

53. Athens, *Violent Criminal Acts and Actors,* pp. 37–38.

54. As quoted by Thomas Cottle, *Boston Sunday Globe,* November 6, 1977, in Straus, Gelles, and Steinmetz, *Behind Closed Doors,* pp. 36–37.

55. Athens, *Violent Criminal Acts and Actors,* pp. 31–32.

56. Ibid., pp. 33–34.

57. Felson and Steadman ("Situational Factors," 67, 72) found that one could predict what an offender would do, not from what he had done earlier in the incident, but only from the behavior of the other.

58. The interest of governments in grounding the metaphor of the state along socially recognized distinctions may have been more significant historically. Compare Paul Starr, "The Sociology of Official Statistics," in *The Politics of Numbers,* ed. William Alonso and Paul Starr (New York: Russell Sage Foundation, 1987), pp. 7–57.

59. By not discussing the results of this form of research, I do not mean to imply that the results have been consistent or widely convincing in the research community. For example, the widely appealing explanation that unemployment causes crime has repeatedly failed to

find support in the data that relate crime rates and unemployment levels across areas or over time. See the literature review in James Q. Wilson and Richard J. Herrnstein, *Crime and Human Nature* (New York: Simon & Schuster, 1985), p. 313; and David Cantor and Kenneth Land, "Unemployment and Crime Rates in the Post-World War II United States," *American Sociological Review* 50 (June 1985): 317–32; compare Elliott Currie, *Confronting Crime* (New York: Pantheon, 1985). Nor do I mean to imply that unemployment and underemployment are not related to violent crime. The point is that for those who would like to find the relationship, an alternative and unjustifiably neglected strategy is to start by working back from the phenomenon itself, the offender's experience of actually doing the crime, rather than beginning with data on the massive reality of unemployment and trying to manipulate them to demonstrate a relationship to an exceptional event like homicide.

60. For a chain of citations to the relevant literature, see Gwynn Nettler, *Killing One Another* (Cincinnati: Anderson, 1982), p. 27; and Marvin E. Wolfgang, ed., *Studies in Homicide* (New York: Harper & Row, 1967), pp. 5–6.

61. Police agencies do not record social-class data about offenders (income, occupational status, standard of living, education, and the like). On these issues, crime witnesses, when available, might not be reliable. The U.S. Bureau of the Census *does* record social-class-relevant data, repeatedly, across the nation, and in large numerical frequencies, but census data describe geographically bounded populations in general, not offenders specifically. Thus, studies that explore socioeconomic theories by relating crime to census data do so without knowing how many of those committing and not committing crimes are poor, unemployed, from the lower classes, uneducated, and so forth, much less how many of those committing and not committing crimes consider themselves poor, regard their job prospects as dim, or are aware of the degree of inequality in the social-class structure of their area.

62. Edward Green and Russell P. Wakefield, "Patterns of Middle and Upper Class Homicide," *Journal of Criminal Law and Criminology* 70 (Summer 1979): 177–78.

63. For a class-conscious account of the case, see Diana Trilling, *Mrs. Harris* (New York: Harcourt Brace Jovanovich, 1981).

64. Elijah Anderson, *A Place in the Corner* (Chicago: University of Chicago Press, 1978), pp. 1, 33, 35. About fifty-five men, aged 22 to over 70, frequented Jelly's during Anderson's fieldwork. Anderson noted that during the three years of his fieldwork, eight members of the group died, six from violence or crime, and others were wounded.

65. Curtis, *Criminal Violence,* pp. 32–34.

66. Robert M. O'Brien, "Exploring the Intersexual Nature of Violent Crimes," *Criminology* 26 (February 1988): 151–70.

67. Marvin E. Wolfgang, "Violence in the Family," in *Violence, Perspectives on Murder and Aggression,* ed. Irwin L. Kutash et al. (San Francisco: Jossey-Bass, 1978), pp. 238–53.

68. Or 38 percent of the spouse homicides in recent national data. See Murray A. Straus, "Domestic Violence and Homicide Antecedents," *Bulletin of the New York Academy of Medicine* 62 (June 1986): 448. In a survey of arrest records conducted in 1967 in seventeen large American cities, for homicides involving black spouses, "44 percent of the reported clearances were husband offender–wife victim and 56 percent wife offender–husband victim." Lynn A. Curtis, *Violence, Race and Crime* (Lexington, Mass.: Lexington Books, 1975), p. 58.

69. For an example of the dynamics, see Melvin R. Lansky, "Shame and Domestic Violence," in *The Many Faces of Shame,* ed. Donald L. Nathanson (New York: Guilford Press, 1987), pp. 335–62. For a study suggesting that patterns of status inequalities between mates might contribute to male violence against spouses, see John E. O'Brien, "Violence in Divorce Prone Families," *Journal of Marriage and the Family* 30 (November 1971): 692–98.

70. Angela Browne, *When Battered Women Kill* (New York: Free Press, 1987).

71. Ibid., p. 104.

72. See table 1.1. See also Wolfgang, *Patterns in Criminal Homicide;* and Ellen Rosenblatt and Cyril Greenland, "Female Crimes of Violence," *Canadian Journal of Criminology and Corrections* 16 (April 1974): 250–58.

73. Wolfgang, *Patterns in Criminal Homicide,* table 8, p. 368.

74. This provocative finding is much less firmly established than the other patterns relating gender to homicide. The frequently cited source is Wolfgang, *Patterns in Criminal Homicide,* p. 213. But Pokorny, "Comparison of Homicide," replicating Wolfgang's Philadelphia study in Houston, found these sites to be less frequent.

75. Jane Totman, *The Murderess: A Psychological Study of Criminal Homicide* (San Francisco: R & E Research Associates, 1978), pp. 49, 55.

76. Elaine Hilberman and Kit Munson, "Sixty Battered Women," *Victimology* 2 (1977): 460–71.

77. Browne, *When Battered Women Kill,* p. 81.

78. Ibid., pp. 138, 142, 154, 187. This pattern does not appear to be an artifact of Browne's methods. For an example from independent studies, see p. 34, n. 45 above ("Ruth" case), and Totman, *Murderess,* p. 57.

79. R. Emerson Dobash and Russell Dobash, *Violence Against Wives* (New York: Free Press, 1979), p. 144; and Mildred Daley Pagelow, *Family Violence* (New York: Praeger, 1984), p. 306. In some cases, an attack by the male on an innocent, defenseless third party—a pet or a child—appears to trigger the woman's switch from suffering to avenging martyr.

Chapter 2. Sneaky Thrills

1. In her study of some 4,600 shoplifters arrested by detectives in a Chicago department store, Mary Cameron found that all the female shoplifters who were arrested at age 10 were shoplifting in groups, but 85 percent of the 19-year-olds who were arrested had been alone. She concluded that shoplifting becomes progressively more a solitary activity with age. See Mary Cameron, *The Booster and the Snitch* (New York: Free Press, 1964), pp. 102–3.

2. John Allen, *Assault with a Deadly Weapon,* ed. Dianne Hall Kelly and Philip Heymann (New York: McGraw-Hill, 1978), p. 13.

3. Bracketed numbers link quotes to cases in a data set, "Autobiographical Accounts of Property Offenses by Youths, UCLA, 1983–1984," no. 8950, Inter-university Consortium for Political Social Research, Ann Arbor, Michigan. The accounts were volunteered by students in three offerings of my criminology class during 1983 and 1984. Because of the age range of the students and because no time limit was placed on the recollection, the events recounted cover acts by 7-year-olds and middle-aged office workers, with most falling within early adolescence.

4. Cameron (*Booster and Snitch,* p. 82) found that males and females shoplift in the same way as they shop. Males go in for particular items and commonly come out with just one new possession, which makes them harder to catch. Females more often "go shopping" when they shoplift, moving through the store to find items that will be especially appealing.

5. For an example of creative middle-class vandalism, see William J. Chambliss, "The Saints and the Roughnecks," *Society* 11 (November–December 1981): 24–31.

6. "Love-at-first-sight" consumer experiences may be a relatively recent phenomenon, or at least enhanced by the modern social structure of the department store. A student of shoplifting in England reports that "the post–Second World War invitation to shoppers to 'walk around without obligation' makes it very much easier for the shoplifter. Before this time it was never assumed that people entering a shop did not know what they wanted, or that they would leave without making a purchase, or would expect to be allowed to wander without supervision and intervention." D. P. Walsh, *Shoplifting* (London: Macmillan, 1978), p. 22. The supervision of a helpful attendant clerk not only makes sleight-of-hand more difficult, it interferes with the privacy that is so helpful in getting good romances started. Merchandisers' complaints about being burned by shoplifting usually neglect to mention their encouragement that consumers play with possessive passions.

7. L. B. Taylor, "Shoplifting: When Honest Ladies Steal," *Ladies Home Journal,* January 1982, pp. 88–89.

8. The seemingly confused metaphysics of the relationship between subject and object—over who is moving whom or what—may appear extraordinarily bizarre if we assume (as does virtually all contemporary social science) that people typically act on the world by first defining features outside themselves, then weighing alternatives and costs, and only then deciding what they will do. But the mutual determination of subject and object is typical of everyday life. To paraphrase both William James and Merleau-Ponty, we do not first see the tiger charging at us with bared teeth, then consider the implications and our alternatives, and only then come to the conclusion that we would be better off somewhere else; we perceive the tiger charging at us with our flying feet. It is not only emotionally turbulent adolescents who "confuse" their own desires with qualities and powers in their environment. We all do, and so consistently that it is not correct to label the phenomenon a "confusion."

9. It may be objected that both shoplifters and paying customers may experience store

goods as provocative, coquettish, enticing; as they play with their legally different projects, their objects play with them. But the process through which paying customers experience a seduction to purchase may also make essential use of the culture of deviance, albeit in wholly legal ways. Thus honest customers who purchase not in the practical attitude of satisfying wants defined before entering a store but in response to the suddenly encountered charms of objects often set up the seductive power of the goods they will buy by considering momentarily why they "really ought not" to pay the price. Consider also the little fuss that is so often made upon ordering desserts in restaurants, along the lines, "It would be sinful, but what the hell. . . ." The main course may be ordered without a sense that it is "irresistible," not because it is less desirable but because no moral injunction was placed in the way of ordering it.

10. See Howard S. Becker, "Becoming a Marihuana User," *American Journal of Sociology* 59 (November 1953): 235–42; and David Matza, *Becoming Deviant* (Englewood Cliffs, N.J.: Prentice-Hall, 1969), pp. 111–17.

11. In the context of opiates, sociologists have analyzed the onset of "addiction" as the subject's acknowledgment of a "craving," which refers to an internal state. See Alfred Lindesmith, *Opiate Addiction* (Bloomington, Ind.: Principia Press, 1947). But the addict's experience is also of an external force, the power of a thing to which he is drawn toward. Thus, in some firsthand accounts, opiate addiction is described with strong romantic imagery; heroin, for example, is a "lady" that seduces its addict-lover. See the poetic account in Richard P. Rettig, Manual J. Torres, and Gerald R. Garrett, *Manny: A Criminal Addict's Story* (Boston: Houghton Mifflin, 1977), p. 52.

12. On the raising of normal appearances to a problematic level in the process of becoming deviant, see Matza, *Becoming Deviant.*

13. Cameron, *Booster and Snitch,* p. 163. Cameron's useful study of shoplifting was based on data files created by department-store detectives after they had arrested the suspects. Those who were arrested were usually so upset on the few occasions when Cameron was present, she found it impossible to obtain a reconstruction of the event from the suspect's perspective.

14. Ibid., pp. 102, 106.

15. Ibid.

16. And perhaps other metaphors as well. There is also the memorable encouragement from the sixties, "Shoplifting gets you high!" Jerry Rubin, *Do It!* (New York: Simon & Schuster, 1970), p. 122.

17. The following discussion was inspired by Arthur Allen Leff, "Law And," *Yale Law Journal* 87 (April 1978): 989–1011.

18. Elliott Leyton, "The Myth of Delinquency," *New Society* 22 (March 1984): 440.

19. Taylor, "Shoplifting."

20. Cameron, *Booster and Snitch,* pp. 79–80. In my reports, as in other studies of adolescent property offenses, females are disproportionately described as shoplifters and males as vandals. Under the influence of the then-prevailing Parsonian framework, analyzing data from Boston courts in the 1940s, George H. Grosser ("Juvenile Delinquency and Contemporary Sex Roles" [Ph.D. diss., Harvard University, 1951]) distinguished the female pattern as "role supportive" and the male pattern as "role expressive." But see Pamela Richards, "Middle-Class Vandalism and Age-Status Conflict," *Social Problems* 26 (April 1979): 490–91: "Junior high school girls are *more* likely than are junior high school boys to report the defacement of schools."

21. Jack Katz, "Essences as Moral Identities," *American Journal of Sociology* 80 (May 1975): 1369–90.

22. Cf. the manifold consequences for deviant self-conception of Bernard's theft of a suitcase in André Gide, *The Counterfeiters* (New York: Modern Library, 1955).

23. Goldilocks tries, but she cannot take the place of the infant nor that of either parent. Her struggle is the child's dilemma between infancy and adulthood, a struggle that becomes extended and intensified in adolescence. See Bruno Bettelheim, *The Uses of Enchantment* (New York: Alfred A. Knopf, 1977). The fable is, in several respects, also an instructive metaphor for understanding adolescent sneak theft. The listener has an unusually ambivalent emotional relationship to the heroine in that Goldilocks is not morally pure; in effect, she vandalizes and burglarizes the bears' home. There is a related and equally unusual tension in the story. That is, Goldilocks does not worry; she eats and goes to sleep, while the listener remains apprehensive about the bears' return. The question that animates the listener's anxiety is not

precisely the same as in Little Red Riding Hood or Hansel and Gretel—Will the good little ones get away?—but has to do with anxiety about the thief: Will she get away with it?

24. Alfred Schutz, *Collected Papers* (The Hague: Martinus Nijhoff, 1962), 1:207–59.

25. As Erikson noted: "The growing and developing youths, faced with [the] physiological revolution within them, and with tangible adult tasks ahead of them are now primarily concerned with what they appear to be in the eyes of others as compared with what they feel they are." See Erik H. Erikson, *Childhood and Society*, 2nd rev. ed. (New York: W. W. Norton, 1963), p. 261.

26. Self reports of 1,189 high school students described a progressive decline in shoplifting, with the peak age coming before 10 and the decline continuing throughout the four high school years, in Lloyd W. Klemke, "Exploring Juvenile Shoplifting," *Sociology and Social Research* 67 (1982): 59–75.

27. Cameron, *Booster and Snitch*, pp. 124–25.

28. See the literature on employee theft, particularly on "fiddling" in Great Britain: Jason Ditton, *Part-Time Crime: An Ethnography of Fiddling and Pilferage* (London: Macmillan, 1977); and Gerald Mars, *Cheats at Work* (London: George Allen & Unwin, 1982).

29. Donald Cressey, "The Criminal Violation of Financial Trust," *American Sociological Review* 15 (December 1950): 738–43. Embarrassing needs, characterized as a "non-sharable financial problem," figured prominently in Cressey's theory of embezzlement.

30. The best available glimpse in the literature is interspersed throughout Ken Mann, *Defending White Collar Crime* (New Haven: Yale University Press, 1985).

31. See also Pamela Richards, Richard A. Berk, and Brenda Forster, *Crime as Play* (Cambridge, Mass.: Ballinger, 1979), a study of about 3,000 middle-class, suburban public school children in the fifth through the twelfth grades.

32. See W. Gordon West, "The Short Term Careers of Serious Thieves," *Canadian Journal of Criminology* 20 (April 1978): 169–90; Mercer L. Sullivan, "Youth Crime: New York's Two Varieties," *New York Affairs* 8 (1983): 31–48; and Terry M. Williams and William Kornblum, *Growing Up Poor* (Lexington, Mass.: Lexington Books, 1985), esp. pp. 52–55. For unique quantitative evidence of social-class differences in persistent delinquency, see Marvin E. Wolfgang, R. Figlio, and T. Sellin, *Delinquency in a Birth Cohort* (Chicago: University of Chicago Press, 1972), pp. 245–48; and Marvin E. Wolfgang, Terence P. Thornberry, and Robert Figlio, *From Boy to Man, From Delinquency to Crime* (Chicago: University of Chicago Press, 1987).

33. Although the need to study the experience of "hedonism" involved in vandalism has been recognized of late, no deep research has as yet been conducted. See V. L. Allen, "Toward an Understanding of the Hedonic Component of Vandalism," in *Vandalism*, ed. Claude Levy-Leboyer (New York: Elsevier North-Holland, 1984).

34. Barry Krisberg, *The Gang and the Community* (San Francisco: R & E Research Associates, 1975), p. 12. See also, Francis A. J. Ianni, *Black Mafia* (New York: Simon & Schuster, 1974); Frederic Thrasher, *The Gang* (Chicago: University of Chicago Press, 1963), pp. 200–202; and Clifford Shaw, "Juvenile Delinquency: A Group Tradition," in *Gang Delinquency and Delinquent Subcultures*, ed. James F. Short, Jr. (New York: Harper & Row, 1968), pp. 82–92.

35. Within local understandings, excessive parental generosity in providing children with spending money was understood to be causally significant. See K. S. Shukla, *Adolescent Thieves: A Study in Socio-Cultural Dynamics* (Delhi, India: Leeladevi Publications, 1979).

36. West, "Short Term Careers."

37. Sullivan ("Youth Crime") also studied white working-class youths.

Chapter 3. Ways of the Badass

1. The differences between the three stages are not on a scale of symbolism versus real action. A physical fight can be nothing more than a show of toughness, while a stare-down can accomplish a consummate act of meanness.

2. As Werthman noted, "Not all black leather jackets communicate the same quality of 'toughness.' . . . One almost has to be committed to a fashion in order to read the nuances of self-image that can be expressed within it." See Carl Werthman, "Delinquency and Authority" (master's thesis, University of California at Berkeley, 1964), p. 118.

3. If these terms seem abstract for the realities of street life, consider the following dialogue

between two Puerto Rican women who were members of a Brooklyn street gang and became uncomfortable with the tough image they embraced in their early adolescent years.

[WEEZA:] We ain't really tough. We don't consider ourselves tough—not me.
[BOOBY:] Because we try to communicate with people. But when they don't want to communicate with us, then that's their problem, not ours.

Anne Campbell, *The Girls in the Gang* (Oxford: Basil Blackwell, 1984), p. 155.

4. For a treatment of such interactions, see Erving Goffman, *Relations in Public* (New York: Harper & Row, 1971), pp. 75–77, 81. For an analysis of "How are you?" as a "greeting substitute," see Harvey Sacks, "Everyone Has to Lie," in *Sociocultural Dimensions of Language Use,* ed. Mary Sanches and Ben Blount (New York: Academic Press, 1975), pp. 57–79.

5. See Harlan Ellison, *Memos from Purgatory* (New York: Berkley, 1983).

6. Gus Frias, *Barrio Warriors: Homeboys of Peace* (n.p.: Diaz Publications, 1982), p. 21.

7. As ethnographic observers have emphasized, toughness, as opposed to socially sensitive, deferential civility, is hardly a constant feature of Mexican-American adolescent society. In the street gangs of Chicago, Horowitz noted, "Most [of these] young men have conventional social skills"; they take a woman's arm when crossing the street and walk on the curb side, skillfully order dinner in a restaurant, and shake hands and make polite conversation when introduced to a stranger. See Ruth Horowitz, *Honor and the American Dream* (New Brunswick, N.J.: Rutgers University Press, 1983), pp. 86–87. The point is that toughness is a contingent social production.

8. R. Lincoln Keiser, *The Vice Lords* (New York: Holt, Rinehart & Winston, 1979), pp. 43–44.

9. On the last point, comments by my colleague, Emanuel Schegloff, were helpful.

10. Werthman, "Delinquency and Authority," p. 88.

11. James Patrick, *A Glasgow Gang Observed* (London: Eyre Methuen, 1973), p. 69.

12. John Allen, *Assault with a Deadly Weapon,* ed. Dianne Hall Kelly and Philip Heymann (New York: McGraw-Hill, 1978), pp. 19, 22–23.

13. Frias, *Barrio Warriors,* p. 19.

14. My thanks here to Paul Price, a sociology graduate student and a staff member in a Los Angeles home for delinquent boys.

15. Patrick, *Glasgow Gang Observed,* p. 83.

16. Florence Rome, *The Tattooed Men* (New York: Delacorte Press, 1975).

17. Allen, *Assault with a Deadly Weapon,* p. 23.

18. Patrick, *Glasgow Gang Observed,* pp. 32, 33.

19. Allen, *Assault with a Deadly Weapon.*

20. See, for example, the photographs of the Maravillos of the 1940s and 1980s, in Frias, *Barrio Warriors,* p. 16.

21. Descriptions of dress and walk are available in Frias, *Barrio Warriors;* Alfredo Guerra Gonzalez, "Mexicano/Chicano Gangs in Los Angeles: A Sociohistorical Case Study" (Ph.D. diss., School of Social Welfare, University of California at Berkeley, 1981); Carlos Manuel Haro, "An Ethnographic Study of Truant and Low Achieving Chicano Barrio Youth in the High School Setting" (Ph.D. diss., School of Education, University of California at Los Angeles, 1976); and Hilary McGuire, *Hopie and the Los Homes Gang* (Canfield, Ohio: Alba House, 1979).

22. Gusmano Cesaretti, *Street Writers: A Guided Tour of Chicano Graffiti* (Los Angeles: Acrobat Books, 1975), p. 8.

23. Jerry Romotsky and Sally R. Romotsky, *Los Angeles Barrio Calligraphy* (Los Angeles: Dawson's Book Shop, 1976), pp. 23–24, 29, 32–33.

24. See, for example, the laughing skull in Cesaretti, *Street Writers,* and in Romotsky and Romotsky, *Los Angeles Barrio Calligraphy,* pp. 58–59.

25. George Carpenter Barker, *Pachuco* (Tucson: University of Arizona Social Science Bulletin, no. 18, 1958).

26. Frias, *Barrio Warriors,* p. 23; and Haro, "Truant and Low Achieving Chicano Barrio Youth," p. 363.

27. Dick Hebdige, *Subculture: The Meaning of Style* (London: Methuen, 1979), p. 65.

28. Ibid., p. 110.

29. Sandy Craig and Chris Schwarz, *Down and Out: Orwell's Paris and London Revisited* (London: Penguin Books, 1984), p. 107.

30. Hunter Thompson, *Hell's Angels* (New York: Ballantine Books, 1967), p. 253.

31. Harold Finestone, "Cats, Kicks, and Color," in *The Other Side*, ed. Howard S. Becker (New York: Free Press, 1964), pp. 281–97.

32. By the 1970s in New York ghettos, being "cool" had been around for decades and had apparently lost some of its force. It was replaced by "too cool" as a superlative in the adolescent lexicon. See Campbell, *Girls in the Gang*, p. 183. Now "chill out" is popular.

33. Allen, *Assault with a Deadly Weapon*, pp. 199–200.

34. Admiration for the "killer" is reported in David Dawley, *A Nation of Lords: The Autobiography of the Vice Lords* (Garden City, N.Y.: Doubleday Anchor Press, 1973), p. 32.

35. Frias, *Barrio Warriors*, p. 45.

36. Being a badass is not a status obtained in a fatefully violent moment and guaranteed for life. Like other charismatic figures, the badass is subject to the double challenge: (1) that he must always be open to challenge—there is no time off for the badass, no vacation from this occupation, which is indeed a vocation; and (2) that he must never fail any challenge. Cf. Max Weber, *Economy and Society* (New York: Bedminster Press, 1968), 3: 1112–13.

37. Patrick, *Glasgow Gang Observed*, p. 49.

38. Pat Doyle et al., *The Paint House: Words from an East End Gang* (Harmondsworth, England: Penguin Books, 1972), p. 31.

39. Richard P. Rettig, Manual J. Torres, and Gerald R. Garrett, *Manny: A Criminal Addict's Story* (Boston: Houghton Mifflin, 1977), p. 19.

40. Barry Alan Krisberg, *The Gang and the Community* (San Francisco: R & E Research Associates, 1975), p. 15.

41. Ibid.

42. Ibid., p. 24.

43. Keiser, *Vice Lords*, p. 18.

44. Doyle et al., *Paint House*, p. 23.

45. Campbell, *Girls in the Gang*, p. 164.

46. Patrick, *Glasgow Gang Observed*, p. 43.

47. Ellison, *Memos from Purgatory*, p. 86.

48. Keiser, *Vice Lords*, p. 35.

49. Craig Castleman, *Getting Up: Subway Graffiti in New York* (Cambridge, Mass.: MIT Press, 1982), p. 93.

50. Patrick, *Glasgow Gang Observed*, p. 77.

51. Doyle et al., *Paint House*, pp. 28, 30.

52. Ellison, *Memos from Purgatory*, pp. 58, 61. Note that the evidence is of a "primer," not of a pattern of violence.

53. Krisberg, *Gang and Community*, p. 14.

54. William Gale, *The Compound* (New York: Rawson Associates, 1977).

55. Horowitz, *Honor and the American Dream*, p. 92.

56. Ellison, *Memos from Purgatory*, pp. 48, 60, 61.

57. Cf. Ellison's account of his practice before a mirror with a twelve-inch Italian stiletto in ibid.

58. Keiser, *Vice Lords*, p. 62.

59. Patrick, *Glasgow Gang Observed*, pp. 54, 56.

60. Cesaretti, *Street Writers*, p. 57.

61. Patrick, *Glasgow Gang Observed*, pp. 52–53.

62. No doubt in some erotic uses, the "bad" quality of "fuck you" is deemed delicious. As many a wag has noted, "fuck" is an especially versatile condiment in courses of conversations. An anonymous list, provided to me by an engineer who found it circulating in a local metal-coating plant, includes "positive" uses, as in "Mary is fucking beautiful"; inquisitive uses, as in "What the fuck?"; and ad hoc, sometimes ambiguous enhancements of emphasis, as in "It's fucking five-thirty." "Fuck" draws attentions beyond civility, and it is therefore widely attractive as a means by which a speaker suggests he has more passion or a more idiosyncratic feeling about a matter than convention will allow him to express. Our concern here is to grasp the specifically hostile and threatening forms, the "bad" power that the phrase can achieve.

63. Rettig, Torres, and Garrett, *Manny*, p. 18.

64. Patrick, *Glasgow Gang Observed*, p. 54.

65. See also ibid., p. 32. At a dance hall, Pat pushed his way onto the floor and bumped into three big guys who said, "Who the fuck are you pushin'?" Pat responded with "Ah'm pushin' you, thug face," whereupon fists began to fly, this time to Pat's great disadvantage.

66. Lewis Yablonsky, *The Violent Gang* (Baltimore: Penguin Books, 1966), pp. 202–3.

67. Keiser, *Vice Lords,* pp. 44, 45. See also Robert Lejeune, "The Management of a Mugging," *Urban Life* 6 (July 1977): 123–48.

Chapter 4. Street Elites

1. For a recent effort to estimate the proportion of gang homicides that might fit this description, see Cheryl L. Maxson, Margaret A. Gordon, and Malcolm W. Klein, "Differences Between Gang and Nongang Homicides," *Criminology* 23 (May 1985): 209–22.

2. R. Lincoln Keiser, *The Vice Lords* (New York: Holt, Rinehart & Winston, 1979), p. 51.

3. Bill Jersey and Jim Belson, producers, *Children of Violence,* documentary film (Berkeley, Calif.: Catticus Corp., 1982). According to Jim Belson, whom I interviewed in April 1987, this film, to which I refer several times in this chapter, began in the summer of 1981 and extended for a year. Belson used *cinema verité* and ethnographic methods, becoming friendly with members of the group and frequently sleeping at the family home of the leading member. See also Terrence A. Sweeney, S.J., *Streets of Anger, Streets of Hope* (Glendale, Calif.: Great Western Publishing Co., 1980), pp. 49, 52, 67.

4. Frederick Thrasher, *The Gang: A Study of 1313 Gangs in Chicago* (Chicago: University of Chicago Press, 1927).

5. See James Patrick, *A Glasgow Gang Observed* (London: Eyre Methuen, 1973), p. 21; Carlos Manuel Haro, "An Ethnographic Study of Truant and Low Achieving Chicano Barrio Youth in the High School Setting" (Ph.D. diss., School of Education, University of California at Los Angeles, 1976), pp. 171, 370–72; Ruth Horowitz, *Honor and the American Dream* (New Brunswick, N.J.: Rutgers University Press, 1983), p. 237; Anne Campbell, *The Girls in the Gang* (Oxford: Basil Blackwell, 1984), p. 145; Irving Spergel, *Racketville, Slumtown, Haulburg* (Chicago: University of Chicago Press, 1964), p. 64; Gerald Suttles, *The Social Order of the Slum* (Chicago: University of Chicago Press, 1968), p. 27, n. 18; Pat Doyle et al., *The Paint House: Words from an East End Gang* (Harmondsworth, England: Penguin Books, 1972); and R. T. Sale, *The Blackstone Rangers* (New York: Popular Library, 1971), p. 68.

6. A report that summarized the views of social workers assigned to maintain field contact with New York's "conflict gangs" of the 1950s attributed resistance to the gang label to a reluctance to identify with adult criminals. Given that the book noted that one of three recurrent, self-generated nomenclatures for adolescent conflict groups is unqualifiedly evil, (giving as examples Hoods, Killers, Daggers), this attribution is an extraordinary indication of how strongly willed was the effort to distort theory so as not to acknowledge direct observations of the phenomena at hand. See *Reaching the Fighting Gang* (New York: New York City Youth Board, 1960), pp. 22, 43.

7. But see Herbert A. Bloch and Arthur Niederhoffer, *The Gang* (New York: Philosophical Library, 1958), pp. 7–10, the themes of which might have been more effectively developed had the work been composed after the dramatic growth in the forms of ethnic-majority, middle-class collective deviance in the 1960s and 1970s.

8. Most notably, Miller's identification of the "focal concerns" of lower-class and gang culture—trouble, toughness, smartness, excitement, fate, and autonomy—does not clearly set low-income adolescents apart from various white middle-class adolescent forms of deviance. See Walter B. Miller, "Lower-class Culture as a Generating Milieu of Gang Delinquency," *Journal of Social Issues* 14 (Fall 1958): 5–19. Research into the more institutionally protected domains of middle-class youths reveals similar "focal concerns," especially in the peer-prestigious college fraternities. See Stuart L. Hills, "Crime and Deviance on a College Campus," *Humanity and Society* 6 (August 1982): 257–66.

9. Considering all causes of death for males aged 15–19, the mortality rate for whites is slightly higher than that for blacks. Teenage white males die from motor vehicle accidents at about three times the rate for their black counterparts. Teenage black males die from "homicide and legal intervention" at almost five times the rate for their white counterparts. See *Vital Statistics of the United States, 1981,* vol. 2, *Mortality,* part A (Hyattsville, Md.: National Center for Health Statistics, 1986), table 1-8, "Death Rates for 72 Selected Causes by 5-year Age Groups, Race and Sex: United States, 1981," p. 32.

10. For a description, see Gary Schwartz, Paul Turner, and Emil Peluso, "Neither Heads nor Freaks," *Urban Life* 2 (October 1973): 288–313.

11. Recent research on Mexican-American fighting groups has clarified that while a reference to territory is fundamental to conflict, actual residence in the homeland is not: "Almost every *klika* has some fictive residents and occasionally a majority of the members live outside the *barrio.*" See Joan Moore, Diego Vigil, and Robert Garcia, "Residence and Territoriality in Chicano Gangs," *Social Problems* 31 (December 1983): 186. These findings highlight the artificial, socially constructed character of deeply felt affiliation with local territory.

12. Cf. Fred Davis, *On Youth Subcultures: The Hippie Variant* (New York: General Learning Press, 1971).

13. In the mid-1970s, Miller surveyed local informants across the nation for a reading on the state of the "gang" problem. He noted the persistence of enemy pairs. Also, despite publicized claims that victims of "gang" violence had become predominately adult in the 1970s, he found reconfirmation of his Boston area results in the 1960s, that 60 percent of the reported victims were gang members and another 12 percent were nongang peers. See Walter B. Miller, *Violence by Youth Gangs and Youth Groups as a Crime Problem in Major American Cities* (Washington, D.C.: U.S. Government Printing Office, 1975), pp. 38, 40, 43.

14. See, for example, the Saints in William J. Chambliss, "The Saints and the Roughnecks," *Society* 11 (November–December 1981): 24–31. See also the absence of intergroup conflict in Dale Hardman, "Small Town Gangs," *Journal of Criminal Law, Criminology and Police Science* 60 (June 1969): 173–81.

15. See Spergel, *Racketville, Slumtown, Haulburg.* Ghetto youths are well aware of alternative nomenclature that would convey no presumption of elite status. Professional sports teams have proliferated in recent history, and while there are examples of names also favored by youth groups in the ghetto, athletic teams tap into many classification orders that have no apparent appeal to ghetto adolescents: industry-related names (Steelers, Packers, Oilers, Pistons); cute but not particularly powerful species of animals (Orioles, Cardinals, Cubs, Dolphins); innocuous features of the natural world (Lakers, Islanders, Maple Leafs). Rock bands emerge far faster than do ghetto fighting groups, and each new band needs a new collective name. In the early days when rock and roll was "bad," black street groups and black rock groups often operated under similar symbols, for example, (Little Anthony and) the Imperials, (the Five) Satins, the Supremes (before they were Diana Ross and the . . .). But only a few of the music group names proved appealing to the street groups (not the Penguins, the Flamingos, or the Miracles); and those that worked on the street tended to be classy (like satin) or regally dominant (for example, imperial).

16. Sherry Cavan, *Hippies of the Haight* (St. Louis: New Critics Press, 1972).

17. Sandy Craig and Chris Schwarz, *Down and Out: Orwell's Paris and London Revisited* (London: Penguin Books, 1984). On the United States, see Kathryn Joan Fox, "Real Punks and Pretenders," *Urban Life* 16 (October 1987): 344–70.

18. Sale, *Blackstone Rangers,* p. 95.

19. See Francisco Ramirez Chavez, "The Impact of a Chicano Gang on an Alternative School in Orange County, California" (master's thesis, University of California at Irvine, 1982), p. 118.

20. Patrick, *Glasgow Gang Observed,* p. 61.

21. For a study of an upper-middle-class, Irish Catholic youth "gang" in a suburb of Chicago in the early 1960s, see Andrew Greeley and James Casey, "An Upper Middle Class Deviant Gang," *American Catholic Sociological Review* 24 (Spring 1963): 33–41. For a rare study of adolescent groups with high levels of criminal activity in a rural, small university town, see Hardman, "Small Town Gangs," 174.

22. Richard P. Rettig, Manual J. Torres, and Gerald R. Garrett, *Manny: A Criminal Addict's Story* (Boston: Houghton Mifflin, 1977), pp. 22, 25; and David Dawley, *A Nation of Lords: The Autobiography of the Vice Lords* (Garden City, N.Y.: Doubleday Anchor Press, 1973), p. 34. On the indifference of "gangs" to an obvious, effective, spying police presence, see William Gale, *The Compound* (New York: Rawson Associates, 1977). A police officer working in South Brooklyn describes an ironic relationship in which the fascination of street youths with police attentions works decidedly to their practical detriment.

I work with some very aggressive individuals. I have two roles: I am their friend, but also their foe. Sometimes I don't understand why they even talk to me, because I personally am responsible for many of them being locked up. When anything happens as far as crime is concerned in the East New York area, and the Sexboys are mentioned, whatever the unit—be it the Homicide Squad, the Robbery Squad or the Rape Squad—they always come to me, to help them bring whoever it is, or whoever they think it is, into the office.

John Galea, "Youth Gangs of New York," in *Aggression and Violence,* ed. Peter Marsh and Anne Campbell (Oxford: Basil Blackwell, 1982), pp. 223–24.

23. Perhaps the most famous case involved the Blackstone Rangers. See Sale, *Blackstone Rangers.*

24. See Horowitz, *Honor and the American Dream.* The documentary film *Children of Violence* shows young men at different moments building bulging muscles, sporting on their clothes images of vampires enjoying a blood feast, and singing of their love for their mothers in soft falsetto voices.

25. Gene Muehlbauer and Laura Dodder, *The Losers* (New York: Praeger, 1983).

26. Ibid., p. 75.

27. Craig and Schwarz, *Down and Out,* pp. 21–22.

28. Keiser, *Vice Lords,* pp. 3, 5.

29. Horowitz, *Honor and the American Dream,* p. 34.

30. Dick Hebdige, *Subculture: The Meaning of Style* (London: Methuen, 1979), pp. 33–35.

31. Jerry Romotsky and Sally R. Romotsky, *Los Angeles Barrio Calligraphy* (Los Angeles: Dawson's Book Shop, 1976), pp. 45–46.

32. Gusmano Cesaretti, *Street Writers: A Guided Tour of Chicano Graffiti* (Los Angeles, Acrobat Books, 1975), unpaginated, at about p. 63. The most artful and less violent regions of ghetto adolescent deviant culture suggest analogies to attractive features of eighteenth-century Enlightenment society. Thus, in the early 1970s, subway graffiti writers from around New York City would gather in the style of the café society at a number of "salons." A particularly well-known "salon" was a doughnut shop across from DeWitt Clinton High School in the Bronx. There they would share greetings, information on where materials might be available, and accounts of adventures with the police while "getting up." Sketches for graffiti would be compared, and novices would seek stylized autographs and advice on craftsmanship from "writers" whose images and tags had brought them fame around the city. Then a group would head off for a session of viewing and commentary at 149th Street and the Grand Concourse, "an ideal spot from which to watch the trains because it is a point of convergence for the 2, 4, and 5 lines of the IRT." See Craig Castleman, *Getting Up: Subway Graffiti in New York* (Cambridge, Mass.: MIT Press, 1982), p. 85.

33. Keiser, *Vice Lords,* p. 49.

34. See Patrick, *Glasgow Gang Observed,* pp. 84–87.

35. Gus Frias, *Barrio Warriors: Homeboys of Peace* (n.p.: Diaz Publications, 1982), pp. 75–77.

36. Bloch and Niederhoffer, *The Gang,* p. 100.

37. Suttles, *Social Order of the Slum,* p. 158.

38. Harlan Ellison, *Memos from Purgatory* (New York: Berkley, 1983), p. 63.

39. Doyle et al., *Paint House,* p. 35.

40. Patrick, *Glasgow Gang Observed,* p. 136.

41. Malcolm W. Klein, *Street Gangs and Street Workers* (Englewood Cliffs, N.J.: Prentice-Hall, 1971), p. 77.

42. Campbell, *Girls in the Gang,* p. 266.

43. See the informant's description in Hilary McGuire, *Hopie and the Los Homes Gang* (Canfield, Ohio: Alba House, 1979), p. 67.

44. Suttles, *Social Order of the Slum,* p. 68.

45. Horowitz, *Honor and the American Dream,* p. 79.

46. Keiser, *Vice Lords,* p. 6. See also Barry Allan Krisberg, *The Gang and the Community* (San Francisco: R & E Research Associates, 1975), p. 62; and Suttles, *Social Order of the Slum,* pp. 31–32.

47. Frias, *Barrio Warriors,* p. 17, has a useful chart of age subdivisions in various East Los Angeles barrios. See also Moore, Vigil, and Garcia, "Residence and Territoriality," 187.

48. Although Miller found that violence is central to the culture and spirit of the group but not to its practices (see Walter B. Miller, "Violent Crimes in City Gangs," *Annals of the American Academy of Political and Social Sciences* 364 [March 1966]: 96–112), he noted, in another report, that from 1972 to 1977, there were one thousand gang-related killings in the six largest gang cities. See Walter B. Miller, "Gangs, Groups, and Serious Youth Crime," in *Critical Issues in Juvenile Delinquency,* ed. David Shichor and Delos H. Kelly (Lexington, Mass: Lexington Books, 1980), pp. 115–39.

49. On the limited geographic mobility of members of street elites in New York City in the 1950s, see Bloch and Niederhoffer, *The Gang*, pp. 6–7; in Philadelphia in the 1960s, see Krisberg, *Gang and Community*; and in New York City in the early 1970s, see Campbell, *Girls in the Gang*, p. 236.

50. Note that this perspective is inconsistent with the cliché, sometimes boasted by members and often imputed by observers, that the ways of gangs are rites that pass members from the status of boy to man.

51. In this respect, my argument takes off from Thrasher's original appreciation of gangs as natural outgrowths of the social organization of childhood. See, Thrasher, *The Gang*.

52. John Edgar Wideman, *Brothers and Keepers* (New York: Holt, Rinehart & Winston, 1984), pp. 10–11.

53. Chavez, "Impact of a Chicano Gang," p. 66.

54. Mary Pardo, "Dress, Social Control and Chicano Cliques in an E.L.A. High School" (unpublished manuscript, Department of Sociology, University of California at Los Angeles, 1983).

55. Castleman, *Getting Up*, p. 78.

56. Doyle et al., *Paint House*, p. 122.

57. Rettig, Torres, and Garrett, *Manny*, pp. 27, 28.

58. Campbell, *Girls in the Gang*, p. 164.

59. Sweeney, *Streets of Anger*, p. 79.

60. Keiser, *Vice Lords*, p. 61. See also Dawley, *Nation of Lords*, p. 75, where the person referred to as "the fool, Wine" in Keiser is described as "Chester (The Fool) Solomon."

61. Chavez, "Impact of a Chicano Gang," p. 73.

62. McGuire, *Hopie*, pp. 123–27.

63. Ellison, *Memos from Purgatory*, p. 89.

64. Sale, *Blackstone Rangers*, p. 7.

65. There is a parallel between the dressing of street gangs in military metaphors and the adornment of the military body with signs associated with street gangs or elite clubs (green berets, ferocious tattoos, strikingly colored cords, and bandanas). Just who in this overlap of symbolic worlds is influencing whom, and the balancing of good and evil themes in each world, deserves study. For a preliminary note, it appears that military recruits more often come from the ranks of street gangs, sometimes through judicially defined alternatives to conviction, than vice versa.

66. Keiser, *Vice Lords*, p. 68.

67. Various cross-generational continuities are noted in Haro, "Truant and Low Achieving Chicano Barrio Youth," pp. 152–53; and Chavez, "Impact of a Chicano Gang," pp. 117–18. For autobiographical information, I thank Rueben Aguilera.

68. Dawley, *Nation of Lords*, pp. 24–25.

69. Patrick, *Glasgow Gang Observed*, p. 30.

70. Gale, *The Compound*, p. 17.

71. Krisberg, *Gang and Community*, p. 81, quoted from a gang member: "The police got a file a mile long on us. Go to court and if they know you're from our corner, they automatically send you away. They know we're bad, man, mean motherfuckers."

72. Thrasher, *The Gang*, p. 193.

73. *Reaching the Fighting Gang*, p. 43.

74. Gary Hoenig, *Reaper: The Story of a Gang Leader* (Indianapolis: Bobbs-Merrill, 1975), p. 146.

75. Suttles, *Social Order of the Slum*, p. 115, n. 27.

76. Dawley, *Nation of Lords*, p. 39.

77. The documentary film *Children of Violence* exhibits all these details.

78. Horowitz, *Honor and the American Dream*, p. 87.

79. Patrick, *Glasgow Gang Observed*, p. 82.

80. Chavez, "Impact of a Chicano Gang," p. 124.

81. Patrick, *Glasgow Gang Observed*, p. 41.

82. James F. Short, Jr., "Introduction to Conflict Gangs and Subcultures," in *Gang Delinquency and Delinquent Subcultures*, ed. James F. Short, Jr. (New York: Harper & Row, 1968), p. 21.

83. Spergel, *Racketville, Slumtown, and Haulburg*, p. 44.

84. Ibid., p. 89.

85. Doyle et al., *Paint House*, p. 83.

86. Ibid., p. 31.

87. Put another way, collective violence is not just quantitatively but qualitatively different

from violence among individuals. The Cambridge Study in Delinquent Development, which repeatedly gathered data on the same group of some four hundred London working-class males from ages 8 and 9 to age 25 (in 1982), contrasted the accounts of group and individual fights and examined differences among the fighters. Group fights appear to have genuinely distinctive, emergent qualities. They are more concentrated in public settings (pubs and streets); they more often involve the use of weapons; and they are more likely to result in injuries. The authors concluded: "There were many significant differences between individual and group *fights* [but] there were very few significant differences between individual and group *fighters.*" David P. Farrington, Leonard Berkowitz, and Donald J. West, "Differences between Individual and Group Fights," *British Journal of Social Psychology* 21 (1982): 332.

88. See Doyle, *Paint House;* Ellison, *Memos from Purgatory,* p. 86; Walter Bernstein, "The Cherubs Are Rumbling," *The New Yorker,* September 21, 1957, pp. 22–52; Haro, "Truant and Low Achieving Chicano Barrio Youth," pp. 371–72; Patrick, *Glasgow Gang Observed,* p. 53; and Miller, *Violence by Youth Gangs and Youth Groups,* p. 48.

89. With respect to vandalism by street "gangs," Miller found that "most damage was inflicted on public and semipublic facilities, little on private residences or other property." Miller, "Violent Crimes in City Gangs," 110.

90. Cf. Ruth Horowitz and Gary Schwartz, "Honor, Normative Ambiguity and Gang Violence, *American Sociological Review* 39 (April 1974): 238–51. Horowitz and Schwartz did not actually refer to the Latin culture of their subjects as the basis of their heightened concern with honor, but their emphatic references to Pitt-Rivers and the context of their study conveys the suggestion.

91. See ibid., 249; and Spergel, *Racketville, Slumtown, and Haulburg,* p. 25.

92. *Reaching the Fighting Gang,* p. 70. Without an appreciation of the street elite's project of sustaining an aura of dread, the provocation of intergroup violence from the simple expression of a "bad" attitude seems senseless, perhaps a sign of psychological pathology. There were many such enigmatic incidents and psychopathological interpretations in the New York City Youth Board's report on gang violence in the 1950s.

93. See, Chavez, "Impact of a Chicano Gang," pp. 106–7. See also the pressure put on Frias by the insistence of fellow homeboys that he revenge the murder of his best friend, in Frias, *Barrio Warriors,* pp. 37, 38.

94. Some aspects of this process of motivational development were introduced into sociology by Becker's concept of "side bets." See Howard S. Becker, *Sociological Work* (Chicago: Aldine, 1970), pp. 261–73.

95. Rettig, Torres, and Garrett, *Manny,* p. 19.

96. Patrick, *Glasgow Gang Observed,* p. 97.

97. Keiser, *Vice Lords,* p. 61.

98. Moore reported recollections of her ex-felon, ex-barrio-street-fighter informants from East Los Angeles to the effect that in addition to the heavy use of opiates, profitable participation in heroin markets has recurrently undermined loyalties to turf-fighting street groups. See Joan Moore, *Homeboys* (Philadelphia: Temple University Press, 1978), p. 85. This is not to deny the significance of illegal drug use and trafficking in the lives of groups of young men who are self-consciously prepared to make criminal use of violence, just that the *territorial* grounds for intergroup violence are undermined rather than supported by the drug market.

99. Gale, *The Compound.*

100. Boredom appears to be an occupational disease among gang researchers. See Ellison, *Memos from Purgatory,* p. 85; Patrick, *Glasgow Gang Observed,* p. 83; and Klein, *Street Gangs and Street Workers,* p. 123.

101. Patrick, *Glasgow Gang Observed,* p. 52. See also Spergel, *Racketville, Slumtown, Haulburg,* p. 42.

102. Patrick, *Glasgow, Gang Observed,* pp. 63, 64, 118.

103. Doyle et al., *Paint House,* p. 27.

104. Ibid., pp. 32–33.

105. See Frias, *Barrio Warriors,* p. 20:

While walking to school about 7:30 A.M., we began meeting more and more homeboys who were also going to school. There was Woody, Nicker, Lil Bear, Conejo, Chemina, Rocky, Pajaro, Puppet, Chito, and various others. All of them were wearing new clothes, mostly Pendletons and Khaki pants, some of them were wearing some beautiful dark colored small-brimmed 1940's style hats. Everybody had short hair combed back with no part whatsoever. . . . After greeting each other we decided to arrive together at school, check it out and terrorize it.

106. On this point there is supporting evidence from a wide range of gang contexts. See James F. Short, Jr., and Fred L. Strotbeck, *Group Process and Gang Delinquency* (Chicago: University of Chicago Press, 1965), p. 231; Short, "Conflict Gangs and Subcultures," p. 20; Patrick, *Glasgow Gang Observed,* p. 33; and Gale, *The Compound.* Klein's unpopular findings were consistent with this pattern. In one of the most controversial arguments in the history of gang research, Klein indicated that formal social work group programming with gangs increased the cohesiveness of gangs, in effect providing the unattached with incentives to join. Programming (outings and meetings) by social work agencies represented the attentions of conventional society out "there." When detached workers were removed, the gang's cohesiveness and rate of delinquency appeared to decline. See Klein, *Street Gangs and Street Workers.*

107. Keiser, *Vice Lords,* p. 68.

108. Horowitz, *Honor and the American Dream,* p. 146. In a personal communication, Charles Moskos recalled that this was a favorite ploy of young enlisted men in the army of the Second World War.

109. Ibid., p. 155.

110. And from its side, the school administration's losses are also its pedagogic successes in socializing students into competent citizenship in a modern world of rational-legal institutions. Compare Howard S. Becker, "A School Is a Lousy Place to Learn Anything In," *American Behavioral Scientist* 16 (September–October 1972): 85–105.

111. Carl Werthman, "Delinquency and Authority" (master's thesis, University of California at Berkeley, 1964), p. 43.

112. Ibid., p. 44.

113. Campbell, *Girls in the Gang,* p. 182.

114. Doyle et al., *Paint House,* p. 40.

115. Castleman, *Getting Up,* p. 93. See also Haro, "Truant and Low Achieving Chicano Barrio Youth," p. 97.

116. Horowitz, *Honor and the American Dream,* p. 147.

117. Chavez, "Impact of a Chicano Gang," pp. 60–61.

118. Patrick, *Glasgow Gang Observed,* p. 79.

119. Wideman, *Brothers and Keepers,* p. 118; See also Piri Thomas, *Down These Mean Streets* (New York: Random House, 1974), pp. 69–74.

120. He did not shoot. Frias, *Barrio Warriors,* pp. 25–26. Because I am trying to document a powerful fantasy, I am not disturbed that Frias purported to quote extensively, without aid of notes, from scenes he experienced about ten years earlier; that the teacher is said to have opened the class with a grammatical analysis of the sentence, "Johnny and Mary killed the Blue Cop"; that the teacher speaks in a stilted tone; and that the narrator's role, which I did not reproduce here, was eminently cool and superior. Frias's autobiography is especially valuable as a documentation of the perspective in which coarse brutality may be experienced as heroic.

121. See Werthman, "Delinquency and Authority," p. 54.

122. Partridge finds a nineteenth- and twentieth-century use of "Jack" as "A low coll. term of address to any man one doesn't know" and, apparently working off of the sailor-Jack predecessor, suggests a nautical origin. Eric Partridge, *Dictionary of Slang and Unconventional English,* 7th ed. (New York: Macmillan, 1970), p. 429. In the United States, the salience of "Jack" was promoted by its frequency among Southern families ("Jackson"), and in the North by the immigration of blacks. It is striking that "Jack" follows in an onomatopoetic tradition of street terms that are uttered like a punch, easily rendered as a smack. "Mac" served for generations when the rough strangers one might expect to meet in American cities were likely to be Irish, or going back even further, Scottish.

123. Keiser, *Vice Lords,* pp. 41–42.

124. Examples of a variety of fighting scenes conducted among friends may be seen in the documentary film *Children of Violence.* For written references see Sale, *Blackstone Rangers,* p. 164; and Elijah Anderson, *A Place on the Corner* (Chicago: University of Chicago Press, 1978), p. 194.

125. Short and Strotbeck, *Group Process and Gang Delinquency,* pp. 251–53.

126. Patrick, *Glasgow Gang Observed,* p. 44.

127. Doyle et al., *Paint House,* pp. 25–26.

128. *Children of Violence.*

129. Krisberg, *Gang and Community*, pp. 79, 80.

130. Bloch and Niederhoffer, *The Gang*, p. 104. Given their theoretical predilections, Bloch and Niederhoffer saw this as "an anomalous note in an otherwise highly masculine emphasis" that was one of various "indications of possible homosexual ambivalence in modern gangs [such as] the increasing use by 'toughs' of pastel-colored silk shirts, and trousers of red, lavender, and green, sartorial touches of color previously reserved for the feminine sex."

131. Klein, *Street Gangs and Street Workers*, p. 85.

132. "Gang bang," which meant group rape in the East twenty years ago, is a common term for intergroup fighting in the Southwest today, perhaps not without a delicious awareness of its historical double entendre. At the least, the phrase has rhyming and onomatopoetic qualities.

133. Werthman, "Delinquency and Authority," p. 95.

134. Ibid.

135. Doyle et al., *Paint House;* Patrick, *Glasgow Gang Observed;* and Richard Jenkins, *Lads, Citizens and Ordinary Kids: Working-class Youth Life-styles in Belfast* (London: Routledge & Kegan Paul, 1983).

136. Horowitz and Schwartz, "Honor, Normative Ambiguity and Gang Violence," 245, 246.

137. Ibid., 245. Spergel's later study of 654 gang homicides in Chicago came to similar conclusions. See Irving Spergel, "Violent Gangs in Chicago: In Search of Social Policy," *Social Service Review* 58 (June 1984): 199–226.

138. See Hunter Thompson, *Hell's Angels* (New York: Ballantine Books, 1967). Reports of "gang" violence have begun to report age ranges for members extending well beyond adolescence. On violent gangs in Chicago see Spergel, "Violent Gangs in Chicago"; and in Los Angeles see Cheryl L. Maxson, Margaret A. Gordon, and Malcolm W. Klein, "Differences Between Gang and Nongang Homicides," *Criminology* 23 (May 1985): 209–22. See also the interviews with Flaco and others in David Weddle, "Turf Wars," *L.A. Weekly,* December 14–20, 1984, pp. 25–31.

139. Professional sports teams also use geographic identifications to call for loyalties that transcend social class and ethnic divisions. In England, fighting "teams" of working-class youths often pick up this geographic differentiation as a basis for organizing football-related violence.

140. One exception was the gang of blacks from south-central Los Angeles in the 1960s, the "Businessmen."

141. Castleman, *Getting Up*, p. 19.

142. Romotsky and Romotsky, *Los Angeles Barrio Calligraphy*.

143. It is not the designation of a separation from family home or formal institution or simply an intimation of physical risk that lends the "street" adjective its deviant undertone. "Outdoor life" and "outdoor people" suggest a health that is robust morally as well as physically. Wilderness journeys may carry substantial risk while remaining morally clean.

144. See Krisberg, *Gang and Community*, pp. 11, 55.

145. Haro, "Truant and Low Achieving Chicano Barrio Youth."

146. Howard L. Myerhoff and Barbara G. Myerhoff, "Field Observations of Middle Class 'Gangs,' " *Social Forces* 42 (1964): 328–36.

147. Mike Brake, *The Sociology of Youth Culture and Youth Subcultures* (London: Routledge & Kegan Paul, 1980), p. 101.

148. Krisberg, *Gang and Community*, p. 51.

149. Howard Erlanger, "Estrangement, Machismo and Gang Violence," *Social Science Quarterly* 60 (September 1979): 235–48.

150. See David Matza, "Poverty and Disrepute," in *Contemporary Social Problems,* ed. Robert K. Merton and Robert A. Nisbet, 2nd ed. (New York: Harcourt, Brace & World, 1966), pp. 619–69, which, although not quite the argument advanced here, has been a valuable inspiration.

151. The original skinheads were self-consciously, proudly working class. An early action of the group in the late 1960s was to dump garbage at the door of the Town Hall to aid the dustmen on strike in a militant working-class protest. See Doyle et al., *Paint House.* At about the time that middle-class suburban whites from the North were traveling in jeans and long hair to help Martin Luther King, Jr., with nonviolent protest on behalf of the Birmingham, Alabama, garbage men, English working-class youths were shaving their heads and rolling up their jeans to reveal high boots to lend an air of aggression to their elders' job complaints. See also Brake, *Youth Culture and Youth Subcultures*, p. 77.

152. A common theme in the autobiographies of ethnic-minority men who were members of fighting gangs as youngsters is their disgust at their parents' meek, humiliated posture before welfare officials, judges, school principals, and other authority figures. For vivid accounts, largely from elderly ghetto blacks, of both god-fearing humility and deep indignation with respect to racial relations, see John Langston Gwaltney, *Drylongso* (New York: Random House, 1980).

153. Herbert Asbury, *The Gangs of New York* (New York: Alfred A. Knopf, 1928); and Thrasher, *The Gang.*

154. Hebdige, *Subculture,* pp. 41–43.

155. For a series of comparative analytical leads on the perspectives on interpersonal authority held by American ethnic poor and working-class groups before and after immigration, see Herbert J. Gans, *The Urban Villagers* (New York: Free Press, 1962), pp. 230–42.

156. Doyle et al., *Paint House,* pp. 68–69.

157. Campbell, *Girls in the Gang,* p. 239.

158. Frias, *Barrio Warriors,* p. 23.

159. Gwen Louise Stern, "Ethnic Identity and Community Action in El Barrio" (Ph.D. diss., Northwestern University, 1976), pp. 163–65.

160. Haro, "Truant and Low Achieving Chicano Barrio Youth," p. 363.

161. See Kevin F. McCarthy and R. Burciaga Valdez, *Current and Future Effects of Mexican Immigration in California* (Santa Monica, Calif.: Rand Corp., 1986), p. 9. The image of the Mexican-American population as concentrated in agricultural labor is grossly outdated. But the California population of Mexican-born workers still has a sizable concentration in agriculture. In Los Angeles County, more than 20 percent of this group is employed in farm work; in the larger Los Angeles region, more than 40 percent. See ibid., p. 38. See also D. S. Massey, "The Settlement Process Among Mexican Migrants to the United States: New Methods and Findings," in *Immigration Statistics: A Story of Neglect,* ed. D. B. Levine, K. Hill, and R. Waren (Washington, D.C.: National Academy Press, 1985), appendix C.

162. Horowitz and Schwartz, "Honor, Normative Ambiguity and Gang Violence," 247.

163. In *Children of Violence,* this is nicely represented in the mother's recollections of her childhood in a family of deferential farm workers and in the sons' affections for her.

164. Campbell, *Girls in the Gang,* pp. 193, 194.

165. Suttles, *Social Order of the Slum,* p. 126. Research has recently begun to take up the controversial but theoretically strategic comparison of the black and the Hispanic expressions of urban gang life. See Spergel, "Violent Gangs in Chicago"; and Maxson, Gordon, and Klein, "Gang and Nongang Homicides."

166. As Thompson noted about the Hell's Angels.

167. Ellison, *Memos from Purgatory,* p. 47. And Campbell, *Girls in the Gang,* p. 237, stated: "Laws are broken as part of the gangs' life-style and values, but gangs are not composed of potential revolutionaries; in fact, quite the opposite. Their views are often conservative."

168. David E. Kaplan and Alec Dubro, *Yakuza* (New York: Collier Books, 1987).

Chapter 5. Doing Stickup

1. Joan Petersilia, Peter W. Greenwood, and Marvin Lavin, *Criminal Careers of Habitual Felons* (Santa Monica, Calif.: Rand Corp., 1977).

2. James F. Haran, "The Losers' Game: A Sociological Profile of 500 Armed Bank Robbers" (Ph.D. diss., Department of Sociology, Fordham University, 1982), p. 87. In 1967, out of 2,200 bank robberies, only 453 were committed by men who knew anything about the inside operation of their target. See D. A. Johnston, "Psychological Observations of Bank Robbery," *American Journal of Psychiatry* 135 (1978): 1377–79.

3. Bureau of Justice Statistics, *Criminal Victimization in the United States, 1985* (Washington, D.C.: U.S. Department of Justice, 1987), table 76, p. 66.

4. The average from robberies of all types was $600. Federal Bureau of Investigation, *Uniform Crime Reports* (Washington, D.C.: U.S. Government Printing Office, 1986), p. 18. For detailed data from one city, Chicago, see Richard Block, *Violent Crime: Environment, Interaction and Death* (Lexington, Mass.: Lexington Books, 1977), p. 70.

5. Alfred Blumstein, Jacqueline Cohen, Jeffrey A. Roth, and Christy A. Visher, eds., *Criminal Careers and "Career Criminals"* (Washington, D.C.: National Academy Press, 1986), 2:60.

6. Federal Bureau of Investigation, *Uniform Crime Reports,* p. 18.

7. The greater reliability of statistics on bank robberies is a product of federal regulatory and insurance requirements and FBI jurisdiction, which make for relatively uniform recording practices. See Haran, "Losers' Game," p. 12.

8. In a small group of intensively interviewed California prison inmates, the estimated arrest probability evidence for armed robbery was 0.21. See Mark A. Peterson and Harriet B. Braker, *Who Commits Crimes* (Cambridge, Mass.: Oelgeschlager, Gunn & Hain, 1981), p. 28.

9. See, for example, the review of evidence in Elliott Currie, *Confronting Crime* (New York: Pantheon, 1985), p. 68.

10. Laurie Taylor, *In the Underworld* (London: Unwin Paperbacks, 1985), p. 79.

11. James D. Wright and Peter H. Rossi, *Armed and Considered Dangerous* (New York: Aldine de Gruyter, 1986), pp. 144–48.

12. Indeed, some studies indicate that for some groups of hard-core offenders, during certain periods of their lives, incarceration may intensify their criminal activity upon release. See the review in Currie, *Confronting Crime,* p. 77.

13. Jan M. Chaiken and Marcia R. Chaiken, *Varieties of Criminal Behavior* (Santa Monica, Calif.: Rand Corp., August 1982).

14. John Allen, *Assault with a Deadly Weapon,* ed. Dianne Hall Kelly and Philip Heymann (New York: McGraw-Hill, 1978), pp. 102, 105, 106, 161–62.

15. Ibid., pp. 108–10.

16. Chaiken and Chaiken, *Varieties of Criminal Behavior,* p. 147.

17. When Zimring and Zuehl published a statistical write-up of their research, they added the provocative note to their qualitative characterization, "recreational violence": "If the term sounds frivolous or abstract, the reader is invited into our files." Indeed, the category seemed so close to the patterns indicated by autobiographies I had been examining that I took up the invitation, which was graciously honored. Franklin E. Zimring and James Zuehl, "Victim Injury and Death in Urban Robbery: A Chicago Study," *Journal of Legal Studies* 15 (January 1986): 1–40.

18. The original narratives are archived in the data set, "Robberies in Chicago, 1982–1983," no. 8951, Inter-university Consortium for Political and Social Research, Ann Arbor, Michigan.

19. When I claim that something is true of "virtually all" or "the typical" stickup, I mean to assert, in a narrow reading, that I have shaped the analysis to fit the information available on all these 437 robberies, as well as the situated criminal practices described in various ethnographies and life histories.

20. For an example of one such career, see Allen, *Assault with a Deadly Weapon,* p. 50. Henry Williamson, who committed numerous street robberies in the Chicago black belt of the 1950s, talked of this strategy frequently. See Henry Williamson, *Hustler! The Autobiography of a Thief,* ed. R. Lincoln Keiser (New York: Doubleday, 1965). Jones, a half-Italian, half-black mugger who was active in the Lower East Side of New York in the 1960s, elaborately demonstrated it. See James Willwerth, *Jones* (New York: M. Evans & Co., 1974).

21. Clifford Shaw, *The Jack-Roller* (Chicago: University of Chicago Press, 1966).

22. Franklin E. Zimring, "American Youth Violence," in *Crime and Justice,* ed. Norval Morris and Michael Tonry (Chicago: University of Chicago Press, 1979), 1:74.

23. Older victims may be especially vulnerable to injury for physical reasons unrelated to offenders' actions, but this, like the question of whether robbers disproportionately select aged victims, is another matter.

24. See the description in Claude Brown, *Manchild in the Promised Land* (New York: Macmillan, 1965), pp. 154–56.

25. Two of the robbery-murder cases (10606, 10809) might fit the nightmare of awakening to find that one is being attacked. A few others came close but had insufficient details to rule out an interpretation that the offenders were responding to their victims' resistance. There is one important exception: sleeping victims are frequently attacked by robbers when their "home" for the night is out in public, say, on a salt box on an El platform at Congress and Kedzie Streets in Chicago.

26. See the discussion of the advantages of such sites in Willwerth, *Jones,* pp. 19, 26–27, 41.

27. See the discussion of asking for change as a street stickup man's strategy in Sally Engle Merry, *Urban Danger* (Philadelphia: Temple University Press, 1981), pp. 169, 176.

28. Working with the same core of robbery-homicides but including additional cases or excluding some of the core for different analytic purposes, Zimring and Zuehl reported a

series of figures indicating that victims and offenders are not strangers. See Franklin E. Zimring and James Zuehl, "Victim Injury and Death," 9, 14, 38, 39.

29. Ibid., table 3, p. 9.

30. Ibid., table 6, p. 14.

31. For a similar strategy in Detroit cases, see Mary Lorenz Dietz, _Killing for Profit: The Social Organization of Felony Homicide_ (Chicago: Nelson-Hall, 1983), p. 61.

32. Edwin H. Sutherland, _The Professional Thief_ (Chicago: University of Chicago Press, 1937), p. 33.

33. Ibid., p. 55, n. 11.

34. Williamson, _Hustler!_, p. 131.

35. Erving Goffman, _Frame Analysis_ (Cambridge, Mass.: Harvard University Press, 1974), p. 313.

36. Allen, _Assault with a Deadly Weapon_, pp. 52, 184–86. Virtually any interview study of robbers contains similar comments. For two from disparate contexts, see Taylor, _In the Underworld_, pp. 90–91; James F. Haran, "Losers' Game," p. 104.

37. Lynn A. Curtis, _Criminal Violence_ (Lexington, Mass.: Lexington Books, 1975); André Normandeau, "Trends and Patterns in Crimes of Robbery" (Ph.D. diss., University of Pennsylvania, 1968); Block, _Violent Crime_, p. 30.

38. See John E. Conklin, _Robbery and the Criminal Justice System_ (Philadelphia: J. B. Lippincott, 1972); David F. Luckenbill, "Patterns of Force in Robbery," _Deviant Behavior_ 1 (1980): 361–7 and Michael J. Hindelang, _Criminal Victimization in Eight American Cities_ (Cambridge, Mass.: Ballinger, 1976), p. 223. But _fatal_ injury is much more likely when the robber uses a gun. See Philip J. Cook, "Robbery Violence," _Journal of Criminal Law and Criminology_ 75 (Summer 1987): 501–20.

39. Robert Lejeune, "The Management of a Mugging," _Urban Life_ 6 (July 1977): 134.

40. P. D. Chimbes, "Violent Crimes in a Nonmetropolitan Area of Ontario," _Crime and/e Justice_ 6, no. 4 (1978): 234–45.

41. Matthew D. Lynes, "Sex Differences in Coercion and Compliance in Robbery Offenses" (unpublished manuscript, Department of Sociology, University of California at Los Angeles, 1984).

42. See Andre Normandeau, "Trends and Patterns in Crimes of Robbery," and his "Armed Robbery in Montreal, and Its Victims," _Victimology_ 6 (1981): 308; Janet L. Barkas, _Victims_ (New York: Scribner, 1978), p. 150; Hindelang, _Criminal Victimization_, p. 348.

43. Michael J. Hindelang, Michael R. Gottfredson, and James Garofalo, _Victims of Personal Crime_ (Cambridge, Mass.: Ballinger, 1978), p. 44.

44. David F. Luckenbill, "Generating Compliance: The Case of Robbery," _Urban Life_ 1 (April 1981): 35.

45. Thomas Aceituno and Michael Matchett, "Street Robbery Victims in Oakland," in _17 Prevention and Control of Robbery_, ed. Floyd Feeney and Adrianne Weir (Davis, Calif.: University of California Center on Administration of Criminal Justice, 1973), pp. 213–310.

46. Conklin, _Robbery and the Criminal Justice System_, p. 119.

47. Block, _Violent Crime_, p. 83. Note that these figures do not always distinguish armed robberies from unarmed robberies. In general, the studies show that victims usually do not resist in robberies. But victims of armed robberies are particularly unlikely to resist. Victims of robbery by gun resisted about half as often (18 percent) as did victims of all other robberies. Block then found that in robberies by gun in which the victim does not resist, the chance of injury is 7 percent; in robberies by gun in which the victim does resist, the rate of injury is 78 percent (pp. 84, 86).

48. Philip J. Cook, "The Relationship Between Victim Resistance and Injury in Noncommercial Robbery," _Journal of Legal Studies_ 15 (June 1986): 405–16; and his "Reducing Injury and Death Rates in Robbery," _Policy Analysis_ 6 (Winter 1980): 21–45.

49. Zimring and Zuehl, "Victim Injury and Death," 30.

50. And as discussed further in chapter 7, when victims are demographically like offenders—who are, disproportionately, young, black, urban males active in vice and other criminal activities—they are especially inaccessible to any form of social survey, as the census experience has indicated.

51. These cases are especially useful for balancing out the usual picture of robbery interactions because they invert the biases in the usual samples of robberies, which underplay violence, especially fatal violence. These data have the additional advantage, for developing

a more complete appreciation of the situated meaning of robbery to offenders, that homicide cases motivate the police to accumulate far more detail on the offense process than does the typical robbery.

52. In her study of police records on robbery homicides in Detroit, Dietz, *Killing for Profit*, p. 70, wrote, "Frequently, when a robbery has been committed, one of the group members will turn and fire a shot while leaving. Ostensibly, this is to keep the robbery victims from following, but then the end result may be deadly for one of the people robbed." By turning and firing a shot on exiting a robbery scene, an offender may simply continue and add a final note to the manifestation of the badass character with which he initiated the event, signaling in a way that is predictably effective for the victims that he comes from a place that is loaded with explosive negative potential, the sort of place, the offender implies, a conventional person does not want to know about.

53. In 7 of the 39 cases for which the information on victim-offender interaction was inadequate to determine whether the victim resisted, the victim was known to have been involved in drug trafficking (n = 5), fencing, or prostitution. Zimring and Zuehl, "Victim Injury and Death," table A3, found that in at least 16 percent and maybe as much as 21 percent of all the cases of robbery killings, the victim was a drug dealer. My coding differs from theirs in that I required evidence that drug dealing was relevant to the unfolding narrative before I would code the case as drug related. It is likely that the police may, at times, impute drug-dealer status to people involved in deviant lifestyles and imply a causal relevance to the robbery killing when the victim was not a drug dealer or when he was but the offender was ignorant of or indifferent to the fact.

54. More precisely, in one of these cases, one of the victims knew of the offender and could establish his identity readily through a third party. Adding the acquaintance and vice cases together, the offenders either knew the victims or chose victims who were active in vice occupations in at least half the current set of cases on robbery-homicide (n = 53 of the 105). For an additional 17 of the 105 cases, there was insufficient information to rule out the possibility that the victim and offender had been acquainted. See also Zimring and Zuehl, "Victim Injury and Death."

55. Zimring and Zuehl, ibid., 25, reported that lone offenders committed fewer than 40 percent of the crimes in each of the sets they counted: robberies without injury, robberies with nonfatal injuries, and robbery killings.

56. Williamson, *Hustler!*, pp. 109, 111–13.

57. Malcolm X, with the assistance of Alex Haley, *The Autobiography of Malcolm X* (New York: Grove Press, 1965).

58. Dietz, *Killing for Profit*, pp. 147, 159.

59. Allen, *Assault with a Deadly Weapon*, p. 185.

60. Williamson, *Hustler!*, p. 41.

61. Dietz, *Killing for Profit*, pp. 157–59.

62. Sociologists of deviance will recognize the oblique respect paid here to Howard S. Becker's influential analysis of the adoption of the Marihuana Tax Act as the result of H. J. Anslinger's "moral entrepreneurship." Howard S. Becker, *Outsiders* (New York: Free Press, 1963), pp. 135–46.

63. Dietz, *Killing for Profit*, p. 84.

64. Ibid., p. 84.

65. Cook, "Victim Resistance and Injury."

66. All but 22 had sufficient information for an analysis on this theme. I used the following categories in coding "whether the fatal violence by offender was 'irrational'":

1. Fatal violence by the offender before the victim resisted or attacked the offender, when the victim eventually resisted or attacked (n = 1).
2. Fatal violence by the offender without any resistance or attack by the victim (n = 22).
3. Fatal violence by the offender after the victim resisted or attacked, but the offender's fatal violence was not necessary for his situational escape (n = 27).
4. The offender's fatal violence was necessary to protect the offender from the victim's violence or other endangering resistance or attack (n = 11).
5. We can't tell if the victim resisted, but circumstances make clear that the offender did not have to kill to escape (n = 18).

6. The victim resisted without physically endangering the offender, who committed the fatal blow and abandoned the robbery to escape (n = 4).

7. Insufficient information to code any of the above (n = 22).

67. These figures are almost certainly underestimates because, in many cases, there was insufficient information to code the question. Excluding cases with insufficient information, Zimring and Zuehl, "Victim Injury and Death," table 10, p. 18, reported "active noncooperation" (refusal, flight, physical force) in 55 percent of the robbery killings and "passive noncooperation" ("the victim usually says he or she has no money") in another 11 percent. They did not report a figure for resistance in their set of robberies with nonfatal injuries but, for a sample of 348 undifferentiated robberies drawn from the same period, they reported a figure of 18 percent.

68. Police records, however, show a rate of only 14 percent. See Richard Block and Carolyn R. Block, "Decisions and Data: The Transformation of Robbery Incidents into Official Robbery Statistics," *Journal of Criminal Law and Criminology* 71 (Winter 1980), 634.

69. Allen, *Assault with a Deadly Weapon*, p. 50.

70. "Because both citizens and police systematically eliminate attempted robberies, 33 percent of total robbery incidents are attempts, but only 6 percent of robberies known to the police are attempts." Block and Block, "Decisions and Data," 633.

71. Williamson, *Hustler!*, p. 202.

72. The current popularity of the term *stickup* is not new. The term has been favored by robbers at least since Stanley's days as an ethnic Polish "jackroller" in 1920s Chicago. Shaw, *The Jack-Roller*, p. 54.

73. See also the experience of David, an experienced robber treated as modal in a study of robbery homicide in Detroit, in Dietz, *Killing for Profit*, p. 1.

74. James Carr, *Bad* (New York: Herman Graf Associates, 1975), p. 53. Years later, Carr became an associate of the black militant prisoner leader George Jackson; the public attention he received motivated him to write an autobiography.

75. Allen, *Assault with a Deadly Weapon*, pp. 186–89. If this seems a "sensational" case, it is because our image of contemporary robbery has been rendered abstract and too lifeless by summary statistical portraits, *ex post facto* rhetoric portraying "professional" styles, and a neglect of rich, qualitative data. In fact, sensationalism is not uncommon in the stickups committed by career robbers. As we will see, the contexts of their robberies generally display hedonistic or emotion-expressive factors that enhance the risks of capture and conviction without contributing instrumentally to the success of the stickup: gratuitous assaults on victims; the presence of illegal drugs; and the accompaniment as passive observers on the stickup of convicts on escape, prostitutes, or drug dealers.

76. Williamson, *Hustler!*, p. 204.

Chapter 6. Action, Chaos, and Control: Persisting with Stickup

1. The first major modern study of robbers—Conklin's literature review and analysis of interviews with sixty-seven Massachusetts prisoners serving time for robberies committed in Boston in the late 1960s—identified a group of "professional" robbers who stole "to support a hedonistic life style." See John E. Conklin, *Robbery and the Criminal Justice System* (Philadelphia: J. B. Lippincott, 1972), p. 63. See also Floyd Feeney, "Robbers as Decision-Makers," in *The Reasoning Criminal*, ed. Derek B. Cornish and Ronald V. Clarke (New York: Springer-Verlag, 1986), p. 55.

2. James F. Haran, "The Losers' Game: A Sociological Profile of 500 Armed Bank Robbers" (Ph.D. diss., Department of Sociology, Fordham University, 1982), pp. 102, 106.

3. Jan M. Chaiken and Marcia R. Chaiken, *Varieties of Criminal Behavior* (Santa Monica, Calif.: Rand Corp., August 1982), p. vii. An earlier study for the Rand Corporation, in which in-depth interviews were conducted with "habitual" armed robbers in a medium security prison in California, found that more than half the forty-nine inmates said that they committed crimes as adults for expressive reasons (thrills, anger) or for high living (drugs, alcohol, women); only 32 percent said they did so for financial reasons (to pay the rent or to support their families). See Joan Petersilia, Peter W. Greenwood, and Marvin Lavin, *Criminal Careers of Habitual Felons* (Santa Monica, Calif.: Rand Corp., 1977), pp. 76, 93–94, 111.

4. James D. Wright and Peter H. Rossi, *Armed and Considered Dangerous: A Survey of Felons and Their Firearms* (New York: Aldine de Gruyter, 1986), pp. 40–41, 44–45, 75–77.

5. This section is inspired by Erving Goffman, "Where the Action Is," in his *Interaction Ritual* (New York: Pantheon, 1977), pp. 149–270.

6. Arthur Allen Leff, "Law And," *Yale Law Journal* 87 (April 1978): 989–1011.

7. It is reasonable to worry that the ubiquitous presence of these "sensational" themes in the life histories says more about the criteria of publishing than about robbers' lives in general. Were it not for the statistical findings of the various studies of career offenders that I have cited repeatedly in chapters 5–7, and the diversity of the authors' personal interests and institutional affiliations, this methodological worry would be overwhelming.

8. The sociologist John Gagnon, as quoted in Bruce Jackson, *Outside the Law: A Thief's Primer* (New Brunswick, N.J.: Transaction Books, 1972), p. 180, n. 9.

9. See Nicholas Pileggi, *Wiseguy* (New York: Simon & Schuster, 1985), p. 62; and Henry Williamson, *Hustler! The Autobiography of a Thief,* ed. R. Lincoln Keiser (New York: Doubleday, 1965).

10. David M. Hayano, *Poker Faces: The Life and Work of Professional Card Players* (Berkeley: University of California Press, 1982), p. 5.

11. See, for example, Haran, "Losers' Game."

12. See Jackson, *Outside the Law;* Williamson, *Hustler!;* and Harry King and William J. Chambliss, *Harry King, A Professional Thief's Journey* (New York: John Wiley & Sons, 1984).

13. Laurie Taylor, *In the Underworld* (London: Unwin Paperbacks, 1985).

14. Pileggi, *Wiseguy,* p. 81.

15. Ibid., pp. 132–33.

16. Billie Miller and David Helwig, *A Book About Billie* (Ottawa: Oberon Press, 1972), p. 147.

17. Williamson, *Hustler!,* pp. 33, 66, 71, 97, 104.

18. James Willwerth, *Jones* (New York: M. Evans & Co., 1974).

19. James Carr, *Bad* (New York: Herman Graf Associates, 1975), p. 38.

20. Claude Brown, *Manchild in the Promised Land* (New York: New American Library, 1965), p. 69.

21. William J. Chambliss, "The Saints and the Roughnecks," *Society* 11 (November–December 1973): 24–31.

22. Williamson, *Hustler!,* p. 116.

23. Pileggi, *Wiseguy,* pp. 24–25.

24. Taylor, *In the Underworld,* p. 39.

25. Piri Thomas, *Down These Mean Streets* (New York: Vintage Books, 1974), pp. 214, 227.

26. Malcolm X, with the assistance of Alex Haley, *The Autobiography of Malcolm X* (New York: Grove Press, 1965), p. 109.

27. Pileggi, *Wiseguy.*

28. Richard P. Rettig, Manual J. Torres, and Gerald R. Garrett, *Manny: A Criminal Addict's Story* (Boston: Houghton Mifflin, 1977).

29. Williamson, *Hustler!,* p. 87.

30. Ibid., p. 128. This is a classic case that supports Lindesmith's theory of opiate addiction. See Alfred R. Lindesmith, *Opiate Addiction* (Bloomington, Ind.: Principia Press, 1947).

31. John Allen, *Assault with a Deadly Weapon,* ed. Dianne Hall Kelly and Philip Heymann (New York: McGraw-Hill, 1978), p. 79.

32. John Edgar Wideman, *Brothers and Keepers* (New York: Penguin Books, 1985). See also the account by "Luis Santos" of robberies and other property crimes committed to finance a projected, fabulous career as a drug dealer (which also failed to materialize) in Francis A. J. Ianni, *Black Mafia* (New York: Pocket Books, 1975), p. 199.

33. Wideman, *Brothers and Keepers,* p. 166.

34. Bill Hanson et al., eds., *Life with Heroin: Voices from the Inner City* (Lexington, Mass.: Lexington Books, 1985), p. 38.

35. Ibid., p. 181.

36. Ibid., p. 36.

37. Ibid., p. 77.

38. Goffman, "Where the Action Is," p. 188; and Howard S. Becker, as cited by Goffman.

39. Of course, different groups of offenders will be familiar with different terms for articulating the connections among the metaphors of action. The terms used here reflect the somewhat dated world of the safecracker, as represented by Sam, in Jackson, *Outside the Law.*

40. Miller and Helwig, *Book About Billie,* p. 9.

41. Williamson, *Hustler!,* p. 4.

42. Wideman, *Brothers and Keepers,* p. 73.

43. Clifford Shaw, *The Jack-Roller* (Chicago: University of Chicago Press, 1966), p. 85.

44. Malcolm X and Haley, *Autobiography of Malcolm X,* p. 51.

45. Hayano, *Poker Faces,* p. 19.

46. Taylor, *In the Underworld,* pp. 8–9.

47. Pileggi, *Wiseguy,* p. 59.

48. Ibid., p. 43.

49. Jackson, *Outside the Law,* pp. 20–22.

50. Of the 500 bank robbers he studied, Haran ("Losers' Game," pp. 113–15) classified 9.2 percent (46, "including one housewife") as "the naive bank robber type" who commits "a usually isolated offense . . . late in life, as a response to a stress induced problem."

51. Carr, *Bad,* p. 53.

52. Ibid.

53. Allen, *Assault with a Deadly Weapon,* p. 96.

54. Pileggi, *Wiseguy,* p. 72.

55. Williamson, *Hustler!,* p. 205.

56. Thomas, *Down These Mean Streets,* pp. 80–81.

57. Carr, *Bad,* pp. 80–81.

58. Pileggi, *Wiseguy,* p. 27.

59. See Shaw, *The Jack-Roller;* Jackson, *Outside the Law;* and King and Chambliss, *Harry King.*

60. Allen, *Assault with a Deadly Weapon,* p. 192.

61. Ibid., p. 112.

62. Ibid., p. 121.

63. Miller and Helwig, *Book about Billie,* p. 141.

64. Jackson, *Outside the Law,* p. 22.

65. Willwerth, *Jones,* pp. 33–34.

66. Pileggi, *Wiseguy,* p. 61.

67. Wideman, *Brothers and Keepers,* p. 131.

68. Malcolm X and Haley, *Autobiography of Malcolm X,* p. 109.

69. Carr, *Bad,* p. 55.

70. Pileggi, *Wiseguy,* p. 126.

71. Hanson et al., eds. *Life with Heroin,* p. 32.

72. Willwerth, *Jones,* p. 33.

73. Malin Åkerström, *Crooks and Squares* (New Brunswick, N.J.: Transaction Books, 1985); Jackson, *Outside the Law;* and King and Chambliss, *Harry King.*

74. Marvin E. Wolfgang, Robert M. Figlio, and Thorsten Sellin, *Delinquency in a Birth Cohort* (Chicago: University of Chicago Press, 1972).

75. Petersilia, Greenwood, and Lavin, *Criminal Careers of Habitual Felons,* p. 110.

76. Chaiken and Chaiken, *Varieties of Criminal Behavior,* p. 29.

77. Wright and Rossi, *Armed and Considered Dangerous,* p. 14.

78. Ibid., p. 107; other referenced data is in text and tables, pp. 100–110.

79. This is the form of criminal career described by the nonviolent professional thieves Harry King (King and Chambliss, *Harry King*), Sam (Jackson, *Outside the Law*), and Chic Conwell (Edwin Sutherland, *The Professional Thief* [Chicago: University of Chicago Press, 1937]).

80. Williamson, *Hustler!,* pp. 55–56.

81. Pileggi, *Wiseguy,* p. 39.

82. Ibid., p. 161.

83. On the organization of the deviant's identity as a "regular suspect," see, David Matza, *Becoming Deviant* (Englewood Cliffs, N.J.: Prentice-Hall, 1969), pp. 177, 180.

84. Pileggi, *Wiseguy,* p. 38.

85. Allen, *Assault with a Deadly Weapon,* p. 107.

86. Willwerth, *Jones,* p. 190.

87. Ibid., p. 24.

88. Ibid., p. 18.

89. Malcolm X and Haley, *Autobiography of Malcolm X,* p. 109.

90. Ibid., p. 132.

91. Ibid., p. 149.

92. Although robbery, in contrast with other crimes, appears to be cleared less often by initial identifications made by victims or witnesses, small samples taken from police files in Los Angeles, Berkeley, Washington, D.C., and Miami in 1973–74 indicate that initial iden-

tifications are responsible for perhaps half of cleared robberies. Of the cases not cleared through initial identifications, only a small fraction, in these samples 10 percent, were cleared through some form of nonroutine, special action by the police (for example, fingerprint investigations). See Peter W. Greenwood, Jan M. Chaiken, and Joan Petersilia, *The Criminal Investigation Process* (Lexington, Mass.: D. C. Heath, 1977), pp. 123–29, 138–39, 226.

93. Williamson, *Hustler!*, p. 127.

94. Thomas, *Down These Mean Streets*, pp. 247–48.

95. Rettig, Torres, and Garrett, *Manny*, p. 63.

96. Wideman, *Brothers and Keepers*, p. 130.

97. Ianni, *Black Mafia*, p. 199.

98. Pileggi, *Wiseguy*, pp. 205, 206.

99. Taylor, *In the Underworld*, pp. 180–81.

100. Allen, *Assault with a Deadly Weapon*, pp. 79–80.

101. Taylor, *In the Underworld*, p. 72.

102. Haran, "Losers' Game."

103. Wideman, *Brothers and Keepers*, p. 157–59.

104. Pileggi, *Wiseguy*, p. 27.

105. Ibid., p. 49.

106. Allen, *Assault with a Deadly Weapon*, p. 96.

107. Ibid., p. 25.

108. Taylor, *In the Underworld*, p. 166.

109. Malcolm X and Haley, *Autobiography of Malcolm X*, pp. 115, 135.

110. Willwerth, *Jones*, p. 93. (emphasis in original).

111. Ibid., p. 166.

112. Brown, *Manchild in the Promised Land*, pp. 113–14.

113. Williamson, *Hustler!*, pp. 123–26.

114. Allen, *Assault with a Deadly Weapon*, p. 66. Compare a theory that was popular during the 1960s, which held that experiences with injustice in initial encounters with the criminal justice system were crucial in promoting a "drift" toward delinquency. See David Matza, *Delinquency and Drifter* (New York: John Wiley & Sons, 1964).

115. Allen, *Assault with a Deadly Weapon*, p. 191.

116. Taylor, *In the Underworld*, p. 93.

117. As might be expected, the biographies are not rich in accounts of sexual life in prison, but a few show a remarkable lack of self-consciousness and reticence in reporting the excitement of mass rapes (see, Carr, *Bad*, pp. 57–58) and the satisfactions of finding, on returning to prison for yet another stint, that friends have picked out homosexual "punks" for them. See Allen, *Assault with a Deadly Weapon*, p. 123.

118. Willwerth, *Jones*, p. 100.

119. Allen, *Assault with a Deadly Weapon*, p. 96.

120. Shaw, *The Jack-Roller*, p. 54.

121. Taylor, *In the Underworld*, pp. 78, 79.

122. Miller and Helwig, *Book about Billie*, p. 106.

123. As Drake and Cayton noted decades ago, the black bourgeoisie shares in the fascination. See St. Clair Drake and Horace R. Cayton, *Black Metropolis* (New York: Harper Torchbooks, 1962), 2:395.

124. Ossie Davis, "On Malcolm X," in Malcolm X and Haley, *Autobiography of Malcolm X*, p. 458.

125. Williamson, *Hustler!*, p. 34.

126. Carr, *Bad*, p. 21.

127. Willwerth, *Jones*, p. 172.

128. Wideman, *Brothers and Keepers*, p. 145.

Chapter 7. Of Hardmen and 'Bad Niggers': Gender and Ethnicity in the Background of Stickup

1. In his study of 500 bank robbers convicted in 281 cases in the New York area, Haran found that 96 percent were male. In the twelve-year period covered by his study, "only one

woman was armed during the commission of the robbery." James F. Haran, "The Losers' Game: A Sociological Profile of 500 Armed Bank Robbers" (Ph.D. diss., Department of Sociology, Fordham University, 1982).

Another source on the issue is self-report questionnaire studies. Conducted primarily with juveniles, usually in-school populations, they may systematically miss the most violent offenders. A review of the most prominent self-report studies showed sex ratios for "strong-arm" offenses, the category closest to robbery, of 4.5 to 1, which was the highest ratio in all the forms of deviance covered. See Michael J. Hindelang, Travis Hirschi, and Joseph G. Weis, "Correlates of Delinquency," *American Sociological Review* 44 (December 1979): 995–1014.

National victim surveys are another source. In their recent study of juvenile offenders identified in National Crime Surveys from 1973 through 1981, Laub and McDermott used the category "robbery," as defined in FBI–Uniform Crime Reports, and a category, "assaultive violence with theft." Among blacks, the sex ratio was 15 to 1; among whites, it was 7.5 or 5.5 to 1, depending on the definition used. See John Laub and M. Joan McDermott, "Young Black Women," *Criminology* 23 (February 1985): 81–99.

2. Surveyed victims are able to identify offender characteristics in only about 5 percent of these "household" crimes. For whites, the male-female ratio was about 8 to 1, for blacks, about 13 to 1. Michael J. Hindelang, "Variations in Sex-Race-Age-Specific Incidence Rates of Offending," *American Sociological Review* 46 (August 1981): 470. In national police statistics, males constitute 92 percent of those arrested for both robbery and burglary, and about 87 percent of those arrested for criminal homicide and for aggravated assault. Federal Bureau of Investigation, *Uniform Crime Reports* (Washington, D.C.: U.S. Government Printing Office, 1986), table 37, p. 181.

3. Laub and McDermott, "Young Black Women," table 2, p. 90.

4. Norval Morris and Michael H. Tonry, editors of the most prestigious periodic series of review essays in criminology, *Crime and Justice: An Annual Review of Research*, noted their difficulty in obtaining submissions on the topic. See Morris and Tonry, "Black Crime, Black Victims" in *The Pursuit of Criminal Justice*, ed. Gordon Hawkins and Franklin E. Zimring (Chicago: University of Chicago Press, 1984), p. 279.

5. There is no escape from this offensiveness, as long as determinist theory is used. Thus, it does not help much to offer the qualification that it is only under certain conditions (economic, historical, and so forth) that blacks tend to commit robbery. Probability statements, applied to all those in the explanatory category, imply guilt by statistical association. Thematically one is left imputing to "blacks" or "blackness" a criminogenic inclination.

6. Michael J. Hindelang, "Race and Involvement in Common Law Personal Crimes," *American Sociological Review* 43 (February 1978): 93–109.

7. Erhard Blankenburg and Johannes Feest, "On the Probability of a Bank Robber Being Sanctioned," *International Journal of Criminology and Penology* 5 (May 1977): 120; Haran, "Losers' Game"; Marvin E. Wolfgang, Robert M. Figlio, Thorsten Sellin, *Delinquency in a Birth Cohort* (Chicago: University of Chicago Press, 1972), table 5.4, pp. 72–73.

8. Hindelang, "Common Law Personal Crimes," table 1, p. 100. (In both national arrest and victim survey data for 1974, blacks were responsible for 62 percent of the robberies, while whites were responsible for about 62 percent of the simple and of the aggravated assaults.)

9. In national police data for 1986, blacks were responsible for 62 percent of the robberies and whites were responsible for 69 percent of the burglaries. Federal Bureau of Investigation, *Uniform Crime Reports*, table 38, p. 182.

10. For a British study, see Philip Stevens and Carole F. Willis, *Race, Crime and Arrests*, Home Office Research Study No. 58 (London: Her Majesty's Stationery Office, 1979).

11. This level of representation of blacks in robbery-homicide is not unique to the 1982–83 period covered by the Chicago data set. In his studies of police records in Chicago, Block found that, from 1965 to 1974, "the percentage of known offenders who were black increased from about 75 percent to 90 percent during the ten-year period." See Richard Block, *Violent Crime: Environment, Interaction, and Death* (Lexington, Mass.: Lexington Books, 1977), p. 49.

12. *U.S. Census of Population, 1980: Subject Reports: Poverty Areas in Large Cities* (PC 80-2-8D), final report (Washington, D.C.: U.S. Government Printing Office, 1985), sec. 2, table P-11, p. 1007.

13. The category Hispanic is about 80 percent Mexican origin. Less than 2 percent of Spanish-origin persons were reported as black. *U.S. Census of Population, 1980: General Population Characteristics: California* (PC 80-1-B6), final report (Washington, D.C.: U.S. Government Printing Office, 1982), table 16, "Total Persons and Spanish Origin Persons by Type of Spanish Origin and Race: 1980."

14. John Allen and Jones both described such early career techniques. See John Allen, *Assault with a Deadly Weapon,* ed. Dianne Hall Kelly and Philip Heymann (New York: McGraw-Hill, 1978); and James Willwerth, *Jones* (New York: M. Evans & Co., 1974).

15. Laub and McDermott, "Young Black Women."

16. It is particularly impressive that heroin-addicted women, who would seem particularly likely to appreciate the attractions of robbery, if the act were attractive for reasons independent of a version of maleness that it can be made to represent, do not commit it. They often have desperate economic, emotional, and physiological needs and are already committed to a criminal lifestyle. See Marsha Rosenbaum, *Women on Heroin* (New Brunswick, N.J.: Rutgers University Press, 1981). Street prostitution is hardly a passive occupational role, and the heroin-prostitution life is not free of female violence. See also Eleanor M. Miller, *Street Women* (Philadelphia: Temple University Press, 1986).

17. For an appreciation of this issue, see Albert J. Reiss, Jr., "Co-Offender Influences on Criminal Careers," in *Criminal Careers and "Career Criminals,"* ed. Alfred Blumstein et al. (Washington, D.C.: National Academy Press, 1986), 2:132–33. Assault is often, in an important respect, a collectively engaged line of criminal conduct, with the "victim" and the "assailant" exchanging blows. On the joint or group nature of robbery, especially by young males, see Franklin E. Zimring, "Kids, Groups, and Crime: Some Implications of a Well-Known Secret," *Journal of Criminology and Criminal Law* 72 (1981): 867–85.

18. Ulf Hannerz, *Soulside* (New York: Columbia University Press, 1969), p. 30; Ned Polsky, *Hustlers, Beats, and Others* (New York: Anchor Books, 1969), p. 21.

19. Edith A. Folb, *Runnin' Down Some Lines: The Language and Culture of Black Teenagers* (Cambridge, Mass.: Harvard University Press, 1980), p. 197.

20. Elliot Liebow, *Tally's Corner* (Boston: Little, Brown, 1967); and Elijah Anderson, *A Place on the Corner* (Chicago: University of Chicago Press, 1978).

21. See, for example, Ann Teresa Cordilia, "Robbery Arising out of a Group Drinking Context," in *Violent Transactions,* ed. Anne Campbell and John J. Gibbs (Oxford: Basil Blackwell, 1986), pp. 167–80.

22. In Great Britain, half the men and two-fifths of the women were reported to gamble regularly on racehorses. A national survey of "who gambles" in the United States in the mid-1970s reported rates of 68 percent for males and 55 percent for females. See Tomas M. Martinez, *The Gambling Scene: Why People Gamble* (Springfield, Ill.: Charles C Thomas, 1983), pp. 3, 4.

23. Regular horse players see risk takers as fools. They seek to work on inside information, systems, and logical inferences from previous performances; at the race track, they respect the taboo against inquiring about the amount others bet—a rule that insures that only money, not face, will be put at risk. See Marvin B. Scott, *The Racing Game* (Chicago: Aldine, 1968). Where this rule of reserve is not observed, for example, in horse rooms or bookie shops in which audiences are present, horse playing can take on the head-to-head action of poker. See, for example, Irving K. Zola, "Observations on Gambling in a Lower-Class Setting," in *The Other Side,* ed. Howard S. Becker (New York: Free Press of Glencoe, 1964), pp. 247–60.

24. David M. Hayano, *Poker Faces: The Life and Work of Professional Card Players* (Berkeley: University of California Press, 1982), p. 83.

25. Ibid., p. 89.

26. Rosenbaum, *Women on Heroin,* p. 50.

27. Terry M. Williams and William Kornblum, *Growing Up Poor* (Lexington, Mass.: Lexington Books, 1985), p. 61.

28. Sally Engle Merry, *Urban Danger* (Philadelphia: Temple University Press, 1981), p. 86.

29. Anderson, *Place on the Corner,* p. 194. In other contexts, "fronting up" captures a related practice. English criminals often become self-consciously manipulative about the skills and techniques of fronting up. See Laurie Taylor, *In the Underworld* (London: Unwin Paperbacks, 1985).

30. The closest documented analogy appears to be the trading of poetic insults among young low-income black women, which may begin playfully but end in pain. See Claudia Mitchell-Kernan, *Language Behavior in a Black Urban Community* (Berkeley, Calif.: Language-Behavior Research Laboratory, Monograph no. 2, 1971).

31. Janet Lever, "Sex Differences in the Complexity of Children's Play and Games," *American Sociological Review* 43 (August 1978): 476 (emphasis in original).

32. In another article, Lever noted that boys' games have a denser structure of rules than does girls' play, affording ready opportunities for arguments and for creative maneuvers to

get around the rules. Girls often treated arguments as antithetical to the essence of play. "Most girls interviewed claimed that when a quarrel begins, the game breaks up, and little effort is made to resolve the problem." See Janet Lever, "Sex Differences in the Games Children Play," *Social Problems* 23 (April 1976): 483.

33. Iris Marion Young, "Throwing like a Girl," *Human Studies* 3 (April 1980): 143.

34. Ray L. Birdwhistell, *Kinesics and Context* (Philadelphia: University of Pennsylvania Press, 1970), pp. 44, 49.

35. Alfred Blumstein, "On the Racial Disproportionality of United States' Prison Population," *Journal of Criminal Law and Criminology* 73 (1983): 1259–81.

36. For a similar finding in St. Louis, about twenty-five years ago, see Lee Rainwater, "Crucible of Identity: The Negro Lower-Class Family," in *The Negro American,* ed. Talcott Parsons and Kenneth B. Clark (Boston: Beacon Press, 1967), p. 187.

The male black deficit is not due simply to mortality. The number of males per female rises substantially later in the life cycle. Nor does the deficit simply continue sex deficits existing when the population was younger. There are, of course, other alternative interpretations of the intra- and interethnic patterns. The effects of out-migration and in-migration on gender imbalances are especially complex. The undocumented immigration from Mexico appears to be disproportionately male (see W. T. Dagodag, "Source Regions and Composites of Illegal Mexican Immigration to California," *International Migration Review* 9 [Winter 1975]: 499–511; and D. North and M. F. Houstoun, *The Characteristics and Role of Illegal Aliens in the U.S. Labor Market: An Exploratory Study* [Washington, D.C.: Linton & Co., 1976]), a pattern that would offset and hide large losses of Hispanic males from census counts but only to the extent that undocumented residents were actually counted in the census. As to the uncounted undocumented male Hispanic residents, all indications are that they come seeking employment rather than action. See R. Walsinger, "The Occupational and Economic Integration of the New Immigrants," *Law and Contemporary Problems* 45 (1982): 197–222; and D. S. Massey, "Dimensions of the New Immigration to the United States and the Prospects for Assimilation," in *Annual Review of Sociology,* ed. Ralph H. Turner and James F. Short, Jr. (Palo Alto, Calif.: Annual Reviews Inc., 1981), 7: 57–85.

37. Ronald Angel and Marta Tienda, "Determinants of Extended Household Structure: Cultural Pattern of Economic Need," *American Journal of Sociology* 87 (May 1982): 1360–83.

38. The most recent statistical indication of a positive relationship between female-headed families and violent crime rates, for blacks and for whites, is in Robert J. Sampson, "Urban Black Violence: The Effect of Male Joblessness and Family Disruption," *American Journal of Sociology* 93 (September 1987): 348–82. (Sampson used aggregate data from the census and the FBI that do not show either the family backgrounds of those who actually commit the crimes or the temporal order of variables.)

39. Other indicators measure participation in the labor force. See William Julius Wilson, "The Urban Underclass," in *Minority Report,* ed. Leslie W. Dunbar (New York: Pantheon Books, 1985), pp. 75–117.

40. Bureau of Justice Statistics, *Criminal Victimization in the United States, 1985* (Washington, D.C.: U.S. Department of Justice, 1987), table 38, p. 40.

41. Ibid., table 6, p. 16.

42. See Robert M. O'Brien, "The Interracial Nature of Violent Crimes: A Reexamination," *American Journal of Sociology* 92 (January 1987): 817–35.

43. One needs at least to take into account the physical proximity of whites and blacks to those blacks who commit robbery. See ibid.

44. There is evidence that black offenders are especially uncooperative with research efforts to describe their criminal experience statistically. Michael J. Hindelang, Travis Hirschi, and Joseph Weis, *Measuring Delinquency* (Beverly Hills, Calif.: Sage, 1981). Consider also the provocative finding from victimization studies that the rate of simple assault, for blacks with 13–15 years of education (i.e., at least a year of college) is 10.6, while the rate for blacks with 0–4 years of education is 2.3; and for whites with 0–4 years of education, the rate is 7.2. Is it more reasonable to interpret these differences as reflecting real differences by education and race, or as reflecting especially strong biases among poorly educated blacks against cooperation in reporting? See Robert M. O'Brien, *Crime and Victimization Data* (Beverly Hills, Calif.: Sage, 1985), p. 56.

45. Lee H. Bowker, *Prison Victimization* (New York: Elsevier, 1980), pp. 71–85. Sociologists who interpret victimization statistics do not seem to be bothered by this gap. It is understandable, if something less than morally neutral, to exclude criminals from the portrayal of *victims*

of crimes; however, it risks serious distortion to theories of *criminals'* motivations if such a vitally significant part of criminal experience is excluded.

46. In his study of police files on robbery in Chicago from 1965 to 1974, Block found that "most victims of robbery and robbery homicide were black. In other cities robbery is predominantly an interracial crime. In Chicago, robbery is geographically and racially concentrated among blacks in predominantly black neighborhoods, both as victims and offender." See, Block, *Violent Crime,* p. 49. To some this finding will suggest that Chicago is an unrepresentative, unfortunate base for understanding contemporary robbery in general. It is also possible to draw a contrary inference that the Chicago data indicate with special clarity how free robbery by blacks is from racist motives.

47. Franklin E. Zimring and James Zuehl, "Victim Injury and Death in Urban Robbery," *Journal of Legal Studies* 15 (January 1986): tables 2, 3, pp. 8, 9. The "relationship unknown" category was much larger in the robbery-homicides (at 24 percent) than in the robberies (at 3 percent).

48. On the victimization of Korean merchants by black robbers in Los Angeles, see Ivan Light and Edna Bonacich, *Immigrant Entrepreneurs: Koreans in Los Angeles, 1965–1982* (Berkeley: University of California Press, 1988), pp. 314–15.

49. Two other patterns of evidence may be drawn from the Chicago data sets on the cross-race issue. First, if black offenders vent racial anger or get some special kick when victimizing whites, there should be more cases of injuries of victims who did not resist in black offender–white victim cases than in black offender–black victim cases. In reanalyzing the set of robberies in which the victims were injured, I found the copresence of the injury and resistance of victims in almost exactly the same proportion of black-black (65 of 173) as black-white (19 of 50) cases.

Second, Zimring and Zuehl created narrative summaries on homicides with unknown motive that occurred in the same twelve-month period. Only ten of the eighty-five cases in this series had white victims and only in one of these cases was the offender identified; he was American Indian.

50. Ronald L. Carter and Kim Q. Hill, *The Criminal's Image of the City* (New York: Pergamon Press, 1979). Even within racial areas, the whites roam much farther from their own residence in their choice of "marks"; for the black property criminals, a familiarity with the area seems to be a stronger influence on the choice of a mark.

51. Carl Werthman and Irving Piliavin, "Gang Members and the Police," in *The Police: Six Sociological Essays,* ed. David Bordua (New York: John Wiley & Sons, 1967), p. 80.

52. James Carr, *Bad* (New York: Herman Graf Associates, 1975), p. 55.

53. Allen, *Assault with a Deadly Weapon,* p. 34.

54. Ibid., pp. 111–12.

55. Dan A. Lewis and Greta Salem, *Fear of Crime: Incivility and the Production of a Social Problem* (New Brunswick, N.J.: Transaction Books, 1986), p. 7.

56. Miller, *Street Women,* p. 124.

57. Gwaltney provided numerous self-portraits of black people over age 60 living in northeastern urban communities who reported having successfully resisted at least one mugging, including that of an elderly woman who, after cutting her assailant, gave him first aid. See John Langston Gwaltney, *Drylongso* (New York: Random House, 1980), p. 27 and passim.

58. Malcolm X, with the assistance of Alex Haley, *The Autobiography of Malcolm X* (New York: Grove Press, 1965), pp. 102–3.

59. Avelardo Valdez, "Chicano Used Car Dealers," *Urban Life* 13 (October 1984): 239.

60. Jenna Weissman Joselit, *Our Gang: Jewish Crime and the New York Jewish Community, 1900–1940* (Bloomington: Indiana University Press, 1983), p. 37.

61. Francis A. J. Ianni, *Black Mafia* (New York: Pocket Books, 1975).

62. The leading explanation of this underrepresentation is in Ivan Light, *Ethnic Entrepreneurs in America* (Berkeley: University of California Press, 1972). Light's work has influenced this section far more than my direct reference to his writings in the subsequent endnotes and text may indicate.

63. Joselit, *Our Gang,* p. 27.

64. Albert Fried, *The Rise and Fall of the Jewish Gangster in America* (New York: Holt, Rinehart & Winston, 1980), p. 33.

65. For an indication of such attempts and their pathetic results in the South Bronx, see William Gales, *The Compound* (New York: Rawson Associates, 1977), p. 73.

66. Joselit, *Our Gang,* p. 28.

67. John Landesco, *Organized Crime in Chicago* (Chicago: University of Chicago Press, 1968).

68. See Light, *Ethnic Entrepreneurs in America.*

69. Francis A. J. Ianni with Elizabeth Reuss Ianni, *The Family Business* (New York: Russell Sage Foundation, 1972).

70. Alan Block, *East Side–West Side: Organizing Crime in New York, 1930–1950* (Cardiff: University College Cardiff Press, 1980), p. 163.

71. Joselit, *Our Gang,* pp. 39–40.

72. There is a suggestive ethnic imbalance in the ethnographic literature. Descriptions of such arrangements are usually of white working-class youths. See W. Gordon West, "The Short Term Careers of Serious Thieves," *Canadian Journal of Criminology* 20 (April 1978): 169–90; Mercer L. Sullivan, "Youth Crime: New York's Two Varieties," *New York Affairs* 8, no. 1 (1983): 31–48; Williams and Kornblum, *Growing Up Poor;* Jay MacLeod, *Ain't No Makin' It* (Boulder, Colo.: Westview Press, 1987); and James Patrick, *A Glasgow Gang Observed* (London: Eyre Methuen, 1973). Young black street criminals are described as engaging in a variety of hustling activities, including pimping, drug sales, and the sale of goods "boosted" from retail stores and of building materials from construction sites. The continuous extraordinarily high level of unemployment among black youths would be consistent with this difference in the forms of crime.

73. Light, *Ethnic Entrepreneurs in America,* p. 14.

74. See Nicholas Pileggi, *Wiseguy* (New York: Simon & Schuster, 1985); and Allen, *Assault with a Deadly Weapon,* p. 189.

75. Ivan Light, "The Ethnic Vice Industry, 1880–1944," *American Sociological Review* 42 (June 1977): 469, 471, 472.

76. Roger Lane, *Roots of Violence in Black Philadelphia, 1860–1900* (Cambridge, Mass.: Harvard University Press, 1986), p. 107. Monkkonen found that from June 1859 to October 1885, blacks were underrepresented in the crime figures of the Columbus, Ohio, area, relative to their percentage of the population. Independent of race, robbery was relatively rare compared to contemporary levels. In figures on prosecutions for Ohio as a whole in 1883, robbery was less frequent than murder. See Eric Monkkonen, *The Dangerous Class: Crime and Poverty in Columbus, Ohio, 1860–1885* (Cambridge, Mass.: Harvard University Press, 1975), pp. 26, 44, 86.

77. Block, *East Side–West Side,* pp. 205–6.

78. Joselit, *Our Gang,* p. 52.

79. Edith A. Folb, *Runnin' Down Some Lines* (Cambridge, Mass.: Harvard University Press, 1980), p. 20. Note the wishful, celebratory use of the term "partner." With its mixture of business and cowboy allusions, the term is popular across ethnic groups in contemporary criminal rhetoric.

80. James B. Jacobs, "Street Gangs Behind Bars," *Social Problems* 3 (Winter 1974): 359–409.

81. A study of all drug offenders sentenced by federal courts in the Southern District of New York between 1969 and 1976 (n = 4,371) found that nearly 80 percent of the "big dealers" were white (compared to 60 percent of the "user" population in these cases and compared to what is surely, because of federal prosecutorial priorities on big dealers, a much lower percentage of whites in the street user-dealer population). See Ruth D. Peterson and John Hagan, "Changing Conceptions of Race: Towards an Account of Anomalous Findings of Sentencing Research," *American Sociological Review* 49 (February 1984): 68.

82. Allen B. Fields, " 'Slinging Weed': The Social Organization of Streetcorner Marijuana Sales," *Urban Life* 13 (October 1984): 255, 265–66.

83. Thomas Mieczkowski, "Geeking Up and Throwing Down," *Criminology* 24 (November 1986): 645–66.

84. Williams and Kornblum, *Growing Up Poor,* p. 50.

85. H. C. Brearley, "Ba-ad Nigger," *South Atlantic Quarterly* 38 (January 1939): 75–81.

86. Maurer reported that "professional" theft groups or "mobs" used self-denigrating titles with pride early in the century. Jewish thieves would refer to themselves as *gonifs* and to their groups as "a mockey jew mob." Jews were overrepresented among pickpockets, and the term "cannon" for pickpocket, Maurer theorized, was an alternative for "gun," which, in turn, was suggested by the word *gonif.* See David Maurer, *Whiz Mob* (New Haven, Conn.: College & University Press, 1964), p. 89.

Each ethnic form of tough, mean, or badass style responds to the peculiar vulnerabilities and strengths implied in ethnically distinct forms of insult. It would be valuable to pursue this line of research for understanding the contribution of other ethnic groups to the rates of predatory violent crimes. At this writing, because of the current weakness of the ethnographic literature on Hispanics, ethnics of European origin, and others, I will suggest only a few minor comparative points.

87. Allen, *Assault with a Deadly Weapon.*

88. Erving Goffman, *The Presentation of Self in Everyday Life* (New York: Anchor, 1959), pp. 151–52.

89. Allen, *Assault with a Deadly Weapon,* pp. 54–55.

90. Lee Rainwater, *Behind Ghetto Walls: Black Families in a Federal Slum* (Chicago: Aldine-Atherton, 1970), p. 259.

91. Ibid., p. 333.

92. Williams and Kornblum, *Growing Up Poor,* p. 119.

93. Ibid., p. 67.

94. Janet K. Mancini, *Coping in the Inner City* (Hanover, N.H.: University Press of New England, 1980), p. 109.

95. Ibid.

96. Claude Brown, *Manchild in the Promised Land* (New York: Macmillan, 1978), p. 19.

97. Williams and Kornblum, *Growing Up Poor,* p. 7.

98. MacLeod, *Aint No Makin' It,* p. 122.

99. William Labov, "Rules for Ritual Insults," in *Studies in Social Interaction,* ed. David Sudnow (New York: Free Press, 1972), p. 137.

100. Thomas Kochman, "Toward an Ethnography of Black American Speech Behavior," in *Rappin' and Stylin' Out,* ed. Thomas Kochman (Urbana: University of Illinois Press, 1972), p. 259.

101. Rainwater, *Behind Ghetto Walls,* p. 278.

102. Folb, *Runnin' Down Some Lines,* p. 92.

103. Ibid., p. 32.

104. Ralph Ellison, *Invisible Man* (New York: Random House, 1982).

105. H. Rap Brown, "Street Talk," in *Rappin' and Stylin' Out,* ed. Kochman pp. 205–6. "Rap" Brown earned his name from rapping.

106. Folb, *Runnin' Down Some Lines,* p. 190.

107. MacLeod, *Ain't No Makin' It,* p. 27.

108. Michael J. Bell, *The World from Brown's Lounge* (Urbana: University of Illinois Press, 1983), p. 20. Ethnic references can be insulting solely because a generic is used to refer to an individual. "Jap," "Chink," and "Spic" signal that the individual merits expecially little consideration by employing an abbreviation for the ethnic group's name (or, with "Mick," an aspect of family name common in the group). For those who are abused with these substantively vacant terms, no particular transcendent response is made relevant, other than an insistence on individual identity.

109. Folb, *Runnin' Down Some Lines,* p. 70.

110. Gwaltney, *Drylongso,* p. 76.

111. Mancini, *Coping in the Inner City,* p. 167.

112. Rainwater, *Behind Ghetto Walls,* p. 21 (emphasis in original).

113. Folb, *Runnin' Down Some Lines,* p. 45.

114. Bettylou Valentine, *Hustling and Other Hard Work: Life Styles in the Ghetto* (New York: Free Press, 1978), pp. 46–47.

115. The most recent documentation of the widespread persistence of this culture is in Williams and Kornblum, *Growing Up Poor.*

116. Douglas C. Glasgow, *The Black Underclass* (New York: Vintage, 1981), p. 94. The pimping culture frames sensual pleasures as secondary to moral domination. At the rhetorical extreme, "any place designated for sex—a motel, a front room . . . [is called] a *killing floor, slaughter house, whip shack.*" There is also some overlap of the terms for sex and physical assault: "to rip off/on someone, to jam, to jackkup, to throw." Folb, *Runnin' Down Some Lines,* p. 152 (emphasis in original). Sex in this regard is a way of destroying the other's moral existence.

117. Ibid., p. 24.

118. Gwaltney, *Drylongso,* p. 130.

119. Folb, *Runnin' Down Some Lines,* p. 111.

120. Ibid., p. 39.

121. Mitchell-Kernan, *Language Behavior in a Black Urban Community,* p. 82. With continued "signifying," the debtor's hand movements toward his pocket could be interpreted by the creditor as dangerous, thus motivating him to shoot the debtor. In such event, the proper

characterization lies somewhere in the overlap of street signifying–loud talking; assault; and, because of the demand for payment, robbery.

122. See Fried, *Jewish Gangster in America*.

123. Dermot Walsh, *Heavy Business: Commercial Burglary* (London: Routledge & Kegan Paul, 1986), p. 60.

124. John Irwin, *The Jail* (Berkeley: University of California Press, 1985), pp. 29–30, 33–34.

Chapter 8. Primordial Evil: Sense and Dynamic in Cold-Blooded, 'Senseless' Murder

1. Friedrich Nietzsche, *Thus Spoke Zarathustra,* in *The Portable Nietzsche,* ed. Walter Kaufmann (New York: Viking, 1968), pp. 150–51.

2. Elliott Leyton, *Compulsive Killers* (New York: New York University Press, 1986); and Jack Levin and James Alan Fox, *Mass Murder* (New York: Plenum Press, 1985).

3. To *Newsweek,* Gary Gilmore committed "a senseless holdup murder (one of two within a couple of days) that profited him about $100." (Walter Clemons, "Gary Gilmore's Saga," *Newsweek,* October 1, 1979, p. 72.) The amount stolen in robberies may be less instructive about robbers' motives which, I have been arguing, are not fundamentally instrumental anyway, than about the materialism that governs the public's view of the event. At what point does the take from a robbery-killing become too large to warrant reporting the event as senseless?

4. Norman Mailer, *The Executioner's Song* (New York: Warner Books, 1979), p. 715.

5. Paul Ricoeur, *The Symbolism of Evil* (Boston: Beacon Press, 1967).

6. David Matza, *Becoming Deviant* (Englewood Cliffs, N.J.: Prentice-Hall, 1969).

7. Truman Capote, *In Cold Blood* (New York: New American Library, 1965).

8. Ibid.; Gary Kinder, *Victim* (New York: Laurel Books, 1982); and Joseph Wambaugh, *The Onion Field* (New York: Dell, 1973).

9. Capote's title, *In Cold Blood,* was an ironic protest against capital punishment, not the author's view of the crime itself.

10. See the classic article by Howard S. Becker, "Problems of Inference and Proof in Participant Observation," in his *Sociological Work* (Chicago: Aldine, 1970), pp. 25–38.

11. An example is Clark Howard, *Brothers in Blood* (New York: St. Martin's Press, 1973). Howard manufactured composite characters and did not hesitate to quote the unexpressed thoughts of murder victims. Although all the authors abjured footnoting sources, a careful reader will often realize when a text is tracking the accounts of particular witnesses, background interviews, police reports, or trial transcripts. But in Howard's account, we are never even told which of the four offenders involved in the killing may have been interviewed. Perhaps what is most essential for producing a high-quality source of data on these exceptionally rare events is a research focus on a short period around the time of the offense. Falling into a common narrative trap, Howard tapped a great number of emotionally powerful theories of pathological psychological development by concentrating his research on the early biographical backgrounds of the killers. But it is in their experience in the nine days between the start of their escapade and their murders (three of the four escaped from a minimum security prison together) that we must locate the emergent dynamics that led to what was, for all of them, an unprecedented event.

12. In crucial places, relying on his extensive personal interviews, Capote imputed otherwise undocumented thoughts to Perry. See the essay by Tompkins, a piece of criticism based on fresh investigative work that indicates that the market, however evil its seductions, may also stimulate more of a commitment to "replication" than is usually undertaken in academic social research. Phillip K. Tompkins, "In Cold Fact," *Esquire* (June 1966), pp. 125, 127, 166–71.

13. Ricoeur, *Symbolism of Evil,* p. 25.

14. Ibid., p. 20.

15. From our modern ethical sensibility, we are tempted to explain the laws of kosher diet as having been medically wise in ancient times. For a phenomenologically more accurate view, see Mary Douglas, "The Laws of Leviticus," in her *Purity and Danger* (London: ARK Paperbacks, 1984), pp. 41–57. What is prohibited is not merely unhealthy but disgusting; the sensual repulsion involved goes beyond rational considerations and reflects a nausea or dread

about existential chaos. In a secular form, it is the violation of our artificial cultural distinctions—our sense of boundaries—that makes sticky icky.

16. Kinder, *Victim*, p. 89.

17. Ibid., p. 91.

18. Ibid., p. 118.

19. Ricoeur, *Symbolism of Evil*, p. 33.

20. Ibid., p. 67.

21. Capote, *In Cold Blood*, pp. 127–28.

22. Ricoeur, *Symbolism of Evil*, p. 30.

23. Ibid., p. 33. There is a justice to the sufferings that Zeus imposes, but it is not grasped clearly if we insist on using a legal-bureaucratic-rationalist understanding of justice. Reading Greek mythology with a modern sensibility that demands that the punished be found guilty before he or she is punished, it is possible to detect mortal defilement or sacrilege somewhere behind the sufferings the gods impose (even if, as in the case of Oedipus, the search for mortal culpability must reach into prior generations before it can rest). See Hugh Lloyd-Jones, *The Justice of Zeus* (Berkeley: University of California Press, 1983), p. 128. But to go too far with an attempt to reconcile the gods' vengeance with modern understandings of fault and justice is to ignore the distinctive theme in primordial evil that the sufferings of human beings transcend mortal predictability, understanding, and moral control. If the gods exacerbate wars whose origins may be traced to human hubris, the godly escalations of conflict also clearly leap beyond the gradations of fault that can be attributed to the mortal warriors. After all, if the gods' curses on mankind simply followed as effect from mortal sins, people could control the gods through perversity.

24. Capote, *In Cold Blood*, p. 34.

25. Wambaugh, *Onion Field*, pp. 118–19.

26. Ricoeur, *Symbolism of Evil*, p. 27.

27. Ibid.

28. Kinder, *Victim*, p. 140.

29. Rene Girard, *Violence and the Sacred* (Baltimore: Johns Hopkins University Press, 1977).

30. Ricoeur, *Symbolism of Evil*, p. 43.

31. See Arthur Allen Leff, "Law And," *Yale Law Journal* 87 (April 1978): 989–1011.

32. Nietzsche, *Twilight of the Idols*, in *Portable Nietzsche*, ed. Kaufmann, p. 550.

33. Capote, *In Cold Blood*, p. 155.

34. Ibid., p. 57, 58.

35. Ibid., p. 59. For this characterization, which Capote presumably reconstructed from his extensive interviews with Perry, we are completely at the author's mercy.

36. Jack Abbott, *In the Belly of the Beast* (New York: Vintage, 1982).

37. Ibid., p. 16.

38. Ibid., pp. 5–6.

39. Ibid., p. 79.

40. Matza, *Becoming Deviant*, pp. 174–75.

41. Mailer, *Executioner's Song*, p. 61.

42. Wambaugh, *Onion Field*, p. 121.

43. Capote, *In Cold Blood*, p. 169.

44. Richard Eugene (Dick) Hickock, as quoted in Mack Nations, "America's Worst Crime in Twenty Years," in *Truman Capote's In Cold Blood: A Critical Handbook*, ed. Irving Malin (Belmont, Calif.: Wadsworth Publishing Co., 1968), p. 12.

45. Nations, "America's Worst Crime," p. 14.

46. Kinder, *Victim*, p. 263.

47. Ricoeur, *Symbolism of Evil*, p. 20. Ricoeur most directly intended a historical meaning for this "entrance," to which I am giving a psychobiographical reading.

48. John Irwin, *The Felon* (Englewood Cliffs, N.J.: Prentice-Hall, 1970), p. 101.

49. Kinder, *Victim*, p. 155.

50. Mailer, *Executioner's Song*, p. 182. Gilmore had long been negotiating with a used car dealer to buy a white truck that, given its age and excessive price, he found inexplicably seductive. After Nicole left him, he acquired the truck on a contractual commitment to come up with $400 in two days—a commitment that he had no hope of meeting legitimately. So instead of bringing him a new, calming source of pride, the truck pushed him on to the robbery-murders.

51. Nietzsche, *Thus Spoke Zarathustra*, in *The Portable Nietzsche*, ed. Walter Kaufmann, p. 150.

Chapter 9. Seductions and Repulsions of Crime

1. Michel Foucault, ed., *I, Pierre Rivière, having slaughtered my mother, my sister, and my brother . . .* (New York: Pantheon Books, 1975), p. 106.

2. In the short essay he included in the volume, Foucault continued his pioneering emphasis on the unique phenomenon of power/knowledge. Some of his colleagues and students, however, were quick to impute causal force to class formations, the hypocrisies of the Enlightenment, the market economy, the contractual form, and so on. We learn of the situational facts essentially though the initial, brief reports of doctors who performed what we would today recognize as a coroner's investigation.

3. Robert K. Merton, "Social Structure and Anomie," in his *Social Theory and Social Structure* (New York: Free Press, 1968), p. 198.

4. Stephen Cole, "The Growth of Scientific Knowledge," in *The Idea of Social Structure*, ed. Lewis A. Coser (New York: Harcourt Brace Jovanovich, 1975), p. 175.

5. Richard A. Cloward and Lloyd E. Ohlin, *Delinquency and Opportunity* (New York: Free Press, 1960).

6. Robert J. Sampson, "Urban Black Violence: The Effect of Male Joblessness and Family Disruption," *American Journal of Sociology* 93 (September 1987): 348–82; William Julius Wilson, *The Truly Disadvantaged: The Inner City, The Underclass, and Public Policy* (Chicago: University of Chicago Press, 1987); David Rauma and Richard A. Berk, "Remuneration and Recidivism: The Long-Term Impact of Unemployment Compensation on Ex-Offenders," *Journal of Quantitative Criminology* 3 (March 1987): 3–27.

7. Merton, "Social Structure and Anomie," p. 198.

8. Gus Frias, *Barrio Warriors: Homeboys of Peace* (n.p.: Diaz Publications, 1982), p. 19.

9. Alfred Blumstein et al., *Criminal Careers and "Career Criminals"* (Washington, D.C.: National Academy Press, 1986), 1:46–47; and Christy A. Visher, "The Rand Inmate Survey: A Reanalysis," in ibid., 2:168. A recent theory sees adolescents as a social class defined—through legal requirements of school attendance, legal restrictions on employing youths, and laws excepting youths from minimum-wage rates—as having a common position in relation to the means of production. Attractive for its historical and theoretical color, these ideas account no more convincingly than do Merton's for vandalism, the use of dope, intergroup fighting, and the character of initial exeriences in property theft as sneaky thrills. David F. Greenberg, "Delinquency and the Age Structure of Society," *Contemporary Crises* 1 (April 1977): 189–224.

10. Cohen, as quoted in Merton, "Social Structure and Anomie," p. 232.

11. John Edgar Wideman, *Brothers and Keepers* (New York: Penguin Books, 1985), p. 131. Recently, the revelations of insider trading in securities markets have produced strikingly similar statements from high-level miscreants. When the take runs into millions of dollars and comes in faster than the criminals can spend it, it is difficult to explain crime with ideas of overly socialized materialistic aspirations. As the offenders themselves put it, at this level, money quickly becomes a way of keeping score.

12. Edith A. Folb, *Runnin' Down Some Lines: The Language and Culture of Black Teenagers* (Cambridge, Mass.: Harvard University Press, 1980), p. 128 (emphasis in original).

13. Indeed, if we look at what is used to make materialism seductive in advertising, it is not clear that we find the American dream of shiny material success more than a version of "street culture": soul-wrenching intonations of black music, whorish styles, fleeting images of men shooting craps in alleys and hustling in pool halls, torn shirts and motorcycles, and all the provocatively sensual evils of "the night." Judging from Madison Avenue, materialism may be less essential to the motivation to become deviant than an association with deviance is essential to the motivation to be acquisitive.

14. As Davis noted, "Each classical social theorist shows how their fundamental factor not only undermines the individual's integrity but also saps the society's vitality." See Murray Davis, " 'That's Classic!' The Phenomenology and Rhetoric of Successful Social Theories," *Philosophy of Social Science* 16 (1986): 290.

15. And here the evidence continues to mount through increasingly sophisticated historical research that demonstrates the many episodes in which more-qualified Northern blacks were pushed aside when jobs were offered to less-qualified white immigrants. See Stanley Lieberson, *A Piece of the Pie* (Berkeley: University of California Press, 1980). Roger Lane, *Roots of Violence in Philadelphia, 1860–1900* (Cambridge, Mass.: Harvard University Press, 1986), is a provocative argument that European ethnic groups who were new to the city in the nineteenth

century (the Irish, then the Italians) initially had high rates of violent crime, sometimes higher than the rates for blacks, but the rates for white ethnics declined as these groups were incorporated into the industrial economy, while the rates for blacks, who were excluded from all but servile and dirty-work jobs by discriminatory preferences for less-qualified whites and by public segregation enforced by violence, continually rose.

16. Or when repeal would be too raw politically, the available alternative is to add constraints on the investigative-prosecutorial process. An obvious example from the 1980s is the move to abolish the office of special prosecutor. A less obvious example from the 1970s was built into the Tax Reform Act of 1976. For this and other examples that marked the closing of the Watergate era, see Jack Katz, "The Social Movement Against White-Collar Crime," in *Criminology Review Yearbook*, ed. Egon Bittner and Sheldon Messinger (Beverly Hills, Calif.: Sage, 1980), 2:161–84. An important appreciation of the distinctively negotiable character of enforcement efforts against white-collar crime in class-related partisan politics is found in Vilhelm Aubert, "White Collar Crime and Social Structure," *American Journal of Sociology* 58 (November 1952): 263–71.

17. See Henry Williamson, *Hustler! The Autobiography of a Thief*, ed. R. Lincoln Keiser (New York: Doubleday, 1965). In his encyclopedic study of bribery, Noonan found an admitted awareness of participating in bribery only in the diaries of Samuel Pepys. See John T. Noonan, Jr., *Bribes* (New York: Macmillan, 1984), p. xiv. In relation to differences in the quality of moral autobiographies written by authors of different social classes, we should consider the differential demands on writing talent. Much more interpersonal insight and attention to subtle interactional detail are required to trace the inside experience of white-collar crimes, given their elaborate diffusion of deceit over long careers and in complex social relations. The extraordinary biographies of Robert Moses and Lyndon Johnson by Robert Caro indicate the dimensions of the task. See Robert A. Caro, *The Power Broker: Robert Moses and the Fall of New York* (New York: Alfred A. Knopf, 1974); and *The Path to Power: The Years of Lyndon Johnson* (New York: Alfred A. Knopf, 1982). Talent aside, we should also consider that, for our deceitful elites, to bare all that was involved might entail unbearable self-disgust. It is notable that our social order is so constructed that it is virtually impossible emotionally for our elites truly to confess.

18. Jack Katz, "Concerted Ignorance: The Social Construction of Cover-up," *Urban Life* 8 (October 1979): 295–316; and Jack Katz, "Cover-up and Collective Integrity," *Social Problems* 25 (Fall 1977): 1–25.

19. See J. C. Goulden, *Truth Is the First Casualty: The Gulf of Tonkin Affair—Illusion and Reality* (Chicago: Rand McNally, 1969); and Anthony Austin, *The President's War* (Philadelphia: J. B. Lippincott, 1971).

20. John Dyson, *Sink the Rainbow! An Inquiry into the 'Greenpeace' Affair* (London: Gollancz, 1986); Leslie Cockburn, *Out of Control* (New York: Atlantic Monthly Press, 1987).

21. Ray Innis of the Congress on Racial Equality stated with regard to Goetz's attack, "Some black men ought to have done it long before. . . . I wish it had been me." And Geoffrey Alpert, director of the University of Miami's Center for the Study of Law and Society, noted, "It's something we'd all like to do. We'd all like to think we'd react the way he did." And Patrick Buchanan, soon to be President Ronald Reagan's press chief, commented, "The universal rejoicing in New York over the gunman's success is a sign of moral health." See Lillian Rubin, *Quiet Rage: Bernie Goetz in a Time of Madness* (New York: Farrar, Straus & Giroux, 1986), pp. 10, 11, and 15, respectively.

22. Kirk Johnson, "Goetz's Account of Shooting 4 Men Is Given on Tape to New York City Jury," *New York Times*, April 30, 1987, p. 14, quotes a tape of Goetz's initial interview with the police.

23. Ibid.

24. There was some indecisive evidence that Goetz responded in kind, with an inverted, morally aggressive, ambiguity. According to one victim, who recalled saying to Goetz, "Mister, give me five dollars," Goetz responded with "You all can have it." Kirk Johnson, "Goetz Shooting Victims Say Youths Weren't Threatening," *New York Times*, May 2, 1987, p. 31. Another version by the same victim, reported in Rubin, *Quiet Rage*, p. 7, had Goetz approached with, "Hey man, you got five dollars for me and my friends to play video games?" and Goetz responding: "Yeah, sure . . . I've got five dollars for each of you." According to a paramedic, shortly after the shooting another victim commented that Goetz had preceded his attack with a threat: "The guys I were with were hassling this guy for some money. He threatened us, then he shot us." Kirk Johnson, "A Reporter's Notebook," *New York Times*, June 15, 1987, p. B1.

25. Johnson, "Goetz's Account of Shooting."

26. And on blocking the public's encounter with the resulting corpses, injuries, and sorrows of relatives, even in popularly supported military conflicts. See Susan Greenberg, *Rejoice! Media Freedom and the Falklands* (London: Campaign for Press and Broadcasting Freedom, 1983), pp. 9–12; and Arthur Gavsnon and Desmond Rice, *The Sinking of the Belgrano* (London: Secker & Warburg, 1984).

INDEX